BATH ABBEY'S MONUMENTS

AN ILLUSTRATED HISTORY

About the Author

Oliver Taylor is Head of Interpretation at Bath Abbey. He received his Ph.D. from Durham University in 2008 and has published widely on literary and local history.

BATH ABBEY'S MONUMENTS

AN ILLUSTRATED HISTORY

OLIVER TAYLOR

The History Press

This book is dedicated to my grandparents, whose children are living monuments of their enduring love.

First published 2023

The History Press
97 St George's Place, Cheltenham,
Gloucestershire, GL50 3QB
www.thehistorypress.co.uk

British Library Cataloguing in Publication Data.
A catalogue record for this book is available from the British Library.

ISBN 978 0 7509 9373 9

Typesetting and origination by The History Press
Printed and bound in Great Britain by TJ Books Limited, Padstow, Cornwall.

MIX
Paper from responsible sources
FSC® C013056
FSC www.fsc.org

Trees for Life

ACKNOWLEDGEMENTS

Thanks are due to the following people who have helped the formation of the book in various ways: Pete Jones, Jeremy Key-Pugh, and Anna Riggs for reading drafts of the chapters; David Stubbs for informing me of John Buckler's drawings of the monuments to Erasmus Philipps and Martin Madan in the British Library (Add MS 36379); Dr Julian Litten for informing me of the manuscript AC/Unlisted/box 32c at Bristol Record Office; Archivists at Bristol Record Office, The Somerset Heritage Centre, and The Society of Antiquaries; Kim Jordan for making his research on Bath's monumental masons available to me; Rich Howman for days of patient photography to show the monuments in their best lights; David Littlefield, Fergus Connolly, Andrew Wardrope, Sam, Tim, and Matt from Sally Strachey Historic Conservation, and the late Mark Hudson for their sensitive thinking about and work on the ledgerstones. Finally, thanks and love are due to my family for the love and time that has enabled this book to be written.

CONTENTS

Opposite: Bath Abbey looking east from the west end showing the Tudor arcades and monuments in the Nave. © Bath Abbey.

LIST OF COLOUR PLATES

Colour Plate A: Monument to Bartholomew Barnes (d. 1606) located on the south side of the Sanctuary. © Bath Abbey.

Colour Plate B: Page 17 of Bath Abbey's *Benefactors' Book* (compiled 1618–25) listing some of the benefactors to the paving of the church 1614–15, including Bishop James Montagu's contribution of £43 6*s* 8*d* which completed the paving of the Nave and the church. © Bath Abbey.

Colour Plate C: Tomb of Bishop James Montagu (d. 1618) in the North Nave of Bath Abbey. In the background, Sir George Gilbert Scott's arrangement of the tablets on the walls of the Nave can be seen. Bath Abbey Archives. © Bath Abbey.

Colour Plate D: Detail of the effigy of Bishop James Montagu (d. 1618), from his tomb located in the North Nave of Bath Abbey, executed by Nicholas Johnson. © Bath Abbey.

Colour Plate D (ii): Silhouette of the tomb of Bishop James Montagu (d. 1618). The window installed in 1951 comprised of the arms and some of the glass given by other seventeenth-century benefactors to the Abbey can be seen in the background. © Bath Abbey

Colour Plate E: Tomb of Lady Jane Waller (d. 1633) on the south wall of the South Transept of Bath Abbey. In *English Church Monuments* (1946), Katherine Esdaile 'unhesitatingly' ascribed the tomb to Epiphanius Evesham. © Bath Abbey.

Colour Plate F: Detail of the effigies of Lady Jane and Sir William Waller from the tomb of Lady Jane Waller (d. 1633). Sir William's vandalised sword hand and 'broken face' described by Samuel Pepys in 1668 can be seen. © Bath Abbey.

Colour Plate F (ii): Detail of the pediment of Lady Jane Waller's tomb (d. 1633) attributed to Epiphanius Evesham. The paint dates to April 1948 when the restorer Pearl Blencowe carried out her 'experiment in cleaning' the monument. © Bath Abbey.

Colour Plate G: *A Service at Bath Abbey* (1788) by Samuel Hieronymus Grimm. The watercolour shows the Nave looking west from the elevated perspective of the organ. Monuments can be seen on the pillars and walls in line with and above the string course of the windows, allowing worshippers to use the benches for prayer. © British Library.

Colour Plate H: *A Perspective View of the Abbey-Church of St. Peter and Paul at Bath* (1750) by James Vertue. © Bath Abbey.

Colour Plate I: Mid-seventeenth-century ledgerstone commemorating three generations of the Wakeman family in the North Aisle of the Nave. © Bath Abbey.

Colour Plate J: Ledgerstone to Mrs Anna Peirce (d. 1688) and Mary A. Court (nee Peirce) (d. 1679). The quotation from Psalm 39 – 'And now Lord what is our hope / truly our hope is even in thee' – is carved at the bottom of the ledgerstone. © Bath Abbey.

Colour Plate K: Monument to Elizabeth Peirce (d. 1671) and her brothers Robert and Charles. The 'verses' on the monument were 'found in her Closet after her decease'. © Bath Abbey.

Colour Plate L: Page 44 of Bath Abbey's *Benefactors' Book* (compiled 1618–25) which records the Christmas gift of 'Two Velvet Palls, and Two Black cloath Palls' from John Baber to the Abbey in 1705. © Bath Abbey.

Colour Plate M: Early eighteenth-century ledgerstone to John William Teshmaker (d. 1713) at the west end of the Nave. Like many monuments in the Abbey, it addresses the reader, asking them to 'Have one Good thought when thus on Graves you tread'. © Bath Abbey.

Colour Plate N: Monument to Jacob Bosanquet (d. 1767) by Thomas Carter the Younger, centre, in its present location on the east wall of the South Transept. The large monuments to Josiah Thomas (d. 1820), by Gahagan, and Joseph Sill (d. 1824) can be seen on the right and left, respectively. © Bath Abbey.

Colour Plate O: Inscription tablet to C.M. (Catherine Malone) (d. 1765) in the North Aisle. It is all that remains on the Abbey's walls of the larger monument that was erected to her in the North Aisle c. 1765–67. © Bath Abbey.

Colour Plate P: Relief carving from Catherine Malone's monument (*c.* 1765–67). It depicts 'a boy sleeping by an urn, with a branch of cypress in his left hand, resting his head on an hour-glass'. The carving was removed in the nineteenth century and discovered by archaeologists beneath the Abbey floor in 2020. © Bath Abbey.

Colour Plate Q: Monument to Leonard (d. 1761) and Elizabeth Coward (d. 1759) erected in 1764. It was probably carved by a Bath sculptor and is similar in design to Catherine Malone's, erected in the Abbey *c.* 1765–67 (shown on Colour Plate P). © Bath Abbey.

Colour Plate R: Monument to James Quin (d. 1766) created by Thomas King between April 1766 and April 1769. © Bath Abbey.

Colour Plate S: Detail of the figures of Liberality (left) and Genius (right) either side of the 'Batheaston Vase' and a medallion portrait of Lady Anna

Miller (d. 1781) from her monument created by John Bacon. © Bath Abbey.
Colour Plate T: Monument to Richard 'Beau' Nash (d. 1761) by John Ford. It was erected in 1791 after Dr Henry Harington invited subscriptions from the Bath public. © Bath Abbey.
Colour Plate U: Group of ledgerstones to members of the Harvey family of sculptors, including 'The Very Ingenious' John Harvey (d. 1742) and his sisters, Sarah (d. 1691/2) and Ann (d. 1696) to the left of it. © Bath Abbey.
Colour Plate V: Tablet to botanist Dr John Sibthorp (d. 1796), centre, by John Flaxman. Sibthorp's *Flora Graeca* introduced the plants of Greece to British readers. Consequently, Flaxman's monument alludes to Greek mythology, depicting Sibthorp crossing the River Styx, stepping from Charon's ferry into the underworld. © Bath Abbey.
Colour Plate W: Detail of monument to Colonel Alexander Champion (d. 1793) by Joseph Nollekens showing '*Fame* on a pedestal, with her trumpet inverted, holding a medallion of the deceased. A coat of mail, cannon, battle-axe, & warlike trophies, surround the pedestal'. © The author.
Colour Plate X: Monument to Sir William Baker (d. 1770), centre, by John Francis Moore, erected in the Abbey at the end of August 1776. Its form was altered in the nineteenth century. Notably, the original black marble pyramid has been removed from the background and its pedestal. © Bath Abbey.
Colour Plate Y: John Francis Moore's original design for the monument to Sir William Baker (d. 1770). In the top right of the watercolour is written 'Erected in Walcot Church at Bath'. It seems that it was ultimately decided that Bath Abbey was a more fitting location for the monument. © Victoria and Albert Museum, London.
Colour Plate Z: South wall of the Gethsemane Chapel, South-East Choir. What remains of the monuments with busts to Mary Frampton (d. 1698) and Dorothy Hobart (d. 1722), left and centre, respectively, after the nineteenth-century works. The inscription to Elizabeth Winkley (d. 1756) sits between Frampton and Hobart, her portrait to the right of Hobart. © Bath Abbey.
Colour Plate Z (ii): Inscription tablet from the monument to Mary Frampton (d. 1698) where the text "by Mr. Dryden" appeared before it was printed as the poem "The Monument of a Fair Maiden Lady". © Bath Abbey.
Colour Plate Z (iii): Details of the monument and bust of Dorothy Hobart (d. 1722) by the "Very Ingenious" Bath sculptor Mr John Harvey. © Bath Abbey.
Colour Plate AA: Photogrammetric survey of the Abbey floor after the removal of the Victorian furniture in 2018. It shows the arrangement of the ledgerstones and heating grates after George Gilbert Scott's work 1864–74.

Small white marbles can be seen inset into the floor, concentrated in the Nave. © Bath Abbey.
Colour Plate AB: Monument to Henry Harington (d. 1816) by Thomas King (centre). Beneath is the tablet to his daughter-in-law Esther Harington (d. 1829), the only tablet beneath the bench seating in the Choir. This helps to illustrate the different approaches to the Victorian rearrangement of the tablets in the Nave and Choir. © Bath Abbey.
Colour Plate AC: *Interior of the Abbey* by J. C. Nattes (1805) showing the Choir looking west. On the left, buildings south of the Abbey block light from the windows. The size, arrangement and placement of monuments under the organ gallery before 1835 can all be seen. © Bath Abbey.
Colour Plate AD: 'Index Plan of the Grave-Stones upon the Floor of the Abbey Church, Bath' by Charles P. Russell (1872). The blank area on the right, in the North-East Choir, was found to have been paved with many marble backing stones from wall monuments when the Corporation Stalls were removed in 2018. © Bath Abbey.
Colour Plate AE: The floor of the North-East Choir paved with marble backing stones removed from wall tablets 1868–72. The outlines of urns, foliage and oval-shaped marbles keyed to receive carvings which originally comprised the tablets can be seen and compared with the designs on the wall behind. © The author.
Colour Plate AF: Arrangement of monuments in the middle bay of the North Nave Aisle. The tablet to Robert Walsh (d. 1788) can be seen in the centre of the bay, with its black marble backing intact, around which the others, which have had their backings removed, have been arranged symmetrically. © Bath Abbey.
Colour Plate AG: Brass plaque to Mary Reeve (d. 1664) and four of her sons, possibly executed by her husband George Reeve, Bath's city goldsmith. It is all that remains of a larger monument originally erected on a pillar on the south side of the Nave. © Bath Abbey.
Colour Plate AH: Monument to the painter William Hoare (d. 1792). Francis Chantrey was commissioned to make it in 1828 by his son Prince Hoare, who directed that it be 'cleaned with pure water only' annually. This appears to have lapsed. It was specially cleaned in 1902. © Bath Abbey.
Colour Plate AI: Tablets of similar design to Anne Wylde (d. 1764) and Mary Belford (d. 1800). Mary Belford's tablet was one of six to be 'left dirty, in order to show what some of the monuments were like before the cleaning and conservation work in 1997'. © Bath Abbey.

Colour Plate AJ 1,2,3,4: Ledgerstone to Christiana Susanna Lucus (d. 1781) showing it: (1) prior to conservation missing pieces and stained by oak tannins; (2) during conservation work with the alternative inscription showing on the back of the stone; (3) with the aramid fibre applied to the back; (4) after conservation work. © Bath Abbey / The author.

Colour Plate AK: Photogrammetric survey of the Abbey floor in 2021. The image shows the new positions of the ledgerstones and of the heating grates, which may be compared with the arrangement of them in the photogrammetric survey of the 1872 arrangement in Colour Plate AA. © Bath Abbey.

Colour Plate AK (ii): Bath Abbey looking east from the west end showing the ledgerstones in the Nave. © Bath Abbey.

LIST OF FIGURES

Fig. 1: Tablet to James Bassett (d. 1819) in the north-east porch, Bath Abbey. © Bath Abbey.
Fig. 2: Tablet to Sir Erasmus Philipps (d. 1743) in the north-east porch, Bath Abbey. © Bath Abbey.
Fig. 3: Monument to Richard and William Chapman probably created after the death of the latter *c.*1627. The date of Richard's death on the monument (1572) should probably read 1579. © Bath Abbey.
Fig. 4: Ground plan of The Abbey Church, Bath, engraved by Richd. Roffe from a drawing by R. Cattermole (1816), published in Britton's history of Bath Abbey 1825. The tombs of John Bellingham (d. 1576) and Margaret Lichfield (d. 1579) are marked at l and n, respectively, in the South Choir. © The author.
Fig. 5: Replica of a tablet to Peter Chapman (d. 1602) donated in 1998. The original monument was wooden and was removed to the vestry in the nineteenth century. It was then lost. © Bath Abbey.
Fig. 6: Undated nineteenth-century print (possibly *c.*1835) depicting the tomb of Bishop James Montagu (d. 1618) in the Nave. The artist has deliberately drawn the pillars and walls without tablets to emphasise the tomb. © The author.
Fig. 7: Detail of the Tomb of Margaret Lichfield (d. 1579) on the right-hand side of James Storer's engraving of 'Prior Bird's Chapel, Bath Cathedral'. © The author.
Fig. 8: Detail of the monuments to Mary Reeve (on the left-most pillar), the oval monument to Calveley Legh M.D. and Granville Pyper (central pillar). On the far right-hand side can be seen Charles Godfrey's monument. © Bath Abbey.
Fig. 9: Detail of monument to Jacob Bosanquet (d. 1767) as originally installed to the left of the Great West Door at the west of the Nave. British Library, London, UK © British Library Board. All Rights Reserved/Bridgeman Images.
Fig. 10: Monument to Dorothy Hobart (d. 1722) in its original form and location on the pillar next to the pulpit in the south of the Nave as depicted by Samuel Grimm in 1788. British Library, London, UK © British Library Board. All Rights Reserved/Bridgeman Images.
Fig. 11: Monument to 'C.M.' (Catherine Malone; d. 1765) in its original form and location in the North Aisle of the Nave as depicted by Samuel Grimm in 1788. British Library, London, UK © British Library Board. All Rights Reserved/Bridgeman Images.

Fig. 12: *Quin's Monument, Bath*, drawn by John Nixon, engraved by Sparrow, which appeared as the frontispiece to the *European Magazine and London Review* in 1792. © The author.
Fig. 13: Plate depicting the monument to Lady Anna Miller (d. 1781) from Collinson's *History and Antiquities of the County of Somerset* (1791). © The author.
Fig. 14: *Study perhaps for the Monument to the Rt. Hon. William Bingham. Bath Abbey* by John Flaxman. © The Trustees of the British Museum.
Fig. 15: Monument to William Bingham (d. 1804) by John Flaxman. © Bath Abbey.
Fig. 16: Monument to Sir Richard Hussey Bickerton (d. 1832) by Sir Francis Chantrey. © Bath Abbey.
Fig. 17: Tablet to the Stibbs family, including Captain Bartholomew Stibbs (d. 1735). © Bath Abbey.
Fig. 18: The 'elegant' monument to Andrew Barkley (d. 1790) by Thomas King. © Bath Abbey.
Fig. 19: Henry Storer's drawing and the engraving of the 'S[outh] Transept, Bath Cathedral' for his father, James Storer's *History and Antiquities of the Cathedral Churches of Great Britain* (1814). © The author.
Fig. 20: *View, looking S.W. of Nave, &c.* (1820) engraved by John Le Keux from a drawing by Frederick Mackenzie, published in John Britton's *History and Antiquities of Bath Abbey Church* (1825). © The author.
Fig. 21: James Storer's etching of the *Interior of Bath Cathedral* (from Henry Gastineau's drawing). © The author.
Fig. 22: Plan of the new Choir Screen signed by Edward Blore (*c.* 1835) showing 'Recesses for Monuments' marked on the north and south side of its central door. © Bath Abbey.
Fig. 23: Marbles removed from wall monuments set into distinctive striated stone *c.* 1835–36 in the south-west Nave. © The author.
Fig. 24: Drawing of Catherine Malone's (d. 1765) monument by James Cross for James Hayward Markland's *Remarks on English Churches* (1843). Cross's depiction appears intentionally distorted to support Markland's description of the monument's 'unrivalled ugliness'. © The author.
Fig. 25: *North Transept, Bath Abbey Church* by James Cross for James Hayward Markland's *Remarks on English Churches* (1843). © The author.
Fig. 26: George Philipps Manners's arrangement of the tablets on the South Nave Aisle wall seen in *The Illustrated London News*, 7 January 1854. © The author.
Fig. 27: Samuel Rogers Jr, mason, Canal Bridge, Widcombe, Bath, *c.* 1864. A cabinet photograph by J. & J. Dutton, photographers, Bath. Samuel Rogers's

firm carved a number of monuments for the Abbey and its cemetery here in the mid-nineteenth century. © Bath & North East Somerset Council.

Fig. 28: Photograph of the North Nave Aisle looking west by Dawson & Dutton, *c.*1860. © The author.

Fig. 29: Photograph of the Nave looking east by J. Dutton, *c.*1860. © The author.

Fig. 30: 'Tablet in the Abbey Church, Bath' to John Bowles (d. 1819) published on p.305 of the *Gentleman's Magazine*, October 1820. © The author.

Fig. 31: Tablet to John Bowles (d. 1819) in the South Aisle today. The tablet has been reduced to its inscription and coat of arms. It is therefore representative of the way in which George Gilbert Scott treated such simple tablets and applied the terms of the 1868 Faculty to his work on them. © Bath Abbey.

Fig. 32: 'Kemble Memorial Screen, Bath Abbey Church', designed by John Oldrid Scott and executed by Harry Hems, published in *The Builder*, 24 April 1886. © The author.

Fig. 33: Tablet to Jesse and William Mead by Bath masons Turvey and Perrin erected in 1929. Like the tablet to William Siddons (d. 1808) it was placed above the string course in the South Nave Aisle. The Faculty paperwork shows that the lettering of the Mead tablet was to be 'like the "Siddons" Tablet'. © Bath Abbey.

Fig. 34: Tablet to Captain Aubrey Reilly (d. 1917) by Farmer and Brindley installed above the string course at the east end of the North Nave Aisle. © Bath Abbey.

Fig. 35: Tablet to Thomas William Dunn by Thomas Baylis Huxley-Jones erected above the string course on the south wall of the East Choir in 1932, opposite the monument to William Hoare and the memorial to those from Bath College who lost their lives in the First World War. © Bath Abbey.

Fig. 36: Tablet to Sarah Fielding (d. 1768) on the north-west wall of the Nave. © Bath Abbey.

Fig. 37: The pieces of the Julian Penny's (d. 1657) ledgerstone undergoing consolidation and conservation work in June 2019. © The author.

Fig. 38: Ledgerstone to Joseph Philips (d. 1703). The portion on the left (with the crest) was all that remained after George Gilbert Scott's work in 1872. Charles Russell's 1872 and Richard Rawlinson's 1719 records of the ledgerstones were used to newly carve the missing inscription. © The author.

Sacred to the Memory of
JOSEPH COLLINS,
who departed this Life in LONDON,
August 30th 1823, Aged 33 Years.
Possessed of the most amiable disposition
he enjoyed the Love and Esteem
of all who knew him.
Also of MARY COLLINS,
Mother of the above JOSEPH COLLINS,
who died Jany 5th 1835, Aged 79.
Also of SUSANNA COLLINS,
Aunt of the above JOSEPH COLLINS,
who died Septr 14th 1836, Aged 83.
SACRED TO THE MEMORY
OF CHARLES PALMER DIMOND, ESQre
OF LONDON
WHO DEPARTED THIS LIFE
ON THE 12th OF JANUARY 1843,
IN HIS 34th YEAR.
"BLESSED ARE THE DEAD WHO DIE IN THE LORD; YEA, SAITH THE SPIRIT, FOR THEY REST FROM THEIR LABOURS AND THEIR WORKS DO FOLLOW THEM."
HIS REMAINS ARE DEPOSITED
IN THE SAME VAULT,
WITH THOSE OF HIS FATHER AND MOTHER,
WILLIAM WYATT DIMOND, ESQre
OF THIS CITY
AND MATILDA MARTHA DIMOND.
SACRED
TO THE MEMORY OF
SUSAN,
ONLY DAUGHTER OF BENJAMIN IFILL ESQre
OF THE ISLAND OF BARBADOES,
WHO DEPARTED THIS LIFE ON
THE 18th OF APRIL 1833,
AGED 28 YEARS.
SACRED
to ye DEAR MEMORY of ANNE only
Daughter of GEORGE FINCH ESQ of
Valentines in Essex
AN EXCELLENT PERSON
well natur'd, discreet, and vertuous
most affectionately beloved by her
Relations & most justly esteemed by all
that knew her.
It pleased God to visit her with a tedious &
Severe illness which (tho in the flower of her age &
Bless'd with a plentiful Fortune) she bore with great
Evenness & Constancy.
She prepared her self by frequent & fervent
Devotion for her dissolution which she waited for
with such pious Resignation as manifested her heart
to be affected with ye POWER of RELIGION and
the well grounded hopes of a Blessed
ETERNITY
Her life being the more desirable
In that the first real occasion
of Greif she gave her
Sorrowful Mother was
her DEATH
LUGE ET IMITARE
Under this place are deposited the remains of
JOHN MOUTRAY Esqr of Roscobie of Fifeshire,
in the Kingdom of Scotland, Twenty eight Years
a Post Captain, and late a Commissioner
of His Majesty's Navy at Antigua.
In his publick Character he was Valuable to his
Country for his long and faithful Services,
and universally beloved for the Integrity of his
Principles and the distinguished Sincerity
of his Heart.
He died Nov. 22d 1785 in the 65t Year of his Age.
This Tablet
is the last sad offering of
the purest conjugal Affection
to the memory of
RAWSON HART BODDAM Esqr
(late of Capel House, Enfield Middlesex)
interred beneath
who died at Bath on the 20th of May 1812
aged 78 Years.
In his early Youth he entered into the
Civil Service of the East India Company,
Anno Dom: 1752,
and having, through a course of the
most zealous Devotion to the Interest
of that great Body,
assiduously promoted
the honor of his KING and COUNTRY,
was in testimony of
his distinguished Merits appointed
GOVERNOR of BOMBAY A.D. 1784.
His administration was characterised by
The Virtues of the Gentleman,
The Philanthropist, and the Patriot.
On quitting that honorable station
He carried with him the Regrets
of the large portion of Society
European and Asiatic
that had experienced the Blessings
of his Government.
His dignified retreat from public life
was but a transition
to the exercise of new Virtues,
In the dispensation of domestic Happiness
to a numerous and affectionate Family
and the pleasures of Society
to the Friends who loved
and the Neighbours who respected him.
Also to the Memory of his Son
RAWSON HART BODDAM,
of the Honble East India Company's
Civil Service, Bengal,
who died at Bath 15th April 1836,
aged 44
Also of ELLEN KEZIA, Née HUNGERFORD, Wife of the last named.
HENRY FORSTER MILLS, A.M.
CHANCELLOR OF YORK MINSTER
DIED 27th APRIL 1827
Sacred to the Memory
of
Sir WILLIAM BOOTHBY Bart
General of his Majesty's Forces
and Colonel of the 6th Regt of Foot,
died 16th April 1787
Aged 68 Years.
Sacred to the Memory
of CECILIA MARY ANN
Daughter of
EDWARD Wm HENSLOW Esqr
(Storekeeper of His Majesty's
Dock Yard Chatham)
and CECILIA MARIA his Wife
Ob: 14th March 1802
Beneath this Pavement
are deposited the Remains of
HENRY and SARAH ROSEWELL ARCHBOULD.
Their Love was disinterested,
their affection mutual,
and their Sensibility equal thus attached,
and thus bound by every tender Cord
which twines about the Heart,
their incessant Prayer was never to be separated,
most indulgent Heaven translated them
from this vale of wretchedness,
and, in kindness to their Prayer,
united them to the blissful Regions
of Eternity.
Sacred
to the beloved Memory
of JOHN STOKES

INTRODUCTION

On Wednesday, 7 July 1819, two days of horse racing began at Lansdown Racecourse, north of Bath. Among the revellers attending the meet was James Bassett, a joiner from Widcombe, south of the city. At the break of day, Bassett left his home at 6 Church Street, where Hannah Bassett worked as a Mantua maker, and set off on the five-mile walk up to the racecourse. He and his friends, a party of young men, were in high spirits. To pass the time, they began horsing around. In a 'frolic', Bassett attempted 'to vault over the head of his companion', John Shepherd, but it went tragically wrong. The two men fell backwards, Shepherd falling back onto Bassett. The 'violence of the concussion', the inquest later found, had burst Bassett's bladder. Although he was 'immediately taken down to the Casualty hospital, where he received the best surgical advice and attention', James Bassett died the following morning.[1] He was a descendent of the Bassett family who for many years were 'proprietors of the manor of Claverton'. By the 'indulgence of the worthy Rector', Bassett was buried at St Mary's, Claverton, 'amongst the remains of his once opulent ancestors' on Monday, 12 July 1819.

On the evening of Bassett's burial, 'a long and melancholy muffled peal was rung' on the Abbey's bells. Bassett had been an Abbey bellringer himself and the peal was a mark of 'respect to their unfortunate young friend'. Bassett's friend, John Shepherd, was 'truly miserable'. He was 'the innocent cause of the fatal event'. Although 'no blame whatever' was 'attributable' to him, he held his friend 'in the highest esteem'. Indeed, all who knew Bassett did, according to the newspaper and the marble tablet erected in Bath Abbey after his death (Fig. 1). Its inscription reads:

Opposite: Detail of the arrangement of the tablets on the wall of the South Nave Aisle. The central placement of the large monument to Anne Finch (d. 1713) and the symmetry attempted in the monuments either side of it exemplifies George Gilbert Scott's approach to the ordering of the tablets in the Nave 1868-71. The tablet to Cecilia Henslow mentioned in the Introduction can be seen in the top-left of the bay. © The author.

Sacred to the Memory of JAMES BASSETT,
of the Parish of Lyncombe and Widcombe;
who died July 9th 1819. Aged 40 Years.
Who in the Moment of Social Pleasure,
received a fall, which soon deprived him of Life,
and sent him (in the Blessed hope)
to another and a better World.
His Companions and Friends as a mark of Esteem
and affection; have subscribed and Placed
this Humble Tablet to his Memory.
READER
Think! in the Midst of life we are in death.

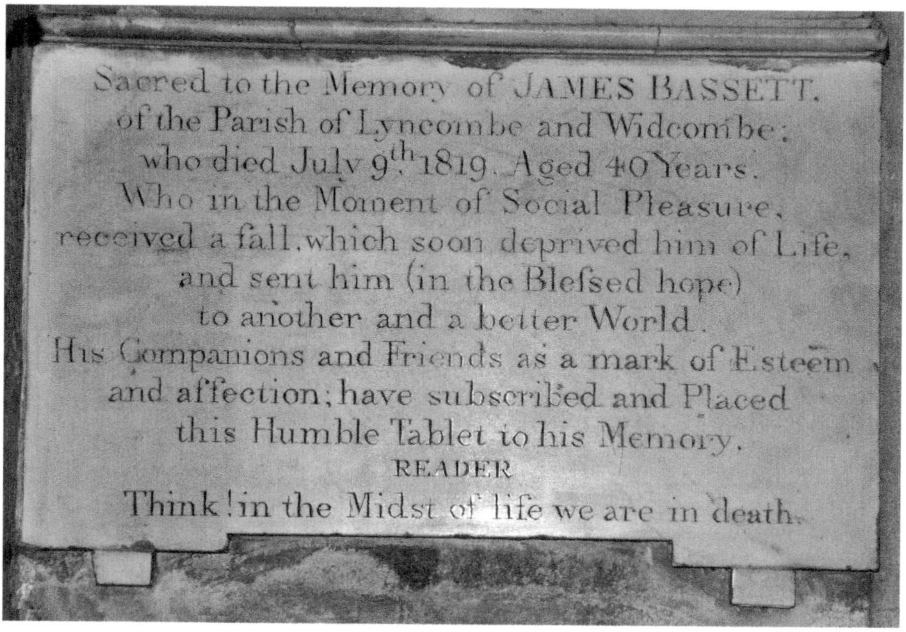

Fig.1: Tablet to James Bassett (d. 1819) in the north-east porch, Bath Abbey. © Bath Abbey.

The tablet is presently placed, perhaps where it always has been, in the north-east porch of the Abbey next to the door to the tower Bassett may have used when he rang the Abbey's bells. There is no record of a fee received by the Abbey for permission to erect the tablet in either the Rector's, Sexton's or Churchwardens' Accounts. Neither is there any record of the tablet's original location, nor if it was moved during the rearrangements of the monuments in the 1830s and 1860s. This, it seems, was very much a tablet for one of the Abbey's own: privately subscribed to, privately erected.

In the summer of 1835, Sir Erasmus Philipps's tablet was removed from the west of the South Aisle, where it had been erected and was drawn by John Buckler on 6 July 1827, and placed opposite Bassett's in the north-east porch (Fig. 2). Perhaps no monument has been moved further from its original location in the Abbey than Philipps's. In the process, the sienna marble of the border and pediment were removed along with the cartouche containing Philipps's coat of arms, leaving only the decorative lintel and the inscription tablet beneath it, which reads:

Sacred
To the Memory of
Sr: ERASMUS PHILIPPS
of Picton Castle in the
County of Pembroke
Bart:, Member of
Parliament for the
Town, and County of
Haverford-west,
who was Unfortunately
Drown'd in the River
Avon, near this City, by
a Fall from his Horse
Octobr: *15*th: *1743*
Aged *43*.

Fig.2: Tablet to Sir Erasmus Philipps (d. 1743) in the north-east porch, Bath Abbey. © Bath Abbey.

Philipps's death was as accidental as Bassett's. Returning to Bath from Italy 'some pigs frightened his horse, which ran back, and threw him into the river'. And so these two tablets, commemorating lives cut short in tragi-comic ways, face each other; the impact of each inscription intensified by its careful placement next to the other.

Bassett's and Philipps's memorials are two of 635 tablets on the walls of Bath Abbey. Unsurprisingly, they are not ones previously mentioned by commentators on the Abbey's monuments. The ones that have attracted comment have traditionally been those by celebrated sculptors whose work has commemorated celebrities of local or national life. But the Abbey's monuments are not simply monuments to those whose rank or income meant they were buried in Bath rather than Westminster Abbey. True, Bath Abbey contains monuments to some who might have been buried and commemorated in Westminster. However, Bath Abbey's monuments are also uniquely a collection through which can be read the story of the parish church building itself and the rise of Bath as a spa. They are a sorely underappreciated aspect of the city's famous Georgian heyday. The Royal Crescent, Circus, Baths, Pump Room, and Assembly Rooms are rightly appreciated as the places frequented by Bath's fashionable eighteenth-century visitors. However, the Abbey, as the church attended by those visitors, is rarely mentioned, and nowhere is it addressed that during the Georgian period the Abbey was a 'gallery of sculpture' that attracted numerous visitors and citizens who wanted to admire the latest works of art by artists working in a serious and respected artform: the English church monument. Certainly monuments to the first rank of politicians, admirals, doctors, philosophers, bishops, soldiers, merchants and others can be found. But so too can those of Bath's teachers, socialites, cloth merchants, poulterers, booksellers, mayors, sculptors, plumbers and publicans, to name but a few. Hidden in the lines of their monuments is an unwritten social history of Bath.

Until now, writers have largely reduced thinking on the Abbey's monuments to two quotable but questionable phrases conceived in the early nineteenth century. Henry Harington's description of the Abbey – 'These ancient walls, with many a mouldering bust, / But show how well Bath waters lay the dust'[2] – and John Britton's statement that 'Perhaps there is not a Church in England, not excepting that national mausoleum, Westminster Abbey, so crowded with sepulchral memorials.'[3] Britton was right to identify Bath Abbey's monuments as on a par with those in Westminster Abbey in 1825. Bath Abbey's over 1,500 monuments are a nationally significant collection. Bath's 635 wall tablets are comparable in number with the 'just over 600 tombs and other substantial monuments'[4] in Westminster Abbey.[5] Add to that number Bath Abbey's 891 ledgerstones (flat inscribed gravestones), almost three times as many as the 'more than 300 memorial stones and stained glass windows'[6] at Westminster, and one could easily correct Britton's statement to say that Bath Abbey has the largest collection of monuments of any church in England. However, the combination of the English church monument's fall out of fashion in the mid-nineteenth century and the extent of the alterations to Bath Abbey's monuments in the 1830s and 1860s has led them to be all but forgotten. A fact all the more surprising given their importance in Georgian Bath. Whilst the Abbey's spectacular medieval architecture, rather than its monuments, contributes to the Outstanding Universal Value of the UNESCO World Heritage City of Bath, the importance of the Abbey's monuments is acknowledged three times in Historic England's Grade I listing of Bath Abbey. The 'monument-crammed interior is of very considerable note for its historical interest' and the 'exceptionally high concentration of memorial tablets (some 640 in all) from the C17 onwards attests to the church's central place in Bath society'.[7]

This book tells the story of the monuments for the first time. How did a ruined Tudor abbey come to have the largest collection of church monuments in the country by 1845? How has this nationally significant collection been seen by those who have visited the Abbey over the centuries, and how has it been cared for and added to by the generations who have looked after the Abbey? What do we encounter today when we look around the Abbey, walk across its floor, and read the monuments? This book argues that the monuments played an important role in the rebuilding of the Abbey as a parish church in the late sixteenth and seventeenth centuries, helped to create a new identity for it in the eighteenth and nineteenth centuries, and that what we encounter of them today is the result of major renovation and conservation work in the nineteenth and twenty-first centuries, respectively. All of which is illustrative of the way in which the Abbey has invited, benefited from, cared for, and managed its monuments for over 400 years.

Having been rebuilt in the early sixteenth century in the perpendicular Gothic style, from 1539 the Abbey Church of St Peter and St Paul (what is now called Bath Abbey) was ruined, its monastery closed, everything of value in its building sold or stolen. The late rebuilding of the church meant that whilst Leland noticed a couple of tombs in the 1540s, the interior was simultaneously like a cathedral and comparatively clear of the large tombs that could be found in medieval cathedrals. The close relationship between the laity and the Abbey, and the Abbey's location at the heart of the city, meant that some local families had been burying and commemorating their ancestors in the church before the Dissolution. The desire to rebuild the church must therefore have been motivated partly by a desire to honour their places of rest and preserve any monuments to them, as well as to see the church building and place of worship restored to its former glory. It is telling that two of the earliest monuments to be erected in the late sixteenth-century Abbey to 'strangers' (that is, visitors to the city) – to John Bellyngham (Bellingham) (d. 1576) and Mrs Margarett Lytchfylde (Lichfield) (d. 1579) – were erected in the South Choir, where the building was sound. These two tombs can be seen to the left of the door to the vestry, in the background of Henry Storer's drawing and engraving of the 'S[outh] Transept, Bath Cathedral' for his father, James Storer's *History and Antiquities of the Cathedral Churches of Great Britain* (1814) later in this book (Fig. 19). Early seventeenth-century benefactors to the rebuilding of the church, such as Bartholomew Barnes (d. 1606), were 'richly entombed therein', in Barnes's case on the south side of the Sanctuary in 1607.

The major benefaction of Bishop James Montagu (d. 1618) made the Nave fit for worship. Ordinarily services were held in the Choir, but large civic services were held in the Nave. The completion of the Nave and Montagu's desire to be entombed conspicuously there in order that his tomb might 'stirr up some more benefactors'[8] to the Abbey had the additional benefits of connecting giving to the church in life with being commemorated in the church after it, and providing a new space, unadorned by monuments, in which executors might take their pick of a place for a monument to their loved ones.

The completion of the post-Dissolution rebuilding of the Abbey in the early seventeenth century and its consequent capacity to be used for burial and house monuments coincided with the rise in importance of Bath as a health resort. Queen Elizabeth I conceived the rebuilt church as one for the city and one that could be used by the 'nobilitie' and others when visiting the city. The Abbey was certainly frequented by this class in the seventeenth and eighteenth centuries (although St James's was sometimes preferred because its service times allowed them to get to the Pump Rooms earlier). As a doctor himself, Henry Harington would have known, as well as anyone, the link between the illusory cure of the waters and the raising of monuments in the church. By the end of the nineteenth century, the class of person buried in the Abbey was not only a commonplace, thanks to Harington, but the subject of further and more prolonged satire in the journal established by Charles Dickens, *All the Year Round*:

In this noble abbey repose knights and beaux, George the Third doctors and barons of Tudor times. Under the well-trodden floor repose the masqueraders of all centuries, waiting for the last trumpet – abbots and fine ladies, friends of Dr. Johnson and Garrick, and stern monks, who opposed kings and beat down the sword with the crozier. Dainty misses, who swam about the baths with floating trays for nosegay and snuff-box, and demure nuns of the early English period; gentlemen who were not admitted to the new assembly-rooms in boots; and young misses who were not allowed to dance minuets without lappets or in aprons, lie beside early English barons and lady prioresses – 'Dust to dust' and 'All is vanity; written largely on many a tomb.'[9]

By then, the Abbey's reputation for monuments was such that even tablets not erected there were being misattributed to it.[10] However, the Abbey certainly was a place where the 'great and the good' were buried and had monuments erected to their memory. But this is only part of a picture that has been obscured by nineteenth-century perspectives on the monuments which have been followed unquestioningly by later writers. Monuments to the class of person Harington and *All Year Round* had in mind certainly made the newspaper and were often those that were executed by celebrated London sculptors. However, monuments to the newly affluent and influential middle classes – merchants, artisans, and their families and children – of parishioners, and of Bath's citizens executed by the city's sculptors, are more numerous. Indeed, by 1814, James Storer felt the Abbey's collection of monuments would have been much more 'becoming' had the 'urnal tablets to infants' given way to 'monuments of divines, philosophers, statesmen, or heroes'. Perhaps this is why such tablets have been pointedly ignored since 1814. But for the city and the Abbey, such monuments were important. Insofar as memorials were concerned, the Abbey became the centre for the city to mourn, to raise monuments to its citizens, to celebrate the city's achievements and values, from the eighteenth century to the two most recent floor stones to the Ropers (2016) and the Brownswords (2020), two major benefactors to the Abbey and the city, which commemorate their gifts but not their burials. Large monuments, such as those to Sir William Baker by John Francis Moore or Herman Katencamp by John Bacon Jr, were good for the revenue of the church (and the smaller sums that could be taken from visitors wishing to view these artworks) but the monuments to Nash, Harington, Josiah Thomas and others show it was equally important for the church to be a place where citizens' monuments could have pride of place.

One of the misconceptions in almost all discussion of the monuments is that they are the product of the deceased's desire to be commemorated.[11] Although some people occasionally specified how they would like to be commemorated in their wills (usually in the seventeenth century), the vast majority of the Abbey's monuments originated from a spouse's, child's, friend's, executor's or community's desire to honour the deceased, perpetuate their memory, and celebrate their virtues. Whilst some executors could pay for them outright, the cost of a marble tablet was a significant investment. At the end of the eighteenth century, the Bathonian sculptor Thomas King advertised his 'neat' (a euphemism for small, simple and generic) monuments for sale at between 8 to 50 guineas each. With the fees the Abbey charged for permission to erect monuments on its walls or pillars (more costly in the Choir than the Nave), the minimum sum required to create and erect such a monument was approximately £20 (about four months' wages for a skilled tradesman). For the larger, bespoke monuments by London sculptors, commissioners could expect to pay at least ten times that sum. Some of the monuments one encounters in the Abbey, especially those from the nineteenth century, were therefore funded by subscription schemes that brought together friends (Bassett), citizens (Harington, Nash), parishioners (Lea), or colleagues (Dunn, Manley Power). Bath Abbey's fees for permission to erect these monuments were occasionally waived and, regardless, were only a few pounds, often less than 10 per cent of the total cost of the monuments. In comparison, by the end of the nineteenth century, at Westminster Abbey the 'fee' alone 'for private monuments' varied 'from £200 for a bust upwards, according to the size of the monument'.[12] The fees went 'entirely to the maintenance of the fabric, and not to the private emolument of the Dean or any other member of the Chapter'. The revenue from burial and monuments also went towards the maintenance of the fabric of Bath Abbey, although, as we will see, the fees for monuments and the hire of funeral silks also helped to supplement what was regarded as an insufficient income for the rector's living. Bath was therefore comparatively affordable to Westminster, and if one could pay there is no record of any other objections (on grounds of class or worth) to being buried or raising a monument in Bath Abbey. The Dean of Westminster Abbey pointed out that by the end of the nineteenth century, 'space in the Abbey' was 'very limited, the honour of a monument being very much coveted, the disfigurement occasioned by disproportionate monuments very incongruous, and the expense of the fabric of the Abbey very great'. In that, Westminster and Bath Abbeys had much in common. Finally, it should be remembered that the cost and supply of marble and the time it took to agree a design, carve a tablet, and even make good any mistakes, meant that, with the exception of ledgerstones (which could be laid directly onto graves within days of a death), tablets were erected months or even years after the death of the person they commemorate.

This book addresses two different types of monuments in Bath Abbey. The first are called ledgerstones. These are flat gravestones inscribed with the details of the deceased and layed into the church floor. All but a handful of these mark burials in the Abbey. However, as we will see, they were occasionally used as cenotaphs to commemorate those buried elsewhere. By the nineteenth century, ledgerstones were usually simple and plain, the letter cutting less flourished and elaborate, the coats of arms seen at the top of many seventeenth- and eighteenth-century stones omitted. However, the beautiful carving and craftsmanship on earlier seventeenth- and eighteenth-century ledgerstones, such as those to John William Teshmaker (d. 1713) or the Harvey family, are arresting when one walks across the Abbey floor, as was surely their intention, judging from how these and many other stones' inscriptions address the reader directly.

There are a number of different-sized ledgerstones on the Abbey floor. By the nineteenth century, a large-sized ledgerstone for the Abbey floor was standardized at 6ft x 2ft 6in (with the option of a small-sized stones, especially used for children). The earliest ledgerstone still presently in the Abbey floor is dated 1623. Anthony Wood's 1676 survey suggests that there were many other, and perhaps earlier, ledgerstones in the floor. However, by the late seventeenth century their inscriptions had been eroded. From around 1620, ledgerstones became increasingly desirable in the Abbey, owing to the facts that all the roofs had been repaired by 1612 and the floor itself repaired 1614–15. The approximately 6,500 burials that took place in the Abbey from around 1576 until 1845 have resulted in a unique, and uniquely large, collection of ledgerstones. Eight hundred and ninety-one ledgerstones were counted prior to the Footprint Project conservation works to the floor between 2018–21, accounting for over a third of the approximately 2,400 stones that comprise the entire Abbey floor.[13] Approximately 8 per cent of all burials in the Abbey are commemorated by a ledgerstone. The different types of stone – blue lias limestone, Welsh pennant, white marble, and others – and the ages of the ledgerstones (covering the period 1623–1845) have given a beautiful texture to the Abbey floor.

This kind of beautiful patina given to a church floor by ledgerstones forms part of George Herbert's poem 'The Church-floor', which was part of his major work *The Temple* (1633):

Mark you the floor? that square and speckled stone,
Which looks so firm and strong,
Is *Patience*:

And th' other black and grave, wherewith each one
is checker'd all along,
Humility:

The gentle rising, which on either hand
Leads to the Choir above,
Is Confidence:

But the sweet cement, which is one sure band
Ties the whole frame, is *Love*
And Charity.

Hither sometimes Sin steals, and stains
The marbles' neat and curious veins:
But all is cleansed when the marble weeps.
Sometimes Death, puffing at the door,
Blows all the dust about the floor:
But while he thinks to spoil the room, he sweeps.
Blest be the *Architect*, whose art
Could build so strong in a weak heart.

Herbert's descriptions of the ledgerstones and floor are emblematic of Christian qualities, from those *italicised* in the first half of the poem, to the stained marble and marble weeping with condensation allegorical of sin and tears of repentance in the second half. Epitaphs on the Abbey's ledgerstones (especially those pre-dating the more simple designs of the nineteenth century) also convey the Christian qualities of the deceased in their epitaphs and often follow conventions in their letter cutting alluded to in the type of Herbert's poem, such as emphasising those qualities, locations, names, and dates through the emphasis of italic lettering. Like Herbert's opening line, they also occasionally address the reader.

The second type of monument is the marble tablets now on the walls of the Abbey: 635 at the last count. The book will also discuss the tombs of Bishop James Montagu (d. 1618) and Lady Jane Waller (d. 1633), but not the Chantry Chapel of Prior Birde (d. 1525). The earliest date that appears to be carved on a mural tablet is 1572 (although taking this date as the year in which the monument was created is problematic, as will be discussed in Chapter 1). After burial ceased within the Abbey in 1845, a small number of tablets were erected as cenotaphs (commemorating burial elsewhere), the latest being dated 1972. As we will see, the tablets' forms and locations were changed radically between 1835–36 and 1868–71. This fact makes the full assessment of them individually problematic in many ways.

As well as covering the walls, before 1835 the Abbey's pillars were covered with marble tablets; some pillars may have had as many as twelve tablets on them. The majority appear to have been generic tablets created by Bath sculptors in the eighteenth and nineteenth centuries. Two early tombs – that of Bishop James Montagu erected in 1619, and that of Lady Jane Waller probably erected before 1635 – survive; however others, such as those to John Bellingham and Margaret Litchfield, were removed from the South Choir Aisle in the nineteenth century. A handful of tablets created by notable eighteenth- and nineteenth-century sculptors from London are part of the collection. These tend to be the larger tablets that have survived the nineteenth-century works relatively intact, although Carter's tablet to Jacob Bosanquet has been cut down. Westminster Abbey unquestionably has more works by well-known London-based sculptors, especially those by John Bacon (1740–99), John Bacon Jr (1777–1859) and Joseph Nollekens (1737–1823). Bath Abbey has no signed monuments by Henry Cheere (1703–81), Louis-Francois Roubiliac (1702–62), John Michael Rysbrack (1694–1770) or Peter Scheemakers (1691–1781). However, Bath and Westminster do have similar numbers of tablets by Sebastian Gahagan (1779–1838), Francis Leggatt Chantrey (1781–1841), John Flaxman (1755–1826) and John Francis Moore (1745–1809).[14]

Today the concentration of the tablets gathered together on the walls of Bath Abbey, mostly beneath the string course, is arresting in itself. But they have largely been reduced to their inscriptions and coats of arms, what George

Herbert would call their 'dusty heraldry and lines' in his poem 'Church Monuments'. To understand the impact these tablets had when their original designs and decorations were present, it is necessary to consider the depictions of the Abbey interior in the eighteenth and nineteenth centuries. It is also necessary to imagine the Abbey interior as it was before George Gilbert Scott's renovations to it in the 1860s and 1870s. Prior to Scott's works, the organ-screen divided the Nave from the Choir, the vista to the east window could not have attracted the visitor's gaze as it now does; no stained glass filled that window and the majority of the windows were plain rather than stained glass; fan vaulting only formed the ceiling in the Choir and that and the rest of the stonework was blackened by decades of candle, gas and coal smoke; no pews covered the Nave floor and the Mayor's seat and monuments disfigured the Birde Chantry Chapel. The whiteness, colours and gilding, as well as the modern artistry and sculptural designs, of newly installed marble tablets would have stood out brightly to visitors and worshippers alike. The monuments were *the* tourist attraction for those walking in or through the church in the eighteenth and nineteenth centuries after 'church time' and the newspaper advertised new works when they could be seen. Throughout the book the words 'monuments' and 'tablets' are used interchangeably to refer to those on the wall (although the former is occasionally used to refer to the entire collection of ledgerstones and tablets; the usage should always be obvious from the context in which it is used). Where 'ledgerstones' or 'tablets' are referred to, the words are used to designate those distinct forms.

Whilst small generic tablets in white ('statuary') marble made by Bath sculptors could be afforded by some of middle classes, as Nicholas Penny has pointed out, bespoke marble monuments 'were luxuries of expensive imported materials made only for the wealthy few who wore Indian muslin, sat on chairs of West Indian mahogany and drank port, claret, and hock'.[15] The rise in popularity of the English church monument coincided with the rise of the British Empire. Consequently, numerous monuments in churches and cathedrals across the country commemorate those involved in colonisation and enslavement. Bath Abbey is no exception. Indeed, in 1950, the Director of Bath's Municipal Libraries and Abbey historian, Reginald Wright, described the Abbey as 'a shrine of the British Empire'.[16] Approximately 20 per cent of the monuments erected in the Abbey commemorate individuals who helped to govern, administrate, expand and protect the British Empire: investors, employees and directors of the East India Company; members of the government of Jamaica, Barbados and other colonies; plantation owners; and many others.

The inscriptions and iconography of their monuments often unquestioningly and patriotically dignify, glorify and idealise the empire and their roles and conduct within it. But not always. The tablet to Captain Bartholomew Stibbs (discussed in Chapter 2) demonstrates that sometimes behind the plainest monuments lie grave histories of enslavement and exploitation.

Bath Abbey benefited from the British Empire in as much as it accepted payments for permission to erect monuments from the families of those involved in it. The fees for erecting monuments in different periods are discussed throughout the book. Such fees were only a fraction (often less than a tenth) of what it would have cost to commission a sculptor to carve the monuments themselves. Whilst there are some instances of fees being waived for both burial and the erection of monuments (as in the case of James Bassett above), they are rare and infrequent. Conversely, if one could pay for a monument, no questions appear to have been asked about Christian denomination, class or where the money came from. For example, Edward Henslow's monument to his wife (Cecilia Maria) and daughter (Cecilia Mary Ann), who died at 'nine Months and three Weeks', cannot help but elicit the reader's immediate empathy for him. However, it would appear that the way in which Edward 'made use of the King's stores' for his own purposes whilst 'Storekeeper of His Majesty's Dock-Yard Chatham' – taking sails, canvas, 'an aviary and beehives, five deliveries of candles – including three boxes each weighing a hundredweight, and five deliveries of hogs lard, each of five pounds', not to mention the 'yard boat', 'a mast, sprit, sculls and oar for her', firewood, lead which was made into 'a water trough and beer coolers', signal colours and 'worn bunting'[17] – would have helped him to put money by to afford the costs of a monument to his loved ones.

Unlike in Westminster Abbey, no serious steps appear to have been taken to curb the number of monuments in Bath Abbey in the late eighteenth and early nineteenth centuries, either by the fees that were charged for permission to erect a monument, or in regulation by the rector or churchwardens. Overcrowding in Westminster Abbey 'eventually brought a government decision that, so far as possible, those soldiers and sailors killed during the Napoleonic Wars would be commemorated in St. Paul's'.[18] St Paul's became 'the chosen location for more than thirty official monuments to men who fought, and usually died, in the wars [*c.* 1793–1815]'.[19] In comparison, the Royal Navy monuments in Bath Abbey are often to those who served but later retired to Bath, such as Admiral Sir Richard Hussey Bickerton (d. 1832) or Admiral Sir William Hargood (d. 1839). An indication of the jingoistic use of such monuments in Bath Abbey may be judged by the fact that the annual tradition of draping the Union Jack over Admiral Sir William Hargood's monument on the anniversary of the Battle of Trafalgar was still being celebrated in the twentieth century. In St Paul's, monuments were 'proposed by the Houses of Parliament, approved by the monarch and paid for by the state, which then entered into contracts with the artists, initially overseen by the Royal Academy and subsequently under the so-called "Committee of Taste" a body composed chiefly of connoisseurs'.[20] A committee of taste was just what Bath Abbey needed, according to John Britton in 1825, to stop what he regarded as the indiscriminate erection of monuments in Bath by those whose 'fancies' were unchecked.

Nevertheless, since the late seventeenth century, antiquarians, journalists, writers and tourists have given the sense that Bath Abbey's monuments are a special collection of artworks, a spectacle worth seeing. What they have felt about that spectacle has naturally changed with different generations' aesthetic, religious and political persuasions. Of course, there have been many vociferous opinions about individual monuments, the aesthetics of the collection of monuments as a whole, and the interior of the Abbey over the years. Yet, there has been no history to contextualise these changing perspectives or explain the monuments' changing importance, place in, and value for the Abbey over four centuries. In the twentieth century, there were calls for such a book, at least on the monuments to those who served in the Royal Navy, but no such book was written, perhaps because the records in the Abbey's archive that shed light on the history of the parish church were not well understood or valued as they should have been. To an extent, the story of the Abbey's monuments follows the fortunes of church monuments in general, rising in popularity in the late sixteenth century in the spaces left in churches stripped during the Dissolution, and falling out of fashion in the nineteenth century with the end of intramural burial in 1852 and the rising popularity of stained glass. However, the story of monuments in Bath Abbey is unique. The size and grandeur of the cathedral-like interior to attract and accommodate monuments, its tradition of being the place well-to-do laity of the city were buried before the Dissolution, its status as the city's parish church for visiting nobility from the Elizabethan period, the rise of Bath as a spa bringing the rich and dying, the lack of extra-mural burial ground around the Abbey, and the number of skilled and sought-after sculptors working in the city all combined to create the potential for the Abbey to fill its interior with monuments that would help the church rise from the ashes.

This book is the first history of the Abbey's monuments, and tells the story of this unique collection. Drawing on a wealth of archival material, it explains why and how Bath's central parish church came to have such a large collection of monuments, how they have been depicted by artists and writers, and how they have come to be positioned where they are in the forms they are today. In so doing, it gets beneath the surface of the prevailing narrative that the Abbey was simply a place of burial and commemoration for 'the great and the good'. In addressing the collection of monuments, the book inevitably does not aim to interpret many individual monuments nor biographies of those commemorated in the Abbey. The reader may consult any number of nineteenth- or twentieth-century guidebooks and histories of Bath and the Abbey that have approached individual monuments and their subjects. A number of monuments, such as Bassett's above, have been selected and discussed at greater length. The purpose of their selection has been to illustrate themes and arguments presented by the book that relate to trends in the Abbey's monuments in general. Naturally some, such as Bishop James Montagu's tomb or William Bingham's and Catherine Malone's monuments, have been chosen because of the richness of the documentary sources relating to them. More could be said about all of these monuments and others and no attempt at exhaustive criticism of individual monuments has been attempted. Rather, the book attempts to provide an historical framework and context for those approaching the Abbey's monuments individually or in thematic groups.

The major architectural changes to Bath Abbey's interior are read in relation to the monuments and there is much new material for those interested in the Abbey in general to enjoy. However, the book is confined to a consideration of the church monuments per se, that is, two- and three-dimensional objects in stone. Consequently, regimental colours, memorial windows, the font, lectern, pulpit, and many other aspects of the church that were given 'in memory of', have fallen outside the scope of the book, as have monumental brasses. The rebuilding of the Abbey as we know it today between 1480–1518 and the ruination of the church at the monastery's dissolution in 1539 means that there are no medieval monuments or brasses in the church. The installation of monuments in the Abbey from 1576 coincides with a period in which church brasses were falling out of fashion. From the period of 1600 onwards, 'the introduction of tombstones and epitaphs, sounded the death-knell of the brass'.[21] Whilst a number of brasses were installed in the Abbey in the seventeenth century (the majority in the mid-to-late century) only a few survive, notably those to Sir George Ivy (d. 1639) and Mary Reeve (d. 1664). These seventeenth-century brasses, and those installed in the nineteenth century when brasses came back into fashion, would make for interesting thematic studies in themselves.

Obviously, in terms of the role of commemoration within the church and the Abbey's central role for the city in this, these aspects are inseparable from the monuments. In terms of the aesthetic and revenue of the church, the donations of heraldic glass to the windows in the first two decades of the seventeenth century certainly functioned like the book argues the monuments did afterwards. However, a detailed history of commemorative windows has been beyond the scope of the book and the windows are only considered insofar as they relate to the monuments (and how they often obscured the light from the windows). Likewise, the book is not a history of burial within the Abbey, neither does it address the Abbey cemetery created by John Claudius Loudon, as important as this is. For a history of burial in Bath, readers would do well to consult the Bath Burial Index.[22] Intramural burial in the Abbey is discussed to the extent that it is helpful to understand the context and placement of the monuments, the relative costs of burial and commemoration, and the extent to which monuments contributed to the Abbey's revenue, and the role of the Abbey's sextons.

The monuments played a key role in the Abbey's aesthetics and income from the early seventeenth to the early nineteenth century, and the two were interlinked from the beginning: the revenue from monuments supplemented the income of the Abbey and contributed to its repair,[23] securing its future so it did not fall into ruin (as it had) and cementing its identity as a reformed and later fashionable parish church, fulfilling its Elizabethan raison d'etre to be a place to receive nobility for divine service in life, and their bodies, monuments, and the fees for them, in death. Each of the book's four chapters outlines a distinct phase in the Abbey's history and how monuments contributed to it.

Chapter 1 looks at the creation of the parish church and its role in becoming the premier place of rest and commemoration in the city. It argues that the opportunity to erect monuments in a cathedral-like church helped the rebuilding of the Abbey, to establish the new Protestant identity as well as new revenues for the reformed parish church. It shows how the completion of the second phase of repairs in 1606 (effectively the completion of the Choir, tower and transepts) coincided with the final burial in the nearby Church of St Mary de Stall, and the formal articulation of fees for burial at the Abbey. From this date a number of important seventeenth-century monuments – such as that to Bartholomew Barnes (d. 1606) – were erected in the Abbey. The completion of the Nave by Bishop James Montagu (d. 1618) and his desire to be buried and memorialised in it in order to 'stir up some more benefactors' encouraged others to follow his suit, thus benefiting and beautifying an interior which was empty of medieval monuments and in which executors could consequently take their pick of a location for them. At the end of the century, the Abbey revised its fees and improved the interior of the church. The revenue from burial services and the hire of palls helped to enable these repairs to the church, which, in turn, would have made the interior all the more attractive to those wanting to erect a monument.

Chapter 2 demonstrates how the Abbey and the city worked together to create an identity for Bath Abbey comparable to Westminster Abbey: it became a desirable place to be commemorated for those who might have been buried at Westminster had they died in London. It shows that monuments created by the country's leading sculptors were placed in the Abbey to show them off to best effect, and that the well-respected work of Bathonian sculptors, such as the Harvey family, Thomas King, and John Ford, were celebrated for their own contributions to the church's civic identity. The Abbey authorities also began consciously managing where burials, ledgerstones and monuments were placed, partly to cope with the number of burials, partly to ensure a certain coherence in where certain similar monuments were placed within the church. By the late eighteenth century, the chapter shows that income from burials and monuments at the Abbey contributed between 4–7 per cent of the total annual income of the rectory (that is the total revenue from the Abbey, St James's and St Michael's Without). It looks at a number of monuments, large and small, and illustrates that, whilst £20 was the minimum needed to commission and a erect a 'neat' tablet by a Bath sculptor in the Abbey, the fees received for erection of these monuments was often only 10 per cent of this sum. A number of important monuments are discussed for what they reveal about the process of commissioning and erecting a monument in the Abbey, and the appearance and location of these monuments, and what they tell us about the values the city was trying to convey through them. Ultimately, one's ability to pay the fees for a monument was what was important about whether one was commemorated in the Abbey: denomination and where the money came from were not questioned.

The installation of a monument in the Abbey was the end of a time-consuming process that involved a number of people. There could sometimes be a delay between the death of the person, burial, and monument, since families had to be notified and decide whether they wanted the deceased to be buried in Bath. When the executors did wish for that to be the case and a monument to be erected to the deceased, the Abbey's sexton would dig the grave, the rector and clerk receive a fee for the burial, and the sexton would receive a fee for arranging for the new ledgerstone. If a monument were also to be erected a fee would be paid, either to the sexton or churchwarden, for permission to erect it (up front to reserve space if the monument were to take months or years to create); a sculptor would be commissioned to carve (and occasionally to design from scratch) the monument; when complete, a mason would be paid to fix it to a wall or pillar with metal (usually iron but sometimes copper) bars and mortar, and (in the twentieth and twenty-first centuries, at least) the rector would occasionally dedicate the monument during a service. It could be months, years, and occasionally decades between the subject's death and the erection of their monument. The Abbey's sextons generally received the fees and coordinated the erection of monuments in the Abbey as well as guided visitors around them. They and their hand in installing and interpreting the monuments has been forgotten today. Chapters 1–3 tell the stories of the Abbey's sextons in the seventeenth to nineteenth centuries.

The third chapter looks at the changing attitudes towards the monuments in the nineteenth century and how this, in turn, led them to be modified and moved as part of the major works to the interior of the Abbey. First under George Philips Manners between 1835–36, when the tablets were removed from the pillars, rearranged on the walls and in the recesses of the new gallery for the organ, or reduced to their inscription tablets, which were set into the floor. The motivation for these works was twofold: firstly, to allow more light through the Abbey's windows, which had recently been cleared of surrounding buildings; secondly, to bring order to the perceived confusion in the arrangement of the tablets. Then George Gilbert Scott's works to the monuments between 1868–72 went much further than Manners's had in reducing the original designs of the monuments to their inscriptions and coats of arms, if they had them. Without the pillars, central organ screen or floor to accommodate them, many of the monuments were altered beyond recognition and moved far from their original locations, first in the Nave between 1868–71, then in the Choir in 1871–72. As we will see, Scott's approach to the arrangement was slightly different in each. The arrangement of the wall tablets today is largely that made by Scott and his Clerk of Works, James T. Irvine, and the arrangement of the ledgerstones is that made by the Footprint Project 2018–21. In the case of the wall tablets, the reader throughout this book must imagine the Abbey and its monuments in very different forms and locations to those where they encounter them today. A number of images of the interior are included to help the reader imagine the arrangement of the monuments prior to the nineteenth-century works.

The final chapter looks at how the Abbey treated its monuments and conserved them after Scott's works. Three major projects are discussed: Sir Thomas Jackson's works to organ and how they effected the arrangement of the monuments in the North Transept in 1895–1915; the cleaning of the monuments in the twentieth century by the Friends of Bath Abbey after the Second World War and by Nimbus Conservation in the 1990s; and the Footprint Project conservation of the floor (2018–2021) when the ledgerstones were lifted, conserved and replaced. It looks at how the Abbey tried to retain the orderliness Scott had achieved in the monuments whilst also wanting to accommodate new monuments that commemorated civic achievements and the city's war dead. Just as the sextons had been passionate custodians of the monuments, the chapter highlights the roles Sydney Adolphus Boyd, Gerald Deacon, The Friends of Bath Abbey and others played in the conservation of the Abbey's special and unique collection of monuments. It is hoped that the book as a whole contributes to the same spirit of care for and enquiry into the monuments that has attracted writers on them since the early seventeenth century.

1

CREATION

'WHAT ELSE DOTH ARISE BY BREAKING GROUND FOR BURIAL PLACES, AND FOR MONUMENTS', 1569–1712

Introduction

By the end of the seventeenth century, Bath Abbey had become the parish church for the city and a place for visitors to worship, walk in and survey its growing number of church monuments. Samuel Pepys himself did as much in 1668, tipping the Abbey sexton 1*s* for the trouble of showing him round the city walls and the Abbey's monuments.[1] Yet only a century earlier the church had lain in ruin and was not even owned by the city. How did a building that was little more than a convenient quarry for stone in the late sixteenth century become a desirable place of burial and commemoration? This chapter will examine the transformation of the church from a ruin to place of rest and remembrance. It will discuss how the Abbey, which was not recognised as a parish church until 1573, can have burial registers dating from 1569 and suggests that burials, in fact, began inside the Abbey from 1576, with the registers beginning to be used properly from 1600. The chapter will demonstrate that reading the burial registers alongside sources that illuminate the repairs to the church from 1573 is important to understanding the viability and desirability of burial in the Abbey

Opposite: Detail of the effigies of Bartholomew Barnes (d. 1606) and his wife from his monument on the south wall of the Sanctuary. © Bath Abbey.

in the late sixteenth century. Reading these sources alongside those that tell the story of the rebuilding of the Abbey allows us to see, in detail, how from 1606 the Abbey replaced St Mary de Stalls and its churchyard as the place of burial for the parish and the city's well-to-do visitors. Those visitors' religious sympathies and professional networks became key to the choice of the Abbey as a place of burial and commemoration for them. What better statement of support for the reformed religion than to contribute to the reforming of an entire abbey-church building?

The stories of key individuals, such as James Montagu, Bishop of Bath and Wells 1608–16, and the part they played in intuiting the great opportunity that a magnificent cathedral-like interior which was all but empty of medieval monuments presented to a city like Bath that attracted the wealthy and infirm, will be told. If, like Bartholomew Barnes's executor, one had the money and desire to commemorate a loved one in the Abbey, the size and location of that monument were there for the choosing. That provided both revenue to supplement the church's 'small' income and seems to have set an example that others followed. As the century progressed, the number of monuments erected in the church grew, which, in turn, attracted interest from antiquaries. Their surveys, made as early as 1656, recorded a number of these early monuments that would otherwise have been lost. At the same time, the Abbey came to develop its charges for various extras around burial services, from tolling the bell to hiring of palls, which enabled it to profit from the wealth and social rank of the city's visitors and consequently ensure the Abbey didn't fall into ruin ever again.

In 1539, however, Bath's Abbey Church did stand in ruins. Its monks were pensioned off and the building left open to the sky. Henry VIII gave 'most of the local property of the Abbey' to his illegitimate daughter Etheldreda (whom he married off to John Harington Sr). The church was offered to the city 'at the bargain price of five hundred marks'. But the citizens were 'suspicious of such a cheap deal' and turned the offer down.[2] Without an owner to care for it, it laid the Abbey open to 'acts of vandalism and opportunism'. The bells from the tower, the lead and timbers from the roofs, the glass from the windows, the stone from the walls and the floor, the cloths and silver from the altar were all taken down and taken away. This shell of a church lay open to the sky. In 1542, the church was bought by Humphrey Colles from Taunton, a wealthy local landowner for whom the Abbey must have been secondary to the lands that came with its purchase. In 1548, it was bought by Matthew Colthurst of Wardour Castle in Wiltshire, who bequeathed it to his son Edmund in 1559.

Edmund, in turn, 'presented the priory church to the mayor and citizens of Bath, to become their parish church'.[3]

By then, the church, as the introduction to the Abbey's seventeenth-century *Benefactors' Book* tells us, was 'uncovered and much Ruined as it had longe stood after the Dissolution yet the walles of the greate tower and of most part of the Church then standing'.[4] From the fifteenth century, rich members of the laity had been buried in the monastic abbey-church and some had even prepared monuments for themselves. In 1534, Isabell Chauncellor willed that she be buried in 'St. Leonard's chapell in the north ile under a stone there all redy by me prepared'.[5] In the 1540s, Leland found the church 'onrofid' (unroofed) and 'wedes grew about' the 'sepulchre' of the first Bishop of Bath, John of Tours (d. 1122).[6] Another bishop's 'fair great marble tumbe' seen by Leland leaked oil probably because 'his body was enbaumid plentifully'.[7] Later in the century, Sir John Harington remarked on the graffiti scrawled onto the Abbey's walls.

These descriptions underline the fact that, shortly after the Dissolution, burial and commemoration in the Abbey were neither viable nor desirable. The Dissolution of the Abbey in 1539 also meant that family members who would otherwise have been buried together were buried separately, as was the case with the Style family: Alderman Thomas Style was buried in the 'cathedral church'[8] in 1536 but Mayor Robert Style was of necessity buried in 'the churchyard of Stalles'[9] in 1541. The church of St Mary de Stalls, in the Abbey churchyard, appears to have become the next best place to be buried. In 1561, Bathonian William Baell asked to be buried in the 'parish churche of our blessed ladie of Stallis in the Ile called Sainte Katheren'. The Chapel of St Katherine in the church was a special place of worship for the city.[10] Likewise, before 1576, well-to-do visitors to the city seem to have chosen St Mary de Stalls. For example, in 1573, a Mr William White paid the city 6*s* 8*d* for Mr Willobie to be 'buried in the ile at Stawles'.[11]

Nonetheless, descendants of those families, including the Styles, who had been buried and commemorated in the Abbey wanted to see it and the final resting place of their ancestors restored. Perhaps none more so than Peter Chapman, whose father, Thomas Chapman, was 'buried in the cathedral church of SS. Petir and Powle in Bath' in 1524. Peter, Thomas's youngest son, may have seen his father buried in the Abbey and perhaps saw the window his father asked to be glazed there. Peter distinguished himself as a soldier under Henry VIII, Edward VI, Mary Tudor and Queen Elizabeth I. At the age of 84, he marched 800 men to Tilbury Camp to fight off the Spanish Armada. Through him, royal grants were secured for Bath in 1552 and 1590, and he was surely one of those behind the 'zealous sute of the Maior & Citizens' that resulted in Queen Elizabeth's proclamation of April 1573:

> Elizabeth by the grace of God Queene of England [...] at the most humble desire and zealous sute of the Maior and Citizens of our Citie of Bathe, have given licence to new builde and erecte one Church, upon the foundations of the late Abbey Church of the late dissolved Monastery of Bathe, for the receavyng of such Nobilitie and other our subjects as resort or shall from tyme to tyme have occasions to resorte to that Citie, there to have convenient place to heare Sermons, and other divine service, which cannot conveniently be in any other Church within our sayd Citie, for the smalenes of the rowmes buildinges of the same, and heretofore for lacke of convenient rowmes [...] in the now Churches within our sayd Citie, the Sermons have ben made in the open market place there, beyng not mete nor convenient for such purpose, which greater Church cannot be of newe buylded and finished without greater sumes of money than the Citizens there be able to beare or sustayne. And albeit they [...] themselves very zealous, and do employ great travayles and charges therein, yet are they not able to finish the same, therefore have made their further humble sute unto us to licence them and theyr assignes & deputies to receave the gratuities [...] within this our Realme of England and Wales for the finishyng of the sayd Church.

Work began the same year, and one can imagine Peter Chapman's pride when 'shew[ing] unto my Lorde [Gilbert Berkeley, Bishop of Bath and Wells, 1560–84]' the letters patent.

'As nere as may be to my anncestoures': Burial and commemoration in the Abbey, 1569–1600?

Although the Abbey's burial registers nominally begin in 1569 (as do the surviving registers of the city's other parish churches) it is hard to imagine how burials could have taken place within the Abbey that early. Until 1572, when Edmund Colthurst gave the unroofed and dilapidated church to the city, the city neither owned nor had the right to use the Abbey (and the following year the church became a building site). Marriages might conceivably have taken place if the porch were used for the sacrament, as the porches of medieval churches were, but the body of the church could not have been used for interments. In 1572, the fate of the Abbey was far from certain. Already partly demolished, the church could not 'be of newe buylded and finished without greater sumes of money than the Citizens there be able to beare or sustayne'. Only in 1573 would the Abbey's fate have seemed hopeful, and even then it would have been tenuous at best. Queen Elizabeth I's licence legitimised the city's intention for the Abbey to become the city's parish church. But that was all. There would be almost half a century of work ahead. Before that took place, the Abbey was little more than 'a sort of quarry, from which building materials could be procured'. From 1568, the old Bishop's Palace was also 'used as a stone quarry'.[12] Would relatives really have wanted to bury and erect expensive monuments to loved ones in such a place? How can the entries in the Abbey's burial registers from 1569 be explained?

Between 1576 and 1599, the Abbey's burial registers contain indications of which burials took place in the 'Abby' and occasionally indicate those which took place in the nearby church of St Mary de Stalls (for example, 'Rose Byam was buried the nineteenth Daie [of March 1588] Stawlls'). Such designations clearly differentiate between intramural burials (burials inside the Abbey itself) and burials elsewhere (in the Abbey churchyard or in the nearby church or churchyard of St Mary de Stalls). By 1576, the Chancel of the Abbey (the only part that was then roofed) would have been an increasingly viable and fitting place of burial for the city's elite and the 'strangers' who visited Bath. Confidence in the progress that had been made on the rebuilding of the church was high. The Burghley Papers at the National Archives 'include a Remembrance from the Mayor and Burgesses of Bath to William Burghley in 1576 asking for permission to complete the Abbey Church'.[13] By 1577, the repair of the Chancel roof and North Transept were almost complete and the mayor and Corporation obviously felt confident enough to show off what had been achieved: 13*s* 4*d* was lavished on 'Mr. henry Newtons dyner when he came to vyewe the new church'.[14] In the same year, 'Sir Hary Adams, Vicar of Stawlls & Witcomb' was buried at the Abbey, rather than in St Mary de Stalls.[15] This in itself is telling in how the tide was turning towards the Abbey as the city's premier place of rest.

All institutional and physical traces of St Mary de Stalls have vanished.[16] The exact date that the church was closed is unclear, but it 'remained in use for worship until 1593, and the last burial in the churchyard was not until 1606'.[17] Peter Davenport has written that the 'new abbey church was not ready for services until around 1600' and that 'burials took place there a little earlier'.[18] His date of 1600 is a little late, given that the Abbey had an incumbent from 1583 and paid visiting preachers for sermons there from 1574. Furthermore,

Fig.3: Monument to Richard and William Chapman probably created after the death of the latter c.*1627. The date of Richard's death on the monument (1572) should probably read 1579. © Bath Abbey.*

monuments were being erected in the Abbey itself from the late 1570s. The oldest surviving monument in the Abbey appears to be inscribed with the date 1572, the year in which the monument states alderman Richard Chapman died (Fig. 3). However, it is probable that this date should read 1579.[19]

The other monuments that were erected in the Abbey in the same decade, to John Bellyngham (Bellingham) (d. 1576) and Mrs Margarett Lytchfylde (Lichfield) (d. 1579), were recorded there by Anthony a Wood in 1676, but did not survive the nineteenth-century rearrangements of the monuments. That burials in the 'Abby' began to be designated as such in 1576, the same year that monuments began to be erected there, is evidence that building work at the Abbey had progressed sufficiently to allow both activities to take place by then. Furthermore, John Britton's plan of the Abbey shows that these two early tombs were located in the South Choir Aisle (Fig. 4). In the early 1570s, work to the roof was focused on the north side and North Transept. Erecting these tombs on the south side of the church would therefore have ensured they were under cover, at least risk of damage from the works, and in the best location to be admired. As we shall see, the south side of the Abbey and South Choir became a desirable place to erect monuments, often by those not from Bath. Bellingham and Lichfield's monuments suggest this trend began in the late sixteenth century, and perhaps for the extremely prosaic reason that the building there was simply in a better state of repair than the north side.

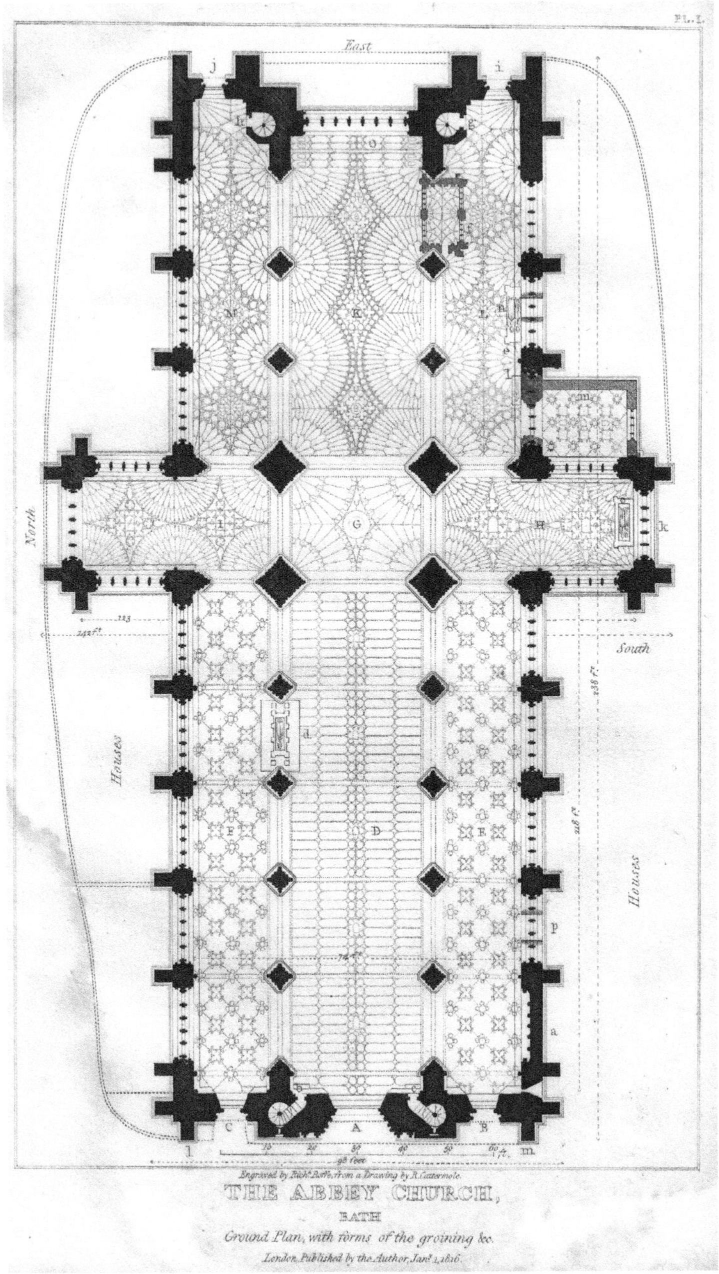

Fig.4: Ground plan of The Abbey Church, Bath, *engraved by Richd. Roffe from a drawing by R. Cattermole (1816), published in Britton's history of Bath Abbey 1825. The tombs of John Bellingham (d. 1576) and Margaret Lichfield (d. 1579) are marked at l and n, respectively, in the South Choir.* © *The author.*

The way in which the Abbey's Parish Registers are written in the late sixteenth century also provides a clue as to what they record. The pages recording the christenings, marriages and burials from 1569 to 1599 are all neatly ruled, margined and carefully written. The entries from 1600 are not so and look like workaday books that were being used day-to-day from this date, with errors and omissions typical of these kinds of documents. By comparison, the neatness and uniformity of the pages for 1569–99 look like they have been copied from another register.[20] The first page of the christenings is even headed 'Chrystninge [...] 1569 unto this present yeare an[n]o 1599', which clearly proves the register of christenings is a copy (probably from another register or registers) made in 1599, and strongly suggests the registers of marriages and burials are too. Insofar as the burial registers are concerned, one possibility is, therefore, that the list of burials 1569–99 were compiled retrospectively using the (now lost) burial register of St Mary de Stalls (which was probably used to record burials in the Abbey from 1576) before the Abbey register was used to record burials there from 1600. That would explain the descriptors 'Abby' and 'Stawlls' to locate burials in what we now call the Abbey burial registers. It would obviously be important to specify the church in which the burials took place (and to carry those forward into the new burial register) in a way that would not be so important for christenings and marriages, hence why such descriptors for those registers may have been felt unnecessary. This theory fails to explain why the surviving registers of the churches that were amalgamated into the Rectory of Bath (St James, St Michael's Without, and the Abbey Church of St Peter and St Paul) all begin in 1569. However, it does explain the difference in the way the Abbey's registers are recorded in 1569–99 and does shed some light on how and when the Abbey subsumed the parish of St Mary de Stalls.

The dating of the phases of repair of the Abbey also helps to support this theory and sheds further light on why the registers of St Mary de Stalls were copied in 1599. Before 1573, when Queen Elizabeth I gave permission for the Abbey to become the city's parish church, there would have been no need for any parish registers for it. In 1576, it seems work on the first phase of repair (making good the Chancel for worship) was sufficiently advanced to allow for burials inside the Abbey and they began to be recorded in the register of St Mary de Stalls. In 1597, the second phase of repair of the Abbey (the rebuilding and reroofing of the transepts and tower) had progressed enough for money to be sought for a bell for the tower. One of the donors, Lord Robert Rich, first Earl of Warwick (1559–1619), was in Bath in that year and was given gifts of wine and sugar by the city, gifts that were customarily given to Abbey benefactors.[21]

His gift of £2 was given 'about the same tyme' as William Ford gathered money 'in the great Church' (the Abbey), as did other aldermen in the city's other parishes (including £10 'Collected in Staules Parish' by Ford himself). By 1600, the work to 'loft and lead' the Abbey's tower was complete. Anticipating this, it would seem the registers of St Mary de Stalls were copied in 1599. After years of uncertainty and disarray (both materially and administratively), it is easy to understand the desire to establish a distinct, new identity for the Abbey in its registers for the new century, a clean break with the past. Reading the burial registers in this way helps us to understand what they record, and that burials in the Abbey itself probably didn't begin until 1576. From 1600, the designations 'Abby' and 'Stalls' cease and it is reasonable to assume that the burials recorded from this date took place in the Abbey itself. It is not until 1684 that qualifiers as to whether a burial is an 'Abbey' burial begin again. Without the complexities discussed above, it must be assumed that these later qualifiers are due to the persuasion or diligence of the individual clerk.

The increasing status of and progress in the Abbey's repairs and the question of what would happen to St Mary de Stalls clearly presented families, such as the Styles, with dilemmas when trying to decide where to bury their loved ones. With relatives buried in St Michael's Without, St Mary de Stalls and the Abbey, Gregory Style did not feel the need to specify his church of choice in his Will in 1577: 'my bodye to be buried in xxon burial as nere as may be to my anncestoures'. His burial on 29 April of that year is recorded in the Abbey registers but not designated 'Abby' or Stalls. However, by the end of the century, the Abbey had become the burial place of choice for both well-to-do visitors to the city and its ruling class. The Chapmans could finally lay family members to rest in the church, something they hadn't been able to do since the days of the monastery.

'To be richly entombed therein': Monuments and the cost of burial and commemoration, 1600–07

By 1595, the Abbey, Sir John Harington wrote to Queen Elizabeth's Lord High Treasurer, Lord Burleigh, 'seemeth more like a church than it has aforetime, when a man could not pray without danger of having good St. Stephen's death, by the stones tumbling about our ears'.[22] With the Choir and transepts roofed by 1600, the Abbey became an increasingly desirable place for burial. That the Chancel of St Mary de Stalls was demolished 'relatively early on after 1583' and most of it 'left as open ground' must have also helped the shift, in local burials at least, to the Abbey.[23] Queen Elizabeth I had envisioned the Abbey as a place 'for the receavyng of such Nobilitie and other our subjects as resort or shall from tyme to tyme have occasions to resorte to that Citie, there to have convenient place to heare Sermons, and other divine service'. From 1576, the Abbey also became the place for those well-to-do visitors to be buried and memorialised. The monuments to John Bellingham, Gentleman of Sussex, and Margaret Lichfield, wife of Thomas Lichfield, lutenist to Queen Elizabeth I, have already been noted above (the latter will be discussed later). To these might be added monuments to William Chapman (d. 1586) and his father Peter (d. 1601/2), the man instrumental in securing the royal patronage for the Abbey (discussed above), whose monuments were located in the North Choir Aisle, which came to be known as the 'Chapman Aisle'. Peter's monument was described by Anthony a Wood in 1676 thus – 'Und' the ar'es of Chapman, on a wooden table joyning to the hatchment of Child, noteth yt und'neath it, lyeth buried' – and the inscription read:

> Nere this place lyeth the body of Peter Chapman of the
> Citie of Bath Gent, who served King Henry the Eighth at
> Bulloigne 6 years. After him King Edward then King
> Phillip and Queen Mary after Queen Elizabeth who when he was
> 84 years old was Sergant Major of 800 men going
> To Tilbury Camp who lived the last year of her Majesties
> Raigne being 96 years old was buried the 23rd of February 1602.[24]

Neither the monument to William nor Peter Chapman survives, although a stone replica of the latter (excluding the arms and hatchment) was donated by descendants of the Chapman family and was erected in the North-East Choir Aisle in 1998 (Fig. 5).

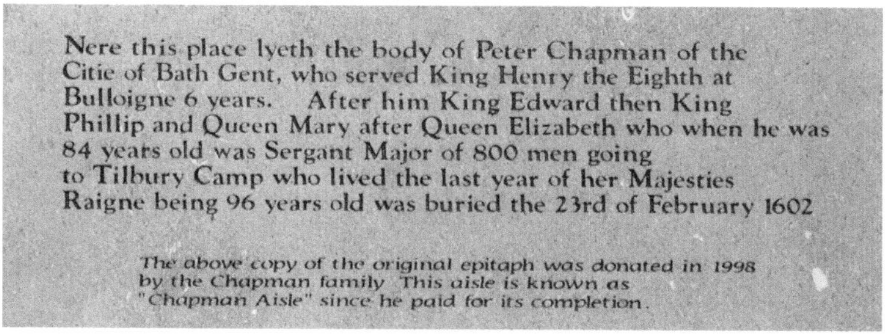
Nere this place lyeth the body of Peter Chapman of the
Citie of Bath Gent, who served King Henry the Eighth at
Bulloigne 6 years. After him King Edward then King
Phillip and Queen Mary after Queen Elizabeth who when he was
84 years old was Sergant Major of 800 men going
to Tilbury Camp who lived the last year of her Majesties
Raigne being 96 years old was buried the 23rd of February 1602
The above copy of the original epitaph was donated in 1998
by the Chapman family This aisle is known as
"Chapman Aisle" since he paid for its completion.

Fig.5: Replica of a tablet to Peter Chapman (d. 1602) donated in 1998. The original monument was wooden and was removed to the vestry in the nineteenth century. It was then lost. © Bath Abbey.

Whilst Harington could write optimistically at the end of the sixteenth century about what had been achieved, by the early 1600s, the fundraising and restoration was faltering: 'how slow it hath rysen again, I may blush to wryte'. Under Elizabeth I's patronage, collections had 'bene made over all England, with which the chauncell [was] covered with blew slate' but now, Harington went on, 'the whole body of the church stands bare'. Elizabeth I died a year after Peter Chapman and their deaths must have been felt by those continuing the restoration of the Abbey. Harington likened the church to 'the poore traveller' in the story of the Good Samaritan, abandoned, 'spoiled and wounded by theeves' (both following the Dissolution and because, according to Harington, not all the money collected under Elizabeth's licence came into the hands of the townsmen of Bath): 'The priest goes by, the levites go by, but doe nothing'. Harington may have also had the lack of diocesan support for the rebuilding in mind in the figure of the priest. Elsewhere, he wrote critically of Bishop John Still's failure to use the bishopric's lead mines to reroof the Nave. Thomas Bellott (1534–1611), the steward to Elizabeth I's Lord Treasurer, William Cecil, was Harington's Good Samaritan. Bellott, like other benefactors to the Abbey in the first decade of the seventeenth century – from the wealthy William Paston in 1604 to the humble tiler-cum-plasterer Richard Beacon in 1606 – both gave generously to the church and created a memorial for himself: in Bellott's case, the 'Billet-wise' glasing of the East Window.

Insofar as monuments per se, Harington worthily commended 'a wealthie cittizen of London' who 'adventured to set his tombe there'. This 'honest citizen did not despaire of the reedifying this church, that gave order to be richly entombed therein'.[25] Harington was, without a doubt, referring to Mr Bartholomew Barnes of the Parish of St Swithen's, who 'being 61 yeeres old, sickened, died, and was buried at Bathe'[26] in the Abbey on 3 October 1606. The Abbey's *Benefactors' Book* describes his contribution to the church as follows:

> Rowland Backhouse of London Merchant & Alderman, free of the Company of Mercers, Executor unto Mr Bartholomew Barnes of the same Cittie Mercer in the behalf of the said Mr. Barnes who lieth buried in the South side of the Quier at the upper end gave 12li.[27]

Backhouse's payment of £12 from Barnes's estate was certainly modest considering Barnes's wealth. In 1599, Barnes, his relative Edward Barnes, and son-in-law and executor Rowland Backhouse (d. 1648), collectively invested £300 in the East India Company,[28] a sum worth approximately £41,000 today.

It is interesting that even in 1607, when Barnes's monument was erected and the Choir, tower and transepts were complete, commissioning a tomb in the Choir could still be described as an 'adventure'. It was certainly less of an adventure than it had been. However, the fact that Backhouse erected two different monuments to Barnes after his death – one in St Swithen's Church, Walbrooke, London, where a small monument on a pillar of the middle aisle was erected and the other in the South-East Choir of the Bath Abbey – perhaps suggests that Barnes's executor shared Harington's uncertainty about whether (and if so, how) the church might be completed. Erecting a monument even in the Choir of the Abbey was an act of faith, in more than one sense. Barnes was described as 'a worshipfull and wise Gentleman, and a worthy friend and favourer of Religion' in *Stow's Survey of London* (1633). This is certainly the impression Backhouse wished to give of Barnes, both in the style and substance of his monument in the Abbey. The Latin inscription, originally inlayed in gold, reads:

> IN OBITVM BARTHOLOMEI BARNES
> DEFVNCIT VIRI VERAE RELIGIONIS
> AMANTISSIMI NVPER MERCATORIS
> LONDINENSIS NVNCQ, COELORVM
> REGNI CIVIS BEATI.
>
> RELIGIO, PIETAS, FACVNDAE GRATIA LINGVAE,
> INGENIVM, VIRTVS, INVIOLATA, FIDES,
> CVM GRAVITATE LEPOS CVM, SIMPLICITATE VENVSTAS,
> LARGA MANVS, PECTVS NOBILE, FIRMVS AMOR,
> DENIQ QVICQVID HABET NATVRA QVOD ADDERE POSSIT,
> ADDERE QVOD POSSIT GRATIA QVICQVID HABET,
> OMNIA BARONEM VIVVM COMITATA FVERVNT,
> OMNIA MORS ATRAX, OBRVIT ISTA SIMVL.
> OBRVAT ISTA LICET, TRISTI MORS SOEVA SEPVLCHRO,
> TTAMEN ILLOREY FAMA SVPERSTES ERIT[29]

In 1825, John Britton found that the lines were 'the earliest specimen of Latin verse' to survive in the Abbey. Barnes's tomb is now the only *prie-Dieu* style monument in the Abbey (Colour Plate A). His wife Margaret (m. 1572) and his children, including a surviving son, Bartholomew, and daughters Margaret, Mary, and three others whose names are lost, have also had their effigies carved onto the monument.

Two different monuments in two different churches were well within Barnes's means. His cenotaph in London, although more modest than his tomb in the Abbey, would have been seen as a fitting perpetuation of his memory and legacy by Barnes's friends and colleagues. Barnes would have probably liked the 'adventure' of a tomb in the Abbey. Both Barnes and his son-in-law Backhouse were Merchant Adventurers, as well as members of the Mercers' livery company.[30] As it happens, Barnes's 'small Memorie on a pillar in the middle Ile' in St Swithen's, Waldbrook, was lost when the church was destroyed in the Great Fire of London in 1666. Backhouse's contribution to the Abbey from Barnes's estate and decision to erect a tomb to him there is illustrative of how, after the money collected under Elizabeth's licence dried up, Bath's ruling class – many of them clothiers and mercers themselves – successfully exploited business, religious and political networks to raise funds for the completion of the church.[31] Barnes was a Puritan and his Will displays 'closer links with the leaders of the presbyterian movement'. Barnes requested that Stephen Egerton give his funeral sermon (and also left him £10): 'Egerton had been suspended from preaching by Bishop Aylmer in 1583 for refusing to subscribe to Archbishop Whitgift's articles demanding conformity with the royal supremacy, the Prayer Book and the Thirty Nine Articles' and at the time Barnes made his Will 'Egerton was curate of St. Anne's Blackfriars, where he ministered to a *strongly puritan congregation, largely made up of merchants' wives*'.[32] By the end of the century, Henry Chapman claimed that 'not any one (that I know of) not of the Religion professed and established, gave one Penny towards its [the Abbey's] Reparation'.[33] This is obviously wishful thinking and a bit rich from the recently reformed old cavalier. Nonetheless, Chapman was right to highlight the link between religious sympathy with the reformed church and those who supported the Abbey's rebuilding financially. Fees for burials and erecting monuments were part of the revenue from these people and would have been used for the church's repair. This type of revenue became all the more important in later centuries.

On 25 May 1606, five months before Barnes was buried in the Abbey, the Mayor of Bath and representatives from the parish of St Mary de Stalls met, considered, and 'agreed' the charges 'concernynge buriells in the greate churche'. The note, written upside down at the back of the register for 1569–1743, is considerably faded and illegible in parts. But it is possible to make out that:

> concernynge buriells in the greate churche [illegible] that [?persons] of the degree of A knight with thatte those buried shall paid for breaking the

grounde xx b [shillings] and vi b [shillings] viii d [pence] ringinge the greate bell [illegible, but probably visitors or non-parishioners which would make this a sliding scale of fees] breakinge ye grounde and v b [shillings] for ringinge the greate bell All [?others to paie?] vi b [shillings] viii d [pence] for breakinge the grounde and ii b [shillings] vi d [pence] for ringinge the bell [illegible] child ii b [shillings] for breakinge ye earthe.[34]

The agreement is significant for two reasons. Firstly, it is the earliest extant expression of burial fees for the Abbey. The premise of setting a sliding scale of fees with higher costings for high-ranking nobility (from out of town) would be one followed in all later tables of fees for burial at the Abbey. This pragmatic response to the increasing numbers of well-to-do visitors to Bath (some of whom were visiting on account of their ill health) made good economic sense for a church in need of funds for its completion. The newly repaired east end of the church would have made an impression on dying visitors and their relatives, who may have been attracted to inter their loved ones there, instead of transporting them to their home parishes for burial. As we will see in the following chapter, even for those who were embalmed and 'carried away', the Abbey was a used as a spectacular mortuary (for which a fee was also charged).

The second reason that the agreement of Abbey burial fees in 1606 is significant is that, in the same year, according to Peter Davenport, the 'last burial in the churchyard'[35] of St Mary de Stalls took place. Furthermore, in 1606, Thomas Bellott was also in Bath, as shown by a payment of 19*s* 6*d* in the Chamberlain's Accounts for 'a gifte given to Mr. Billett'.[36] The gift perhaps marked a significant moment in, or conceivably even the completion of, the second phase of repairs, to which Bellott was the principal benefactor. The convergence of these three things – the first articulation of the Abbey's burial fees, the end of burials in St Mary de Stalls churchyard, and the completion of the second phase of repairs to the Abbey – is no coincidence and demonstrates a significant milestone in Bath's project to make the Abbey the parish church for the city and its visitors. In 1606, then, thirty years after burials began to take place in the Abbey, it seems it was sufficiently restored to replace St Mary de Stalls as a place of burial. This piece of logistical and administrative tidying up is echoed by smaller payments in the Chamberlain's Accounts that suggest a tidying up of the two churchyards, also in 1606: 'the pavyor for worke don in Stalls Churchyarde' was paid 9*d* and 'John Pavyor' was paid 12*d* 'for leavyinge the Waie to the Abbye'.[37]

A comparison with the earliest Churchwardens' Accounts for the nearby Church of St James, from 1654, show that the Abbey's fees were in line with other churches: 6*s* 8*d* was received for 'the Buriall of a Stranger'; 3*s* 4*d* was received for the burial of two local men, Walter Werratt and Nicholas Byam (the latter 'in Snt. Georges Isle'); and 2*s* was generally received for the burial of children (although 'Willm Adlington's Daughter' was buried at a cost of 3*s* 4*d* and in 1655 the burial of 'a Strangers Child' cost 3*s*). In 1655, John Farr, either the mason or sexton, was paid 1*s* 'for laying the toombestone on Captane Constants grave'.[38]

The Chamberlain's Accounts show that the city occasionally paid the necessary fees for burial, albeit less frequently at the Abbey than at the other churches. Richard Gillian (or Gyllian) appears to have acted as a sexton for a number of churches and probably at the Abbey too. In 1594, he was paid 4*d* by the city for digging the grave of John Swayne, whose burial is recorded in the Abbey register on 23 April. However, the entry is neither qualified 'Abby' nor 'Stalls', so it is likely Swayne was buried in the Abbey churchyard or that of St Mary de Stalls. Gillian was paid a stipend of 10*s* and given a coat annually between 1595 and 1597.

Later in the century, Mr Spincke and Thomas Dale were paid for 'buryinge' (gravedigging) in 1635 and 1636; however, neither of them took place in the Abbey. The cost of digging a grave in the Abbey remained the same into the 1600s as can be seen from the payment of fourpence for 'Digginge the widdowe Chapmans grave' (Mrs Joane Chapman, widow, was buried in the Abbey on 20 February 1633). However, by 1662 Richard Wakelie and James Davis were paid 1*s* (or 6*d* each) for digging a grave for Thomas Poole at St John's Hospital.

Occasionally, where 'strangers', that is people from outside the parish (usually visitors to the city from elsewhere in the country), were unable to pay for their burial in the Abbey, the city paid the bill, as was the case in September 1656 when Richard Wakelie was paid 2*s* 'for Candles and Chardges for burieinge of One Honny [William Honey] That Dyed in the Church yard by Mr Mayors Order', or in 1676 when George Spering was paid 10*s* 2*d* for 'buriell & other expences for on drouned' at the weirs. Like Richard Gillian, Richard Wakelie and George Spering were paid by the city to dig graves at other burial places, as well as the Abbey. In 1676, 'George Spearing' was listed as sexton at the vestry meeting of St James' Church.[39] Richard Wakely was buried in the Abbey on 9 May 1684. His entry is written with particular care in the register, suggesting Wakely may have been the sexton and known to the clerk. The cost for the burial of the drowned man is unusually high and other records suggest this sum probably included a ledgerstone for him: he was Dr Henry Stubbs.[40] Two shillings seems to have been about the going rate for a burial in the middle of the seventeenth century: the clerk of St James' was paid 2*s* in 1660–61 'for Ringing the Bell & digging a Grave for the Widd.[ow] Ball'. The gradual increase in this cost can be seen by comparing it with the payment of 12*d* (1*s*) 'to the Prist & Clarcke & Bellman for Mother Wardes buryall' at St John's Hospital in 1597 and 1*s* 4*d* 'payd to the Minister Clarke and Sexton for burieinge of Joane Moore' in 1640. The location of this last burial is not known but a Joane, daughter of Mr Walter Chapman, was buried in the Abbey on 1 May 1640. Burial of children in the Abbey appears to have attracted similar fees to those charged by St James' (given above). For example, in 1651 the mayor ordered that a widow, Thomasin Webbe, be paid 2*s* 6*d* towards the burial of her daughter, Elizabeth, in the Abbey. In subsequent centuries, burials of children in the Abbey attracted lower fees than adult burials.

The cost of shrouds for burials at the Abbey (and other churches) were also occasionally paid for by the city. In 1600, the city paid 3*s* 10*d* for a shroud for Hugh Hill. The cost of his burial in the Abbey (6*d*) on 10 May was also met by the city. The cloth for shrouds was supplied by the city's clothiers, including the Chapmans. In this way the expansion of burials into the Abbey would have had a small financial benefit to those in that line who had supported the rebuilding of the Abbey. In 1632, Mr William Chapman was paid 6*s* 'for his six ells of narrowe holland Delivered to John Ady for a couple of Shroudes'. Those for children were proportionally cheaper at 1*s* 2*d*, the cost of Sara, daughter of Walter Werratt's shroud for her burial in the Abbey on 5 January 1649. By 1670, 4*s* 8*d* appears to have been a standard costing for an adult's shroud. In comparison, in 1694, 'a Coffin for a souldier that dyed at Kingsmead house and for men to carry him & for digging ye grave & ringing ye bell' cost 12*s*.[41] In 1705, new arrangements (discussed at the end of this chapter) were made for the use of palls.

'To stirr up some more benefactors to that place': Bishop James Montagu and the repair of the Abbey floor, 1608–18

As Sir John Harington intimated, fundraising and works to the church had faltered by the first decade of the seventeenth century. Yes, the Abbey was sufficiently repaired by 1606 to establish itself as a place of burial to replace St Mary de Stalls and its churchyard. But the income from burials alone (at this time) would not be enough to undertake the work required in the Nave, let alone put a roof on it. East of the tower was complete enough to attract executors like Backhouse to erect tombs there, but the larger space of the Nave not so. New revenue streams and a major patron were needed in the new century to finish the project begun a generation before.

On 26 February 1608, Dr John Still, Bishop of Bath and Wells, died. Amongst other things, for the Abbey this meant a new potential benefactor, one who might bring the diocese's resources, and in particular the lead from its mines, to help roof the Nave. Still had given modestly to the second phase of repair (the rebuilding and reroofing of the South Transept and tower): he is third in the list of such benefactors, having given £20, probably before May 1603, when William Powell, his Archdeacon of Bath, gave £10.[42] However, he appears to have been hesitant to use the diocese's lead mines to help the Abbey. Harington recalls that Still was approached by Sir Arthur Hopton (d. 1607) about the roof, since Still was 'well bestowed' with the 'the lead mines of Mendip'. Hopton 'was wont betweene earnest and sport to motion [him] "to give toward it but the lead to cover it [the Abbey] which would cost him nothing"'. But Still replied, 'Well said, gentle Sir Arthur, you will coffe me as you scoffe me', which, as Harington says, 'is no great token that he liketh the motion'. However, when Still was in Bath, Harington remembers 'he promised them very faire', which the city and its supporters reminded him of, but which appears to have come to nothing.[43]

Such a promise seems only to have been made good by Still's successor as Bishop of Bath and Wells, Reverend James Montagu. Montagu was enthroned at Wells Cathedral on 14 May 1608, and within a month had visited Bath. In Bath he was courted by the mayor and aldermen, who presented him with 'a Cupp' worth £10 4*s* wrapped in a 'Green cloth'. However, if John Harington is to be believed, it was the weather more than the cup that seems to have encouraged Montagu to support the Abbey so generously. During the same visit, he was caught in a late spring shower, the incident that gave rise to the story about how Harington convinced the Bishop to give to the church:

> Conversing one day with bishop Montague, near the abbey, it happened to rain, which afforded an opportunity of asking the bishop to shelter himself within the church. Especial care was taken to convey the prelate into that aisle which had been spoiled of its lead, and was nearly roofless. As this situation was far from securing his lordship against the weather, he remarked to his merry companion that it did not shelter him from the rain. 'Doth it not, my lord?' said Sir John, 'then let me sue your bounty towards covering our poor church; for if it keep not us safe from the *waters* above, how shall it ever save others from the *fire* beneath?' At which

> jest the bishop was so well pleased, that he became a liberal benefactor both of timber and lead; and this benefaction procured a complete roofing to the north aisle of the abbey church, after it had lain in ruins for many years.[44]

In *A collection of treatises relating to the city and waters of Bath* (1725) Henry Chapman printed the 'Historico-Poetical Account' of the Abbey that Harington 'delivered' to Montagu, and the Bishop's 'prophetic' reply concerning its 'happy restoration' (although the poem is obviously an imagining after the fact, as is made clear by its 1609 date). In answer to Harington, Montagu is said to have replied: 'I have long desired to see and contemplate these Ruins and Rubbish; and now it grieves me to behold Them: However, I will enter; but with this Intent, Never to re-enter 'till I see them better cover'd'.[45] Lead, timber and money for the workmanship were secured. Montagu was in Bath again in 1609. It is just as unthinkable that the Nave roof was completed by then as it is that he didn't enter the unfinished church. By 1612, however, the Nave roof was complete, a new stone pulpit given by Montagu was installed on the south side of it, and a lavish, celebratory 'Supper for the Lorde Bishopp provided at Mr. Clifts howse ye whole chardge amountinge to xiij.li ij.s 4.d'[46] (almost a year's wages for one of the skilled tradesmen working on the Abbey).

With the roof complete, the Nave could begin being used for services and monuments could begin to be erected without the risk of being damaged by the wind, rain, frost, and worse. Montagu's gift towards the roofing, valued at £1,000 in the Abbey *Benefactors' Book* written shortly after Montagu's death in 1618, has found its way into most historical accounts of the Abbey. What have not been remarked on are Montagu's other gifts to the church and how he galvanised the fundraising for other important repairs – notably, for our purposes, the floor of the church, which the *Benefactors' Book* records Montagu completed: 'The Greate Middle space of the Bodie of the Church was Paved at the Charge of the Lo: Bishopp Montague the Charge came to 43li. 6s. 8d. Thus came this Church to be all Paved' (Colour Plate B).[47] These repairs began with the paving of the cross aisle (the area connecting the two transepts) before Thomas Bellott's death in 1611, and then took place across the rest of the Abbey floor (with the exception of the centre of the Choir) between 1614–15. They would have been necessary to make good the floor after decades of being open to the sky. The entry recording Montagu's completion of the paving suggests that the paving of the church had generally been removed at the Dissolution and that the majority of the church was unpaved. Another reason that repairs may have been necessary is because the Nave may have already begun to be used for burials, despite being unroofed.

The 'Benefactors to the Paving of the Church', as recorded in the Abbey's *Benefactors' Book*, all had a good reason to want the paving to be well repaired: either because they themselves had asked to be buried there in their Wills, or because they had buried family members there, or both. Cross-referencing the *Benefactors' Book* with the burial register helps to date some of the payments towards the repair of areas of the Abbey floor. The clothier Francis Allin (who paid for the paving of the South Choir Aisle) and lady's maid Mrs Margaret Mannering (who contributed towards the paving of the North Nave Aisle) were buried in the Abbey on 2 January and 18 August 1615, respectively. In the same year, Mrs Gertrude Wood, wife of the Alderman John Wood, was buried in the Abbey on 23 November 1615. A year earlier, 'Lady Marie wife to Sr Augustine Nicols, Judge of the Comon Pleas' was also buried in the Abbey (Anthony a Wood also recorded a monument to her on the north wall of the North Transept in 1676).[48] Both husbands (Wood and Nicols) are named as benefactors to the paving and it is likely their gifts were given at the time of their wives' burials (his wife's health and funeral must surely have been the reasons Sir Augustine Nicholls was in Bath). Equally, it would make sense for Lady Booth's gift towards the paving of the majority of the North Choir Aisle to have been given in 1615, the year 'her cosen' Margaret Mannering who was 'dwelling' with her was buried. It is beyond the historical record to date the gift of the 'three Seafayring men', Richard Stanly, John Smith and Ellis Wood. However, since it is written as a continuation of the gift of the Lady Booth, rather than a separate entry in its own right, it may also date to 1615. John Webb, the octogenarian gentleman farmer of Swainswick, who also gave to the paving of the North Nave Aisle, was buried '80 years and upward' at Swainswick on 4 April 1616, so his gift may also date to the 1614–15 period.[49] The *Benefactors' Book* records a total of £81 8*s* 7*d* given towards the repair of the Abbey floor in the early seventeenth century, with a further £30 donated by Dr Robert Peirce at the end of the century towards the paving of the South Aisle (Peirce and his family's monuments there will be discussed at greater length at the end of this chapter).

From the late 1500s, the paving of the city in general had become a concern for the Corporation and there are numerous entries in the Chamberlain's Accounts concerning the city's streets. Insofar as the paving in the churches is concerned, the Chamberlain's Accounts help us to understand the costs involved in paving the Abbey and even suggest who carried out the work. In 1589, 'paving over a grave in Stalles Church' cost 6*d* (and 5*d* the following year).

In 1602, several payments to a pavier named John shed some light on the cost per yard of paving when the High Street and Westgate were paved by him: 'paid for fower [4] load of stones to pave att the Weste gate iiij.s [4*s*]'; 'paid for xxiiij.tie [24] yeards of pavinge at the weste gate unto John Pavier at j.d [1*d*] ob [of] the yeard iii.s'; 'paid for a hundred & three score yeards of pavinge in the high streete unto John Pavier at j.d [1*d*] ob the yeard xx.s [20*s*]'. Thomas Masey may well have been the quarryman from whom the stone was bought ('paid for eighteen loades of stones for to pave in the high streete unto Thomas Masey xviij.s [18*s*]'). The Corporation bought stone from Masey on many other occasions. Richard Baker and Thomas Beaker also laboured for John on these occasions, transporting the rubble and sand.[50]

In 1602, John the Pavier was also paid 'to goe unto Bristoll to gett paviers' ahead of Queen Elizabeth I's intended visit. The anxiety over the state of the paving in Bath generally can be felt by the fact that Robert Vernam was sent to Tetbury and Chichester, Roger Ffeilde's man was sent to Frome, and others were also sent to Warminster and Chippenham. Although Elizabeth ultimately didn't visit the city, a payment for 'a hammer for the strange paviors vi.d' suggests that some came and that some work was carried out by them.[51] With so many specialist paviers in Bath and the prospect of showing off the progress in the Abbey to the Queen, it is tempting to wonder if any of them were shown what was needed in the Abbey, and even if any of them advised on or carried out early work to the paving of the Cross Aisle or Choir.

John Bigg is almost certainly the local pavier (John Pavier) who carried out the work on the Abbey. In 1613 he paved St Michael's Church[52] and in 1615 made the 'floure' [floor] in the town hall, for which he was paid 5*s*. Christopher Oulden, his labourer, was paid 20*d* to 'sift and carry sand from the Churche to the same floure'.[53] This suggests that Oulden was moving materials the pair had used in paving the Abbey in 1614–15 the short distance from the church to the new town hall. The work would have been especially personal to Bigg, since on 22 March 1581 'Jone wife of John Bigg' was buried in the 'Abby'.

The repair of both the Nave roof and the floor of the church led to an increasing number of Wills asking to be buried and commemorated in the Abbey by ledgerstones alone. In 1615, the wealthy clothier Francis Allin willed 'his body to be buried in the greate churche of Peter and Paule in Bathe' and that his son and executor John Allin should 'bestowe xxv [shillings] [illegible] at the leaste upon a tombe stone to laye over my corpes where at Bathe buried'. The cost suggests Allin had an elaborately inscribed ledgerstone in mind when compared with the sixpence for simple 'paving over a grave in Stalles Church' in 1589.

Likewise, in 1624, Dame Elizabeth Booth (d. 1628), who, like Allin, might easily have afforded a spectacular monument, preferred to be buried in the South Aisle 'by my cosen Margarett Manneringe without any Tombe erected for me after my death, but a Tombestone with a short Epitaph *I have chosen the Lord for my keeper* or such like'.[54] Sadly, neither Allin's nor Booth's ledgerstones has survived today (the earliest surviving ledgerstone dates to 1623, and since 1874 has been covered by the Corporation Stalls). But their Wills show that, after 1615, a ledgerstone in the Abbey was seen as fitting memorial, even for the upper classes.

In 1616, Montagu's translation to the Bishopric of Winchester left the Abbey, once again, without a patron (although it could be argued that the rector, John Pelling, discussed below, continued the spirit of selfless giving that Montagu had shown to the church until his death in 1620 – although his gifts were, strangely, neither recorded in the *Benefactors' Book* nor quantified elsewhere). Montagu's Will, made in April 1618, only months before his death in July of that year, appears to both recognise the problem for his beloved Abbey church and the solution that his patronage seems to have helped emerge for it. With the exception of Prior Birde's Chantry Chapel, all medieval monuments appear to have been removed from the church at the Dissolution. Unlike many cathedrals, then, the interior of the church was a blank canvas for both old and new money to erect monuments in. The combination of monied, ailing visitors to Bath and a church with plentiful space for spectacular monuments could be an endless source of revenue for the Abbey. In his Will, Montagu set the example he hoped others would follow:

> My body I comit to the earth whence it was taken, there to rest in hope of a glorious resurrection, beseechinge my executor that it may be decently buryed, without cuttinge or manglinge, if it be possible, in the great church of Bath, in some convenient place in the body of that church, to stirr up some more benefactors to that place.[55]

Being 'buryed in a remote place', such as Bath, as he described it in his Will, Montagu saw 'no great reason to be at any extraordinary charge' for his funeral expenses. Yet, he went on, 'my will is to have 300li bestowed uppon a monument in the body of the church of Bath, and for all other charges I would not have my executor to exceed the sum of 400li'. Whilst the monument appears to have been within the sum Montagu asked for, his funeral expenses were certainly not. The itemised expenses of the funeral allow us to build up a detailed picture of the customs and costs of a high-profile burial at the Abbey at the beginning of the seventeenth century.

On Montagu's death in Greenwich on 20 July 1618, three surgeons were employed to 'imbowell' him. His bowels were buried (by torchlight) at a cost of £2.[56] Charges were also incurred for 'breakeing the ground in the chauncell' (£2), 'makeing the grave' (2*s*), 'an afternoones knell' (6*s* 8*d*), 'the minister' (£2) and 'the clark' (2*s*). A coach and horses were then hired 'to carrye the corpps to Bathe' and 'stuffe to new imbalme the bodye and for scareclothing to carrie it stanch to the Bathe' purchased. The journey took the company from London to Reading, Newbury and Marlborough to Bath, where a payment to 'Mr Walter Chapman for 3 houses, plate, linnen, pvisions' suggest the party may have stayed at The White Hart. Chapman was paid a further £36 8*s* for arranging 'for 30 poore men, to be distributed at Bathe as followeth, vidz: to – for his gowne & xij d in reward'. A similar payment was made for the '20 poore men that came from Wells to attend the funerall'.

Preparations were then made for the Abbey to be suitably decked in mourning (a tradition continued into later centuries for high-profile funerals). Timber 'rayles to hang the blacks about the church' were set up at a cost of £1 19*s* 6*d* and 'black bays [baize]' hired 'to hang round the church & the 3 houses at Bathe £5' (presumably where the company stayed). A further £2 was paid 'for the spoyleing of 80 yerds of black bayes', which indicates the amount of fabric used for these decorations, not to mention the hundreds of yards of black cloth for the mourners and their gowns.

Montagu's funeral took place on 20 August. If the accounts were not enough to tell us how well-attended it was, Thomas Fuller's anecdote about the crush emphasises it. Fuller tells the story of a 'certain officer of Bath church' who was 'appointed to keep the doors' on the day of the bishop's burial. Such was the role of the sexton in later centuries and likely here also. The funeral expenses record a payment 'to the beadles that kept the church doore £1' so more than one person may have occupied the role, which was also not uncommon at the Abbey. Unfortunately, for one of them, Fuller writes, being a 'very corpulent man' he was 'bruised to death by the pressing-in of people' and was buried before the night.[57] The only entry for 20 August 1618 in the Abbey's burial register is for Bishop Montagu. However, there is only one entry the following day (21 August) for a man named John Broade, perhaps the unidentified sexton. His counterpart would have taken a share of the £2 for 'breakeing the ground in the church'. Sixteen shillings were paid 'for the ringers'. The 'sum total of funerall charges', according to the accounts, was £1,240 18*s* 11*d*. This sum included the £300 for 'makeing and finishing the toombe, with the grate of iron, and for the carriage of it from London to Bathe and all other charges about it' and £10 for 'makeing the epitaphs for the toombe'.

On 25 November 1618, Sir Charles Montagu commissioned the freemason William Cuer and carver Nycholas Johnson to 'make, compose, frame, erect, set up, perfect, and finish [...] one tombe or monument of alabaster and touchstone wth armes to be carved and engraven, and to be set in their proper coulours and metals'. The detailed specification for the tomb, transcribed in Dingley's *History from Marble*, reveal the inscriptions were 'appoynted by the said Sr Charles or his assignes' and the 'figure representing the said Ld Bishop of Winchester' was 'well laid in oyle colours'. The tomb was to be 'transported, erected, set up, and finished in the said Cathedrall Church of Bath at or before the eight daie of October next [1619]'. Rather than £300, Sir Charles Montagu appears to have paid Cuer and Johnson 'two hundredth pounds' for the tombe and then, in addition, paid for the 'iron grate' surrounding it at his own charge. In 1767, the Duke of Montagu 'gave £20 towards re-beautifying this monument', which was also restored in the nineteenth century by John Stone, when he was town clerk (Colour Plates C and D).[58]

Fig. 6: Undated nineteenth-century print (possibly c.*1835) depicting the tomb of Bishop James Montagu (d. 1618) in the Nave. The artist has deliberately drawn the pillars and walls without tablets to emphasise the tomb. © The author.*

The eventual location of the tomb, situated beneath the second-most easterly arch of the Nave between the central and north aisles, ensured maximum visibility of this most 'stately Monument' for it to function as Montagu intended (Fig. 6). Wealthy would-be benefactors, drawn to Bath because of their poor health, would see the tomb, learn the story of Montagu's generosity, and respond in kind. By paying for their own monuments they, too, would do what Montagu desired: contribute both materially and monetarily to the beautification and upkeep of the church. As the century progressed, the number of monuments in the Abbey increased. Montagu intuited that these material contributions both to the coffers and the beautification of the interior of the Abbey would transform the church from a bare, whitewashed shell into desirable place of rest and commemoration. The success of Montagu's plan was confirmed in 1673 by Henry Chapman. As a churchwarden of the Abbey in 1666, the church's finances would have been well known to him. At the end of the seventeenth century, Chapman put the revenue of the church at about £20 per annum. This was, he went on, 'but a small maintenance for so great a Building, yet with this, and with what else doth arise by breaking ground for Burial places, and for Monuments, it is as well kept in Repair as any Church I know of'.[59]

'One or two observable monuments': Seventeenth-century surveys and descriptions of the monuments

Although seventeenth-century accounts of Bath naturally focus on the baths themselves, several of them do provide a picture of the Abbey's monuments from the 1630s, albeit with most attention paid to the large tombs. In July 1635, Sir William Brereton described the Abbey as 'as lightsome a pleasant church as any I have seen' but 'only one or two observable monuments', picking out the Montagu tomb in particular. The only aspect of 'the greatt Church' remarked on by Peter Mundy in June 1639 was the 'pretty passionate Monumentt off the Lady Mary Walles [sic], wife to Sir [William] Wales, knight, hee yet alive' (that is, the tomb of Lady Jane Waller). Towards the end of the century, Celia Fiennes was less enamoured with the 'lofty and spacious' church, whose Choir she found 'neat but nothing extraordinary'. Her observation that 'much Company walke there especially in wet weather' shows the growing attraction of the church and its monuments to the city's visitors in the late seventeenth century. Among them Samuel Pepys, who, on 14 June 1668, took his wife and maid to see the church 'and look over the monuments, where, among others, Dr. Venner and Pelling, and a lady of Sir W. Waller's; he lying with his face broken' (Colour Plates E and F).

As well as casual visitors, from the middle of the seventeenth century the Abbey's monuments were sufficiently important to attract antiquaries, who recorded them in various levels of detail. The earliest extant survey, dated 1656–57, was made by Maurice Price, servant to Timothy Baldwin, then Doctor of Civil Law and Fellow of All Souls College in Oxford, as part of his *Transcript of several Coates of armes belonging to several Noble Familyes their plaices of Buriall together wth the Epitaphes and Inscriptions upon their several Tablets & Grave Stones*. Strangely, Price only recorded a handful of monuments in the North Aisle of the Nave, principally those to Bishop James Montagu, Reverend John Pelling and Robert Culliford. He also recorded two hatchments and the inscription on Montagu's pulpit (also recorded by Dingley in his *History from Marble*). His most valuable record, which is unique, is that of the only ledgerstone he recorded. This was the ledgerstone to Maria, the beautiful, chaste and loving wife of Richard Wakeman Jr, who died in 1655. Were it not for Price's record of it, the monument would have been lost to history, unrecorded as it is by later antiquaries: 'Quae jacet hic quaris. desir hinc Wakemanam Maria, provida, quae conjux pulchra pudica pia. 1655'.[60] This was possibly one of the monuments to the Wakeman family paid for by the city in 1655 (see below).

Henry Chapman's *Thermae Redivivae; or, The City of Bath described* (1673) also recorded a number of monuments and inscriptions now lost. In his account of the city, Chapman consciously tried to honour those of earlier generations who had repaired the Abbey. Unsurprisingly, then, he picked out Montagu's 'noble Monument' first for special mention, followed by Montagu's contemporary Rev. John Pelling (Rector of the Abbey, 1608–20). Pelling's monument was located opposite Montagu's on the wall of the North Aisle. According to Chapman, 'the City, in Testimony of the Respects they owed' him erected the monument for his indefatigable zeal in promoting the repair of the church. Chapman recounts that 'in that generous and benefactory Age' if any 'Person of Honour offered to him', Pelling would respond '*Non Mihi, sed Ecclesiae*, which occasioned that Motto over his Tomb'.[61] The full inscription, including the motto, was recorded in 1778 when the monument was described as '*A Freestone Monument, Erected to the memory of* Johanni Pellings [sic]': 'With a 3-qr. Length of the deceased in a nitch. In his right hand he holds a book; his left, is on a skull resting on a cushion. On each side is two small figures, one holding a skull, the other an hour-glass'.[62]

The monument can be seen in the North Aisle beneath the window on the right-hand side of Samuel Grimm's drawing of 'A Service at Bath Abbey' (1788) (Colour Plate G). The large monument on the very far right of the drawing, which also contains a three-quarter length figure, is the monument to Robert Mason (d. 1662).[63] No payment for Pelling's monument has been identified in the city's Chamberlain's Accounts. In the eighteenth and nineteenth centuries, such monuments were funded by private subscriptions and this may have been the case here. However, as Chapman suggests, such payments for monuments to significant members of the city were made. One probable example is the unusually high payment of £11 to 'Mr Wakeman the elder by Mr Maiors Order as by a note appears' in 1655. Three generations of the Wakeman family were Bath's town clerks. The note has not survived, but it may be that the payment was for monuments to the family. Richard Wakeman Jr's wife (Mary) and son (William) were both buried in the Abbey on 27 April and 24 September 1655, respectively. As we have seen, Mary was commemorated with a ledgerstone, recorded by Maurice Price (1656–57). And, in 1676, Anthony a Wood recorded 'A Hathment or an escocheon of Wakeman hanging on a pillar next below B'p Mountague's mon[ument]' recording the deaths of Richard Sr (d. 1656), Richard Jr (d. 1675) and Theodore Wakeman (d. 1675). James Vertue's 'A Perspective View of the Abbey-Church of St. Peter and Paul at Bath' shows the hatchment with the 'saltire wavey' was still there in 1750 but was likely removed by the end of the eighteenth century (Colour Plate H). The Wakeman family's diamond-shaped hatchment can be seen on the left-hand side of the drawing, to the west of the Montagu tomb. The ledgerstone commemorating Theodore is still in the North Aisle where it was originally laid (Colour Plate I). Understandably, it was important for the city to commemorate its own in the Abbey, especially when, like Pelling and the Wakemans, individuals had themselves given generously of their time, talents and wealth to the Abbey itself. A marble tablet obviously created sometime later, now placed above the entrance to the Abbey shop in the South Aisle, records that in 1675 'Theodore Wakeman gave a silver flagon' to the church.

Another monument, now also lost, singled out for special description by Henry Chapman was that to Margarett (d. 1579) and Thomas Lichfield, 'Lutenist as they say to Q. Eliz.'. Chapman described it thus: 'In the South-east Isle, is a pretty, somewhat stately, and doubtless conceited Monument, all of Free-stone, having Originally no Inscription, as to time, person, or quality, therefore vulgarly called the *Speechless Monument*, but now not so'. Chapman recorded two 'Scribled Inscription[s]' in the form of couplets – 'Fancy may think one hid within this Tomb, / But reason sayes his grave was Mothers Womb' and 'Nameless not Fameless, here one lyes, / Believe not me, believe thine Eyes' – which were answered with a longer verse:

Nameless then Fameless, for how can Fame
Attend that man that wants a known-by Name?
Anonymus here might very well share Fame
With *Alexander*, bating but his Name.
Harry Spicer like to *Caesar* and't had nt spread,
But Caesar's living, and Harry Spicer's dead.
Then Name makes fame, and nothing else for Fame
'S no more in sense then a Recorded Name.

To prevent future defacing 'by such scribling and scratching', Chapman noted that someone 'acquainted with the name and quality of the there interred' had 'silenc'd' the vandals with the following couplet: 'If any man my Name and Life enquire, / *Lichfield* my Name, my Life was Musicks hire'.[64] Anthony a Wood was silent on such inscriptions in 1676, but his description of the 'statelie monument of free stone of two stories high on pillars, & an altar stone monument of free stone curiouslie wrought within the lower story pillars'[65] confirms that this is the monument that can be seen on the right-hand side of the engraving of 'Prior Bird's Chapel, Bath Cathedral' that was included in Volume I of James Storer's *History and Antiquities of the Cathedral Churches of Great Britain* (1814) (Fig. 7). More will be said about how the Abbey came to use this monument to engage and profit from curious visitors in the following chapter.

No monument in the Abbey demonstrates the fragility and vulnerability to damage and graffiti better than the tomb Sir William Waller erected to his first wife Jane (Colour Plates E and F). Jane was the only daughter and heir of Sir Richard Reynell. The Reynells were an old Devon family with country estates at Forde House, Wolborough. On 12 August 1622, Jane married Sir William Waller, who would later become a famous Parliamentarian officer during the English Civil War. The couple had two children, Richard (b. 1631) and Margaret (b. 1633). Jane died in Bath in May 1633. The Wallers' children, Richard and Margaret, are depicted sitting on the left and right of the tomb that Waller commissioned for Jane. He recalled that Jane was a 'virtuous, discreet, loving and beloved wife'. He listed these, and other qualities, in the epitaph that can be seen on the left-hand side of the monument.

Engd. by J. Storer from a Drawing by H. Gastineau.
Pl. 5.
Prior Birds Chapel, Bath Cathedral.
Published Sep 1 1816, by Sherwood, Neely & Jones, Paternoster Row.

Fig. 7: Detail of the Tomb of Margaret Lichfield (d. 1579) on the right-hand side of James Storer's engraving of Prior Bird's Chapel, Bath Cathedral. © *The author.*

The niche on the right-hand side has been left blank. Presumably it was intended for Waller himself. However, after Jane's death he married twice more and was buried in 1668 in the New Chapel at Tothill Street, London.

The history of Jane Waller's tomb has attracted much speculation. Some believe it was the work of Epiphanius Evesham (fl. 1570–*c.*1623). However, no maker's signature has been found. The words 'ERECTED 1663 RESTORED 1880' are carved on the west face of the plinth. But this seems to be misleading, since visitors to the church in 1635 and 1639 commented on Lady Waller's 'pretty passionate monument'. However, the story that Royalist soldiers defaced the tomb, cutting off William Waller's face and sword arm, is probably true. It had certainly been damaged by 1668 when Samuel Pepys visited the Abbey and saw Waller's effigy 'lying with his face broken'. An inspection of the tomb today also reveals hundreds of pieces of graffiti on the tomb, much dating from the Second World War.

Sir William Waller was in Bath in 1635 (possibly to see or oversee his wife's newly erected tomb) when he was given 1*s* 10*d* in sugar (wine and sugar were gifts traditionally given by the city to Abbey benefactors). His old friend, Robert Hopton, also received a share in a gift of £1 11*s* 3*d*. In the same year there is also a payment of 15*s* to Mr Gally 'for his chardges about the conveyannce of Sr. William Walleys [sic] hundred pound'. This is obviously Waller's part in the donation, recorded on a marble tablet above the doorway in the South Aisle of the Nave, which reads: '1646 Sir William Waller Lady Booth And William Edward Sturridge Gave £300 To The Chamber Of This City In Trust For The Repairs Of This Church The Interest Of Which Is £15 Yearly'.[66] Waller was in Bath again in 1643 during the English Civil War, notably taking sanctuary in the Abbey with his wounded troops after fighting against Hopton at the Battle of Lansdown. It is not hard to imagine him taking refuge in the South Transept near his first wife's tomb, reflecting on love lost and friendships sullied. Waller had honoured the memory of his old friendship with Hopton in the letter he wrote to him before the battle. Insofar as his wife's memory was concerned, he adopted an equally practical response. From 1643, a series of sporadic payments begin to appear in Bath's Chamberlain's Accounts, which suggest that some of the interest from the money given by Waller to the church was used to keep his wife's tomb in good order. There are three payments in 1643: one of £2 to 'the Sexton for keepinge Cleane Sr. William Wallers Ladies Tombe of the last two yeares'; another of £1 'Item payd Thomas Singer for keepeinge Cleane the Lady Wallies Toumbe'; and the last of £2 to Henry Gay (possibly the same sexton who received the first payment of £2) 'for keepeinge Cleane the Ladie Wallers Tombe last yeare and the yeare also'.[67] Waller was quartered in Bath again in 1648 and probably saw the damage the Royalist soldiers had done to his wife's tomb. However, there is no indication in the accounts that Waller sought to repair it.[68] There is also a significant hiatus in the payments for the cleaning of the tomb until 1688, when Mr John Masters and John Sugar were paid £2 'the gift of Sr. Will. Waller'. John Sugar was listed as the sexton of St James in April 1679.[69] Masters and Sugar (sometimes Suger) were paid the same sum in 1689, once for 'for cleansing Sr. William Wallers Tombe as by their Receipt appears' and again for 'cleaning Sr. Wm. Wallers tomb'.[70] There is a final payment of £2 to 'John Masters and John Shugar' in 1690–91 for 'cleaning Sr. William Wallers Tombe'[71] before the accounts are silent on the payments for cleaning the tombe. However, John Shugar clearly continued to carry out the office of sexton, as can be seen by a number of other payments to him for digging graves in the same years.[72] The payments to Sugar and Masters for keeping the Waller tomb clean were competitive compared with similar payments to sextons for the regular cleaning of other large monuments in the county. The accounts for the Wellington Estate for 1706, 1722 and 1735 record payments of 5*s* 'to the Sexton for cleaning the Monument', probably that to Sir John Popham (*c.* 1532–1607) in the Church of St John the Baptist, Wellington, Somerset.[73]

The desire to keep one's family monuments in good repair was naturally a common concern. Perhaps for none more so than Dr Robert Peirce, who, despite being the city's 'Physician for Poor Strangers', tragically had to bury his closest family members in the Abbey. In 1659, Dr Peirce took up residence in the Abbey House (the former Prior's quarters), where he lived until his death in 1710. The house had a private door into the church. Although the house was demolished in 1755, the door still exists in the south-west corner of the Abbey (although it was walled up in 1811). No doubt Peirce made use of the private door to visit the monuments he commissioned for his family members. Ledgerstones are known to have existed for his wife Anna (d. 1688), daughters Elizabeth (d. 1671) and Mary (d. 1679), and for Dr Peirce himself after his death in 1710. Dr Peirce's Will suggests that there was no ledgerstone carved to his son Charles (d. 1665, aged 4), who is named, along with his younger son Robert (d. 1655, aged 1), on the wall monument he erected in memory of his daughter Elizabeth (d. 1671):

> I Give and Bequeath to the Church of St. Peter and St. Paul in Bath The sume of Ten pounds towards the keeping of the South Isle in necessary Repair on which I have already been at some charge and where my nearest Relations lye Buried and where I desire to be Interred also provided that the Monument already Erected for my Daughter Elizabeth is kept cleane and undefaced and the Three Blew [Blue lias] Stones under which they doe and I must lye be kept unmoved Except by consent of my Executor.[74]

Only the ledgerstone to Anna and Mary (Colour Plate J) and the wall monument to Elizabeth has survived (Colour Plate K). The quotation from Psalm 39 – 'And now Lord what is our hope / truly our hope is even in thee' – carved at the bottom of the ledgerstone united the stone with the others from the Peirce family group. The Reverend Richard Rawlinson's 1719 survey recorded lines also taken from the Psalms on Elizabeth's ('When I awake up after / thy likeness, I shall be Satisfied / with it', Psalm 17) and Dr Robert Peirce's 'black Marble Grave-Stones'. The lines 'Thy loving kindnesse is better than life it self [sic]' from Psalm 63 on Dr Peirce's stone are a fitting tribute to a compassionate physician who treated patients of different sexes, nationalities, classes and religious persuasions with equal kindness. The care taken to select and include lines from the Psalms on all his family's ledgerstones would have made a touching sight for visitors to the church and helped them to read these monuments as a family group (a coherence that was only lost during the nineteenth-century works to the floor).

An entry on page 42 of the Abbey's *Benefactors' Book* indicates the ongoing need for the repair of the South Aisle in this early period and contextualises the bequest concerning the South Aisle in Dr Peirce's Will: 'Robert Peirce Doctor of Physick at his own charge repaired the paving of the whole south-isle, & erected a pinacle on the south-side of the Church £30'. Peirce obviously had very personal reasons for wanting the floor of the South Aisle where his family were buried to be in a good state of repair. He would have known the paving there in intimate detail, having walked it countless times from his private door into the church to visit his family's ledgerstones and the monument he erected to his daughter, Elizabeth, on the west wall of the South Transept (where Rawlinson recorded it in 1719). Elizabeth Peirce's memorial is both unusual and poignant because the verses commissioned to be carved on it were 'found in her Closet after her decease', presumably by Dr Peirce himself:

To the deare memory of
Elizabeth, daughter of Dr. Robert Peirce and
Anna his wife, who ended a sickly life by a
Sudden death (caus'd by an inward imposthume)
Febr: eighteenth 1671. aged 19 years
Though sudden to her friends yet not so to her,
As appeares by these verses found in her
Closet after her decease.

Death is the common lot of all,
It Spareth neither greate nor small.
Then (since the time's not in our pow'r)
Let's liue a though't were our last hovr.
For come when't will; t will sudden seem,
Although the warning long hath been.
And be not troubled, if your friends.
Come suddenly vnto their ends.
For't is a debt, that all must pay,
Though some do goe a neerer way
Then others, yet the iourney's sure,
And some paine in't we must endure.
How necessary 'tis to be
Prepar'd for death, pray, learne of me.

Neere this place also ly the bodies of
Robert and Charles Peirce brothers of
the said Elizabeth: Robert Peirce aged one
year, died Nouemb: 15th. 1655; Charles Peirce
aged foure years died Febr: 12th 1665.

No wonder, then, that he wished to keep the aisle he walked and where members of his family were buried in good order. Elizabeth's monument was unrecorded by Anthony a Wood 1676–78. Assuming that he did not simply ignore it (and it is large and unusual enough for him not to miss it), this would date the erection of Elizabeth Peirce's monument and the repair of the South Aisle pavement between 1678 and 1710.

Peirce's *Memoirs* of his practice at Bath also illuminate late seventeenth-century burial practice in the Abbey, as shown by his account of his treatment of Robert Grierson. After attempts by 'Physitians, Chyrurgeons, and [...] *Bonesetters*' in Scotland to treat his 'Sciatica', the 18-year-old was sent to Bath at the beginning of October 1665 and treated by Peirce.[75] Peirce records that 'all that was attempted, signified not, for in *February* following he dy'd'. Initially, Grierson was 'Embalmed' and 'wrapped in Cerecloths' (strips of fabric impregnated with wax and wrapped snugly around the body to exclude air) since it was thought that 'his Corps was to be cary'd back into *Scotland* to be interr'd there'. Eventually, the order came to bury him in the Abbey and 'a Stone laid upon him'. Anthony a Wood recorded it as being in the south cross aisle (transept) of the Abbey, giving his date of death as 17 March 1666 [sic]. The Abbey's burial register reveals that he was only buried on 10 April, almost a month later, underlining the same difficulties Peirce identified in knowing how to deal with visitors to the city who died hundreds of miles from home. Fourteen years later, Peirce 'happen'd to be walking in the Church', perhaps to visit his family's graves. On entering the South Transept, Peirce found 'the Sexton opening his [Greirson's] Grave; to interr another'. Peirce 'reprov'd' the sexton 'for uncovering, his Corps so soon'. The sexton defended himself by saying 'That Ground would consume a Corps in less time'. Peering into the earth, Peirce noticed that what the sexton had said 'prov'd very true, for there was not so much as a Hands-breadth left together whole of the Cerecloth, and nothing at all of the Flesh'. With the exception of Grierson's lame hip and leg, his bones were 'white and as smooth as if prepar'd for a Scelliton'.[76] The anecdote illustrates how the interment of visitors to the city in addition to the Abbey's parishioners had, over the course of a century, begun to put pressure on the space available for burial in the confined space of the Abbey by the end of the seventeenth century. Consequently, this would lead to existing burials being disturbed and in later centuries disarticulated to make room for new burials.

Increasing numbers of burials also meant increasing numbers of mourners' feet and damage to the ledgerstones and pavement, both from erosion and the frequent lifting and relaying of the stones (hence the need for Peirce and others to repair the floor). This was already a problem by 1676, when Oxford antiquary Anthony a Wood, in his survey of the 'Monumentall Inscriptions in S. Peter's Church in the Citie of Bathe' (1676–78), observed that in the South Choir Aisle were: 'many flat free stones laying on graves of a late date, but their inscriptions by the often pushing of people over them to the bowling green &

walkes at the east end of the church are woren out'.[77] Like many who followed in his footsteps, Wood's survey was hampered by the state of the church, and especially its floor. He acknowledged that his was not a comprehensive record of all the monuments he saw. The stones in the North Choir Aisle were a particular problem for him: 'Here are severall of the Chapmans buried und' flat stones, but the inscriptions wch are on those stones inlaid with black pitch, or other stuff, are woren out, or covered with dirt so much yt they are not legible'.[78] Seats built over 'severall other flat stones' in the Chancel, the number of ledgerstones (especially in the North Aisle) 'being free and soft' (made from local Bath stone (oolitic limestone), and their erosion from foot-traffic (noted especially in both transepts and the aisles) also frustrated him. Occasionally, then, Wood used the burial register and the writings of Thomas Guidot to supply information he could not find on the stones themselves.

Although not the first seventeenth-century antiquary to survey the Abbey's monuments, Wood's survey is by far the most concentrated and comprehensive. It begins in the centre of the chancel before documenting the North Aisle then South Aisle, the North and South Cross Aisles (Transepts), the centre of the Nave and, finally, the North and South Nave Aisles. Of the eighty-six monuments he recorded, forty-nine were ledgerstones, thirty-one were wall tablets (this figure includes hatchments and the Lichfield, Montagu and Waller tombs, but excludes the Birde Chantry), and it is unclear what six of them were (but they are probably all ledgerstones). Excluding these six, altogether there were thirty-three monuments in the Chancel (including the Choir Aisles), twenty-one in the Transepts, and 26 in the Nave (including the side aisles). The ledgerstones he noted dated between 1615–77 and other monuments between 1572[/9]–1675. The monuments Wood recorded were spread evenly around the church. However, twenty-six of the forty-nine ledgerstones are located in the North Aisle (Nave, Cross and Choir), mostly commemorating the Chapmans, the family that spearheaded the rebuilding of the church after the Dissolution, and other members of the city's elite. It must be remembered that the desirability of being buried here is linked to the north side's completion before the south side of the church. Choosing to be buried there was therefore a statement, like Barnes's, of the support for and faith in the completion of the Abbey as a reformed parish church.

'For ye use of strangers Resorting to this Citty': How developments and repairs led to revenue from burials and monuments, 1691–1712

From the beginning of the seventeenth century, the revenue from burials and monuments had helped to supplement larger sums from high-profile benefactors for the rebuilding of the church. As the majority of the works to the church completed by the late 1620s, the frequency of large donations also decreased. This meant the Abbey needed to rely on the parish's regular income, which included burials and, in later centuries, the charges made for the permission to erect monuments in different parts of the building. The Abbey's accounts before the nineteenth century have, unfortunately, been lost, so the extent to which monuments contributed to its income cannot be known definitively until then. However, the Abbey's late seventeenth- and early eighteenth-century vestry minutes do present a picture of the church expanding in three distinct but interrelated ways in which it could profit from burials, especially those of 'strangers' or visitors to the city, an increasing number of whom also paid for monuments.

The first way was by formalising and refining the charges for the ringing of the bells before and after the funeral service. On 14 April 1691, the vestry met and agreed that:

> at the Buriall of any Man or Woman yt the Bell shall not Toll above two hours; and for a child under twelve years of Age, no above an hour. And that if they Toll longer they shall pay two shillings, & sixpence; and so for every hour afterwards to the use of the Church.[79]

On 8 August 1698, the vestry reduced the amount of time that the bell was permitted to ring for: 'at ye death or Buriall of any person within this parish noe bell shall Ring more yn halfe an houre and after ye Buriall but a quarter of an houre'.[80] It was also agreed that 'noe bell shall toll till ye corpes be brought out of the house upon the forfiture of fourtie shillinge to be paid by ym that desire it'. The vestry also seemingly increased the sexton's fee for 'ringing and tolling the great bell' for the new duration to 'six shillings & Eight pence' (charges for the 'other bells' were already an agreed 'custome' but were, unfortunately, not written down in 1698). John Davice was likely the man to benefit, albeit temporarily, from this increased fee. He was named as the 'sextone' at his burial in the Abbey on 6 May 1700. In 1700, the Abbey's six bells were 'new cast into eight bells by Abraham Rudhall of Gloucester Bellfounder', although not all Bathonians were willing contributors to the project. By 13 November 1701, the new ring of bells were back in the tower and the vestry reduced the amount that the 'Great bell', that is the tenor bell given by the Hopton family in 1627, was permitted to toll after the funeral: 'at Any funeral ye Great bell shall be tolled fourty strokes in one houre fter the Bell have Done. Ringing wch bell shall be called the notice bell.' The bells' reinstatement would have been especially welcomed by the church for their revenue: by December 1704, the Abbey had made a rate 'for the Repairing the Church' (and its organ), which had, by then, amounted to £35 19*s* 2*d* (a sum worth approximately £4,000 today). Later in the century, John Wood noted that the Abbey bells tolled to welcome visitors to the city, and that the visitors for whom the bells rang, in turn, gave to support the Abbey's curates.

The second improvement was to make the Abbey's accommodation feel more luxurious and exclusive for wealthy potential patrons. At the vestry held on 9 February 1707/8, it was agreed to pay the freemason Thomas Greenway £24 'for Six Colloums wth their Basses & Capitalls Sixteen foote in heightth [sic] & two foote diamiter'. These are obviously the six columns supporting the organ loft that can be seen directly beneath the instrument in James Vertue's 1750 etching of the interior. The old and new galleries that the columns supported were to 'Remaine as Publique Gallarys, for ye use of strangers Resorting to this Citty' (but 'ye old Wanscoat of the East front of the gallery' and screen paid for by Thomas Bellott was to be taken down and 'made wth ye same sort of Oake that ye new Organ is done wth'). The phrasing and emphasis on 'strangers Resorting to this Citty' is telling and echoes that of Elizabeth I's licence over a century earlier. The motivation behind the repair work here seems in the same spirit of those earlier improvements; namely, to improve the look, quality and comfort of the Abbey, especially for (noble and wealthy) visitors to the resort.

In the absence of the accounts, which would probably have shown how successful these improvements were in attracting gifts from those using and ultimately being buried in the church, the burial register for the period under discussion is surprisingly illuminating. During William Clement's incumbency (1680–1712) there is a tendency to record where strangers died (e.g. which lodging house they died at and were buried from) in the burial register. Whereas during William Hunt's incumbency (1712–33) there is a tendency to record payments from strangers for burial within the register. The latter will be discussed at greater length in the following chapter. However, there are several payments in the burial register during Clement's years that record the gifts of strangers (or more precisely their relatives or executors) following their burials, or payments over and above the agreed rate for services such as ringing the bells. For example, on 1

January 1695, 'Mrs Henerita wife of Mr Charles Cornwell, Captain, a stranger' was buried 'in ye chancel'. The burial register also includes the receipt of '40 shillings for the church'.[81] Eight days later, 'Mrs An Ince was carried away from Mr William Webb's' and 10*s* (not the standard charge) received 'for goeing the bell'.[82] The burial register shows that even where burial did not take place in the Abbey, a charge was made; presumably these are early charges for mortuaries (something the Abbey would charge for formally in the eighteenth and nineteenth centuries). For example, Lady Bridgeman 'was carried away' on 11 June 1701, but 10*s* 6*d* was marked as 'due' in the burial register. Bodies were transported just down the road to Twerton, or further to London, Yorkshire, and even across the sea to Ireland. Payments are not generally recorded in the burial register for those 'carried away' in the period, but those that are are obviously cost-covering (for the minister and clerk's time) at between 10 and 24 shillings. However, a note at the end of the burial register for 1720 suggests that such payments were recorded elsewhere and generally taken as read: 'Where any persons are found register (carried away) the minister and clerk's dues, etc., were paid'. The entry on 15 May 1706 suggests a weariness with this kind of payment from those who *could*, and in this case it seems *should*, have paid more: 'George Frome, gent., of Salisbury. Pd. Roger Waters, church-warden, *but* 19s. for breaking the ground & goeing of the great bell [my emphasis]'.[83]

On the other hand, where visitors to the city were buried in the Abbey, the burial register records a couple of especially high payments, which certainly go beyond simply covering costs. The highest, made on 20 September 1700, is either an example of outstanding generosity to the church, or a figure that, more likely, incorporated both burial and commemoration with a monument: 'Mirriam Phillips, a Knight's Lady yt died at Dr. Peirce's house, a stranger. Paid £10 4s 0d'.[84] This was definitely the case with the burial on 3 April 1705 of 'John Killingworth, Esquir, of Hampton-wick in ye par. of Hampton Court in Middlesex. Paid £5 4s 0d'.[85] In 1719, Richard Rawlinson recorded Killingworth's ledgerstone as follows:

> On another black Marble Grave-Stone, in Capitals is this Inscription
>
> Under this Stone lyeth interred
> the Body of John Killingworth, of
> the *Middle Temple* Esqr. Son of
> *Wm. Killingworth* Esqr. Serjt. at Law,
> who departed this Life the 1st day of *April*
> 1705. *Aetat.* 41.[86]

Rawlinson's survey makes it hard to be precise about the location, but it seems, from the context, that the ledgerstone was laid in the region of the South Transept alongside ledgerstones to others practising in law from the Inner Temple and Cliffords Inn, respectively. Killingworth's entry in the burial register, therefore, gives us an indicative cost for the burial and commemoration of a non-parishioner outside the Choir of the Abbey in the early eighteenth century. Sadly, no record of a monument to Mirriam Phillips has survived, but it is likely this cost corresponded to a modest monument on the wall of the Chancel.

Finally, the third and most obvious way in which the Abbey expanded a system of charges to profit from burials was through its control and hire of the palls used to cover the body or coffin before burial in the church. The *Benefactors' Book* illustrates how in the seventeenth century Bath's connections with London's cloth industry helped to bring in gifts to the church, from sympathetic mercers like Bartholomew Barnes and Rowland Backhouse at the beginning of the century to drapers such as Mr John Withers (d. 1658), who gave a 'Carpett for the Communion table of Greene broad cloth', and Mr Hudsonne, probably a descendent of an upholsterer from Cheapside, who 'gave a Black Buriall Cloth'. The most significant gift in this respect in terms of how it benefited the revenue of the church was given on Christmas Day 1705 by John Baber, 'one of her majestys Justices of ye Peace for the Cty of Westminster'. The Babers had been especially generous and given a variety of gifts throughout the seventeenth century, from a window to the weathervane and standard on the tower, a weight for the chimes, and a clapper for the bell. John Baber's Christmas presents to the Abbey were:

> Two Velvet Palls, and Two Black Cloath Palls, to be continued for ever; according to a Deed made for that Purpose, wch. Deed, is kept in a Large Chest in ye Library of the Parrish church of St. Peter, and Paul; and after the Renewing, them, as they are wanting, out of what moneys the said Palls, & cloaths, bring in yearly (an account of wch is kep in a Book appointed for that purpose) The Remaining Sums to be disposed of (according to directions of ye said Deed) in Two Equall parts for placing out Poor Freemen's children, and The Bennifitt of the said Parrish Church. &c.[87] [Colour Plate L]

The palls were hired out by the church for use in funeral services. On 16 April 1707, the vestry reviewed and outlined the charges as follows:

Every inhabittant [sic] and Cittyzen of the said Citty, wch. Shall make use of the Larg[e] velvet pall the sum of Ten shillings
and every Stranger for the use of the Larg[e] velvet pall, the sum of Twenty shillings
Every inhabitant and Cittyzen of the said Citty, wch shall make use of the Lesser velvet pall the sum of five shillings,
and every stranger that shall make use of the said Lesser velvet pall Ten Shillings.
Every inhabitant and Cittyzen of the said Citty, that shall make use of the Larg[e] Black cloath pall the sum of two shillings & sixpence
and every stranger that shall make use of the said Larg[e] Black pall the sum of five shillings
And all and every of the inhabitants of the said Citty, shall make use of the Lesser Black cloath pall gratis
And every stranger that shall make use of the Lesser Black Cloath pall, shall pay the sum of Two Shillings.

Without any surviving contemporary accounts to contextualise these costs, it is only possible to estimate the impact of Baber's gift on the Abbey's revenue. It is worth noting, however, that those choosing to be buried at St James' were also required to use Baber's palls. Anyone who refused to comply with this simultaneous order of St James' vestry by using any other pall would 'pay for each default to ye use of Saint James' Church double [illegible] for breaking ground and ringing ye bell at ye same Church'.[88] It paid for the Rectory of Bath to join up its thinking.

Taking the Abbey burials in 1708 as an example of how Baber's palls enhanced its revenue, then, an extremely conservative (and deliberately unrealistic) estimate – assuming that the three high-ranking strangers (the Lord, the Lady and the Knight's daughter) and the nine other strangers (including the children) all used 'the said Lesser velvet pall' at 10*s* each; and that all twenty inhabitants of the city made use of the black cloth pall 'gratis' – would mean the Abbey received a minimum of £6 (approximately £630 today) from the hire of the palls for the year. A more realistic estimate – assuming that the three high-ranking strangers (the Lord, the Lady and the Knight's daughter) each used of the 'Larg[e] velvet pall' at 20*s* each; the nine other strangers (including the children) all used 'the said Lesser velvet pall' at 10*s* each; and that nineteen of the twenty other inhabitants (including the children), given their social statuses, each used 'the Lesser velvet pall' at 5*s* each, and that Richard Brown, the only one buried in the 'Churchyard', used the black cloth pall 'gratis' – would put the revenue just from the hire of palls for 1708 at

£20 10*s* (approximately £2,150 today). This sum would increase to a maximum of £21 5*s* (approximately £2,230 today) assuming that the nineteen citizens (amongst them artisans and aldermen) each 'used the Larg[e] velvet pall' at 10*s* each (which is perhaps as unrealistic as the first sum). However, by the late eighteenth century the Abbey was making a similar annual profit from 'Funeral Silks & Gloves' (hatbands, scarves, gloves and suits made from silk and satin made for mourners). In 1770, a book of accounts show the Abbey made at least £21 profit from these items alone (approximately £2,000 today). This will be discussed at greater length in the following chapter. Taken in the context of Henry Chapman's assessment of the 'small' revenue of the church in 1673, the effect of Baber's gift was highly significant. Chapman lauded Dame Elizabeth Booth's investment, which generated nearly £20 per annum. On a good year, Baber's gift and the hire of palls for Abbey burials alone in the early eighteenth century would have made a similar contribution to its revenue.

The revenue from the hire of the palls at St James would have been important for the Abbey too. Baber's Deed states that the first £25 from the annual hire be 'kept & set apart for keeping the said Palls in Repair & Buying New Ones'. After that half of the annual remainder was to be applied 'toward Repairing the Parish Church of ye Parish of St Peter & Paule', the other half to apprenticeships for 'the sons of such poor ffreemen Inhabitants of the said City'.[89] By the early eighteenth century, therefore, the business of burial in the Abbey and St James' was directly supporting the repair of the building. Two notes pasted onto the blue-marbled front papers of the Abbey's Churchwardens Accounts beginning in 1801 indicate that the £5 fine for not burying in woollen shrouds was also being collected, half of which went to the poor of the parish: 'Received March 26 1799 of Mr Wm Bally two Pounds ten Shillings being a fine due to the Poor for burying Miss Mary Kelawley May in Linen in the Parish Church of Saint Peter & Paul Bath'. In 1765, John Wood put the income of the Abbey 'not above 200 l. a Year in Value'. Assuming the figure was similar at the beginning of the eighteenth century, the hire of palls contributed at least 10 per cent of this sum.

Conclusion

By the end of the seventeenth century, the Abbey was able to fulfil the destiny chosen for it by the city and the Crown. Not only was the church able to receive the large numbers of nobility and parishioners 'to heare Sermons, and other divine service' (not previously possible in the city's small churches), it replaced

St Mary de Stalls and increasingly became the place where the upper-middle classes chose to be buried. Structural works could give way to maintenance and even beautification, which, in turn, attracted wealthy donors and executors. Apparently, by March 1695, there was so little to repair that Benjamin Baber employed workmen who 'cleaned & swept downe all the cobwebs and dust from the tops of the walls and high windowes both of the Chancell & bodie of the church & after of the North and South Iles'.[90] Naturally, keeping the worship space spick and span was devotional. But keeping the monuments in a good state of repair would have been important when families wishing to commemorate a loved one saw the interior. However, 'so great a Building' in fact needed constant revenue and repair. By 1700, Edward Ward wrote favourably that the Abbey was as 'Crowded, during *Divine Service*, as much as *St. Pauls*'. However, Bath's church was a 'very ancient *Cathedral* piece of *Antiquity*' and was, according to Ward, 'kept as badly in Repair'.[91] In the later part of the seventeenth century, therefore, we have seen the Abbey's vestry – comprised of many successful businessmen, some of them descendants of those who put their professional minds and networks to the rebuilding and improvement of the church at the beginning of the century – putting in place mechanisms to optimise its growing revenues from burial and monuments from both parishioners and, especially, visitors to the city and their executors, who would want and could afford to pay for commemoration equal to their loved one's social rank. Tolling the bell and the length of time one paid for, and choosing the best pall, were conspicuously public statements about social worth. Bringing in systems whereby those who could afford to could signify status through these commemorative acts was an intelligent move for a church and city that attracted those with both money and vanity. Ward reports William Clement addressing the congregation present in 1700 and saying that, 'He was afraid most of them came more out of Custom and formality, than in Devotion to the Sacred Deity, or a suitable Reverence to the Place of Worship'. Ward himself thought this 'very true' and was confident 'the Ladies were the only Saints several came there to Adore'. In the eighteenth century, the Abbey would make a virtue of social spectacle in its walls in its expanding collection of church monuments. However, by the end of the century this would come at a cost, and the tension between reverence and revenue insofar as what so many church monuments meant for the worship space would come to a head. The seventeenth century had seen the Abbey transformed from a ruinous blot on the city's landscape to a reformed place of worship and civic pride. In the eighteenth century, the city created a unique identity for the Abbey by accommodating and celebrating the monuments of those who came to the spa but who didn't find a cure.

2

IDENTITY

'AS MUCH SPECULATION AS CAN BE MET WITH, PERHAPS, IN ANY PAROCHIAL CHURCH', 1712–1807

The transformation of the Abbey from Benedictine monastery to reformed parish church, described in the previous chapter, was written in rhyme by Mary Chandler in a verse of her *A Description of Bath* (1733):

SURROUNDED by the AVON'S winding Streams,
Beneath the Hills, a peopled Island Seems;
An ancient *Abbey* in its Centre stands,
The labour'd Work of superstitious Hands;
When *Holy Craft* supreme did guide the Helm,
And *Gothic Darkness* overspread the Realm;
The *artful Priest* amaz'd the gaping Croud,
And *sacred Truth* was veil'd in *mystic* Cloud;
When living Saints for true Devotion bled;
And *Rites profane* were offer'd to the *Dead*;
When *Idol Images* Devotion drew,
And *Idol Gods* were worshipp'd as the *True*;
Witness yon *Front* : how impiously design'd
In *Stone* to represent th'*Eternal* MIND!
Witness the *Saints* and *Angels* on the *Wall!*
Deaf to their Vot'ries *Prayers*, and *silent* to their Call.

Opposite: Light from stained glass falls onto the relief carving of the monument to Jonathan Henshaw (d. 1764) and his wife Mary (d. 1778) on the wall of the North Nave Aisle. © Bath Abbey.

Welcom, fair LIBERTY, and LIGHT *divine!*
Yet *wider* spread your Wings; and brighter shine;
Dart *livelier* Beams on ev'ry *British* Soul,
And scatter *Slavish Darkness* to the Pole.
Now for *pure Worship* is the *Church* design'd;
O that the Muse could say to *that* confin'd!
Ev'n there, by meaning Looks, and cringing Bows,
The Female Idol her Adorer knows!
Fly hence, *Profane*, not taint this sacred Place;
Mock not thy GOD, to flatter CELIA'S Face.
This sacred Pile incloses honour'd Dust,
And pompous *Monuments* secure the Trust:
There MONTAGUE, the Noble Prelate, lies,
With pious Hands up-lifted to the Skies:
A VIRGIN here enjoys eternal Fame,
Joine'd on the Marble with great DRYDEN'S Name.[1]

One measure of the change sensed by Chandler (and other eighteenth-century writers) was how the English church monument had come to define the new, Protestant identity of the building, perhaps even more so than the carving of its West Front. Several other notable eighteenth-century writers contrast the carving of the West Front with the rebuilt church to this end. To name but two, Daniel Defoe remarked that 'The *Abbey-church* is a venerable Pile, and has many Monuments in it'. But, he continued, 'the principal Front is almost blasphemously decorated, if it may be called decorated, with the Figures of God the Father, and Saints and Angels, the Work of Superstition'.[2] Similarly, towards the end of the century, the famous Bath architect John Wood wrote that the 'Flock of Angels on each Side the Figure of the Holy Trinity' looked like 'so many Bats clung Against the Wall'. On the other hand, once it was 'converted to a Parochial Church' the 'Monuments erected in it, as Memorials of the Dead, together with the Arms and other Marks of the Benefactors to the Building' would 'yield the curious Stranger as much Speculation as can be met with, perhaps, in any Parochial Church, of the same standing in the whole World'.[3] Apparently these eighteenth-century writers saw no self-contradiction in scorning Catholic carvings on the one hand and celebrating effigies, busts and gilded monumental sculpture on the other.[4]

In the eighteenth century, the Abbey became, perhaps more than ever, a place to see others and be seen. In Smollett's *Humphry Clinker* (1771), Lydia Melford writes to

Miss Willis that her aunt 'says every person of fashion should make her appearance in the bath, as well as in the Abbey Church'. Thirty years later an anonymous pamphleteer bemoaned the 'rows and rows of young and healthy women carelessly sitting, their backs to the Ministers and the Altar, their eyes wandering about the Church'.[5] If no potential beau were to be seen, their eyes would likely have been drawn to the sculpture that increasingly defined the aesthetic of the Abbey interior. The Abbey, and in particular its monuments, became an eighteenth-century spectacle, to be taken in, preferably after the service was over.

Depictions of the Abbey interior from the middle of the eighteenth century illustrate how the monuments proliferated. Read alongside the antiquarian surveys of the monuments and guidebooks, they enable us to see for ourselves where the monuments were originally positioned and how they were originally designed for the Abbey. We will begin by looking at these to understand what the monuments looked like in the eighteenth century, how they defined the appearance of the interior, how the Abbey began to consciously manage the placement of its increasing numbers of monuments, and the rate at which they were being installed in the church by the end of the eighteenth century. Having looked at the objects and what they tell us about the eighteenth-century aesthetics of the Abbey, we will then consider their cost, both the fees that the Abbey commanded for their installation in the church and the sculptors' costs for creating them. The story of how the Abbey profited from its monuments and burials is told principally through two early sets of accounts kept by two eighteenth-century rectors, Rev. Duel Taylor and Rev. John Chapman. Monuments such as those to Sir William Baker and Captain Bartholomew Stibbs will be discussed in detail for what they reveal about the patriotic narrative the Abbey and the city wished to create through its monuments, and how the source of the wealth that enabled families to pay for approximately 20 per cent of the monuments in the Abbey came from the exploitation and enslavement of people through the British Empire. The chapter concludes by looking at the Abbey's burial registers 1774–92 and the detailed picture the entries give us about burial and the location of ledgerstones. The period coincides with the time the Handcock family held the position of Abbey sextons. The chapter concludes by considering the eighteenth-century sextons and the important roles they played in burial and commemoration at the Abbey. The picture that emerges is one of the church and city working together to build on the work in the seventeenth century to create an identity for the Abbey that was sympathetic and desirable to the city's visitors, as a cathedral-like interior for commemoration comparable to that at Westminster Abbey or St Paul's Cathedral.

'By this Method no Monument will escape your Observation': Antiquarian surveys and artists' impressions, 1719–91

The lack of extant financial records for the Abbey until the mid-eighteenth century makes it impossible to begin definitively quantifying the number of monuments erected in the Abbey until 1801, from which date the Churchwardens' Accounts survive. Two short series of accounts, discussed below, give an insight into the monuments erected at the end of the century: the first, kept by Reverend Duel Taylor, Rector of Bath 1752–67, records 'The Income of the Rectory of Bath' between 1756 and 1765; the second, kept by Reverend John Chapman, Rector of Bath 1768–86, records 'The Profits arising from the Rectory of Bath' between 1768 and 1782. Reading these alongside the Abbey's burial register, especially for the years 1774–92, kept by Henry Sperring, parish clerk until the end of September 1791, allow us to understand burial and commemorative practice and their resulting benefit to the Abbey's finances and aesthetic in the late eighteenth century (these sources will be discussed in detail below). For the first half of the eighteenth century at least, one must rely on the antiquarian surveys and artists' impressions of the monuments. Read together, these sources shed a surprising amount of light on the monuments, especially on their original location in the church and their intended appearance. Both the original designs and the positions of the monuments would be altered in the nineteenth-century reorderings of them. They were the lucky ones; some monuments would be entirely destroyed.

Reverend Richard Rawlinson's *History and Antiquities of the Cathedral Church of Salisbury, And the Abbey Church of Bath* (1719) became a touchstone for later recorders of the monuments in Bath. Its value as a survey is arguably unmatched, even by later surveys, because of the relatively unbiased method Rawlinson seems to have adopted when recording monuments. It is hard to believe it is a comprehensive survey of all the monuments he might have recorded (the ledgerstone to Maria Wakeman recorded by Maurice Price in 1656–57 is one omission). However, the fact that Rawlinson, unlike later writers and more so than Anthony a Wood, seems not to have privileged wall tablets over ledgerstones, but rather seems to have carried out the record valuing both equally, provided later writers with the only survey of the ledgerstones until Charles P. Russell's in 1872. Crucially, Rawlinson's is the only survey of the ledgerstones to have been carried out prior to Sir George Gilbert Scott's works to the floor in the late nineteenth century. Rawlinson surveyed 160 monuments in Bath Abbey in total: he recorded 113 ledgerstones and 47 wall tablets (this figure includes hatchments and the tombs of Montagu, Lichfield and Waller, but excludes Birde's Chantry Chapel). The ledgerstones Rawlinson recorded date between 1621 and 1717. The earliest wall tablet he recorded was that to Richard Chapman with the dubious 1572/9 date (discussed in the Chapter 1); the latest wall tablet Rawlinson recorded was dated 1714, unsurprising given that, as we will see, wall tablets often took months or sometimes years to produce.

Rawlinson's survey begins in the south-west of the nave and proceeds east down the South Aisle and into the south of the Chancel. He then returns to the 'middle ile' of the Nave and surveys it from west to east, before returning to the west of the North Nave Aisle, ending his survey in the north-east corner of the Chancel. Patterns appear in Rawlinson's survey that illustrate the ways in which the Abbey managed the increasing numbers of burials and monuments within its walls in the late seventeenth and early eighteenth century. The forty-seven wall monuments are concentrated in the side aisles (including the transepts) and evenly distributed between the north and south sides: a total of twenty-two on the north side of the church, eighteen on the south side, and only seven in the centre of the Nave or Choir (e.g. on the pillars). The impact of this arrangement and concentration of the monuments was noticed by the Cambridge undergraduate Charles Perry, who recorded his visit to Bath in 1725 as part of 'A Tour from Cambridge to Halifax and Wakefield, returning via Oxford, Bath, and Bristol'. On 12 September 1725, Perry visited the Abbey, which he described as 'large & handsome and built like a Cathedral, tho' tis not one; there is a fine Organ, and in the outward Isles several good monuments'.[6]

Comparison of no. of ledgerstones and their locations in Bath Abbey in 1676 and 1719		
Location	**1676**	**1719**
North Choir Aisle	13	11
North Transept	7	15
North Nave Aisle	6	15
Central Nave	9	28
South Nave Aisle	2	9

South Transept	3	9
South Choir Aisle	3	15
Central Choir	6	11
Total number of ledgerstones recorded	**49**	**113**

In comparison with the very small increase in the number of wall monuments between 1676 and 1719, Rawlinson's survey shows the number of ledgerstones more than doubled in the same period, from forty-nine in 1676 to 113 in 1719. Whilst one or two monuments were added to the pillars of the central Nave and Choir, the number of ledgerstones in the centre of the Nave tripled and in the Choir almost doubled. In the Nave, all but four of the ledgerstones date to the eighteenth century, and twenty date between 1712 and 1717. The change is much more conservative in the centre of the Choir, with only four eighteenth-century ledgerstones and the remainder from the late seventeenth century. All of the monuments in the centre of the Choir are to 'strangers' (visitors to the city) and in the centre of the Nave the only monuments commemorating people 'of this City' date to the seventeenth century. The 'Middle Ile' (and the centre of the Nave in particular) therefore became the place non-parishioners were buried and commemorated. The most commonly mentioned locations these non-parishioners were from were London (and the Home Counties), Ireland and Cornwall. Unsurprising, given the journey times from Bath – London being the swiftest to get to, with a journey time of about three days – that these wealthy visitors were buried and commemorated in the Abbey.

On the other hand, Rawlinson's survey shows the transepts and especially the Choir Aisles to have been the places reserved by the church for the commemoration of its faithful parishioners. This was most pronounced in his survey of the North Choir Aisle, where nineteen of the twenty monuments there commemorated someone 'of this City'. Likewise, on the south side of the church, the further one progressed east in 1719 the greater the concentration of monuments to people from Bath. However, there was not so great a concentration as on the north side. This was probably due to a number of factors. The North Choir Aisle was the first to be repaired in the late sixteenth century and consequently became a special site of commemoration for Bath families such as the Chapmans. Since the South Transept needed to be rebuilt, the south side lagged behind the structural repairs. As we saw in Chapter 1, Anthony a Wood found many of the older inscriptions on the ledgerstones in the South Aisle to be 'woren out' because of the 'often pushing of people over them to the bowling green & walkes at the east end of the church'[7] and Dr Peirce paid for the repair of the pavement on the south side of the Abbey between 1678 and 1710. Repairs to the pavement, and possibly the replacement of damaged and eroded stones Anthony a Wood could not record, would have created space for new ledgerstones to be laid. The fact that the aisle was well-walked would have been an additional incentive to those who wanted their loved ones to be well-remembered. It is interesting that all of the ledgerstones to those not from Bath that Rawlinson recorded in the South Choir Aisle date from the early eighteenth century.

James Vertue's etching of *A Perspective View of the Abbey-Church of St Peter and Paul at Bath* (1750) largely corroborates the picture of the monuments presented by Rawlinson in 1719 (Colour Plate H). Vertue's view of the Nave looking east seems to have consciously omitted the smaller monuments known to have been on the walls of the side aisles. However, the large monuments he does record on the Nave pillars are drawn with a high degree of accuracy. On the south side of the Nave it is possible to see the monument to Mary Reeve ('On the next Pillar below the Pulpit, under a Tent, is a Woman kneeling, with [a] Hat on her Head, between 2 Children')[8] and, on the pillar to the right, Granville Pyper's:

> Large vein'd Marble Monument, in the full Corinthian Order. Within two columns is an urn with a gold flame, resting on a pedestal, standing on each side, two weeping boys, over the urn are two cherubims heads and draperies, resting on the cornish [cornice] is the shield and crest, on each side of which are two crying boys, sitting, on the table between two pedestals [Fig. 8].[9]

The 'Chevron between three Crows'[10] that Rawlinson described on Pyper's ledgerstone can clearly be seen in the shield at the top of the monument. In the background, between Reeve's and Pyper's monuments, is the oval marble with the shield on top to Calveley Legh M.D (d. 1727). On the right-hand side of the etching, to the right of the window on the wall of the South Aisle, can be seen the monument to Charles Godfrey: 'four handsome Corinthian columns and caps, with arcative frize and cornish of the same order, resting on the cornish is a large shield with the arms and crest of the family, surrounded with trophies of arms'.[11] The hatchment on the pillar on the south side cannot been identified with certainty but, given its location, it is possible that it is the 'Painted Coat of Arms. – On the Frame' commemorating Colonel John Duncombe (d. 1747) discussed below. Erected almost thirty years after Rawlinson's survey, it was recorded in the Middle Aisle in 1778.

Fig.8: Detail of the monuments to Mary Reeve (on the left-most pillar), the oval monument to Calveley Legh M.D., and Granville Pyper (central pillar). On the far right-hand side can be seen Charles Godfrey's monument. © Bath Abbey.

However, on the north side of the Nave, on the left-hand side of Vertue's etching, the hatchment of arms in the diamond on the pillar to the west of the Montagu tomb is undoubtedly that of Richard Wakeman: 'A Hathment or an escocheon of Wakeman hanging on a pillar next below B'p Mountague's mon.'[12] Within the central shield can be seen a 'Saltire Wavy', the description used by Rawlinson when describing the arms on Wakeman's ledgerstone.[13] The monument directly to the left of Wakeman's hatchment, that Vertue obviously tried to represent slightly in shadow, is probably that to Henry Southouse: 'On a Northward Pillar is a fair white Marble Monument supported by two Ionick Pillars'.[14] The inscription begins 'Near the West Corner of this Pillar', so it would make sense for the monument to be on the west side of the pillar above the ledgerstone, as appears to be shown by Vertue's etching. The open pediment and some of the other details described in 1778 can just about be seen: '*An elegant Marble Monument*, With black marble pillars and trusses, resting on two skulls; between the trusses, a shield with the family arms and crest, neatly ornamented; in the opening of the pediment is a vause, decorated with flowers'. The inscription is given 'On a circle Tablet'.[15] Given its position and shape, it is possible that the monument to the left of this is that to John

Taylor (d. 1711), described in 1778 as a 'Marble Monument, with a Round Top'. Like Southouse's monument, the inscription uses the pillar to locate the burial and ledgerstone beneath it: 'Near this pillar lyes the body of JOHN TAYLOR'.[16] Vertue's etching gives a good sense of the impact that these large early monuments made, both on promenading visitors and on the aesthetic of the interior. It also shows the exclusivity that erecting a monument on a pillar provided in the early 1700s, something that, by the end of the century, would be lost when two (and sometimes three) monuments would be erected on every face of each pillar.

What Rawlinson's survey captures in variety and volume of monuments, it perhaps loses in descriptive detail. His repeated description of the ledgerstones in the 'Middle Ile' dated 1712–17 ('On another black Marble Grave-Stone, is this Inscription') undervalues the beauty and individuality of some ledgerstones, such as John William Teshmaker's (d. 1713), one of many commemorating people from the Home Counties there in the early 1700s (Colour Plate M). Teshmaker's ledgerstone would have been one of the most arresting and newly laid ledgerstones seen by Rawlinson. In his Will of 1707, Teshmaker, had asked to be 'decently buried without great pomp under my pew in the church of Edmonton [Middlesex]'.[17] It seems to have been decided not to carry him the 113 miles there so he was buried in the Abbey, a day after his death, on 26 June 1713. Like Bartholomew Barnes and others, Teshmaker appears to have been another textile merchant choosing the Abbey as their place of rest, judging from 'the yarne or inckle now in the Barne and House' left to his wife. Given the short time between Teshmaker's death and burial, and the inscription on his ledgerstone, it seems likely that his wife (and sole Executrix) Esther had accompanied him to Bath:

> In Hopes of ye Blessed Resurrection
> Here Lyeth ye Body of Mr. JOHN
> WILLIAM TESHMAKER late of
> ye Parish of Edmunton in ye
> County of Midx Merchant
> Deceased ye 25th of June Anno
> Domini 1713 Aged 50 yeares
> he was an afectionate and
> Prudent Husband a Carefull
> & Indulgent Father Loving &
> Charityable to ye Poor to whose

Pious Memory his Disconsolat
widow Erected this Tombe

O reader stay one Moment with the dead
Have one Good thought when thus on Graves you tread
Think where now my soul abodes in heaven I trust
It there in bliss my Bodys hear in dust
O reader Go & live & learn & dye like men
that have immortall souls & then come hear agen.

The ledgerstone's inscription is both touching and personalised. Teshmaker's 1707 Will and that made on 20 June 1713, five days before his death, bears out all of the qualities the 'Tombe' expresses, including generous bequests to both 'Mr. Chandler Minister of the Gospell at Bath' and 'five pounds apiece to such poor people of the City of Bath as my wife shall in her discretion think [fit]'.[18] John Thomas Smith's 1793 etching *Near Mrs Teshmaker's, Edmonton* gives a sense of the kind of poverty John William Teshmaker may have seen (and wished to relieve) first-hand.[19]

The survey of the monuments published in 1778 as part of *An Historical Description of the Church Dedicated to St. Peter and St. Paul, in Bath; (Commonly called the Abbey) with its Monuments and Curiosities* might justly be called the first survey of the monuments to be conducted by the Abbey itself, as well as the first to be focused on the wall monuments. The book, as its subtitle made clear, was purposely '*Designed as a Guide to Strangers, in viewing this Venerable Pile, And, to point out to them the most valuable Remains of Antiquity, contained therein, As well as the Beauties of Modern Statuaries*'. As such, it is the Abbey's earliest guidebook and was 'Sold by W. Handcock, Sexton to the Abbey'. It was obviously popular, since it ran to at least one edition. The first edition numbered 147 monuments and the second appended six more that had 'been erected since this Book was first published'.[20] The second edition must have been published after 28 March 1783, which was the date the Rector John Chapman received £5 5*s* in part payment for the erection of the monument to Mrs Scriven (chronologically, the last monument to have been erected to be named in the second edition) and before the death of the sexton, William Handcock, on 16 August 1792.

Whilst casual visitors to the Abbey might have found the guide edifying and useful, a detailed reading of the book reveals its lack of rigor when compared with the surveys conducted by antiquarians such as Anthony a Wood or Rawlinson. Its simple list of 147 monuments and transcriptions of their inscriptions contains a number of errors. For example, the number 134 is used twice to record two very different monuments: the '*Elegant Painting in a Wood Frame.* With five figures, and the following inscriptions, SIC TRANSIT GLORIA MUNDI, *Death is swallowed up in Victory* To the pious memory of Dame GRACE GETHIN' in the South Choir Aisle, and the 'Pyramid Marble Monument, with a Urn in Front' to the memory of Thomas Brocas in the Chancel. Secondly, whilst the survey is almost exclusively a record of the marble monuments attached to walls and pillars, the book occasionally and idiosyncratically interpolates short notes of other, unnumbered memorials. For example, between numbers 73 and 74 is written: 'Painted Coat of Arms. – On the Frame, / Colonel JOHN DUNCOMBE, Obiit. Octo. 6, 1747. / Mors Janua Vitae'.[21] After number 81, the record of the marble monument to the actor James Quin, is written: 'Near the Middle of the Church is his Tomb-stone, / *with this inscription*, / Here lies the body of JAMES QUIN, / The scene is chang'd, I am no more, / Death's the last Act: Now all is o'er.'[22] This is the only explicit record of a ledgerstone in the book.

The structure of the guide is also potentially misleading. Its 'Survey' of the monuments begins 'from the East Door of the North Isle', proceeds down the aisle 'round the North Cross' (transept) and onto the 'North Side of the West Door'. From there, it takes in the 'South Side of the North Isle, till we come to the lower Pillar' then goes 'up the North Side of the Middle Isle, and cross over to the South Side'. It then moves down the south side of the Nave before entering 'the South Isle', taking in first its north and then its south sides, before surveying the 'South Cross' (transept), where the 'Christening Font' was situated, and finally going up the South Choir Aisle to the 'East Door, and conclude[ing] with the Monuments in the Choir and Chancel'. The introduction boasted that 'by this Method no Monument will escape your Observation'.[23] Subheadings were given to help readers follow this circuitous route, with separate sections for the monuments in 'The Middle Isle' (from number 55) and those 'In the Choir of the Church' (from number 134). Whilst these may have been helpful to guide visitors around the monuments in 1778, they are potentially misleading to the casual reader today without qualification. For example, whilst the subheading for 'The Middle Isle' obviously distinguishes between the first 54 numbered monuments in the North Choir and North Nave Aisles and those beginning in the Middle Aisle from number 55, there is no subsequent subheading distinguishing between those in the Middle Aisle and those in the South Aisles. However, comparison of the 1778 survey with earlier and later surveys enables the reader to accurately locate the monuments' exact positions in 1778. The following table gives the locations of the monuments in the 1778 survey and indicates the growth in the number of wall monuments in the eighteenth century:

Comparison of numbers of wall tablets in Bath Abbey from seventeenth- and eighteenth-century surveys (excluding ledgerstones)				
Location	**1676**	**1719**	**1778**	**1794**
North Choir Aisle	6	9	11	
North Transept	5	7	8	97
North Nave Aisle	5	6[24]	35	
Central Nave	3[25]	4	29	
South Nave Aisle	1	4	31	
South Transept	6	10	13	100
South Choir Aisle	4	4	7	
Central Choir	1	3	14	20
Total number of wall tablets	**31**	**47**	**148**	**217**

Looking at the wall tablets listed and their locations in detail enables an understanding of how, by 1778, they had come to be arranged. The oldest continued to be concentrated in the North Choir Aisle and North and South Transepts, where 7/11, 6/8 and 7/13, respectively, pre-dated the eighteenth century. In contrast, 27/29 monuments in 'The Middle Isle' and 13/14 monuments 'In the Choir and Chancel' were from the eighteenth century, with the vast majority dating from the 1720s onwards. It seems that the Abbey's beautiful Perpendicular Gothic columns were the desirable place on which relatives wished to erect monuments. The Abbey seems not to have resisted this, although neither is there any evidence to suggest that it charged more for the erection of monuments on the columns as it seems it might have done. Cost, class, perhaps a greater oversight by the rector because regular services were held there, and simply what might reasonably be erected in a small, galleried area may have been limiting factors in the slow rate of growth in the number of monuments in the Choir. However, in the Nave, the number of monuments erected on the walls and pillars increased sevenfold between 1719–78. In October 1794, *The Bath Chronicle* reported that a gentleman whose curiosity had led him to 'enumerate the monuments in the Abbey church' put 'the number on the South-side [at] 100; on the North 97, in the Choir 20 – Total 217'.[26] In comparison, there were 'only about 150 monuments' in the whole of Westminster Abbey by the 1720s.[27]

The effect of that increase can be seen in Samuel Hieronymous Grimm's watercolour of *A Service at Bath Abbey* (1788) (Colour Plate G). Looking west, from the elevated perspective of the organ loft seen in Vertue's 1750 etching, Grimm depicts in his characteristic detail forty-five monuments (including the Montagu tomb). Read alongside Vertue's etching and Rawlinson's survey, Grimm's drawing makes clear that by the end of the century the walls and pillars were incredibly congested. Comparing Grimm's drawing with the 1778 survey is extremely instructive of the original appearance and exact location of many monuments before the nineteenth-century alterations to them. Obviously the smaller, generic monuments that are described in 1778 simply as 'Small Marble Monument[s]' are difficult to identify with certainty (the same is true of the 'Large Marble Monuments'). However, the more 'curious' monuments (to use the eighteenth-century phrase) are easy to identify, if one remembers that their current form and location is different from those encountered in the Abbey today.

The significance of where they were originally located in the Abbey is also important to understand. One of the best examples of this is the large monument to the left of the West Door in Grimm's drawing that is unquestionably the monument to Jacob Bosanquet (d. 1767). It was described in 1778 as follows:

> *A large curious Monument*, Erected to the memory of JACOB BOSANQUET, esq. In a frame of Sienna marble is a Basso-Relievo of the good Samaritan; on the bottom stone is a wreath of palms on a demi-circle table of Sienna marble: Over the ledger is scroul with the following verses, *Go and do thou likewise! So shalt thou die the death of the Righteous; and, thy last end be like his* – It has a small vause with drapery on each side the inscription-table, over which is a large black urn, decorated with flowers; the back ground, a sheet of drapery, fring'd, within which is a shield with the arms and crest. The whole supported by trusses of Sienna and statuary marble [Fig. 9].[28]

Fig.9: Detail of monument to Jacob Bosanquet (d. 1767) as originally installed to the left of the Great West Door at the west of the Nave. British Library, London, UK © British Library Board. All Rights Reserved/Bridgeman Images.

After which the inscription was given:

Near this Place lyeth the Body
Of JACOB BOSANQUET,
Of the City of London Esqr:
A truly good, and honest Man.
A tender Husband,
Affectionate Father;
And faithful Friend;
Not more industrious in acquiring a Fortune,
Than generous in dispensing it;
Thus happily furnish'd,
With every social Virtue,
He liv'd belov'd,
And dyed lamented;
On the 9th day of June,
1767
And in the 54th Year of his Age.

Go and do thou
likewise
So shalt thou die
the death of the
righteous and thy
last end be like his.

Bosanquet's monument is now on the east wall of the South Transept without either the 'a small vause with drapery on each side the inscription-table' or the 'large black urn, decorated with flowers' (Colour Plate N). Its original location suggests the careful consideration in the placement of the monument and its subject matter by the church. Nicholas Penny has pointed out that in the late eighteenth century, church monuments exhibit a desire to illustrate the virtues of the deceased by means of narrative reliefs (like Bosanquet's) which were 'designed less to flatter the family of the deceased than to stir the public to go and do likewise'.[29] He traces this convention to the middle of the eighteenth century and the origination of the use of the Good Samaritan story on monuments in works by Scheemakers, the Bath-based sculptor Prince Hoare, and the unsigned monument to Jacob Bosanquet in Bath Abbey, which he attributes to Thomas Carter the Younger.[30] Thanks to Bacon in 1770 and Banks in 1788, thereafter 'the convention can be said to have become truly popular'.[31]

Such a monument in the Abbey would have been strikingly modern to eighteenth-century eyes when it was erected next to the Great West Door in the summer of 1771. The account book for 23 July of that year records a payment of £3 'For Mr Bosanquet's Monument', a profit equivalent to approximately £260 today, for the permission to erect the monument on the wall there. This sum would have been only a small fraction (perhaps less than 1 per cent) of the cost of such a large and complicated monument in statuary and Sienna marbles. Naturally the immediate income was good for the Abbey, but the Bosanquet monument's modernity, visibility (next to the Abbey's main exit after services) and subject matter must have made a profound impression on visitors and may have benefited the Abbey and its charitable aims after the 1771 payment in ways that may be guessed at but not quantified. For example, in the eighteenth century, sermons were regularly given and collections made at them in support of the hospital. Many of the sermons of John Chapman (Rector of Bath 1768–86) were concerned with 'cheerful giving'. Before the introduction of stained glass depicting Bible stories in the Abbey in the nineteenth century, a monument like Bosanquet's would have been ready material to illustrate these sermons, giving the congregation pause when passing the monument after the service. Although long before Bosanquet's monument was erected, it is hard not to imagine Reverend Edward Bayley gesticulating from the pulpit to the walls of the Abbey and to its monuments when concluding his sermon for the hospital in 1749 thus: '*Works of* CHARITY *will not deceive you* [...] On the Contrary, they will support thee on *the Bed of Languishing*, they will attend thee to thy Grave; and make thy Memory revered far more, than gaudy Escutcheons on thy Hearse, or pompous Titles on thy Monument'.[32] As the century progressed, so the narratives about the health of visitors to the city and church and the effects of the Abbey's monuments on them became increasingly intertwined.

Generally, the monuments on the south of the Abbey are harder to identify in Grimm's drawing, especially those in the South Aisle. Only one monument in the South Aisle in 1778 is dated to the seventeenth century, compared with five (not including the Montagu tomb) in the North Aisle. Without the existing arrangement of these large, older monuments, even more monuments to 'strangers' could be crammed into the South Aisle in what appears to be a more haphazard arrangement than in the North Aisle in Grimm's drawing in 1788. Indeed, the ordered arrangement and greater size of the monuments in the North Aisle makes it possible to identify the monuments on the north wall of the North Aisle in Grimm's drawing (Colour Plate G). Starting on the right-hand side can be seen the *Old Freestone Monument* to Robert Mason (d. 1662):

> With a 3-qr. Length of the deceased in an oval frame, under a canopy of drapery; with a figure of a woman on each side. Above appears, in a square frame, in Basso Relievo; the deceased rising from the dead, at the sound of the trumpet. Beneath is the inscription-table, on each side of which is an angel, extinguishing a lighted tapor. – The whole may be called a good piece of antiquity.[33]

Moving west down the aisle, to the left of this is the small marble monument to Thomas Morris (d. 1763) and the large monument with the three-quarter-length bust to John Pelling (d. 1620) described in Chapter 1. The pillar then obscures the monuments to Edward Alchordus (d. 1652), Elvedale Price (d. 1764), Charles James (n.d.) and Lucia Thomson (d. 1765) before the 'Marble Monument, with an Urn upon Top' to Elizabeth Kelly (d. 1761) can be seen to the left of the pillar. The inscription on this monument begins 'Near the Centre of *St. JAMES's* Burial Ground Lie the Remains of ELIZABETH'. Richard Warner reminded his readers in 1811 that 'No monuments [were] permitted to be placed in this church', a regulation that, he thought, preserved 'its elegant simplicity entire'.[34] Other monuments were erected in the Abbey to commemorate burials at St James'.[35] Notably, ledgerstones were also used as cenotaphs, as in the case of John Boylston (son of Zabdiel Boylston, the physician credited with introducing inoculation for smallpox in North America) who died in Bath on 17 January 1795 and was buried 'in the yard' of St James' Church on 22 January. Boylston had wanted his body, 'born by poor men early in the morning', to be interred decently 'in the nearest parish church yard with a Grave Stone Inscribed viz. – "Here repose the remains of Mr. John Boylston of Boston in New England who died in the humble hope of a happy Immortality Aged [blank] years"'. The inscription on his ledgerstone in the Abbey conveniently omitted the first six words. To the left of Kelly's monument is the monument 'with a Pyramid of Dove Marble and an Oval Tablet' in memory of 'C.M.' (d. 1765) (discussed below), followed by that to both Walter (d. 1729) and Reverend Robert Chapman (d. 1728). The monument to the left of this, partly obscured by the pillar, does not match the description of any subsequent monument in the North Aisle in the 1778 guide. This method could be applied to other areas of Grimm's drawing but the above has allowed us to

Left: *Fig.10: Monument to Dorothy Hobart (d. 1722) in its original form and location on the pillar next to the pulpit in the south of the Nave, as depicted by Samuel Grimm in 1788. British Library, London, UK © British Library Board. All Rights Reserved/Bridgeman Images.*

Right: *Fig.11: Monument to 'C.M.' (Catherine Malone, d. 1765) in its original form and location in the North Aisle of the Nave, as depicted by Samuel Grimm in 1788. British Library, London, UK © British Library Board. All Rights Reserved/Bridgeman Images.*

see just how profoundly the appearance of the North Aisle alone was altered by the monuments by the mid-1760s.

The accuracy of Grimm's drawing generally gives a good sense of monuments' original appearance, especially those in the foreground. The bust on the pillar directly to the left of the pulpit in Grimm's drawing is clearly that to Dorothy Hobart (d. 1722) carved by the Bathonian sculptor John Harvey (discussed below) (Fig. 10):

> *A Monument of Statuary and vein'd Marble*. Erected to the memory of DOROTHY HOBART. On a pedestal is her bust, surrounded with cherubims heads, a crown of glory and festoons of flowers, over which is a lozenge shield, with golden balls and palms on each side, under the bust is an inscription-table, supported by a bottom stone and trusses, curiously carved.[36]

The extent to which the monument was altered in the nineteenth century will be discussed in the following chapter. However, a comparison of Hobart's monument in the Grimm drawing with the monument to Frances Fry (d. 1718) in the Church of St John the Baptist, Membury, Devon, shows the two monuments to be identical. The inscription on the monument to Fry reveals it to have been erected 'to her dear Memory Anno D:1723', a year after Hobart's death. Clearly, Harvey carved both monuments *c.* 1723, probably using the Fry monument as the model for the Hobart monument.[37]

As with Grimm's depiction of the Bosanquet monument, the relief carving of the monuments in the background of his drawing – but not in the periphery of the drawing, as seen by the detail in Mason, Pelling and Montagu – are inevitably simplified squiggles. In the case of the monument to 'C.M.', depicted in the North Aisle, the detail is omitted entirely and a blank rectangle at the bottom of the monument stands in for a poignant piece of sculpture (Fig. 11). The monument is one that continues to delight and fascinate visitors to the Abbey, despite being extremely different from its original design, because of its intriguing inscription. All that remains from the monument depicted by Grimm is the oval tablet with the following inscription (Colour Plate O):

In Memory of C.M.
One of the most valuable Women
that ever lived;
Whose principal Happiness consisted
(altho' she was of some rank,)
in a real & unbounded
Affection & Tenderness
for her Husband & Children;
This Monument is erected;
from the sorrow of their Hearts,
and their Love & Respect for her,
without the vanity or weakness,
of proclaiming her Virtues,
or their own Misfortune,
in so inestimable a Loss.
Lett others therefore celebrate
the Name, Family, & Condition,
of so amiable & rare a Character;
She dyed 1st Jany 1765
in the 47th Year of her Age,
and lyes interr'd
near this place.

The inscription is unusual in the way that it purposely obscures the subject commemorated. The text is consciously reserved, almost stoic, broken only by the parenthetical allusions to the subject's 'rank' and the family's 'misfortune'. Given that monuments in churches like Bath Abbey became public spectacles as soon as they were erected, the privacy this monument keeps for its subject and her family is interesting and its decorum did not go unnoticed by contemporary commentators. James Storer remarked that the tablet was 'most modestly inscribed' and would not 'escape the observation of the tasteful inquirer'.[38] Monumental inscriptions are generally not so reserved in proclaiming the virtues of their subjects and often seek to engage the reader in sparing a thought or a prayer for the deceased. Of course, in withholding 'the Name, Family, & Condition of so amiable & rare a Character' it makes the reader even more curious. And in not satisfying the reader with these details it makes this tablet and the woman commemorated by it all the more memorable; the tablet's reticence serves to intensify the little it does tell about the qualities of its subject (affectionate, tender, etc.). Of course, in so doing, the monument finds itself in the same territory of idealising its subject as the more verbose monuments. The way it goes about it is simply more cultured, almost literary in its approach. This, in turn, suggests who may have commissioned C.M.'s monument.

Catherine Malone (C.M.) was born Catherine Collyer (or Collier) on 2 April 1718 to Mr Benjamin and Catherine Collyer and baptised at St Dionis Backchurch in the City of London. Her father was a merchant (of some standing, according to her monument), well-to-do, self-important and rather eccentric. In 1736, at the age of 18, Catherine was living in the growing parish of All Hallows, Barking.[39] Barking town and Ilford village were the main centres of population with 'undeveloped marshland' in the extreme south of the parish and 'Hainault Forest, in the north [...] about half of which was in Barking.' In the early eighteenth century, the parish had 'relatively good communications with the outside world' and in 1740 'there was a daily coach service from London to Ilford and Barking'.[40] This link to the city may have been important in Catherine's courtship with her husband-to-be, Edmund Malone, who had arrived in London from Dublin in 1722 to study law at the Middle Temple. He was called to the English bar on 16 May 1729 and was a student of the Inner Temple in 1734, later establishing himself as a successful barrister and member of the Irish House of Commons.[41] Malone asked for a licence to marry Catherine 'either in the Parish Church of East Greenwich in the County of Kent or Mordaunt College upon Blackheath also in Kent'. The couple eventually married on 26 May 1736.

In his biography of Edmund and Catherine's second son, the writer and Shakespearian critic Edmond Malone (1741–1812), James Prior recounts a story of Edmund and Catherine's wedding night and Catherine's embarrassment at her father's eccentric behaviour:

> Old Mr. Collier was a very vain man who had made his fortune in the South Sea year; and having been originally a merchant, was fond, after he had retired to live upon his fortune, of a great deal of display and parade. On his daughter's wedding, therefore, he invited nearly fifty persons, and got two or three capital cooks from London to prepare a magnificent entertainment in honour of the day. When other ceremonies had concluded, the young couple were put to bed, and every one of this numerous assemblage came into the room to make their congratulations to my father and mother, who sat up in bed to receive them: 'Madam, I wish you a very good night! Sir, all happiness to you, and a very good night!' – and so on through the party. My father, who

hated all parade, but was forced to submit to the old gentleman's humour, must have been in a fine fume; and my mother, who was then but seventeen or eighteen, sufficiently embarrassed.[42]

This was hardly an auspicious start to their marriage and the couple must have longed to get away from Old Mr Collier's sphere of influence.

The opportunity came when Edmund was called to the Irish bar in 1740 and the couple moved to Dublin, where they had six children, two of whom died in infancy. In the summer of 1759, Edmund and Catherine returned to London with their son Edmond. This was Edmond's first trip to England. He would return to London in January 1763 to follow in the family tradition of becoming an Irish barrister. There, in 1764, he would meet Samuel Johnson, who turned Edmond's mind 'increasingly toward the muses and away from the law'. Edmond would go on to become a distinguished scholar and literary biographer. In 1790, he published *The Plays and Poems of William Shakespeare* in ten volumes. This 'monumental achievement in Shakespearian studies' was the fruit of Malone's 'unprecedented documentary and textual research' and 'heralded a new age of scholarship in which he helped define the scholar's code for generations to come'.[43]

Catherine's health had been 'deteriorating for some time and she increasingly found it difficult to walk [...] it was decided a stint in England might be tonic'. According to Peter Martin, another of Edmond's biographers, father and son left Catherine at Highgate and went on to the Midlands, where his father had business. Catherine soon moved to Bath, where she wrote to her son Edmond, her 'dear nedy'. As Martin says, 'Drinking the supposedly health-giving waters "constantly", brought to her at her lodging because she "almost always [sic] got cold" at the Pump Room, does not appear to have done her much good', but she assured him she would persevere. Catherine 'longed' to see her son and family: 'the time will I hope come when we shall all meet & till then shall never injoy perfect happiness'. The 'expenses at Bath left little money to spare, and the family legal practice presented the best route to a secure future' for Edmond, who visited his mother in Bath when he could.[44]

During the spring of 1760, the news from Bath of Catherine was 'worrying', although her letter of 11 March 'brought some happy if temporary relief: "I just begin to use my limbs with a can[e] after very near 3 months confinement [...] If I have many more fits they will soon wear me out ... I shall not repine at a severe one provided I have you & *all* my children with me".'[45] Edmond continued to visit Catherine from London, where he was studying to become a barrister, although her invalidism continued. She never fully recovered.

Catherine's death in Bath on 1 January 1765 'deeply demoralized' and 'shattered the Malone family'.[46] She was buried in the Abbey on 6 January. Edmond may have attended the funeral but it is unlikely the rest of her family in Ireland would have been able to be present. In the North Aisle, where Catherine was buried, Edmond would have encountered both the large, stately monuments of the seventeenth century and those from the same decade to those who, like his mother, had sought the cure at Bath. Edmond's literary sensibility may have been offended by the self-aggrandising and lengthy inscriptions to the dead, which might, in turn, have led him to consider the kind of text we find on his mother's monument: spare, private and reserved. Catherine's letters to her 'dear nedy' and family bear out her character as portrayed on the monument: her 'principal Happiness consisted / (altho' she was of some rank,) / in a real & unbounded / Affection & Tenderness / for her Husband & Children'. Being separated from them for so much time must have been just as painful as the physical ailments she suffered, for which she spent so much time in Bath.

There is no record of the cost for permission to erect Catherine's monument in the North Aisle, only a receipt for 'Mrs Malone's Linen Hatband & Scarf left £1 11s 6d' on 6 January 1765 in Rev. Duel Taylor's account of 'The Income of the Rectory of Bath 1756–65'. However, it is not unreasonable to assume it was between £2 (the fixed fee for permission to erect monuments between 1756–65) and £3 (the cost for the permission for Bosanquet's monument in 1771). Early in 1765, the Malones suffered another blow: 'an expected legacy from a relative named Mrs. Weaver did not materialize; she had died in March without leaving them a penny'.[47] The Malones, therefore, like the Bosanquets and other relatives in the late eighteenth century, might not have hurried to commission the monument to Catherine immediately.

On the other hand, the budding Shakespearean scholar, Edmond, may have remembered Benedick's reflection in *Much Ado About Nothing*: 'If a man do not erect / in this age his own tomb ere he dies, he shall live / no longer in monument than the bell rings and the / widow weeps' (Act 5, Scene 2). The Abbey's records strongly suggest, if not provide conclusive evidence, that Catherine's monument was erected between 1765 and 1767.[48] Furthermore, the inscription would only really have been accessible to those who knew that C.M. was Catherine Malone; without knowing to whom the monument is dedicated, its commemorative function is extremely limited. The monument was erected out of 'Love & Respect'. But in order for it to also enable others to celebrate the 'Name, Family, & Condition, of so amiable & rare a Character' from her initials alone relied on it being erected promptly, when Catherine was still in living memory for those who knew her in Bath and beyond.

The carving of the monument, described in 1778, included 'a Pyramid of Dove Marble, and an Oval Tablet. Over which are two branches of Palm; beneath, in a Basso Relievo, is a boy sleeping by an urn, with a branch of cyprus in his left hand, resting his head on an hour-glass, with other statuary ornaments.'[49] The 'two branches of Palm' (alluding to the Bible and symbolising the triumph of a martyr over death) described in 1778 are visible in Grimm's 1788 drawing, as a circle or wreath above the 'Oval Tablet'. The monument's original pyramidal form is clear and the drawing also shows that the bottom of the monument included a shield (no doubt showing the Malone family's coat of arms) and decorative volutes. Amazingly, the carving of the boy sleeping by the urn, removed in the nineteenth century, was recovered intact by archaeologists in June 2020 as part of excavations in the South Aisle (discussed further in the following chapter) (Colour Plate P).

It is worth comparing Catherine Malone's monument with that to Leonard and Elizabeth Coward, originally erected in the South Aisle (Colour Plate Q). Both monuments are dedicated to a parent or parents by their children and were erected within a matter of years of each other in the Abbey: that to Leonard and Elizabeth Coward in 'A:D: 1764' (Elizabeth died in 1759 and Leonard in 1761), and that to Catherine Malone between 1765 and 1767. The form of these monuments is almost identical: both were originally pyramidal, on coloured marble backgrounds, with symbolic relief carving in a rectangular frame at the bottom. The main differences are in how the form and proportion are achieved: the Coward monument has a pediment above the pyramid and inscription tablet, whereas the Malone monument originally had decorative volutes beneath the pyramid, either side of the relief carving, as can be seen from the etching of it in James Hayward Markland's *Remarks on English Churches*. A further minor difference is that the inscription on the Malone monument is carved onto the oval tablet and attached to the pyramid background, whereas the inscription is carved directly onto the pyramid on the Coward monument. It would have been easier – and significantly cheaper – to correct any mistakes by carving onto the oval tablet rather than directly onto the larger pyramid marble, and this may represent a development in the sculptor's style or way of working. Carvers of ledgerstones could hide their mistakes by turning the stone over and carving again on its reverse, as in the case of Christiana Susanna Lucas's ledgerstone (d. 1781), which contains two different versions of the inscription. Constructing the monument's inscription tablet would have given the creator of this type of monument a similar option. Finally, the relief carvings of the Malone and Coward monuments are extremely similar: both appear on a background that has been prepared in the same way, textured vertical lines form the background of both carvings from which the polished carvings stand out, which also share some of the same symbolic elements, from a generic tomb and an urn to the ground blooming with flowers (symbolising resurrection). The base of both of the tombs carved on the relief is almost identical: it is only the decoration of them that distinguishes them (Malone's has an oval, whereas Coward's has a rectangular area where the epitaph would be; height is given to the Malone tomb by the pyramidal brickwork, whereas height is achieved on Coward's through the skull and the palm tree (palm being used in both monuments)).

The figures have obvious superficial differences – the boy sleeps holding a branch of cypress on Malone's monument, whereas the cherub weeps holding a handkerchief (appropriate for the lace merchant Coward family) – but are strikingly similar, especially the way in which the tousled, curly hair has been achieved so successfully and almost identically in each monument. It is likely that both were carried out by the same local sculptor, although both monuments are now unsigned. Comparison of the monuments shows how the carving and composition of this particular relief has been refined: the cherub's rather awkward wings on the Coward monument (1764) have been dispensed with on the Malone monument's boy (1765–67) and the figure is the better for it. Being able to fully appreciate the design and intention of Catherine's monument through this relief carving and Grimm's drawing, one can see that, for all of the inscription's reticence, the monument's original design speaks powerfully of her own endurance, hope and faithfulness, and of the affection and tenderness shared between her and her family, and especially her son, Catherine's 'dear nedy'. It is not hard to read the boy sleeping on her tomb as her son, who probably commissioned the tomb, waiting patiently – as he must have done so many times by her bedside in Bath – for her to come back to life. To eighteenth-century commentators, the monument was tasteful. By the nineteenth century, its carving was described as 'of almost unrivalled ugliness'.[50]

★★★

Of all the monuments erected in the Abbey in the eighteenth century, none has attracted more comment than that commemorating the actor James Quin (perhaps with the exception of Catherine Malone's). Quin was 'privately interred' in the Abbey on 25 January 1766. His tablet was erected three years later on 'a pillar at the south-eastern end of the nave', 'the opposite pillar of the nave' to the Montagu tomb (Colour Plate R). The 1778 survey described it thus:

> On the pyramid of Sienna marble is a medallion of Namur black marble, with a striking Likeness of the deceased, and Cyprus branches on each side; underneath is a sarcophagus, of statuary marble, on which is a table, with the following epitaph, wrote by MR. GARRICK, under which is a mask and a dagger, representing Tragedy and Comedy.

The inscription reads:

> OB: MDCCLXVI
> AETAT: LXXIII
>
> That tongue which set the table on a roar,
> And charm'd the public ear, is heard no more:
> Clos'd are those eyes, the harbingers of wit,
> Which spake before the tongue what ***SHAKESPEAR*** writ:
> Cold is that hand, which living was stretch'd forth,
> At friendship's call, to succour modest worth:
> Here lies **JAMES QUIN**: deign, reader, to be taught,
> Whate'er thy strength of body, force of thought,
> In nature's happiest mould however cast,
> To this complexion thou must come at last.

Garrick's epitaph was printed in *The Bath Chronicle* on 24 April 1766, three months after Quin's death, and reprinted in the 'Poets Corner' section of the same paper three years later, when the 'elegant Monument' was 'now erecting in the Abbey Church'.[51] As soon as the following week, the monument was drawing comment. The anonymous correspondent 'W.W.' pastiched Garrick's verse:

Fig.12: Quin's Monument, Bath, *drawn by John Nixon, engraved by Sparrow, which appeared as the frontispiece to the* European Magazine and London Review *in 1792. © The author.*

Lines occasioned by reading an EPITAPH on Mr. QUIN, in last Week's Paper.

LO! now the man, (who when of late he fum'd,
A little brief authority assum'd)
In verse that darts the fire of Shakespeare's page,
Blazons the glory once of Drury's stage,
Immortal QUIN! thy grave with flow'rs he strews,
Cull'd from the garden of thy favourite muse.
GARRICK and QUIN! – take them for all in all,
Their equals ne'er to the world's lot did fall![52]

The writer and diarist Fanny Burney also remarked on Quin's epitaph. In June 1780, she attended the Abbey one Sunday morning and 'after church-time [...] spent an hour or two looking over the abbey-church, and reading epitaphs,– among which, Garrick's on Quin was much the best'. The monument to another eighteenth-century female novelist also caught her eye: 'There is a monument erected, also, for Sarah Fielding, who wrote "David Simple," by Dr. Hoadley. Will any future doctor do as much by me?'[53] John Nixon's drawing of 'Quins monument, Bath', which appeared as the frontispiece to the *European Magazine and London Review* in 1792, gives a picture of the Abbey 'after church-time' at the end of the eighteenth century (Fig. 12). Like the other eighteenth-century images of the interior of the Abbey discussed above, it shows a number of people walking around the church taking in the monuments. Nixon's drawing is especially interesting in that it contrasts a trio of well-to-do male mourners for Quin with a working-class woman in an apron and a boy looking at another monument. In the background, a pair of elderly ladies observe a large monument in the North Aisle. For rich and poor, old and young, by the end of eighteenth century the Abbey's monuments were a spectacular collection of ancient and contemporary sculpture, by some of the most celebrated local and national sculptors. They were a chance for viewers to see the most recent works of a popular artform from London, including those to famous individuals drawn out for special mention by local commentators, and to see Bible stories, symbols of Christian faith, and representations of resurrection before their eyes.

In the last two decades of the eighteenth century, lists of the Abbey's monuments were published that selected for readers the most remarkable monuments to noteworthy individuals in the church. The table of 166 'Monumental Inscriptions' published in *The Gentleman's Magazine* for 1783 gives only a name, rank, date and (usually) a geographical location related to the deceased for each entry. What was intended to be an attractive list of well-to-do names to inform the magazine's readers is, in fact, incredibly misleading and the informed reader would take this list at face value at their peril. The table is obviously based on the longer, second edition of the 1778 survey, which the magazine writes was authored (rather than sold) 'by William Hancock, Sexton'. It is probably no coincidence that the list in *The Gentleman's Magazine* was published in 1783 and it may be indicative of the date that the second edition of the original 1778 survey appeared. However, the editor of the *Gentleman's Magazine* list omitted the Lichfield Tomb and the monuments to Catherine Malone (C.M.) and James Antonio Migliorucci, in favour of reprinting the names of family members who appear on the same monument, names that presumably were intended to be more appealing to the magazine's readership. No monument appears in the *Gentleman's Magazine* table that does not appear in the second edition of the 1778 survey. The number of errors in the magazine's table shows a considerable lack of care in re-presenting the 1778 survey. The printers' errors include incorrect dates (e.g. 1561 rather than 1761 for Elizabeth Kelly's monument mentioned above), incorrect geographical locations attributed to monuments (e.g. 'London' appears next to Mary Reeve's monument, whose inscription only mentions 'of this citty', that is, Bath), and slapdash typesetting (e.g. the parenthesis '*(the Tragedian)*' appears after the name of James Roffey (d. 1769) rather than after the name of the actor James Quin (d. 1766)). In making the table a list of names rather than monuments, the editor also misreads certain inscriptions in the 1778 survey. For example, monument number 62 in the 1778 survey was a 'Square plain Marble Monument', the inscription of which began: 'Near this place lies the body of ELIZABETH, third daughter of the late Rev. Doctor WALDO, of Harrow on the hill; and late wife to Capt. Norton Hutchinson, fourth son of Julius Hutchinson, esq. of Outhorp, in the county of Nottingham'.[54] *The Gentleman's Magazine* contains no entry for 'this most affectionate Wife', Mrs. Elizabeth Hutchinson, whose 'Monument [was] erected by her aforemention'd Husband'. Instead, it gives an entry for 'Waldo, Elizabeth, *Middlesex*, 1763'. Whilst the table, at face value, lists the Abbey's monumental inscriptions, its partial and haphazard use of the 1778 survey results in neither a complete list of inscriptions (names) nor an accurate list of monuments.[55]

In the following decade, John Collinson's *History and Antiquities of the County of Somerset* (1791) printed a by no means comprehensive alphabetical list of 250 monumental inscriptions in the Abbey. It is almost certainly a list of some of the names found on mural monuments only, but includes the large tombs of Montagu, Lichfield and Waller recorded in all the earlier surveys.

The list gives the name, place name and date on the monuments, but no further information about the inscriptions themselves. Of course, Collinson's appraisal of the monuments was only part of his broader history of the church (and county), whereas the monuments were the primary focus of the earlier surveys. Where the 1719 and 1778 surveys described different but nonetheless systematic routes around the church to appraise the monuments in each area of it, Collinson prefaced his list by picking out a handful of monuments for detailed description, guided by the subject or inscription of the monument, rather than its location. With the exception of the 'small marble monument' inscribed to William Clements Esq., these were exclusively the large monuments against the walls of the transepts, pillars and Chancel, and usually had a local connection (such as those to James Quin and Lady Anna Miller).

Fig.13: Plate depicting the monument to Lady Anna Miller (d. 1781) from Collinson's History and Antiquities of the County of Somerset *(1791). © The author.*

That Lady Anna Miller's monument is singled out for special treatment (a plate showing the monument is dedicated to Sir John Miller by 'his Obliged H'ble Servants J. Collinson & E. Rack') is unsurprising given that Edmund Rack, who was responsible for compiling the information on Bath for Collinson, knew both Sir John and Lady Miller and was invited as a contributor to their poetry evenings (Fig. 13).[56] Lady Miller died at the Hot Wells, Bristol, on 24 June 1781, aged 41. Four years later, a 'beautiful monument of statuary marble, elegantly designed, and most exquisitely finished' was executed by John Bacon and installed north of the altar in the sanctuary in August 1785 (indicative of the time it took for large, unique monuments by eminent London sculptors to be commissioned, executed and installed in the Abbey). It was described at length by *The Bath Chronicle* on 1 September 1785, which interpreted the figures either side of Miller's famous Batheaston vase as Liberality (on the left) and Genius (on the right) (Colour Plate S). The plate of the monument was the only one to illustrate the Abbey's monuments in Collinson's *History*. Beneath the sculpture is the fittingly poetic inscription by the poet Anna Seward (the enjambment 'tear / Drop' in the second quatrain is elegantly achieved):

> Devoted stone! amidst the wrecks of time,
> Uninjur'd bear thy MILLER'S spotless name:
> The virtues of her youth and ripen'd prime,
> The tender thought, th'enduring record claim.
>
> When clos'd the num'rous eyes that round this bier
> Have wept the loss of wide-extended worth,
> O gentle stranger, may one gen'rous tear
> Drop, as thou bendest o'er this hallow'd earth!
>
> Are truth and genius, love and pity thine,
> With lib'ral charity, and faith sincere?
> Then rest thy wand'ring step beneath this shrine,
> And greet a kindred spirit hov'ring near.

The inscription adopts and subverts certain conventions of eighteenth-century monumental inscriptions. Unlike Teshmaker's or Bosanquet's monuments, the address to the reader does not didactically instruct them to emulate the qualities of the deceased that have gained them a place in heaven. Neither does it simply act as a *memento mori* like Quin's. Instead, the voice assumes in the final verse that the reader shares these qualities with the 'kindred Spirit' of Miller 'hov'ring near' them. Such flattery would have been welcomed by the literate, well-to-do visitors to the Abbey and its monuments in the Choir. However, whilst the writer of the inscription might have considered who might read it, it is hard to imagine how visitors would have been able to see anything but Bacon's figures. There would have been no more desirable place for a monument than the sanctuary for someone of Miller's status (for her family and, indeed, for the sculptor). Its position would have ensured it could be seen by priests and communicants. However, on 20 May 1726 the vestry had agreed that the altar be at the top of three steps, that 'the distance from the Altar Piece to the first Step be fifteen foot' and that 'Iron Rails of the lightest work [...] inclose the sd. Altar'.[57] At such a distance, the inscription on Miller's monument, behind the altar, would be illegible to the ordinary visitor. Whereas the carving and inscription on Bosanquet's monument may have been easily consumed by (and perhaps even influential on) the congregation and visitors, the eventual position of Miller's monument eventually worked against its inscription's commemorative function. Arguably, the inscription (and monument) would have been best-known through its reproduction in publications such as Collinson's *History* than by its being viewed in the Abbey.

A comparison of a manuscript version of the list of 'Monumental Inscriptions' with the printed version in Collinson's *History* sheds additional light on the Abbey's monuments and the rate at which they were installed in the 1780s and 1790s.[58] The manuscript indicates thirteen monuments that were 'in the Choir of the Abbey', a detail that does not appear in the published version. Further comparison is instructive of the rate at which (noteworthy) monuments were installed in the Abbey between 1787–91. The manuscript records 210 monumental inscriptions, forty fewer than the printed list. The manuscript lists no inscriptions later than two dating to 1787, whereas the printed version lists monuments with dates of 1791. The two 1787 monuments still survive in the Abbey,[59] and both record deaths in April 1787, making it impossible for Edmund Rack to have been the author of the manuscript list of monuments (since he died in February 1787). Of the forty additional inscriptions included in the printed survey (1791), thirty date from 1787 or later.[60] Seven of the remainder of the inscriptions absent from the manuscript are dated 1762–86 (suggesting that the monuments, like the thirty above, were created between 1788 and 1791), with two dating to the seventeenth century and one undated (e.g. those simply missed by the manuscript's author). Therefore, it is possible to say that between 1788 and 1791 a minimum of thirty-seven mural monuments were erected in the Abbey. That only thirteen of the 210 monuments were described as 'in the Choir' in Collinson's manuscript list (comparable with the one recorded as being erected there between 1768 and 1783 in Reverend John Chapman's accounts) emphasises the sharp increase in monuments in the Nave in the last two decades of the eighteenth century.

'Monstrous high': Making money from burials and monuments, 1721–87

With such an interest in the Abbey's monuments by the late eighteenth century, it must not have been unusual for visitors to be seen making records of their own to inform and entertain friends and family. Such was the intention of Reverend John Penrose (1713–76), Vicar of St Gluvias (Penryn) with Budock in Cornwall, who made two visits to Bath to take the waters, first in 1766 and then again in 1767. Penrose's letters from Bath 1766–67 provide a unique insight into the churches in Bath, especially the Abbey, in regard to their architecture, worshipping life and their monuments. For Penrose, such a list was intended to be a 'Supplement' to his 'Bath Memoirs':

> It was my full Design, if the Weather proved dry and warm, and my Strength would permit, to copy those Inscriptions on the Monuments in the Abby, which relate to Devonshire and Cornish Families. But Mr. Heard says, he will save me this Trouble. For he has a copy in London of all the Inscriptions in the Abbey, and has promised to send me a copy of those I intended to take. Which Copy shall be Peggy's Property, and serve as a Supplement to our Bath Memoirs.[61]

He had intended to say more about the Abbey's 'innumerable' monuments in his letters after he had made further 'Observations' of them, but sadly never made good on this.[62] Penrose had frequent opportunity to do so both from the pulpit of the Abbey – which he was invited to preach and pray from – and as a member of its congregation. He also frequently worshipped at St James' Church (before it was rebuilt between 1768 and 1773) and remarked that 'like the Abbey' the church was 'lined all round, both Walls and Pillars, with monumental Inscriptions, which has a venerable Aspect'.[63] He also visited other local churches near Bath, including Walcot ('small, but pretty; [with] many monuments about it')[64] and Widcombe ('a little Church in a Village the South-East side the Avon, not far from Lyncombe'),[65] as well as those further afield such as St Mary Redcliffe, Bristol, and Wells Cathedral, which he found 'poorly paved'.[66]

On his return to Bath in 1767, he found that the Abbey 'hath lately been cleansed and beautified; all the monuments, the Roofs, the Windows, the whole Church throughout is as neat as possible'.[67] We have seen that the Waller Tomb was cleaned periodically, and this was true of the other monuments, too. Prince Hoare specified as much in his Will:

> The Treasurer [of the General Hospital in Bath] for the time being shall once a year at the least cause the monument erected to the Memory of my late father William Hoare in the Abbey Church at Bath to be well and fairly cleaned with pure water only and preserved as far as may be from all injury as also another Monument erected in Walcot Church to the memory of my father and mother which the said Treasurer for the time being shall cause to be kept clean and in good repair.[68]

The pressure that the thousands of visitors to the city put on the places of worship was such that, according to Penrose, not even 10 per cent could attend church: 'Bath is so enlarged, that the Places of Public Worship, will not contain a Tythe of the Inhabitants, and Strangers resorting hither'.[69] This was problematic insofar as burials were concerned, but created a significant source of income for the Abbey when burials did take place there:

> So numerous as the People here are, of some Sort or other, here is no Place of Burial but in the Churches; or none worth mentioning: and the Fees for Breaking Ground in Churches monstrous high, Ten Pounds at the Abbey. So all the Poor, and middling People, nay all except the rich and great, are carried, when dead to the Church-yards of Widcombe or chiefly at Bathwicke, two neighbouring Parishes the other side the river Avon, which is crossed in a Ferry-Boat; and four or five shillings are paid as a Fee for breaking the ground.[70]

Penrose may have been shocked by the 'monstrous' fees but the Abbey authorities appear to have consciously chosen to promote intramural burial in the church, thus enabling the rectory to profit from the fees it could command for burials and monuments within the cathedral-like interior. On 6 August 1722, the following question was raised at the Abbey vestry meeting:

> Whether that Piece of Ground belonging to Sir Philip Parker Bart. lying under the City Wall opposite to Monk's Mill shall be purchased at the Charge of this Parish By the Church Wardens for a burying Place for the said Parish?[71]

The vestry agreed that the ground should not be purchased: forty-two names are signed in support of the resolution, including the mayor's, which suggests the decision was also one supported by the city. The decision was really only the logical continuation of the practice of supplementing the church's revenue with that from monuments and breaking ground that Henry Chapman remarked on at the end of the seventeenth century. In that sense it was a formality. From the city's point of view, it can only have been good for the living to have been enhanced with the extra income. Had the vestry resolved otherwise, the Abbey would not have the number of monuments that it does (and the city would possibly have had to consider selling the advowson sooner than it eventually did in 1836). However, in less than half a century, it was thought that the Abbey's monuments would 'yield the curious stranger as much Speculation as can be met with, perhaps, in any Parochial Church, of the same standing, in the whole World'.[72] The same is still true today.

In the 1720s, money, burial fees and the repair and improvement of the church were important, interrelated concerns for the Abbey authorities. In the spring of 1720, a 'Mr Lockey Hill' had broken into the church, 'Robbing the Vestry'. It is not known what was taken or whether it was recovered, but the churchwarden Mr John Masters seems to have been successful in his prosecution (and Hill protested his innocence from Ilchester Gaol).[73] The Abbey had plans to repair the organ, to replace the pulpit and reading desk, and put new chimes in the tower, and the robbery could not have helped matters. In any case, to carry out these works the Abbey would need substantial sums, £50 for the organ alone. The relationship with the city may also have been slightly strained after Thomas Attwood had erected 'a House against the great North Window', 'Darkening ye Said Window, and obstruct[ing] ye light from that part of ye church'.[74] It is telling that the mayor was not present at the meeting in 1718/9 (as he usually was at meetings of the vestry) when it was agreed that 'there ought to be no Building there at all'.[75] The vestry's opinion must have been expressed in no uncertain terms because, in 1719, when Mr William Collibee (then mayor) took a new lease of the 'plot of garden ground Situate on ye North side of ye parish Church of Saint Peter and Paul', the Corporation stipulated that he should only 'have liberty to build on the sd garden' if he did not 'obstruct or darken any of ye lights of ye said Church'. Such a building was 'not to exceed 24 feet in depth from East to west. Nor to inclose or take in Either of the buttresses belonging to the sd Church into such a building.'[76]

The Corporation had been chastened and was now even considerate of how its decisions about the buildings abutting the Abbey affected the worship space of the interior.[77] However, perhaps the Abbey felt it could not be relied on to fully consider its needs in the Corporation's many building projects around its walls. Ironically, the Abbey's policy of erecting large monuments around the walls of its interior would do as much to obstruct the light and obscure the worship space of those in the Chancel by the middle of the eighteenth century. The scale of this will be discussed in the following chapter. For now, it is worth noting that by the middle of the eighteenth century small works were being carried out on individual monuments to address the problem. In 1814, James Storer, in his description of the Lichfield tomb, wrote: 'Originally there was another sarcophagus above the present containing the woman's body; but as it obstructed the light to the mayor's seat [in the Birde Chantry], it was removed about sixty years ago and laid with the man.'[78] In 1721, the Abbey took matters into its own hands and revised its burial fees. On 10 April 1721, the vestry agreed that 'hereafter shall be paid to the Church Warden towards the repairing of ye Church for every Grave yt shall be Walled round in the Church ye Sum of fifty Shillings for an Inhabitant of ye City and off five pounds for a Stranger buried in such Grave'.[79] Five years later, on 11 April 1726, it was ordered and agreed that:

> if any Person shall desire or that a due observance be not had to prevent it yt after the hour of ten a clock at night that the Sum of forty shillings shall be paid (viz.) twenty shillings to the Arch Deacon and twenty shillings for the use of the church for each Person yt shall be buryed after that hour over and above the usual Fees.[80]

Unfortunately, the 'usual Fees' were not also given and are not extant, but the formalisation of these charges for walled graves and burial after 10 p.m. probably coincides with them being increased to subsidise the works the church wanted to carry out in the decade. After all, the church had used such charges as these, for example in the hire of funeral palls, to generate income for the repair of the church since 1705.

The earliest extant accounts that relate to the Abbey help to illustrate how these fees supplemented the regular income of the rectory. A small, brown leather-bound volume kept by Reverend Duel Taylor (1733–67), Rector of

Bath 1752–67, records 'The Income of the Rectory of Bath' from 1756 to 1765. The accounts cover the general income of the rectory over a seven-year period from 1756 to 1763, with the income in 1764–65 recording only that from 'Hatbands and Scarves'. The extent to which the Abbey continued this source of income from 'Funeral Silks' at the end of the eighteenth century will be discussed below. The table below illustrates the extent to which burial fees[81] and the fees for the erection of monuments contributed to the rectory's income in the middle of the eighteenth century. Between 1756 and 1763, the fee for a burial in the Abbey was 1*s* or 2*s* (4*s* or more if buried in the Choir) and that for a mortuary 6*s* 8*d*. The increase in total income from 1759 is explained by a note at the end of that year's accounts that reads: 'The extraordinary Income of this year has been owing to the Discovery of upward of eighteen Pounds Arrears due to the Rectory of Bath'. This appears to be arrears from the income arising from ground rents. From 1758–59, the accounts show that the Abbey was used less frequently than St James' and St Michael's Without, possibly a reflection of the size of the Abbey parish and the extent to which the Abbey became a place of burial and commemoration for those visiting the city. In the 1760s, the accounts also show an increase in income from involvement in the proving of Wills. In the most extraordinary (and lucrative) case, on 9 April 1762, Duel Taylor received £4 4*s* for 'attending ye Examination of [...] Mrs Tylson's Will 4 Days'. Generally, the fees for this kind of clerical work were more modest, as on 30 January 1756, when the fee of 2*s* 6*d* was 'Rec[eived] for a Marriage Certificate'. Although there is no entry for the issuing of a burial certificate in Duel Taylor's accounts, such certificates were issued by the Abbey. Given that it became a place of interment for those not from Bath, their families sometimes needed proof of their loved one's burial there (as can be seen by a copy of a burial certificate recording that 'Mr. William Ingram was Buried at the Abbey Church at Bath April 29 1737').[82]

Year	**Total Income of the Rectory**	**Income from Abbey Burial Fees**	**Income from Abbey Monuments**
1756	£291 13*s* 3*d*	£11 11*s* 8*d*	£10
1757	£276 1*s* 7½*d*	£12 5*s* 10*d*	
1758	£290 8*s* 9½*d*	£10 1*s* 8*d*	£6
1759	£316 18*s* 9*d*	£14 2*s* 4*d*	£4

1760	£301 3*s* 0*d*	£11 15*s* 8*d*	
1761	£303 8*s* 5*d*	£10 7*s* 8*d*	£4
1762	£329 18*s* 8*d*	£13 10*s* 0*d*	£4
1763	£334 0*s* 9*d*	£24 2*s* 4*d*	£6

With the fees for erecting monuments included, the income from burials and monuments at the Abbey represent between 4 and 7 per cent of the total annual income of the rectory. The fee for erecting a monument in the Abbey was fixed at £2 in the period. This is considerably more than the 10*s* that was charged for erecting monuments at St Michael's Without and a reflection of the type of people who were buried and commemorated in the Abbey. In 1756, monuments were erected to a captain, a colonel and a knight.

The amount of time between a burial and the payment of a fee for a monument was generally a matter of months, as can be seen from the following table. All but two of the monuments for which payments were received by Duel Taylor are named in his accounts. In this period, for the smaller monuments the payments may relate to the date the monument was erected. However, it should be remembered that monuments that now appear small and uncomplicated had much of their finer, decorative work removed in the nineteenth century. For example, the monument to Erasmus Philipps, who was drowned when 'some pigs frightened his horse, which ran back and threw him into the river'[83] on his return to Bath, was originally framed by Sienna marble and included his coat of arms at the top, both since removed, but recorded by John Buckler in 1827.[84] For the larger monuments the date that the payment was received probably indicates the date the family members, executors or sculptor reserved the wall space for a monument, rather than the date when the monument was erected. For instance, it is inconceivable that a large and complicated monument such as that to Miss Sarah Currer could be commissioned, executed by Benjamin Carter (brother of the late Thomas Carter, of Hyde Park Corner, London), packed, transported, and erected in the Abbey in two and a half months. As we will see below, monuments commissioned by London sculptors often took years from commissioning to installation.

Name	Date of Burial	Date Fee for Monument Received
Mrs Rebecca Leyborne	22 February 1756	14 April 1756
Captain John Bowdler	23 April 1754	20 April 1756
Miss Elizabeth Winkley	15 February 1756	29 April 1756
Colonel Madan	12 March 1756	28 May 1756
Sir Erasmus Philipps	22 October 1743	25 September 1756
Dr Aubery	13 November 1757	2 February 1758
Mr Richard Crowle, Esq.	24 June 1757	16 March 1758
Mrs Elizabeth Grieve	24 March 1758	9 May 1758
Miss [Sarah] Currer	2 March 1759	14 May 1759
Mrs Margaret Cunliffe	23 December 1759	26 December 1759
Dr Leyborne	19 May 1759	22 March 1761
Mrs Hannah Alleyne	13 February 1762	11 June 1762
Mrs Cowper	5 August 1762	31 December 1762
King's Serjeant David Pool	4 November 1762	2 March 1763
Mr Webb	?Mrs Ann Webb 10 March 1759?	17 March 1763

Fees for a monument in St James' were either 10*s* or £2 (the latter probably for those erected in the Choir), but £1 in St James' churchyard. The additional £1 fee for burial early in the morning or late at night at all the churches are similar to the fees articulated in 1726 above, as is the system of halving the fees for those living in the parish. This is neatly demonstrated by comparing the fees received for the burials of Mr Henry Dixon and Abraham Gilbert Esquire at the Abbey in the autumn of 1760. Dixon, who was 'Master of the Charity School', was buried in the 'Choir' of the Abbey on 28 October, for which the rector received 10*s* 'for breaking ye Ground for Mr Dixon' and 4*s* 'for his Funeral'. The rector also received a separate payment of 10*s* 6*d* to administrate Dixon's Will. Gilbert was buried in the 'Chancel' of the Abbey on 13 November, for which the rector received £2 10*s* 'for breaking ye Ground in ye Chancel at ye Abby' (five times Dixon's fee) and 8*s* 'for burying ye same

Corpse' (double Dixon's fee). The families electing to bury and commemorate loved ones at the Abbey were frequently of a class where money was no object and could afford to pay over and above the fees asked. This can be seen in Duel Taylor's accounts on more than one occasion where a guinea (£1 1*s*) was paid 'over & above ye Dues'. The impact that such fees from rich 'strangers' could have on the annual income can be seen from those received for the burial of William Maynard Esquire on 25 November 1763. Taylor's account records the following: '26 Novbr Recd for breaking ye Ground in ye Choir £1 0s 0d Recd for walling a Grave £5 0s 0d Recd for burying early in ye Morning £1 0s 0d Recd for Burial Fees at ye Abbey £0 16s 0d'. The £7 16*s* received for this single burial represents a quarter of the Abbey's income from burials, and 2 per cent of the entire income for the rectory for 1763.

As at Westminster Abbey, fees for permission to erect monuments were supplemented by charges for those wishing to view them. By 1843, Westminster 'was charging an extra 3d' to see 'Poets' Corner and the nave, and an extra shilling for the royal tombs and north transept'.[85] In Bath, the sexton received a fee for showing visitors the monuments and, every seven years, a bizarre and macabre event took place: the opening of Thomas and Margaret Lichfield's Tomb. A report of it was given in *The Bath Chronicle* on 12 November 1778 (which erroneously used the surname Fletcher instead of Lichfield). The previous Wednesday, the report began, 'according to septennial custom, the tomb of Thomas Fletcher, who was Lutenist to Queen Elizabeth, was opened in the Abbey-Church, and the bodies of him and his wife exposed to such as paid 3d. to enter the church'. The report conveys something of the grotesque theatricality of the event, designed to titillate the readership, and the almost forensic scrutiny that the human remains were subjected to during the day. Margaret Lichfield's bones were 'all in their proper places, and she appeared a complete skeleton'. Whereas Thomas's body was 'inclosed in a paste, not unlike that composition which surrounds the Egyptian mummies, and his bones would be quite invisible, had not a little bit of the upper crust been broken in'. The report concluded with the fact that there was 'no inscription on the monument', suggesting that the words recorded by Henry Chapman a century earlier had, by then, been effaced.[86]

The thoughts of the then rector, John Chapman, on the custom may never be known, but the fact that it was allowed to take place suggests he respected the 'directions in [Thomas Lichfield's] will to be thus exposed at certain stated times'.[87] Chapman had narrowly missed out on becoming rector in 1752, when the Corporation voted Duel Taylor to the post (with sixteen votes) over Chapman (who had fourteen votes).[88] However, when Taylor died 'at three o'clock'[89] on 11 May 1767, Chapman became first 'the new Reader'[90] at the Abbey, then after the death of Duel Taylor's successor, John, 'wch happened on ye 22d of August 1768'[91] (probably from 'an abscess in his side' which was 'complicated with other Disorders'),[92] Chapman became Rector on the '7th Day of Sept:r 1768'.[93]

One of the first things Chapman did was to begin a set of accounts detailing the 'Proffitts arising from the Rectory of Bath'.[94] Like Taylor's accounts, Chapman's demonstrate the importance of burials and monuments to its finances in the period covered by them (1768–83). They also show their relative importance to other sources of income such as marriages and churchings, and allow comparison with fees for burials and monuments at other churches within the rectory. Whilst Chapman was rector, the profit from a burial in the Nave of the Abbey ranged from 1*s* to 12*s*, with 4*s* and 8*s* being the most common sums. Burials resulting in a profit of 4*s* were just over twice as frequent than those of 8*s* (297 entries for 4*s* compared with 135 for 8*s*). All but one of the thirteen entries for 1*s* are marked 'poor', or, as on 20 January 1775, 'For a burying at ye Abbey from ye Poor House'.[95] At the other end of the social spectrum, profits from burials in the Chancel or Choir ranged from 16*s* to £3 6*s*, with six of the nine entries at £1 12*s*.[96] These profits are comparable with those recorded in the accounts from other churches in Bath: there are six payments of 4*s* each in 1780 for burials at Widcombe, and a payment of 4*s* in 1775 and one of 8*s* in 1782 for burials at St James' (although it should be remembered that in 1768, the same year that the accounts begin, building work also began at St James'). The fee for breaking ground in the Chancel of the Abbey, St James' and St Michael's Without was the same at £2 10*s*, as was the fee for burials before nine o'clock in the morning at £1 8*s*.[97]

The table below shows the range of payments for the erection of a monument inside the different churches between 1768 and 1783. The most common payments are given in **bold** and those for monuments in the Choir given in *italics*.

Type	Bath Abbey	St James'	St Michael's Without
'Flat stone'	10*s* 6*d* – **£1 1*s***	10*s* 6d – **£1 1*s*** *(£3)*	10*s* 6*d*
Monument	£2 2*s* – **£3** *(£4 – £6)*	**£1 1*s*** – £3	10*s* 6*d*

Regarding 'flat stones' (ledgerstones), the accounts show twice as many payments for those at St James' (sixteen) than for those at the Abbey (seven) and St Michael's Without (one).[98] Two entries have been omitted and do not appear in either the Abbey, St James' or St Michael's Without burial registers. At St Michael's Without, flat stones in the churchyard were more common than in the church, as were 'head and foot stones', and half as expensive at 5*s* 3*d*. The cost of a child's stone was slightly reduced at St Michael's Without to 5*s*. Stones in the churchyard of St Michael's Without were by far the most common option for that parish than the Abbey or St James', perhaps in part because the church had 'only a Timber Floor to separate the Living from the Dead!'[99] In contrast, the flat stones laid at the Abbey and St James' appear to have been inside the respective churches, with only one 'head and foot stone' (at 10*s* 6*d*) paid for at St James' in the period. The £2 2*s* paid in 1783 'for a raised tomb in St James churchyard' shows that higher fees were charged for more elaborate monuments there. The single payment of £3 'for a Flat Stone at St James' is surely for a ledgerstone in the Chancel, since the majority (ten) of the payments for flat stones at St James' are for £1 1*s*.

In terms of the monuments erected on the pillars and walls of the churches, the payments for monuments at the Abbey are by far the most numerous. The accounts record twenty-six payments for monuments at the Abbey between 1768 and 1783, compared with four at St James' and one at St Michael's Without. Twenty-one of the twenty-six monuments at the Abbey resulted in a payment of £3 to Chapman, whereas only one of the four payments for monuments at St James' cost £3 (the other three cost £1 1*s*). This shows that permission for erecting monuments in the Nave of the Abbey cost three times that of monuments in the Nave of St James'. Permission for the erection of monuments in the Choir of the Abbey cost £4 or £6. Of course, this was only a fraction of the cost of the monuments themselves. For example, in Chapman's own Will, he asked for a 'small Monument' – with an inscription written by himself in the Will – to be 'affixed' to 'the Wall' behind his pew in the Chancel of the church of Newton St Loe, near Bath, where he asked to be buried. The cost of this was not to exceed 'the Sum of twenty pounds'.[100]

Chapman records the names of twenty-three of the individuals for whom he received payment for a monument. Comparing these payments with the dates of burial allows us to better understand the time between burial and commemoration in the Abbey, and compare the production times of monuments by local sculptors with those executed by London sculptors.

Monuments to individuals named in John Chapman's accounts 1768–83		
Name and Title	**Burial Date**[101]	**Date fee received**
John Roebuck, Esq.	6 February 1767	19 December 1768
Lady Mary Bedingfield	23 September 1767	31 March 1769
James Quin, Esq.	25 January 1766	14 April 1769
Sarah Fielding[102]	14 April 1768	5 January 1770
Dr John Marten Butt	22 October 1769	25 June 1770
Mr [William] Clement, [Esq.][103]	6 June 1770	21 December 1770
Jacob Bosanquet, Esq.	15 June 1767	23 July 1771
John Lamb, Esq.	5 January 1772	28 February 1772
The Hon. Mrs Elizabeth Webb	9 July 1772	28 July 1773
Admiral Robert Hughes	18 January 1774	2 September 1774
Sir Marmaduke [Asty] Wyvil	2 March 1774	5 August 1774
James Pedder, Esq.	26 November 1775	9 February 1776
Dr [Erasmus] Saunders, D.D.[104]	3 January 1776	24 April 1776
Sir William Baker[105]	4 February 1770	28 August 1776
Mr [Robert] Sutton, [Esq.]	9 April 1775	24 January 1776
Mr John Wall, M.D.	29 June 1776	6 February 1777
Rev. Mr Luke Robinson	7 February 1776	2 September 1777
Mr [Edward] Ward, [Esq.][106]	22 October 1776	4 April 1778
Mr [George] Gordon, [Esq.][107]	15 January 1779	20 September 1779
Governor [Roger Hope Elletson Esq.][108]	7 December 1775	23 August 1779
Mr [Roger] Gee, [Esq.][109]	12 September 1778	11 May 1781
Mrs Scriven	9 December 1782	28 March 1783
Mrs Ann Flood	7 June 1774	31 March 1783

Between 1767 and 1769 there appears to be at least an eighteen-month period between burial and the erection of a monument. From the end of 1769, the time between burial and commemoration shortens considerably. The exceptions to this are the larger monuments, such as those to Bosanquet or Baker, created by London sculptors. However, it should be noted that larger monuments by local sculptors in the 1760s also required similar production times. For example, the monument Leonard Coward commissioned for his parents is dated 'A:D: 1764', years after the deaths of Leonard (d. 1761) and Elizabeth (d. 1759). Sadly, the nineteenth-century alterations to the monuments mean that many of these are now unsigned and their designs unrecognisably different from their sculptor's original intention. Nonetheless, many share features that suggest they were produced by the same sculptor. Most obviously, the monuments to Roebuck, Sutton and Ward all have a similar and distinctive border of Sienna marble (which also comprises the entire backing slab of the monument to George Gordon). The letter carving of these four monuments is also identical. The inscriptions on the monuments to Luke and Anne Flood, James Pedder and John Wall are certainly in the same unaccomplished style (and it is arguable that the letter carving on those to Webb, Lamb, Butt and Bedingfield also share certain of these features). The similarity of the brief epitaphs to Gordon ('an Honest Man'), the Floods ('An honest Man. / A good Woman.') and Lamb ('He was a loving Husband / And a true and Sincere Friend') is another obvious link between them. These epitaphs were all commissioned by family members (that to the Floods' 'the grateful Tribute of a Daughters [sic] Affection') with the same being true of that to Pedder ('the best of Husbands & tenderest of Fathers') and Sutton:

> Reflect, O Reader on the Distress of
> Conjugal Affection,
> and pity the fond endeavour
> which in seeking to alleviate
> perpetuates its Sorrows,
> by inscribing this Marble
> To the Memory of
> ROBERT SUTTON Esq:r

Although the letter carving of the monument to Sarah Scriven (d. 1782) is much more refined than that to Robert Sutton (d. 1775), its border of Siena marble and dedication to 'the Best of *MOTHERS*' puts it with this group and illustrates the shared aesthetics and turns of phrase used by Bath's sculptors in the 1770s and 1780s.

Of the monuments to named individuals listed in Chapman's book above, only those to Quin and Butt are signed by Thomas King, Bath's leading 'statuary'. These monuments are much more refined and the letter carving much more assured than the others discussed above (although the similarities between the lettering on the monuments to Quin and Saunders should not be overlooked). King was the best-regarded and most prolific sculptor in Bath in the late eighteenth century, producing work that can also be found in the south-west of England and in the West Indies. Kim Jordan has identified eighty-eight monuments signed by Thomas King (and sons) in Bath's churches, twenty-four of which were in the Abbey. The King studio's output dates between 1760 and 1838, a figure only surpassed by W. Reeves, Son, and Grandson's 122 signed monuments between 1791 and 1862, seventeen of which are in the Abbey. The nineteenth-century treatments of the Abbey's monuments and their name-plates mean that attribution of specific monuments in the Abbey to sculptors needs to be done with care (especially if the signature is not integral to the work). However, Jordan's survey shows that King was the sculptor of choice for monuments in the Abbey in the late eighteenth and early nineteenth centuries.[110] It should also be noted that the reuse of certain monuments' backing stones as paving in the Abbey floor in the nineteenth century also shows monuments now currently unsigned might also be attributed to King. For example, a fragment near the door to the Abbey shop contains the inscription '[KIN]G Invt. et Sculp.' (King invented and sculpted the design), a signature seen on other pieces of marble found by archaeologists during the Footprint works of 2018–21 (discussed in Chapter 4).

Known as a 'Gentleman of Walcot', Thomas King also acted as an intermediary between the Abbey and families commissioning monuments from outside the city, as can be seen by correspondence between King and the Willes family in 1787, which reveals another way in which the Abbey made money from the monuments already erected in its walls in this period and beyond. After the death of the Reverend Dr Edmund Aubery, Archdeacon of Wells, on 7 November 1757, a 'Square Marble Monument' was erected to him in the Abbey.[111]

When his widow, Ann, died on 27 December 1786, her brother, Francis Willes, 'apply'd for leave to take the old one down for the purpose of erecting the new one' that would also commemorate his sister. To that end, Willes engaged Thomas King. On 24 June 1787, King wrote to Willes informing him that 'The Monument to be put up to the Memory of the Dr. Aubery & Will[es] in the Abey Church Bath is finished'. But, he went on:

> Dr. Phillott [the rector] and Churchwardens expect the customary Fees for erecting the same although it stands on the same ground the old one did. I thought it my Duty to [tell you] of it fearing you might misunderstand the Corr[espondence] received from Dr. Phillott.

These 'customary Fees' were, King informed Willes, 'to the Rector is £4.4.0 the Parish £4.4.0 the Sexton 10[s] 6[d] making in all Eight Guineas and a half which [you] pay on your signifying your approbation'.[112] Should he do so, 'The Mont. To the Memory of the late Dr Revd Aubery [will be] put up in the Chancel at West[erly] aisel [aisle]' and would look 'very well'.

Understandably, such fees and such an approach by the Abbey were hard to swallow for the recently bereaved. After all, the family had already paid 8*s* for Dr Aubery's burial in the Abbey in 1757, and on 2 February 1758 the Rector, Duel Taylor, had 'Recd for Dr Aubery's Monument £2 0s 0d'. The fees outlined by King in 1787 were quadruple what had been paid thirty years earlier. On 3 July, Willes replied to King, saying that: 'Mr Aubery and myself are of opinion that as the Fees have been formerly paid for the Ground occupyed by Dr. Aubery's Monument some Abatement ought to be made of the new Fees demanded & a Moity seems reasonable.' However, King was to be the one to negotiate on the family's behalf: 'We must leave this matter to be settled by you as well as you can as We don't wish to do any thing unhandsome that might give offence'. When the monument was finally 'put up' he asked King to write to him in Mayfair 'with an accot. of all the Charges attending both Monuments & you shall not be long without your Money'.[113] Whether the 'customary Fee', the 'Moity', or another fee negotiated by King was eventually paid is unknown. The correspondence gives an extremely interesting insight into the role of Bath's sculptors in relation to the Abbey in the late eighteenth century and the inflexible way in which fees for these monuments were commanded by the Abbey, with no exceptions made even for a former archdeacon of the diocese in this period. This is in stark contrast to the waiving of all fees for Archdeacon Thomas's burial and monument by Gahagan in the early nineteenth century (discussed in the following chapter). King's expression of the 'customary Fees' in 1787 suggests that the normal income of £3 for a monument in the Abbey between 1768 and 1783, recorded in John Chapman's account book, may have been only half of the total fee asked for by the Abbey for the permission to erect a monument. That is, a corresponding £3 for the church for each monument may have been recorded in the Churchwardens' Accounts, which are now lost.

John Chapman's accounts show the significant contribution that the fees for burial services and the erection of monuments in the churches of the rectory made to the living. The table below shows that the income from 'Fees recd for Buryings – Mortuaries – Monuments within the Rectory of Bath' was the second-best source of regular income behind the fees for marriages.

Table showing the income of the Rector of Bath by income stream, 1770–83					
Year	**Burials, Mortuaries, Monuments**	**Marriages**	**Churchings**	**Funeral Silks**	**Silks Cut Off**
1770	£57 3*s* 10*d*	£101 12*s* 6*d*	£22 3*s* 3*d*	£22 7*s* 0*d*	N/A
1771	£52 3*s* 4*d*	£76 18*s* 6*d*	£22 13*s* 3*d*	£28 4*s* 0*d*	£20 2*s* 0*d*
1772	£54 2*s* 8*d*	£64 18*s* 6*d*	£20 7*s* 0*d*	£25 1*s* 9*d*	£11 11*s* 0*d*
1773	£34 6*s* 0*d*	£109 16*s* 0*d*	£22 9*s* 9*d*	£51 16*s* 3*d*	N/A
1774	£48 3*s* 6*d*	£113 3*s* 9*d*	£17 14*s* 6*d*	£17 19*s* 6*d*	£15 2*s* 8*d*
1775	£72 1*s* 0*d*	£91 19*s* 9*d*	£18 3*s* 3*d*	£41 18*s* 0*d*	£23 17*s* 6*d*
1776	£54 18*s* 3*d*	£95 18*s* 9*d*	£18 8*s* 6*d*	£19 3*s* 0*d*	£12 1*s* 0*d*
1777	£51 10*s* 0*d*	£85 12*s* 6*d*	£15 17*s* 6*d*	£17 2*s* 6*d*	£16 1*s* 6*d*
1778	£47 13*s* 0*d*	£99 7*s* 0*d*	£16 17*s* 6*d*	£29 11*s* 6*d*	£7 17*s* 6*d*[114]
1779	£48 13*s* 9*d*	£74 9*s* 0*d*	£16 8*s* 6*d*	£27 12*s* 0*d*	£7 7*s* 6*d*
1780	£43 2*s* 0*d*	£88 14*s* 6*d*	£16 4*s* 0*d*	£20 2*s* 0*d*	£25 18*s* 0*d*
1781	£56 3*s* 8*d*	£85 0*s* 0*d*	£19 2*s* 6*d*	£0 5*s* 6*d* *£14 11s 6d*	£20 12*s* 0*d*
1782	£49 16*s* 9*d*	£86 3*s* 6*d*	£16 7*s* 0*d*	£10 6*s* 6*d* *£16 11s 0d*[115]	£14 16*s* 6*d*
1783	£50 3*s* 0*d*	£69 18*s* 6*d*	£13 9*s* 6*d*	£2 14*s* 0*d* *£6 16s 6d*	£8 5*s* 0*d*

However, when the income from the sale of garments for the deceased and mourners was added to that for burials, mortuaries and monuments, the income from these items was equivalent to, and occasionally exceeded, that for marriages. Chapman accounted for the income from the 'silks' in two separate categories: the first, 'Funeral silks &caet: left uncut with ye several Undertakers', tended to be larger items such as suits (but also included gloves, hatbands and scarves) commissioned in black or white silk or satin (or, rarely, in linen); the second, 'Funeral Silks &caet cut off & remaining with me', tended to be smaller items such as hatbands or scarves. These were presumably the off-cuts saved from the production of the suits and other items that remained with the rector and could be made into these smaller items, which also supplemented his income.[116] The 'Funeral Silks' were left with the various undertakers, some of whom are named in the accounts. 'Mr Cross', 'Mr Plura' and 'Mrs Pember' are all described as 'undertakers' in Chapman's accounts; others, such as 'Mr Geo:[rge] Chapman' (described as a 'Mercer in the City of Bath' in Chapman's Will, who was also, coincidently, John Chapman's godson) and 'Mr [Leonard] Coward' (descendent of a 'Lace-Merchant'), were dealers in the fabrics who may have offered an undertakers' service.[117] Coward's Will gives a sense of the amount and variety of fabrics required and what would have been considered the best taste in mourning at a high-profile funeral at the Abbey in the late eighteenth century:

> the Rector [of the Abbey] and the Rector of Walcot that there be given them hatbands and scarves of the best Black Sattin and also silk hatbands and Gloves to the Clerk and Sexton and to each of the under bearers half a Crown in money and a pair of Gloves that the mourners have Crape hatbands Gloves and Cloaks [...] And I order that Thomas Coward my namesake Linen Draper of Bond Street to bury me and to find mourning.

Generally, the rector's profits were in cash, although in 1770 and 1774 a proportion of the totals shown in the table for the 'Funeral Silks' are from a combination of cash and goods valued by Chapman. From 1781, the payments in goods (marked in italics) exceed those in cash. These were nonetheless beneficial to Chapman, as can be seen from a note in the accounts on 8 June 1782: 'Left with Messrs Collins & Prynne A B[lack] Sattin Suit / Mr Eagle – St James's – allowed in Goods wch I gave my Maids £2 12s 6d.'

Two loose notes, one inserted into the book between the 'Dues – Easter Offerings & Tithes of Widcombe within the Rectory of Bath 1774' and the page for 'Funeral Silks &c.' for the same year related to churchings in 1776, the other at the beginning of the 1780 accounts related to churchings in 1779, indicate that where the rector received a payment for a churching, the clerk received a payment of half the value of the rector's payment. The same arrangement was probably also the case for the payments for burials, as was the case in the nineteenth century. In 1765, John Wood wrote that 'The Rectory of Bath is not above 200 l. a Year in Value'. Chapman's accounts show this was an underestimation, when sums for Easter offerings were included. Wood thought that the Corporation of Bath should 'think of some Expedient to augment the Income of the Rector' so that he need not make 'Collections among the Strangers, and Subscriptions among the Inhabitants'. It was fanciful of Wood to imagine that the Abbey could do without 'Strangers'. After all, since the seventeenth century, the income of the Abbey, at various times and to varying degrees, had relied on the greater revenues that wealthier 'Strangers' could afford, either as benefactors to the fabric or as payees of higher fees. However, in lieu of any augmentations to his income from the Corporation, the way John Chapman appears to have worked with the city's drapers, lace and linen merchants to the benefit of the rectory was a continuation of a model established in the late sixteenth century, and a shrewd way of further diversifying the Abbey's income from burial services begun with the hire of palls enabled by Benjamin Baber (described in Chapter 1). In turn, his successor as rector, the well-liked Dr Phillott, appears to have raised and insisted upon the customary fees for the benefit of himself and the church.

Identity and Empire: The costs of burial and monuments in the Abbey in the eighteenth century

In 1786, Thomas King took out an advert in *The Bath Chronicle* to inform his friends and the public that he had 'fitted up in his Warehouse, sundry elegant *Marble Chimney-Pieces* for sale, from 6l. to 60l. each, which may be packed up at a day's notice. He has likewise several neat monuments for inspection, from 8 to 50 guineas each'.[118] King's price range for a 'neat' monument (a euphemism for a small and generic monument) is comparable with those of his in-laws, the Paty family of Bristol. On 6 May 1779, King married Elizabeth Paty, the daughter of Thomas Paty. A note written by Thomas Paty, or possibly his brother James, under a monument drawn in *The Paty Copybook* (a collection of 125 drawings for funerary monuments dating to the eighteenth and nineteenth century made by the Paty family) reveals that 'A monument of this design', approximately 4ft high and 2½ft wide, largely undecorated, on what appears to be a Sienna marble background (probably a veneer onto Bath stone) 'may be executed from £10:10:0 – 12 or 14 according to the size'. The 'Letters of the Inscription' were charged separately '@ 1¼ each'.[119]

These figures suggest that the sum of £20 (that allowed for by Reverend John Chapman for his monument) would have been about the minimum required for the creation and permission to erect a small monument in the Abbey in the late eighteenth century. Thomas King, Bath's leading late eighteenth-century statuary, also asked that 'a monument to the value of twenty Guineas [£21] be erected'[120] to his memory in his Will. He is not buried in the Abbey but created many monuments that were admired there for such a sum. The example of the monument to Richard Nash (d. 1761) – better known as 'Beau Nash', Bath's Master of Ceremonies and 'Arbiter Elegantiae', who 'shaped the emerging culture of Bath fashionable society'[121] – provides further evidence for the £20 minimum for a monument in the Abbey (Colour Plate T). Nash's monument is almost unique in the Abbey in that it was originally erected thirty years after his death.[122] Dr Henry Harington is credited with having 'originated the idea' for Nash's monument and his initials 'HH' beneath the 'beautiful classic epitaph' show it was written by him.[123] In December 1789, an advertisement was placed in *The Bath Chronicle* publishing the intention 'to erect a TABLET in the ABBEY CHURCH' to 'rescue from oblivion the name of RICHARD NASH, Esq'. Generous subscribers were invited to contribute, to whom the eventual drawings of the monument would be submitted. Since 'the skill of the Artist' was 'not to be displayed, nor any unmerited praise' conferred, the advert assured its readers that 'a FEW POUNDS may suffice for the execution of the design'. Fittingly for Nash, subscriptions could be 'received at the Pump-Rooms, Libraries, and Coffee-Houses'.[124] In April 1791, the same gentleman who made the advertisement above (possibly Harington) published another, thanking 'the Rev. Dr. Phillott [Rector of the Abbey 1786–1815], and the Churchwardens of St. Peter and Paul, for kindly remitting the usual fees', the sculptor 'Mr. John Ford, for his very moderate charge for the work', and the subscribers. Ford's modest fee for carving the monument was £15 15*s* and, with the cost of the 'Advertisements and other expences £3 3s', the total cost £18 18*s*. By which time the fifteen subscribers (including Harington) had given £13 13*s*.[125] Taking the fees articulated for the re-erection of Aubery's monument in 1787 above as a guide illustrates just how great and kind a contribution was made by Phillott's remittance of them, and that, had they been included, the total cost of the erection of Nash's monument would have been more than £20. It is not clear how the remaining £5 5*s* was found, but the advertisement and the discussion of church fees suggests the monument was to be erected imminently. The figures suggest that Harington's scheme for funding Nash's monument had not been entirely successful. However, as we will see in the following chapter, the popularity of raising monuments in the Abbey by public subscription would increase in the early nineteenth century.

Local sculptors like King and Ford helped to create a new identity for the Abbey interior through their work. Earlier in the century, the Harvey family had done the same, especially the third John Harvey (1692–1742), whose own ledgerstone commemorating him as 'The Very Ingenious MR. HARVEY' can be found, with others to his family, in the South Aisle. The Harveys were intimately connected to the Abbey. John Harvey III was the 'son of John Harvie' (d. 1729) and was baptised in the Abbey on 20 January 1692. His grandfather, described on his ledgerstone as a 'carver', was also called John (d. 1673). The young John Harvey III grew up in Westgate Street, a stone's throw from the Abbey. The family's close relationship with the Abbey can be seen in the fact that John's father was elected as one of two Sidesmen for 1703. His father was also an occasional member of the vestry (the decision-making body of the Abbey). He was one of the signatories in 1707–08 at meetings in which the vestry agreed to masonry and joinery work. No doubt the vestry valued Harvey's practical expertise when planning work and assessing the proposals of another Bath mason, Thomas Greenway. Harvey's presence at the vestry in 1713 speaks of a continued devotion to the Abbey as the centre point of his community and his place of worship. It was also the place where many family members were buried and memorialised. John Harvey III's sisters all died when he was also young: Sarah (d. 19 February 1691/2, aged 8), Ann (d. 1 December 1696, aged 8) and Jane (d. 10 June 1700, aged 4). He would have watched the way his father lovingly designed and carved ledgerstones to their memories in the Abbey. Although eroded for over three centuries, the ledgerstone to Sarah and Ann, with its cartouche, cherubs, fruit and blossom (symbols of resurrection), remains one of the most beautiful in the Abbey floor (Colour Plate U).

These experiences would shape the young John and obviously instilled in him a passion to become a monumental mason like his father and grandfather before him. He was apprenticed to his father as a 'carver' for seven years on 26 November 1709. In this capacity he would have helped work on the monument to Mary, wife of William Blathwayt, and her parents, John and Frances Wynter, commissioned by William Blathwayt for Dyrham Church. The agreement between William Blathwayt and Harvey dated 1 November 1710 details the cost and timescale for such a large monument in different-coloured marbles by the Bath sculptor. Harvey (and his 'assigns', which would have included his son) was 'in good and workmanlike manner and according to the best of his Art and skill' to 'Carve erect set up and finish' a monument to an agreed drawing or model in Dyrham Church 'within five Months'. He was to 'compose the same with such Marble and Stone as the s:d William Blathwayt or his Assignes shall find & provide'. Blathwayt would also at his own expense, 'find & provide all the Stone Marble and Sand necessary for making and building the s.d Monument'. Whereas Harvey would 'find & provide all matterials workmanship Clamps Mortar [and] plaister of pallas [sic]'. Harvey would then 'Erect & build all the sd. Monument as above mentioned Except the Table thereof, with the Marble which Mr Blathwayt now has at Dirham'. The cost of the work was agreed at £90 in total (approximately £9,500 in today's money), with £10 'to be paid at the beginning of the work', £15 'at Xmas next [Christmas 1710]', £15 more in March 1711, and the final £50 when the work was 'fulfilled to Mr Blathwayt's satisfaction'.

A note on the back of the agreement dated 27 July 1711 suggests that the monument may have taken longer than the five months to complete and cost more than the £90 originally agreed. It records the receipt of £7 by Harvey, 'which with nine poundes to be payd to Will: Harford of Marshfilde' was 'In full for the worck of the Monument'. A further memorandum below it records that 'at the same time' Blathwayt gave Harvey 'one Guinea more for the Black marble' that he had obviously sourced himself. Marble was an expensive, imported commodity, one for which Harvey would have needed full recompense. Such was its value to sculptors that, in 1720, Harvey III's payment for the monument to Sir Bevil Grenville for Lord Lansdown was paid 'in three Blocks, or more, of fine Marble, which his Lordship procured for him from abroad'. The costs for Blathwayt's monument give us a guide to those Harvey III may have charged for the monument to Dorothy Hobart *c.*1722 (described above).

By the 1720s, Harvey III was in demand for jobs large and small, including decorating existing ledgerstones. In 1719, the West Country physician Claver Morris rode from Wells to Bath to see Mr Harvey (John Harvey III's father). During their 'discourse', Morris 'agreed to give for his [Harvey II's] Son's Cutting a Coat of Arms in my Brother Farewells Tomb-Stone 40s'. In addition, Morris was to 'send an Horse for him to Wells, and to supply him with Diet and Lodging; If he did it within a month from this time'.[126] Harvey's reputation as 'Very Ingenious' – an epithet begun by the physician John Wynter in his *Of Bathing in the Hot-Baths at Bathe* (1728) to describe the quality of Harvey's draughtsmanship, specifically the 'Face and the Profile' of the then recently excavated head of Sulis Minerva – was maligned by John Wood and Richard Warner in the late eighteenth and early nineteenth centuries, but later recovered by writers such as Rowland Mainwaring. The family's body of work on the ledgerstones in the Abbey demonstrates the quality of carving of local sculptors and how interlinked the Abbey's worshipping community, commissioners and creators of monuments were in the early eighteenth century. Doubtless many other monuments now unattributable or lost were carved by the family in the late seventeenth and early eighteenth centuries.

At about £20 and above, when the Abbey's fees were added, even the most modest monument erected in the church cost the equivalent of about four months' wages of a skilled tradesman in the late eighteenth century. Consequently, monuments (and, to an extent, burial) in the Abbey, as elsewhere, were, with few exceptions, the preserve of the upper-middle classes and above. This was especially true of burial and commemoration in the Chancel or Choir. The example of John Bacon (or 'John Beken, Esq.', as he was described in the burial register on 1 July 1752) might be given here. Bacon was buried in the 'Chancel' of Bath Abbey and had desired 'to be buried in Westminster Abbey if I dye in or near London' and if he died 'in or near Bath at the Cathedral Church there at the discretion of my Executors'. The expense of the funeral at either Abbey was not to 'exceed the sum of fifty pounds / the Expences at Westminster Abbey the Embalming of my Body and my Coffin being considered as no part thereof'. Bacon's Will reveals that, for eighteenth-century individuals, burial at Bath and Westminster Abbeys were held in equivalent regard and the sums allowed for burial at each not dissimilar. Wills of others, like Bacon, who travelled to Bath and London, either for the season, health or business, also express the desire to be buried in Bath Abbey should they die in the city. However, Bath would come to be regarded as the poor relation of Westminster in these respects in the nineteenth century.

The allowance for Bacon's funeral was almost as much as that set aside by the Corporation of Bath to 'defray' the expense of Beau Nash's funeral on 17 February 1761 'at a Sum not exceeding Fifty Guineas'. However, the character of Nash's 'state'-style funeral at the Abbey was exceptional (if fitting for his larger-than-life persona as Bath's most famous Master of Ceremonies). The account of John Bacon's funeral printed in the *Bath Journal* on 6 July 1752 (and later relayed by James Tunstall) makes it sound like a slightly showy affair, with Bacon desirous 'that he should be buried in his best wig, a ruffled shirt with sleeve buttons, a ring on his finger, velvet breeches, a new pair of pumps, with buckles, and white stockings, and that he should be carried by his servants in full dress liveries'.[127] However, that is not the spirit that Bacon seems to have wished for in his Will, in which he stated that 'no Rings Scarfs or hatbands be given to any person whatsoever nor any thing offered by way of Entertainment at my funeral except Bread or Biscuit and Wine for Refreshment'. Of course, such funerals were inevitably public affairs, unless they took place at night or early in the morning. This brought a certain amount of spectacle, pomp and public mourning. But, as Reverend John Penrose's description of a funeral procession to the Abbey held on 9 May 1766 shows, this was counterbalanced with a solemnity and respectfulness that Penrose had not seen in his hometown of Penryn, Cornwall, and which seems to have been representative of other such processions he must have witnessed during his years in Bath:

> The first Thing to be mentioned is an Occurrence yesterday, which was too late to be inserted in yesterday's Letter, and That is, we saw a Funeral Procession pass before our Window, a Hearse preceded by men carrying Streamers, and followed by two mourning Coaches. Fanny had never seen a mourning Coach before, That is one remarkable Thing; another is, that no Mob attended the Procession, no not so much as one rude Boy, whereas such a Scene at Penryn would have alarmed the whole Town; and whereas at Penryn on such an Occasion, it would have been known e're this to every Body, who was buried, what his family, what his Faults, etc. a third thing remarkable, is, that we cannot learn by much Inquiry, who was buried, tho' buried in the Abbey.[128]

The procession described was for Miss Ann Parker Wynter, daughter of the late Dr Wynter of Bath (mentioned above). Given that Penrose preached and led prayers at the Abbey during his time in Bath, the fact that he could not find out the deceased's name perhaps suggests a great degree of tight-lipped respectfulness for her. The sense of decency that Bacon wished to surround his funeral at the Abbey also comes through in his gift of 'one hundred pounds to be distributed amongst the poor housekeepers of the parish where I dye without any regard to their happening to differ in Religion'.[129] Gifts to the poor are common in Wills. However, the size and terms of Bacon's gift illustrate how funerals of the wealthy could benefit the parish, even if many of the parishioners themselves could not afford the kind of burial afforded by such 'strangers'.

Burial and commemoration at the Abbey were nonetheless desirable by working-class people. For one, Thomas Trahern, who 'was interred in the Abbey Church' on the evening of Sunday, 13 June 1773, it seems to have been one of the aspirations of his life. Trahern, 'a shoe-black' of the city, 'by industry and extreme parsimony, had scraped together near 300l.', the principal part of which he bequeathed to his brother. This alone might have been worthy of report in the newspaper, but *The Bath Chronicle* thought it important to inform its readers that though Trahern 'would scarcely allow himself necessaries while alive, he ordered in his will that 15l. should be laid out for his funeral expences, and that the Abbey Church should be the place of his interment'.[130] John Chapman's account book does not record a specific payment from Traherne, nor any payment on 13 June (the closest is a payment of 4*s* 'For a Burying at ye Abbey' on 17 June). No record of either a ledgerstone or monument to Traherne has survived, but as we have seen, the sum of £15 would not have been sufficient for a marble wall tablet anyway.

Whilst Bath's sculptors executed the majority of the monuments in the Abbey (some, like Dorothy Hobart's, complicated and expensive) the 'neat' tablets they generally produced were significantly less costly than the bespoke monuments by renowned London sculptors. For example, on 25 July 1799, Thomas Platt Esq., one of the executors of the Oxford Botanist Dr John Sibthorp (d. 1796), paid John Flaxman £20 to begin the commission of a monument to him in Bath Abbey (Colour Plate V). Three years later, on 24 July 1802, the monument, which cost a further £52 10*s*, was sent to Bath. With the £1 14*s* 10*d* for 'Packing Cases', £1 6*s* for 'Iron & Brass Cramps & Plugs' to fix it to the North Aisle where it was originally installed, and 10*s* for 'Cartage & booking', the total cost of the monument came to £76 0*s* 10*d* (approximately £3,500 today).[131]

Fig.14: 'Study perhaps for the Monument to the Rt. Hon. William Bingham. Bath Abbey' by John Flaxman. © The Trustees of the British Museum.

Fig.15: Monument to William Bingham (d. 1804) by John Flaxman. © Bath Abbey.

Another of Flaxman's monuments in Bath Abbey, this time to the American Senator and founder of the Pennsylvania Bank, William Bingham (d. 1804), was, unsurprisingly given its subject, even costlier. The production time for the monument was similar to Sibthorp's. Bingham died in 1804 and the monument was commissioned on 21 May 1806. Comparison of Flaxman's 'study' for the 'Monument to the Rt. Hon. William Bingham' with the finished monument helps to illustrate that time was needed for agreement on the final design of bespoke monuments.[132] Flaxman's study shows a pair of female angels holding a banner that reads 'GLORY TO GOD' standing either side of a crown of laurel above the inscription tablet (Fig. 14). The final design retains the pair of angels and their flowing robes and top-knot hairstyles. However, the banner and their slightly awkward poses have been dispensed with. Instead, they are holding smaller laurel crowns in each hand and are stood on pedestals either side of the inscription tablet (Fig. 15). The final design is much more elegant, broken only by the awkward, conventional carving of the coat of arms beneath the inscription. Bingham's monument was finally delivered to and installed in Bath Abbey in September 1808. Flaxman received a deposit of £87 10*s* for the commission, and his itemised expenses for the commission are insightful not only of the costings of monuments from London studios, but also the way in which such commissions eventually found their way onto the walls of the Abbey in Bath:[133]

Bill for William Bingham's Monument from an Account Book of John Flaxman

Item	**£**	***s***	***d***
Church Fee paid	17	8	6
Mr Binghams Monu.	262	10	0
Cases	9	12	6
Carriage	6	16	0
Mason travelling & living	5	19	0
8 days' work	2	4	0
Bath Mason	5	5	8
Cramps	2	2	0

[Subtotal]	294	9	2
[Minus Deposit]	87	10	0
[Total Paid]	206	19	2

Like Thomas King, Flaxman appears to have liaised with the Abbey to arrange the payment of the 'Church Fee' for the erection of the monument on behalf of his client. It was erected in the 'South Aisle' and is currently located beneath the first window from the west in the Nave. The fee of £17 8*s* 6*d* was a significant increase on the £3 generally paid for a monument in the Nave in John Chapman's day, and is another piece of evidence to suggest Chapman's successor, Dr James Phillott, reviewed and increased the burial fees. In the nineteenth century, a formal charge for monuments that exceeded twelve square feet was brought in (called an 'overmeasure'). This will be discussed at greater length in the following chapter. But it is worth noting here that the size of the 'Church Fee' for Bingham's monument suggests that the overmeasure charge had been brought in by Phillott before 1808. The use of a Bath mason to help erect the monument over the eight days needed to install it suggests that local firms may have benefited from monuments created by London sculptors, even if they were not the creators of the works themselves. In total, the cost of Bingham's monument in 1808 is worth approximately £9,500 today. The sum underlines the fact that such monuments were only affordable for the upper classes.

This continued to be the case into the early nineteenth century. Sir Francis Chantrey's monument to Sir Richard Hussey Bickerton (d. 1832) (Fig. 16) illustrates this and the way in which London sculptors continued to work with Bath's masons when it came to the erection of their monuments in the Abbey. In April 1833, Chantrey 'Recd. an order from Lady Bickerton through P:Marriot Esqr. of Bath for a Monument pursuant to an approved design to the memory of Admiral Bickerton'. At the time Alison Yarrington published her edition of Chantrey's ledger, 'P. Marriot' remained 'untraced'.[134] One plausible candidate, not suggested by Yarrington, might be the 'P. Marriott' who was a member of Bath's town council in 1839.[135] If so, it would be further evidence of Bath's elite acting as intermediaries between those commissioning monuments, sculptors, and the Abbey. It also helps to illustrate the hand the city's elite continued to have in creating the aesthetic they desired for the Abbey interior through its monuments. As we have seen, this had happened since the seventeenth century, and had economic as well as aesthetic benefits for the church.

Fig.16: Monument to Sir Richard Hussey Bickerton (d. 1832) by Sir Francis Chantrey. © Bath Abbey.

Harington's monument to Beau Nash can be seen as a continuation of this trend, as can the decision to finally erect Sir William Baker's monument by John Francis Moore as a cenotaph in the Abbey rather than in the parish church of St Swithin's, Walcot, outside Bath's city centre, where Baker was buried (discussed below). Bickerton's monument is dated 1834 and was paid for in 1835, when it was erected in the Abbey in July. The cost of 'executing the Monument' was £500 (equivalent of approximately £34,000 today). The price was 'exclusive of package, conveyance and erection', which totalled a further £27 1*s*. Like Flaxman, Chantrey appears to have sub-contracted part of the cost of the erection of the monument to a Bath mason, as can be seen from the charge (included in the sum of £27 1*s* above) of £5 5*s* 'for Masons wages & Expenses on 27 July 1835' (only 8*d* less than the mason charged Flaxman in 1808). By 1835, it seems Chantrey preferred 'Strong Copper cramps & Plaster £1 10' to the 'Iron & Brass Cramps & Plugs' used by Flaxman to erect the Sibthorps' monument in 1802.[136]

Chantrey's costs for Bickerton's monument are almost identical to those for the monument he executed to the painter William Hoare (d. 1792), commissioned in 1828.[137] Its erection in the Abbey was recorded in *The Bath Chronicle*, emphasising the 'value', 'good taste and benevolence' of the commissioner, Prince Hoare, naming Chantrey as the sculptor, describing the subject of the relief carving ('the Recording Angel placing a Medallion of the deceased on the tomb beneath'), and the writer of the inscription 'Rev. H. J. Rose, author of "Inscriptiones Graecae"' (Colour Plate AH).[138] All which was intended to impress. It was also effectively a notice of a new work in a public gallery of sculpture. The piece is printed in the column between a notice about where various hunts will meet and a review of theatre productions. Such monuments were just as much public artworks as personal memorials, and the placement of the piece underlines that they were often seen as the preserve of the upper-middle classes.

The erection of a monument by a famous, London sculptor in Bath Abbey was a newsworthy event. Such monuments were, without exaggeration, new contemporary artworks, for public consumption as much as private mourning. One of the most anticipated and well-received was the sculptor John Bacon's monument to the literary hostess Lady Ann Miller of Batheaston (d. 1781), which was erected on the north wall of the sanctuary in 1785, four years after her death (Colour Plate S). On 1 September 1785, *The Bath Chronicle* informed its readers, in unusually detailed and poetic manner:

An elegant and beautiful Monument has been lately opened in our Abbey Church to the memory of LADY MILLER, late of Batheaston Villa. It is designed with the greatest possible simplicity: In the middle, a circular pedestal supports a vase of white marble, copied from the *beautiful antique* so well known at Batheaston Villa; grouped with which are two figures, *Liberality* and *Genius*; the first suspending a medallion of Lady Miller, while the latter decorates it with a festoon of laurel. *Liberality* is bending over the portrait, and by her superior attention and the more important part she bears as supporting the profile, the artist has made a distinction between what is a *virtue*, and what only an *ornament*, of human nature. The head of *Genius* is turned upward, yet supported by her hand, the fingers of which are intermingled with the ringlets of her hair; her animated countenance is blended with a pathetic concern, expressive of the spirit which breathes in the inscription beneath. *Liberality* in one hand holds an inverted cornucopia, and by the gracefulness of her attitude and gentleness of her air, adds force to every obligation she confers, while she entirely takes away the burthen of it. The drapery of the figures vary according to their characters; that of *Genius* being light, airy, and spirited – that of *Liberality*, rich, ample, and flowing, its folds being more large and noble than that of its companion. This group is of one entire piece of the finest statuary marble; every other part is of the same material, except the pyramid behind, which forms a back ground for the sculpture, and is of dove marble highly polished.

The article then gave the inscription of the monument (discussed above) before continuing in florid terms: 'The aptness and propriety of allusion, as well in the component members as in the general implication of this monument, will be felt and acknowledged until time shall erase from the memory of many the fairest impressions of Genius and of Mercy.' Concerning the sculptor, the writer concluded that: 'The execution of this monument will take nothing from the fame of one of the first artists of England, perhaps of Europe, *Mr. Bacon*.'[139]

Likewise, on 15 October 1795, *The Bath Chronicle* informed its readers that 'A very superb monument is just erected in the Abbey Church, to the memory of the late Colonel Champion.' The sculpture was by London sculptor Joseph Nollekens, and represented:'*Fame* on a pedestal, with her trumpet inverted, holding a medallion of the deceased. A coat of mail, cannon, battle-axe, & warlike trophies, surround the pedestal.' (Colour Plate W)[140] These kinds of articles were good publicity for a church wanting to attract executors who were considering a place to erect a monument. As we will see, they would also have encouraged curious visitors to see the monuments, for which the sexton would have taken a small fee for showing them around the church.

The monuments to Sibthorp, Bingham, Bickerton, Miller and Champion are representative of those to 'divines, philosophers, statesmen, or heroes' created by London sculptors for the Abbey in the eighteenth century. These, combined with the prolific output of Bath's sculptors, especially Thomas King, meant that the Abbey had 'justly attracted general attention, and a kind of traditional celebrity' for the 'sculptor's art and muse's praise' by the early nineteenth century.[141] To these might be added John Francis Moore's monument to Sir William Baker (d. 1770) (Colour Plate X). Baker was MP for Plympton Erle (1747–68), Director of the East India Company (1741–53) and Deputy Governor and later Governor of the Hudson Bay Company (1750–70). He was 'one of the foremost merchants trading with America' with 'very considerable' interests 'in the Carolinas and New York, extended over the whole length of the seaboard' and, with others, 'held the 'Hobcaw Barony' in South Carolina', 'which he and his partners sold off in pieces to form individual plantations'. Baker was a 'Mortgagee of Maynard's estate on Barbados' between 1759–70 and reportedly 'mortgagee of Baxters, Mount Edge, and The Spring, three estates belonging to the Dottin family, also on Barbados'. On Baker's death in 1770 his executors reportedly 'seized Maynard's estate and sold it'. Baker's Will was 'silent on West India property, mortgages, and enslaved people'. The description of Baker's monument by the Abbey's 1778 guidebook was also predictably silent on enslaved people:

> An elegant large Marble Monument, To the memory of WILLIAM BAKER. On a base is a pedestal of statuary and other marble; on which are two lighted torches, tied with ribband, urns and burning lamps. Over is a large black pyramid, on which is a sarcophagus of statuary and Sienna marble, over which is a basso-relievo, with figures representing Asia, Africa, America, and Europe; to all which places, he carried on an extensive trad. On the plynth of the basso-relievo is wrote ORBIS TERRARUM FELICITAS. Resting on the basso-relievo are two Saxon shields, with the arms of him and his lady.

Elements of Moore's original design, including the pedestal, torches, urns, burning lamps and 'large black pyramid', were all removed in the nineteenth century. However, they can be seen in Moore's original design for the monument. The design in pen and ink and watercolour shows how it was originally intended to look, and a note in the top left indicates that it was intended to be 'Erected in Walcot Church at Bath', where Baker was buried on 4 February 1770 (Colour Plate Y). The inscription, unusually for the period, is in Latin and describes Baker as the father of the country ('patrem patriae') and asks the reader emulate ('aemulari') Baker's qualities. Clearly, in the six years between Baker's death and the erection of his monument in the Abbey at the end of August 1776, it had been decided by Baker's executors and the rector, John Chapman, that the Abbey was a more suitable place for such a monument. A place that would both provide a more splendid setting for the monument itself amongst other examples of noteworthy sculpture, and where it might be seen by a greater number of worshippers, tourists interested in monuments, and sympathetic colonial administrators who might view the monument, mourn, and emulate Baker.

Late eighteenth-century spectators and commentators obviously found the scene Moore carved unproblematic, in a way that we do not today. At the centre of the low relief is a female figure, in classical drapery with a battlemented crown on her head. Aloof, she holds a cornucopia and most likely represents the City of London, where Baker, the son of a draper from Basinghall Street, began his career as a merchant, finally becoming the city's senior alderman. Moore would use the figure of Britannia receiving tribute on his different designs for the monument to Jonas Hanway (d. 1786), founder of the Marine Society. The monument that was eventually erected to Hanway in Westminster Abbey includes a figure kneeling at Britannia's feet, and the monuments to Baker and Hanway share many other similarities. The kneeling boy on Baker's monument holds a beaver that symbolises Baker's trade with Canada and America and roles in the Hudson Bay Company, although Nicholas Penny has suggested that this 'suppliant native boy with an eager beaver' is 'perhaps an emblem of Industry, perhaps an allusion to the fur-trade'. A turbaned man holding a censer (not, as Penny suggests, a 'lamp-bearing oriental') who is leading a camel with panniers no doubt laden with tea and textiles, represents Baker's trade with Asia and his roles in the East India Company. By the 1750s, the East India Company:

> generated nearly £1 million out of Britain's total £8 million import trade. Sales of tea alone cleared half a million sterling, which represented the import of some 3 million pounds of tea leaves. The rest of the EIC's accounts were made up of sales of saltpetre, silk, gorgeously painted palampores (bed covers) and luxurious Indian cotton cloth, around 30 million square yards of which was now imported annually.[142]

Other symbols include the elephant tusk (the ivory trade), the cow and the ram (Baker as cloth merchant), and the horse (Baker as soldier). On the left-hand side, the figure of Trade or Justice (holding her scales) stands next to a boy reading a book and a ship's mast, sails and anchor (these maritime elements are rendered similarly to those on the Hanway monument).

The whole scene is captioned with the words 'ORBIS TERRARUM FELICITAS'. This is a picture of what eighteenth-century Britons considered global happiness. Penny considered that the 'whole does convey the idea of international commercial goodwill'. However, contemporary historians, such as William Dalrymple, have exposed the increasingly 'symbiotic' relationship between the East India Company and the British Parliament throughout the eighteenth century, and how the former (with the support of the latter) 'executed a corporate coup unparalleled in history; the military conquest, subjugation and plunder of vast tracts of southern Asia' in 'the supreme act of corporate violence in world history'.[143] Generally, as Penny has shrewdly observed, 'members of the East India Company chose to be portrayed as kindly administrators concerned to abolish suttee, rather than as men making money out of shawls or tusks or spices'.[144] Baker's monument falls between the two: it portrays an imperial fantasy of Britain at the centre world, adored by the orientalised, subjugated peoples who paid tribute to her, which, the sculpture suggests, was out of nothing more than devotion to her beauty and superiority.

Jacob Bosanquet's monument fits Penny's mould precisely: 'Not more industrious in acquiring a Fortune / Than generous in dispensing it', the inscription reads (Colour Plate N). In the eighteenth century, how that fortune was acquired was less problematic than it is now. But Bosanquet, too, was Director of the East India and Levant Companies in 1759, and by 1742 could claim 'large dealings in Callicoes and Muslins and do yearly sell 2 or 300 bales'. He also 'imported diamonds from Madras and dealt in other Indian specie'. After 1759, Bosanquet 'sold off most of his stock', which must have contributed to the wealth at his death, which in today's money made him a multi-millionaire.[145] A fraction of this wealth would have been spent on his memorial, which must be nonetheless seen as the fruit of some of these profits. Both Bosanquet's and Baker's monuments were carefully designed and conspicuously placed in the Abbey (rather than, say, St Swithin's, Walcot, where Baker was buried, or the 'French Church' in Threadneedle Street, London, where Bosanquet was baptised in 1713 and to which he left £100 in his Will) to be tangible objects created for the instruction and edification of the public. As such, both monuments idealise their subjects and the means through which their 'fortunes' were acquired, setting

Near
this Place is
Buried IOHN
STIBBS late
Alderman Iuſtice of
the Peace, and three
times Mayor of this City.
He married ALICE
Daughter of ANTHONY
HARDING Esqr. by IOANE
his wife, widow of Colonel
Wm. BAMPFYLDE and had
Iſsue IOHN STIBBS and
others who died young.
His 2d. wife was IANE Daughter
of FRANCIS SWANTON of this
City Gent: who dying without Iſsue.
He married ALICE Daughter and
Coheir of EDWARD PARKER of
Walcot Gent; and by her had ſix
Sons and Four Daughters he died
February the 6th; 1708. Aged 71.
In the Vault, with the Remains of his
Parents, is depoſited IOHN STIBBS
Gent; their Eldeſt Son who died
Iuly 27th, 1732. Aged 55.
EDWARD STIBBS Esqr. Cheſter Herald
their 2d. Son, with the greateſt Duty and
affection Erected this Monument.
Captain BARTHo. STIBBS died Auguſt 24th. 1735.
Aged 50.
EDWARD STIBBS Esqr. Cheſter Herald. died
Ianuary the 10th 1739 Aged 58 Years.
JAMES DOTTIN MAYCOCK, ESQUIRE.
BACHELOR OF ARTS, TRINITY COLLEGE, CAMBRIDGE,
ELDEST SON OF THE LATE JAMES DOTTIN MAYCOCK,
ESQUIRE, M.D., F.L.S., DEPARTED THIS LIFE ON THE
22ND APRIL 1858, AGED 42 YEARS. HIS REMAINS ARE
DEPOSITED IN A VAULT IN BATHWICK CHURCHYARD.
THIS TABLET IS INSCRIBED BY HIS MOTHER
TO THE MEMORY OF A MOST AFFECTIONATE
AND BELOVED SON.
"IT IS THE LORD: LET HIM DO WHAT SEEMETH HIM GOOD."

Fig.17: Tablet to the Stibbs family, including Captain Bartholomew Stibbs (d. 1735).
© Bath Abbey.

in stone the idea of colonial trade as a globally enriching enterprise, with simple philanthropic benefits, without any human cost.

★★★

Yet perhaps no monument in Bath Abbey conceals its links with colonialism, and in particular the slave trade, more so than the monument to the Stibbs family (Fig. 17). The family were part of the Abbey's worshipping community. John Stibbs had married his third wife, Alice Parker, in the Abbey on 7 November 1664, their children were baptised there in the 1670s and 1680s, and John regularly attended vestry meetings, three times in the capacity of mayor of the city in 1686, 1699 and 1708.[146] John Stibbs was obviously highly respected and influential in the city, holding many posts with Bath's Corporation from 1669. John was 'perhaps a baker' but perhaps more likely a publican (he had interests in 'The Unicorn' and 'The Rose & Crown' in Westgate Street and 'The Royal Oak' in Broad Street). When John died on 6 February 1708, aged 71, 'A Marble Monument, with a Pyramid Front' was erected 'with the greatest Duty and affection' by his '2d. Son', Edward Stibbs, Esq, in the Abbey's North Choir Aisle, nearby other important members of Bath's ruling class, such as the Chapman family. By 1708, Edward Stibbs had become Chester Herald, so naturally included the family's coat of arms and motto '*Nec Splendide ec Misere*' above the inscription (both arms and motto have since been removed from the monument, possibly when it was moved to the wall of the North Transept in the nineteenth century). Edward Stibbs was described as 'a sensible man and good officer, but not 5 feet tall, squat and bandy-legged; an eternal gossip and knew more private history than any man in the Kingdom which made him an entertaining companion'.

His younger brother, Bartholomew, was baptised in the Abbey on 1 September 1685. He, too, left Bath for London, and by 1715 was living in the Parish of Stepney married to Elizabeth Simes, daughter of 'John Boyce of London, Mariner'. On 25 November 1715, John Boyce's house was burgled by a John Chance, who took '1 Silver Coffee-pot, value 8 l. 12 Silver Spoons, 6 l. and other Goods, the Property of Bartholomew Stibbs'. Chance was caught and sentenced to death. Stibbs, on the other hand, continued to flourish. On 30 December 1718, he became Commander of the *Cornwall Gally*, a ship of about 150 tons 'mounted with Twelve Guns, and Navigated with Twenty-five Men'. Under the terms of his commission, Captain Bartholomew Stibbs was 'To set forth, in warlike Manner' and 'apprehend, seize, and take the ships, Vessels and Goods, belonging to *Spain*, the Vassals and Subjects thereof, or others inhabiting within any of its Countries, Territories, or Dominions'. Another clause required Stibbs 'to keep an exact Journal of his Proceedings; and therein particularly to take Notice of all Prizes which shall be taken by him'.[147] No such journal of his privateering with the *Cornwall Gally* is extant. However, Stibbs was obviously in the habit of doing so, as shown by a journal kept by him between 1723–24 that documents his voyage to the Gambia and his enslavement of people there.[148]

In 1720, the Duke of Chandos 'concluded it would be right to make some noble Attempts for the opening a Trade into the Inland Parts of Africa'. By the beginning of October 1723, Bartholomew Stibbs had 'arrived at the Mouth of the River Gambia with the African Company of England's Ship *Dispatch*'. He had been tasked by the company to proceed as far as possible up the river 'in quest of the Gold Mines' that were said to be near the waterfalls at Barracunda, 500 miles upriver, and to make any 'other Discoveries in this Country'.

In his *Journal of a VOYAGE up the Gambia* (1723–24), Stibbs recorded his journey. It is revealing of both his character and the atrocities that he observed and participated in. Before setting out upriver on 26 December 1723, Stibbs spent three months at Fort James on James Island (Kunta Kinteh Island). In that time, he saw almost 400 enslaved people trafficked to Senegal, Jamaica and Carolina (America), as well as approximately half a tonne of ivory ('Elephants Teeth'). Compared with his companions, Stibbs was a 'passionate Admirer' of the land and its creatures. Whereas Stibbs seemed to feel a sense of awe at seeing 'two or three Hundred Elephants in a Drove come down to the River to drink', his metallurgist, Richard Hull, wrote dispassionately about the 'pursuit of a wounded Elephant, which pass'd the River just above us'. Stibbs's turn of phrase sometimes even approached the poetic – describing the dust 'rais'd' by the elephants as 'like the Smoke of a Glasshouse or Brewhouse Fire', or 'the great Overfall' (waterfall) near Barracunda as 'roaring almost like *London-Bridge* at Low Water' – and revealed a touch of homesickness, possibly for his father's brewhouses he would have known as a boy in Bath.

Stibbs's views of his 'Linguister', 'Baram Fatty' (the only enslaved person named in Stibbs's narrative), and 'hired Servants' were contemptuous and racist. Their 'Ignorance and Fear both of the People and Country' they are being made to travel to with Stibbs are summarised by him as 'ridiculous Stories' and 'the Palaver concluded with a never-failing reconciling Bottle of Brandy' (appearing to use alcohol to pacify the enslaved people). Stibbs is open enough to at least consider their feelings and agree a compromise (Stibbs 'prevail'd with them to go as far by Water as we did, and no father', that is, he does not make them go over land into the 'barbarous' country they are afraid of). However, his businesslike account of his trading in enslaved people shows how his misplaced sense of purpose and duty ultimately overrode his empathy and humanity:

> On the 5th [February 1724], in the Afternoon, the Merchants came down, and after a long Dispute we found ourselves under a Necessity of contracting with them for ten Slaves, at 23 Barrs [of iron] *per* Head, or else they would not sell us their Gold and Teeth [ivory], which 'twas our Design only to buy, till our Return, by reason we had not Conveniences for Slaves till then. But what was a further Inducement, on our buying these Slaves, one of the Merchants, named *Gaye*, had promis'd to go up the River with us as far as *Tinda*, (where he lives) by which means we should have the Opportunity of knowing the Country on both Sides the River, which otherwise is impossible.

For Stibbs, practicality took precedence over principle, even where people's lives were concerned. His desire to add a knowledgeable guide to his party gives him 'a further Inducement' to trade in human lives, something it seems he had intended to do on his 'Return' from finding the gold. The following day, Stibbs was 'able to purchase but three' of the 'ten Slaves we the Day before contracted for', chiefly owing to 'the Badness of our Goods'. The only thing which 'concern'd' Stibbs about this was that 'by our not purchasing them ten Slaves, we lost the Opportunity of having *Gaye* the Merchant with us'. However, this was not the reason Stibbs did not eventually locate the gold mines he had been asked to find. On 25 February, the party received letters from the new Governor of Fort James aborting the mission and asking for them to return because their boat was needed for trade, including that in enslaved people. Stibbs disappointedly obliged. On route, he 'sent down three Canoas with 31 Slaves for James Fort, under the Care of Mr Thomas Harrison; the Reason of our sending them before was on account of Governor Plunkett's advising us of a Charter'd Ship for Carolina being expected daily at the Fort.' Such acts show Stibbs to be as complicit in the systems of colonialism and enslavement as someone such as Sir William Baker, who owned plantation land in the Carolinas. In spite of his failure to locate the gold mines at Barracunda, Stibbs stayed on at Fort James as its 'Second [Chief Merchant] and Warehouse-Keeper'. Given what Stibbs observed on his arrival, and the proportion of the island set aside for keeping enslaved people captive, this would surely have included slavery.

Stibbs 'went home on account of his ill State of Health' on 17 June 1731 after almost eight years with the Royal Africa Company at Fort James. Almost nothing is known about his life on his return to England. He died on 25 August 1735, aged 50. The bill for his burial was sent to the Chancery Petty Bag Office and an additional rectangular piece of marble added beneath the original pyramid marble inscribed to his father in Bath Abbey (possibly at the instigation of his brother Edward). Although Stibbs's name does not appear in the Abbey's burial register, these two pieces of evidence confirm that he was buried in Bath Abbey. The bill for his burial is written in the same hand as the clerk who wrote the Abbey's burial register for 1735. The register for that year is incomplete, breaking off on 20 June with only one further entry, for 5 October, written in a new hand that continues the register in 1736 beyond. Consequently, Stibbs is not named in the Abbey's burial register. However, in addition to that palaeographic evidence, the fees were signed as 'Received [on] Octr. 4th. 1735' by one 'Jno [John] Blatchly', discussed below, who was sexton of the Abbey between 1728 and 1749. The bill for Bartholomew Stibbs's burial sheds light on the costs of burial and memorialisation, probably near his family's grave, in the north-east of the Choir in the early eighteenth century.

The bill for burying Mr Bartholomew Stibbs (1735)[149]	
Item	**Cost**
Due to the Church	£1 8*s* 4*d*
Ministers dues	£0 2*s* 0*d*
Clerks dues	£0 1*s* 6*d*
for Ringing the bell	£0 6*s* 8*d*
for the Grave	£0 8*s* 0*d*
for laying the Stones	£0 2*s* 0*d*
[Total]	£2 8*s* 6*d*

The 'Due to the Church' is possibly a reflection of an early fee for modifying an existing monument in the church and erecting the rectangular piece of marble beneath the original pyramid (as we saw with Dr Aubery's monument in 1787). Like Sir William Baker, Stibbs's monument aggrandises, commemorates and titles him. Whereas Baker's monument alludes to the human cost of his wealth, Stibbs's monument is entirely silent on the source of his title, wealth, and the enslavement of people.

Approximately 20 per cent of all the monuments in Bath Abbey are directly connected to the British Empire. Chapman's list of the twenty-three monuments installed in 1768–83 is a microcosm of them, containing six prominent examples. Directors of the East India Company, like Bosanquet and Baker, could afford large conspicuous monuments by London sculptors to attract and instruct the public of their virtues. The families of plantation owners in Jamaica, like John Lamb and James Pedder, and even the Governor of the island, Roger Hope Elletson, erected 'neat' monuments lamenting them. Likewise, Robert Hughes, Admiral of the Red, helped to promote and protect British interests in the West Indies. For members of the plantocracy, such as the Alleynes and Maycocks, the grandeur of the Abbey was a befitting and the preferred place of rest and commemoration for their dynasties. The historic context and resonances of the Abbey naturally legitimised and confirmed their place amongst Britain's social elite. Hannah Alleyne (d. 1762) was commemorated with a monument by Bath's leading sculptor, Thomas King. The Alleynes intermarried with the Lowe family who, like the Alleynes, are also now commemorated in the South Nave Aisle, but who were buried and commemorated on the north side of the church in the early nineteenth century. Elizabeth Lowe was buried in the 'N.[orth] Aisle in Lead' on 26 October 1818, and a month later Joseph Lowe was buried identically. The difference being he was 'carried from St. Michael's Parish Church London' to be interred in the Abbey.[150] A large monument to Elizabeth and to another of her sons called Joseph (d. 1816) was erected in the North Transept. For the Abbey (and city), such monuments helped to convey to visitors that the status of Bath Abbey as a place of rest was on par with Westminster Abbey or St Paul's Cathedral (a fact that seems to have been accepted by eighteenth-century visitors to Bath, like John Bacon Esq.), which in turn helped the Abbey to profit from executors wishing to bury and commemorate their loved ones there. Collectively, these monuments created a narrative about eighteenth-century values as much as class for their viewers. The pair of Sir William Baker's and Beau Nash's monuments (which still sit conveniently next to each other in the South Aisle of the Nave, where they were originally erected) exemplify the axis on which these values turned: at home, one should mourn the elegance and social virtues of those like Nash, and abroad, emulate the nation-building (imperial) industry of those like Baker.

At the same time, as Joan Coutu has pointed out, several monuments in the colonies were executed by sculptors from Bath. These include 'primarily stock-in-trade urns and inscription plaques by Thomas King and Charles Reeves and son, but also William Lancashire's monument for Sir John Gay Alleyne with its highly individual design'. Furthermore, the 'often peripatetic lifestyle of the colonial elite' led Henry Crichlow of Barbados to commission 'two monuments (both unsigned) to his wife Lucy Crichlow'. One was erected in Bath Abbey, where Lucy was buried on 14 January 1801; 'the other (damaged) is in St Michael's Church, Bridgetown'.[151]

The context of and decisions about burial in the Abbey in this period are also relevant here. Between 1717 and 1756, twelve black people in Bath were baptised in the Abbey. None were commemorated or even interred within the walls of the church in the eighteenth century. On 2 January 1723, 'Edward Kent (a blacmore) was buried in the Churchyard'. With the exception of 'Christopher Margerum (a child)' and 'Elizabeth Stewart (a poor woman)', Edward Kent was the only person to be buried outside of the church (and, indeed, was the only man to be buried outside of the church) in 1723. Similarly, on 27 November 1778, 'A blackmoor' was buried in the 'Skullhouse'. Hardly anything is known about the skullhouse, which begins to be recorded in the burial registers in 1774. It was the place where the poor and children were often buried. As we will see later, the Abbey did occasionally waive the fees for intramural burial for the poor who could not afford to be buried within the Abbey. However, it appears that no such exceptions were made for black people, whilst at the same time the Abbey unquestioningly received fees for the burial and memorialisation of those who helped to expand Britain's colonies and enslave and profit from the enslavement of people. The Abbey's monuments, therefore, are memorials to a particular race and class of person, those who could afford to pay for such privileges, some by ill-gotten gains. Where the money came from for each monument may never be known, but monuments such as that to Stibbs, and even Catherine Malone, whose father 'made his fortune in the South Sea year', illustrate that the ability to commission and pay the Abbey's fees to erect some monuments were sometimes because of the exploitation of peoples and lands in Britain's 'dominions', even when the monuments themselves do not indicate it. The simultaneous rise in popularity of Bath as a fashionable spa, the popularity of the church monument as an artform, and the increasing affluence that the colonies brought to the upper-middle classes combined in the eighteenth century to leave the Abbey with a uniquely large collection of monuments, which shout loudly about the glory of empire, and which are silent about its evils.

'Almost invariably appended to each burial'?: Bath Abbey's burial register and ledgerstones, 1774–92

What of the ledgerstones in the eighteenth century? We saw in Chapter 1 that, after the repair of the church in the early seventeenth century, such stones were the preferred means of commemoration for some who might have afforded something considerably more lavish in marble on the walls or pillars of the Abbey. Of course, the cost of marble monuments was prohibitively expensive for some, yet for others being commemorated by their 'own stone' (or on their family's stone) was just as desirable. Stones on the floor of the Abbey, which before the Assembly Rooms were built in 1771 was a popular place to promenade, were obviously eroded by the feet of walkers and worshippers. Seating could obscure them and the weekly burials damage existing stones as they were lifted to accommodate more burials. The original inscriptions of these older stones were then sometimes added to, and occasionally obliterated altogether, by newer inscriptions. Historical interest in the ledgerstones also seems to have waned after Rawlinson's 1719 survey. One correspondent to *The Bath Chronicle* in 1792 even suggested that 'matts' be put 'on the stone floors' as part of a series of changes suggested for the church to improve congregational worship and keep out the cold.[152]

The lack of documentary sources makes it difficult to appraise the ledgerstones in the eighteenth century (unlike marble wall tablets, there are no contemporary drawings that reveal their detail). The burial register for the period 1774–92 is the best source for understanding the original layout of the ledgerstones in this period. It was probably kept by Henry Sperring, who was parish clerk until the end of September 1791 (his death, aged 80, on 25 November 1791 is recorded in the register by another hand). As with other parish registers, the burial registers for this period contain a wealth of information about the parish and the church, from the swearing in of church wardens to which undertakers were used for funerals and mortuaries, as well as information about burials, ledgerstones and monuments. What can be learned about the Abbey's monuments and burial practice in the Abbey in this period is both detailed and informative thanks to Sperring's diligent record keeping. However, the Abbey's parish registers have been ignored by researchers, even those who have written on the Abbey's monuments. This is in spite of the fact that the Abbey's registers were published in two volumes by the Harleian Society in 1900 and 1901. The editor, Arthur John Jewers, was an antiquarian with a particular interest in church records and monumental inscriptions.[153] In his preface, Jewers explains that his volumes were based on 'a transcript made by Mr. A. Strother some years since (who was at that time residing in Bath)'. Strothers's transcript 'only brought the Baptisms and Marriages down to 1754', which led Jewers to 'compare' it with the original and continue it to the end of 1800 'to which date the Burials were already transcribed'. This seems to imply that Jewers did not compare Strothers's transcript with the burial registers themselves.

Whether the fault is with Strothers or Jewers, the transcription of the burial registers for this period is particularly poor. For example, the entry for 23 June 1775 in Jewers's published volume reads 'Mrs Elizabeth Hawker', whereas the entry in the burial register reads: 'Mrs Elizabeth Hawker was Buried in ye Church at ye head of the Stone Mark[ed] T:W: by ye Poor Box in ye Middle Isle.' Unfortunately, this kind of silent omission is common and arbitrary in Jewers's volumes, and extremely misleading given his footnote to the entries from 1774 stating that 'entries that mention an inscribed stone are noted here, as they shew such existed, and in some cases indicate relationships'. It is noticeable and disappointing that entries concerning women and the poor tend to be treated in this way more so than those concerning well-known and well-to-do men. This problem is compounded by Jewers's preface to his edition of the burial registers in which he wrongly and misleadingly claims that he has included the 'notes' that 'in the original for a considerable period are almost invariably appended to each burial indicating the place of interment, when they give any information as to the name of the person near or beneath whose stone the interment took place'. In fact, of the 605 entries in the burial register that record burials in the Abbey between 1774 and 1792, only 125 of those printed in Jewers's edition fully and accurately transcribe the entry. A good proportion of the silent omissions concern the lack of transcription of this kind of location information. This suggests that Jewers did not compare Strothers's transcription with the burial registers. Jewers's opinion that the entries in the burial registers that state that burials took place 'under a "white," "large," or "small" stone' are 'useless' because 'large numbers of stones disappeared' during Sir George Gilbert Scott's 'reconstruction of the floor' in the 1860s and 1870s also badly undervalued what can be learnt from the burial registers. In focusing on the facts that 'Burials were generally, during the latter part of the seventeenth and most of the eighteenth centuries, within the Church' and that some notes in the registers state where 'strangers sojourning in the place for health, pleasure, or business' were 'carried away to be buried', Jewers ignored that the burial registers for this period tell us much about burial practice, class and commemoration in the Abbey. The following analysis, therefore, is based on the original burial registers 1774–92, not Jewers's edition of them.

With such vast numbers of burials and ledgerstones being laid in the Abbey by the end of the eighteenth century, the way in which Henry Sperring recorded them is both surprising and indicative of the high degree of thought and care he gave to them. The example of 'Mrs Elizabeth Hawker' above is representative of this, and at the end of 1786 the entries show him amending his initial wording to increase their accuracy: 'Oct 30 Mrs Elizth. East was Buried in ye Church ~~under~~ by ye side [of] Mr Haddens Stone Middle Isle'; 'Nov 27 George Keysell a Child was Buried in ye Church ~~under~~ by their own Stone Middle Isle'.[154] These and many other examples also illustrate that by the end of the eighteenth century, whether one had a ledgerstone or not, the sheer volume of existing burials and ledgerstones sometimes made it impossible to be buried beneath a particular stone. On other occasions, entries in the burial register that record the location of burial are left blank. For example, on 31 May 1788 'William Kettle Esqr was Buried in ye Church under [blank] S Isle',[155] on 24 December 1789 'Mrs Mary Holman was Buried in ye Church under [blank] South Isle',[156] and on 12 August 1790 'Mrs Sarah Croft was Buried in ye Church under Mr [blank] Stone in Lead Mid Isle'.[157] Jewers's edition simply gives the name and title of the burial and omits the location information. These kinds of lacunae in the originals suggest a breakdown of communication between the sexton making the grave and the clerk recording it (at a time when, Thomas Handcock, the sexton's father, was filling in for his son and elected sexton, William, during his long illness).

However, these kinds of entries do tell us that a ledgerstone for these people was not laid at the time of burial. They are also indicative of the state of the ledgerstones themselves in the heavily trafficked Middle and South Aisles. The state of the floor in the Nave can also be inferred from earlier entries. For example, on 31 July 1785 'William Bell Esqr was Buried in ye Church under Gulielmus Livess in ye Middle Isle H:J:S' and, just over a month later, on 9 September, 'The Revd Mr John Ellis Arch Deacon of Bangor was Buried in the Church in the Midle [sic] Isle under the Stone H:J:S:'.[158] It is again a marker of the lack of space for burials in the Abbey by the end of the eighteenth century that two burials take place under the same, older stone in such a short space of time. The inscription 'H:J:S' ('Hic Jacet Sepultus' or 'Here lies buried') is obviously all that remained legible of a longer inscription that had been eroded away.[159] Conversely, entries relating to less-trafficked areas such as the South Transept, where the font was situated, such as that on 27 March 1776 – 'Miss Charlotte Lewis was Buried in the Church under James Keigwin's Stone by ye Christning Vaunt [sic]' – show that even inscriptions on stones laid over sixty years earlier were still perfectly legible there.[160]

Ledgerstones and monuments, as well as the font, its 'rails', the organ, and the church's many doors,[161] seats,[162] stairs,[163] pillars and galleries, were often used to locate burials. Occasionally, 'ye Engines' (the city's fire engine in the North Transept), the poor boxes in the North Aisle and Middle Aisle of the Nave, 'ye North Window [of the] Cross Isle' (the North Transept), 'the [Birde] Chapel in the South Isle', and 'the wall in the North Isle' were used. The amount of seating assigned to individuals in the Choir (for example, rented pews) meant that particular seats were often used to locate burials there (e.g. 'in ye Choir close by ye Seat No: 15' or 'in ye Choir under ye Clerks Seat'). The notes obviously require one to imagine the layout of the interior of the Abbey in the eighteenth century. This is easier to do for some entries than others. For example, one can easily locate where 'Theobald Bourke Esqr was Buried in ye Church at ye Head of ye Bishop's Monument under Mr Price's Stone' on 1 December 1783, whereas 'ye first blue Stone' by 'ye Door' in the North Aisle under which 'Sr: Noah Thomas M.D.' was buried on 24 May 1792 would be impossible to identify today (and subsequent stones laid there would have made such an entry obscure relatively quickly).

The system appears to have enabled the clerk and the sexton to bury family members together when they were not commemorated by their own ledgerstone or monument over a number of years. For example, on 1 December 1775 'Charles Quarman a Child was Buried in ye Church at ye foot of Mr Russell's in ye Middle Isle'. Mr Charles Russell's stone was one commonly used to locate burials, and had been lifted as recently as 23 October 1775 when 'Sarah Bishop was Buried in ye Church at the feet of Mr Russell's Stone'. The stone was then used again on 29 November 1776 to bury Charles Quarman's sister ('Elizabeth Quarman a Child was Buried in ye Church under the White Stones by the left side of Mr Russell's Stone in ye Middle Isle') and on 23 July 1778 to bury his brother ('Thomas Quarman a Child was Buried in ye Church under the White Stones the left side of Mr Chas Russell's Stone in ye Middle Isle').

Unlike wall monuments, where the minimum time between burial and erection in the Abbey appears to have been about six months, ledgerstones could be laid upon burials. The burial register for this period records this with the designation 'own stone' (discussed at greater length below). These stones almost immediately became markers to orientate and locate later burials, as with the stone for Dr Guynon Griffeths, who was buried under his 'own stone in ye North X Isle' (that is, the North Cross Aisle or North Transept) on 8 January 1784. A fortnight later, this stone was used by the clerk to record that on 23 January 'Mr. Richard Page was Buried in ye Church at ye side of Dr Griffith's [sic] Stone North X Isle'. Other ledgerstones clearly took longer to create, if they required more extensive carving than simply a name and date of death. A good example of this is the burial of 'Baron Theodore De Ludere [who] was buried in ye Church at ye end of the Charity School Girls Seat under Mr Joseph Smith's Stone M. Isle' on 15 December 1774. His ledgerstone, 'a White Slab', originally included a beautifully decorative crest of an eagle 'displayed' on top of a crown above the following inscription:

Here lie the Remains
of Theodore Luders
of Widcombe near this City
Knight of the Empire
who died December 6th 1774.
Aged 68
And likewise
Of Anna his Wife
Who died May twenty-first 1792
Aged 76.

The stone was clearly created after Luders's burial beneath Smith's stone and laid later in the middle of the Nave. When his wife Anna was buried, the following was entered in the burial register on 26 May 1792: 'Mrs: Ann Luders was buried under their own Stone Middle Aisle.' The five days between her death and burial was clearly enough time for a mason to add the four lines of text to her husband's stone, and for her burial to therefore be recorded as being under her 'own Stone'.

Where a stone was laid in the church had a significance beyond whether it was simply in the Nave or Chancel, a fact well illustrated by Edward Orpwood's stone. Orpwood was 'Buried in ye Church at ye head of Mr Willsher's Stone in ye North Isle Paid the Church Warden' on 24 March 1776. Probably soon after, and certainly by 28 November 1783, his ledgerstone had been laid when it was used to locate 'Mr Michael Reilly M.D.' who 'was Buried in ye Church under Mr Orpwoods Stone in ye North Isle'. The inscription read:

> Here lieth the Body of
> Edward Orpwood Esq.
> who departed this Life
> the nineteenth day of March
> in the Year of our Lord 1776
> Aged 58.
> He walked in the old Paths
> because he thought them best.

Here the ledgerstone's inscription helps us to understand the significance of the location of Orpwood's, and probably Reilly's, burial. The final two lines allude to Orpwood's Catholicism (as does his Will, in which he bequeathed to his son the 'sword that was given by the Queen of Spain to the Duke of Ormond'). Burial of other Catholics took place in the Abbey in the eighteenth century, and the burial register demonstrates that the North Aisle was frequently the location where this took place. For example, on 3 May 1792, the burial register records that 'Revd: Wm: Heetley was buried under Saml: Wilson's Esqr. Stone North Aisle.' This was Dom Heatley, 'a monk of Lamspring and a nephew of Abbot Maurus Heatley', whose work in Bath from 1787 to 1792 'ended while he was still young, for he died there of typhus fever at the age of thirty three, on 29th April 1792'. Another example is that of John Tobin, whose burial took place in the Abbey on 8 January 1795, almost a month after his death on 12 December 1794. *The Bath Chronicle* sensationalised the event, informing its readers that the 'reason of this rite being so long deferred was a dread often expressed by Mr. Tobin of premature interment, which he suspected often to be the case in the West-Indies'.[164] Tobin, a shipman of Southampton, no doubt heard all kinds of sailors' tales. In his lengthy Will, Tobin asked that 'in case I should depart this life at Bath that I may be Buried in a plain decent manner in the North Isle of the Abby Church where persons professing the Roman Catholick faith are commonly Interred'. Orpwood, Tobin and other Catholics, such as Richard Bostock M.D. (d. 1747), a lodger at Bell Tree House from 1729–37, were all buried and commemorated in the North Aisle.

Further research would pinpoint the beginnings of this tradition and the area of the north side of the church that was used for it. The monuments to Sir Philip Frowde (d. 1674), 'a royalist colonel in the civil war', and Mary Frampton (d. 1698) (Colour Plate Z), whose father, Richard, was described as a 'prominent papist', originally erected in the North Transept suggest that it had been established by the end of the seventeenth century and that it included more than simply the North Aisle. Frampton's monument contains an epitaph written by the poet John Dryden, who had converted to Catholicism. In fact, the 'poem's first appearance was as an inscription'.[165] Sometimes titled 'The Monument of a Fair Maiden Lady', Dryden's lines begin by asking the 'Sacred Tomb' to preserve Frampton, 'a virgin Saint'. The Luders – who were married 'in the German Lutheran Chapel, off the Strand' – and the Krauters – 'Philip David Krauter D.D. / many years minister of the / Lutheran Church in London' – are other examples of non-conformists and non-Anglicans buried and commemorated in the Abbey. Collectively, these monuments demonstrate that, in the eighteenth century, class and one's ability to pay the burial and mason's fees were the deciding factors as to whether one could be buried and commemorated in the Abbey, rather than one's Christian denomination.

A 'shoe-black' like Thomas Traherne could afford to be buried in the Abbey only by being extremely parsimonious. Generally, the churchyard, 'Skullhouse' (from 1774), or 'Poor House ground' (from 1784) were used to bury the 'poor'. Like other records of their type, the Abbey's burial registers illustrate the fates of people closely related in life but divided in death by their class. One example in this period is the burials of the Lansdown family, beginning with Mr Robert Lansdown, who 'was Buried in ye Church under Aldm. [alderman] Saunders's Stone in the South Isle' on 20 November 1777, followed by Elizabeth Lansdown, who was buried under the same stone on 22 November 1782, and another Elizabeth Lansdown who was buried nearby 'under Mr Sheiler's Stone in ye South Isle' on 12 September 1783. On the other hand, 'Mrs Lansdown's Cook was Buried in ye Skull House' on 1 January 1779. Only twenty-four of the 605 burials in the Abbey between 1774 and 1792 were of people described as 'Poor' or (from 1784) 'a Pauper', eight of them children. Unlike the majority of burials, the locations in the church where these poor people were buried was only given on five occasions between 1774 and 1792: two in the 'Middle Isle' (one under 'Mrs Russell['s] Stone'), two in the 'South Isle' (one 'under James Davis's Stone') and one 'by ye blue seat' (like the others, presumably somewhere in the Nave). None of the poor children's burials were given a location.

On ten occasions between May 1776 and March 1790, the burial registers indicate that the Abbey 'forgave' the fee for burial. All of these burials were in the Nave. Only once does the fee appear to have been 'forgiven' for one of the poor discussed above, when 'Mary Whittick was Buried in the Church forgave A Pauper' on 11 March 1785. Three are children, so it is not hard to imagine the compassion behind those fees being forgiven. The reason for waving the fee for the others is not always clear, although forgiving the fees for the burials of Ann Collibee and Mrs Margaret Webb was probably because they were related to members of the town council: the '6th bell' was tolled for Collibee and Webb was buried under her 'own Stone' in the South Aisle.

Between 1774 and 1792, 605 burials took place in the Abbey. Most are described in sufficient detail to allow one to know the area in which the burial took place. However, fifty-seven either omit locations entirely (e.g. 'Mrs. Susanna Lucas was Buried in ye Church under their own Stone') or contain descriptors that no longer enable one to accurately discern the location (e.g. 'George Brickman a Child was Buried at the Head of his Grandfather's Stone'). Seventy-nine of the 605 burials, or 13 per cent, took place under the deceased's 'own stone', an indicator of the number of ledgerstones that were laid (or at the very least modified to include a new inscription) in the period.[166] The following table shows the number of burials by location and number of ledgerstones laid in each area between 1774 and 1792.

Location	**Burials**	**Burials under 'Own Stone'**
Choir and Chancel	27	4
Middle Aisle	172	27
South Aisle	163	18
South Transept	37	5
'Cross Aisle'	3	1
North Transept	30	6
North Aisle	116	16
Unlocated	57	2
Total	**605**	**79**

Burials in the Choir or Chancel were the most uncommon, reserved almost exclusively for knights, ladies and esquires. Between 1775 and 1785, the burial register locates these burials in relation to particular named or numbered seats, whereas between 1786 and 1790 burials in the Choir tend to be recorded 'under ye Organ', 'under ye Organ Loft', or 'under ye Organ Gallery'. Six burials took place in the Choir or Chancel in 1775 before a hiatus in 1776–79, when no burials took place there. From 1780, a maximum of four burials took place in the Choir annually.

The majority of the burials took place outside of the Choir, with 75 per cent of all burials in the period taking place in the middle of the Nave and Nave Aisles. Noticeably more burials took place in the South Nave Aisle than the North, most apparent in 1780, when one burial took place in the North Aisle compared with ten in the South Aisle. Rawlinson's survey showed the increasing use of the middle of the Nave for the burial of 'strangers' in the early eighteenth century and the higher concentration of burials in the South Aisle probably reflects the expansion of burials into this area of the church to accommodate the burial of visitors to the city by the end of the century. Certainly well-known Bath families, such as the Chapmans, Haywards and Henshaws, preferred the North Aisle for their burial and commemoration in the late 1770s and early 1780s. Burial in the transepts was more occasional and sporadic. For example, no burials took place in the North Transept in 1774, 1779, 1781 or 1782.

The burial register for this period shows that where no ledgerstone was laid to an individual, often their burial was recorded under another's stone. Locating a burial in the Middle Aisle would have been especially difficult if a ledgerstone were not laid to the individual. Certain stones, therefore, came to be used as frequent locators of burials. The ledgerstones commemorating Mr Thomas Haviland (d. 1770), for 'many years an Eminent Apothecary' of Bath, and John Orme Esquire (d. 1779) in the middle of the Nave were frequently used to locate burials (e.g. 'Norton Hutchenson Esqr was Buried in ye Church under ye blue Stone the left of Mr Haviland's Stone in ye Middle Isle') or lifted to enable new burials to take place under them (e.g. 'George Raitt M: D: was Buried in ye Church under Mr Orms Stone Middle Isle'). Furthermore, having one's own ledgerstone did not guarantee that one could be buried beneath it by the end of the eighteenth century, especially in the middle of the Nave. For example, on 28 September 1784 'Robert Russell a Child was Buried in ye Church near their own Stone Middle Isle', and on 22 February 1786 'Mrs. Betty Ball was Buried in ye Church next to their own Stone Middle Isle.' Even Bathonian families whose members were commemorated in the middle of the Nave, such as the Farrs, could not be guaranteed to be buried beneath the family ledgerstone by the end of the century. For example, on 14 January 1787 'Rebecca Farr was Buried in ye Church by ye side of her Father's Grave M:[iddle] I[sle]'.

Two entries in the burial register for 1791 perhaps suggest an early system of numbering vaults or graves to locate burials that has since been lost. On 14 July the entry reads, 'Mrs. Sarah Rudge was Buried in ye Church in their own Grave North X Isle 20', and on 1 October the entry reads, 'Child was Buried in ye Church 23.' These are obviously not the same as the entries in the late 1770s recording which bell was used to toll the knell, e.g. '9th Bell', nor related to the numbering of pillars to locate burials and ledgerstones, e.g. '20 December 1778 John Viner Read Esqr was Buried in ye Church under Johnsons Ruddall's Stone between ye 5th & 6th Pillar of ye South Isle.' Neither are they sums of money: it is common to see 'Paid the Churchwarden' following entries in 1775–76 (but not afterwards) and amounts are never recorded. Vaults were numbered by the middle of the nineteenth century, as can be seen by the following carved onto the bottom of the ledgerstone commemorating Louisa Maxwell Macdougall (d. 1841), presumably to locate her burial more accurately than the circumspect 'Here rest / the mortal remains of' which begins the stone's inscription: '3rd vault from bis.p montague / 14 feet from front of skreen'.

Of the 605 burials, 136 of them (22 per cent), were of children. Only fifteen of these burials (11 per cent) took place beneath the child's 'own stone'. However, the Abbey appears to have established a system of burying children who were not buried beneath their own ledgerstones beneath 'white stones' in the floor. This occurred twenty-one times, and only between 1775 and 1786, accounting for 15 per cent of all burials of children in 1774–92. The majority of these (eight) were in the south of the Abbey and middle of the Nave (seven), with only four of them on the north side of the Abbey. We have seen that the Quarman children, discussed above, were buried 'under the White Stones by the left side of Mr Russell's Stone', and 'Serjeant Jephson's Stone by the Library [now vestry] door' appears to have been another locator of a group of 'small white Stones' in the South Choir Aisle. Other groups of white stones appear to have been located 'at ye head of William Tagg's Stone by ye Abbey House door' in the South Aisle, 'between ye blue Stones opposite ye Charity School Girl's Seats N. Isle', 'by ye Engines in ye North Isle' (North Transept), 'by the West door in ye North Isle', 'Near Bennett's door' (unlocated), 'by ye Bishops Mont.' (the Montagu Tomb) in the 'Middle Aisle' (that is to the south of the tomb), and various other locations in the middle of the Nave. The survey of the floor completed before the beginning of the Footprint Project conservation work to the ledgerstones in 2018 clearly shows the locations of the 'white stones' in Sir George Gilbert Scott's arrangement of the floor (Colour Plate AA). This should not be taken as a literal indication of where the stones lay before the Victorian rearrangement of the floor. Scott's introduction of the heating grates into the floor in the early 1870s necessitated the movement, and in some cases removal, of ledgerstones. However, the image does show how, even after the Victorian works, the white stones were concentrated in the South Aisle and middle of the Nave, giving us the impression that late eighteenth-century visitors may have had of the floor, if not its exact layout in this respect.

Opposite: Colour Plate A: Monument to Bartholomew Barnes (d. 1606) located on the south side of the Sanctuary. © Bath Abbey.

widow of the above James Cladell
& daughter of Thomas
a daughter of Alexander Thistlethwayte
Aged

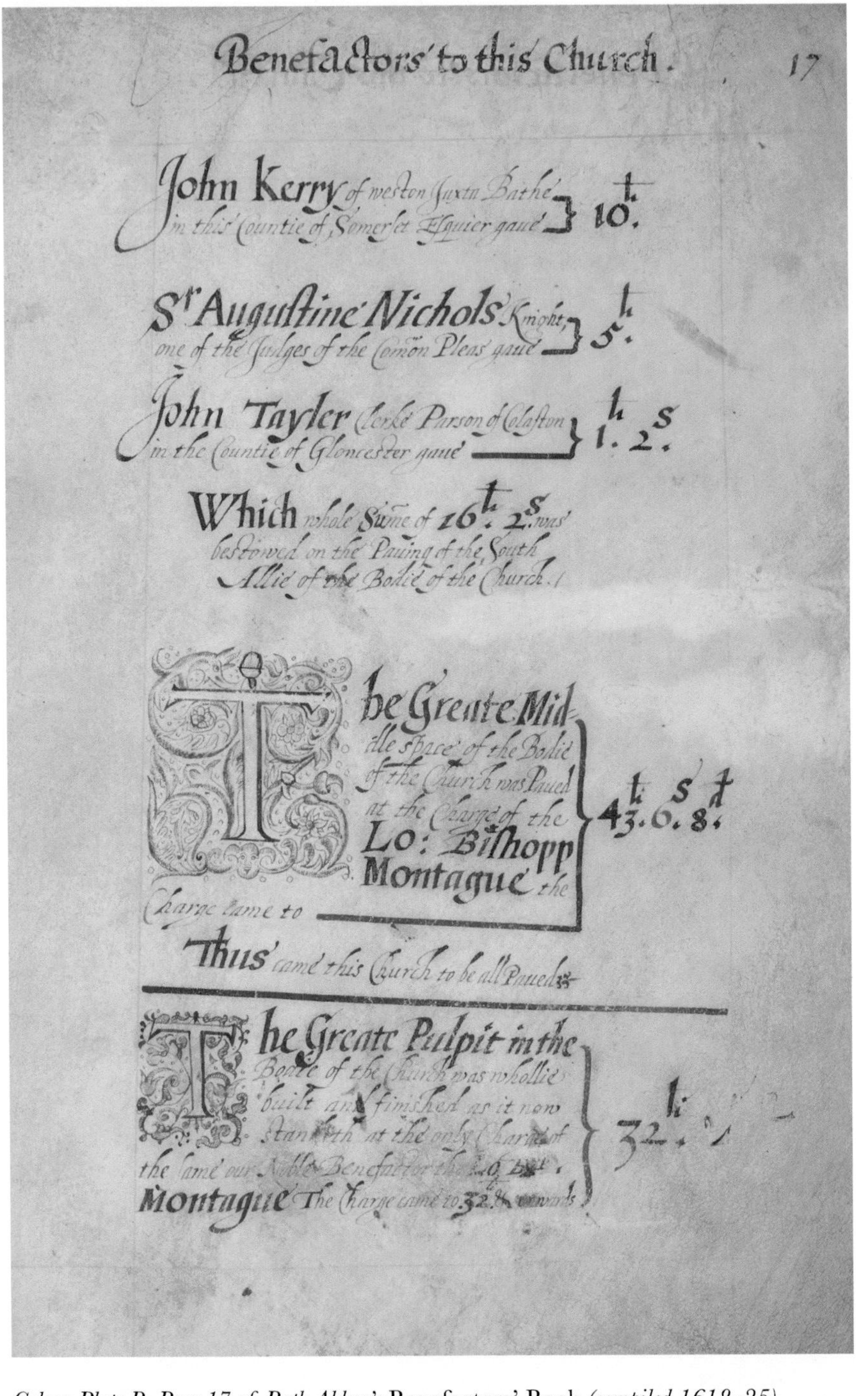

Benefactors to this Church. 17

John Kerry of weston Juxta Bathe in this Countie of Somerset Esquier gave } 10.li

Sr Augustine Nichols Knight, one of the Judges of the Comon Pleas gave } 5.li

John Tayler Clerke Parson of Colaston in the Countie of Gloncester gave } 1.li 2.s

Which whole Sume of 16.li 2.s was bestowed on the Paving of the South Allie of the Bodie of the Church.

The Greate Middle space of the Bodie of the Church was Paued at the Charge of the Lo: Bishopp Montague the Charge came to } 43.li 6.s 8.d

Thus came this Church to be all Paued.

The Greate Pulpit in the Bodie of the Church was whollie built and finished as it now standeth at the only Charge of the same our Noble Benefactor the Lo: Bis: Montague The Charge came to 32.li & upwards } 32.li

Colour Plate B: Page 17 of Bath Abbey's Benefactors' Book *(compiled 1618–25) listing some of the benefactors to the paving of the church 1614–15, including Bishop James Montagu's contribution of £43 6s 8d, which completed the paving of the Nave and the church. © Bath Abbey.*

Colour Plate C: Tomb of Bishop James Montagu (d. 1618) in the north Nave of Bath Abbey. In the background, Sir George Gilbert Scott's arrangement of the tablets on the walls of the Nave can be seen. Bath Abbey Archives. © Bath Abbey.

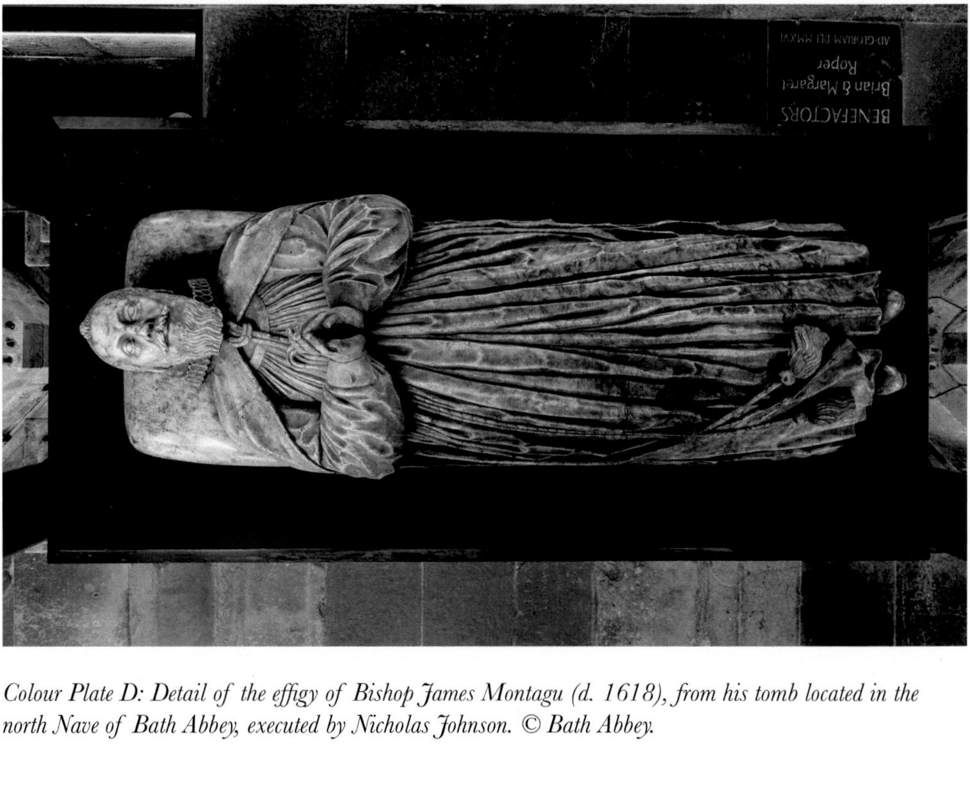

Colour Plate D: Detail of the effigy of Bishop James Montagu (d. 1618), from his tomb located in the north Nave of Bath Abbey, executed by Nicholas Johnson. © Bath Abbey.

Colour Plate D (ii): Silhouette of the tomb of Bishop James Montagu (d. 1618). The window installed in 1951 comprised of the arms and some of the glass given by other seventeenth-century benefactors to the Abbey can be seen in the background. © Bath Abbey.

Colour Plate E: Tomb of Lady Jane Waller (d. 1633) on the south wall of the South Transept of Bath Abbey. In English Church Monuments *(1946), Katherine Esdaile 'unhesitatingly' ascribed the tomb to Epiphanius Evesham.* © Bath Abbey

Colour Plate F: Detail of the effigies of Lady Jane and Sir William Waller from the tomb of Lady Jane Waller (d. 1633). Sir William's vandalised sword hand and 'broken face' described by Samuel Pepys in 1668 can be seen. © Bath Abbey.

Opposite: Colour Plate F(ii): Detail of the pediment of Lady Jane Waller's tomb (d. 1633) attributed to Epiphanius Evesham. The paint dates to April 1948 when the restorer Pearl Blencowe carried out her 'experiment in cleaning' the monument. © Bath Abbey.

Colour Plate H: A Perspective View of the Abbey-Church of St. Peter and Paul at Bath *(1750) by James Vertue. © Bath Abbey.*

Colour Plate G: A Service at Bath Abbey *(1788) by Samuel Hieronymus Grimm. The watercolour shows the Nave looking west from the elevated perspective of the organ. Monuments can be seen on the pillars and walls in line with and above the string course of the windows, allowing worshippers to use the benches for prayer. British Library, London, UK © British Library Board. All Rights Reserved/Bridgeman Images.*

BENEATH THIS STONE INTERRED LYES WHAT
REMAINES OF YE BODY OF RICHD WAKEMAN
YE ELDER WHOSE EMINENT KNOWLEDGE IN YE
LAWS & OTHER LEARNING MADE HIS LIFE AN
HONOUR TO BOTH HE DEPARTED ON THE 15 OF
OCTOBER 1656 ALSO HIS GRANDSON
THEODORE WHO SUCCEEDING IN YE PLACE
OF TOWN-CLERK OF THIS CITY AFTER THE
DECEASE OF RICHARD HIS FATHER & DYING
THE 28 OF DECEMBER WAS BURIED IN YE
GRAUE OF HIS GRANDFATHER
AGED 28

Colour Plate I: Mid-seventeenth-century ledgerstone commemorating three generations of the Wakeman family in the North Aisle of the Nave. © Bath Abbey.

Colour Plate J: Ledgerstone to Mrs Anna Peirce (d. 1688) and Mary a Court (nee Peirce, d. 1679). The quotation from Psalm 39 – 'And now Lord what is our hope / truly our hope is even in thee' – is carved at the bottom of the ledgerstone. © Bath Abbey.

To the deare memory of
Elizabeth, daughter of Dr. Robert Peirce and
Anna his wife, who ended a sickly life by a
sudden death (caus'd by an inward imposthume)
Febr: 18th 1671, aged 19 years
Though sudden to her friends yet not so to her,
As appeares by these verses found in her
Closet after her decease,
Death is the common lot of all,
It spareth neither greate nor small.
Then (since the time's not in our powr)
Let's live as though't were our last hour.
For come when't will, t'will sudden seem,
Although the warning long hath been.
And be not troubled, if your friends,
Come suddenly unto their ends.
For't is a debt, that all must pay,
Though some do goe a neerer way
Then others, yet the iourney's sure,
And some paine in't we must endure.
How necessary 'tis to be
Prepar'd for death, pray, learne of me.
Neere this place also ly the bodies of
Robert and Charles Peirce brothers of
the said Elizabeth: Robert Peirce aged one
year, died Nouemb: 15, 1677: Charles Peirce
SELINA IRWIN, DAUGHTER OF THE ABOVE MAJOR WILLIAM BROOKE,
AND RELICT OF JAMES IRWIN ESQr. OF DEVONSHIRE PLACE LONDON,
ONE OF THE DIRECTORS
OF THE HONOURABLE EAST INDIA COMPANY,
WHO DIED OCTR 1ST 1820, AGED 66.
Near this Place is Interr'd ye Body
WILLIAM STEUART, who died
To the Memory
ELEANORA WALSH

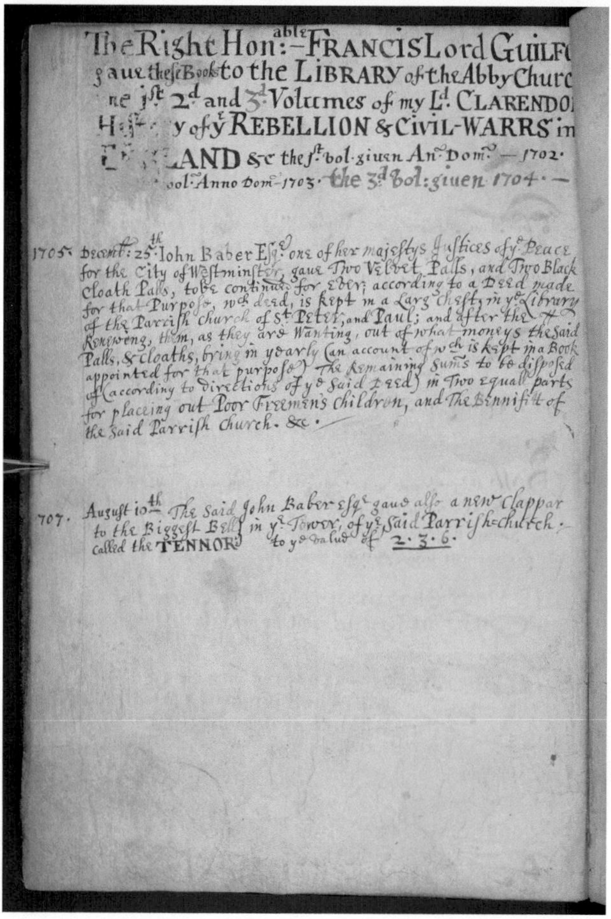
The Right Honble. FRANCIS Lord GUILF[ORD]
gave these Books to the LIBRARY of the Abby Churc[h]
the 1st 2d and 3d Volumes of my Ld. CLARENDO[N's]
History of ye REBELLION & CIVIL-WARRS in
ENGLAND &c the 1st vol: given An: Dom: 1702.
vol: Anno Dom: 1703. the 3d vol: given 1704.

1705. Decembr: 25th John Baber Esqr. one of her majestys Justices of ye Peace for the City of Westminster, gave Two Velvet Palls, and Two Black Cloath Palls, to be continued for Ever; according to a Deed made for that Purpose, wch deed, is kept in a Larg Chest, in ye Library of the Parrish church of St. Peter, and Paul; and after the Renewing, them, as they are Wanting, out of what moneys the said Palls, & cloaths, bring in yearly (an account of wch is kept in a Book appointed for that purpose) The Remaining Sums to be disposed of (according to directions of ye said Deed) in Two equall parts for placeing out Poor Freemen's Children, and The Bennifitt of the said Parrish Church. &c.

1707. August 10th The said John Baber Esqr. gave also a New Clappar to the Biggest Bell in ye Tower, of ye said Parrish church. called the TENNOR to ye value of 2. 3. 6.

Colour Plate K: Monument to Elizabeth Peirce (d. 1671) and her brothers Robert and Charles. The 'verses' on the monument were 'found in her Closet after her decease'. © Bath Abbey.

Colour Plate L: Page 44 of Bath Abbey's Benefactors' Book *(compiled 1618–25), which records the Christmas gift of 'Two Velvet Palls, and Two Black cloath Palls' from John Baber to the Abbey in 1705. © Bath Abbey.*

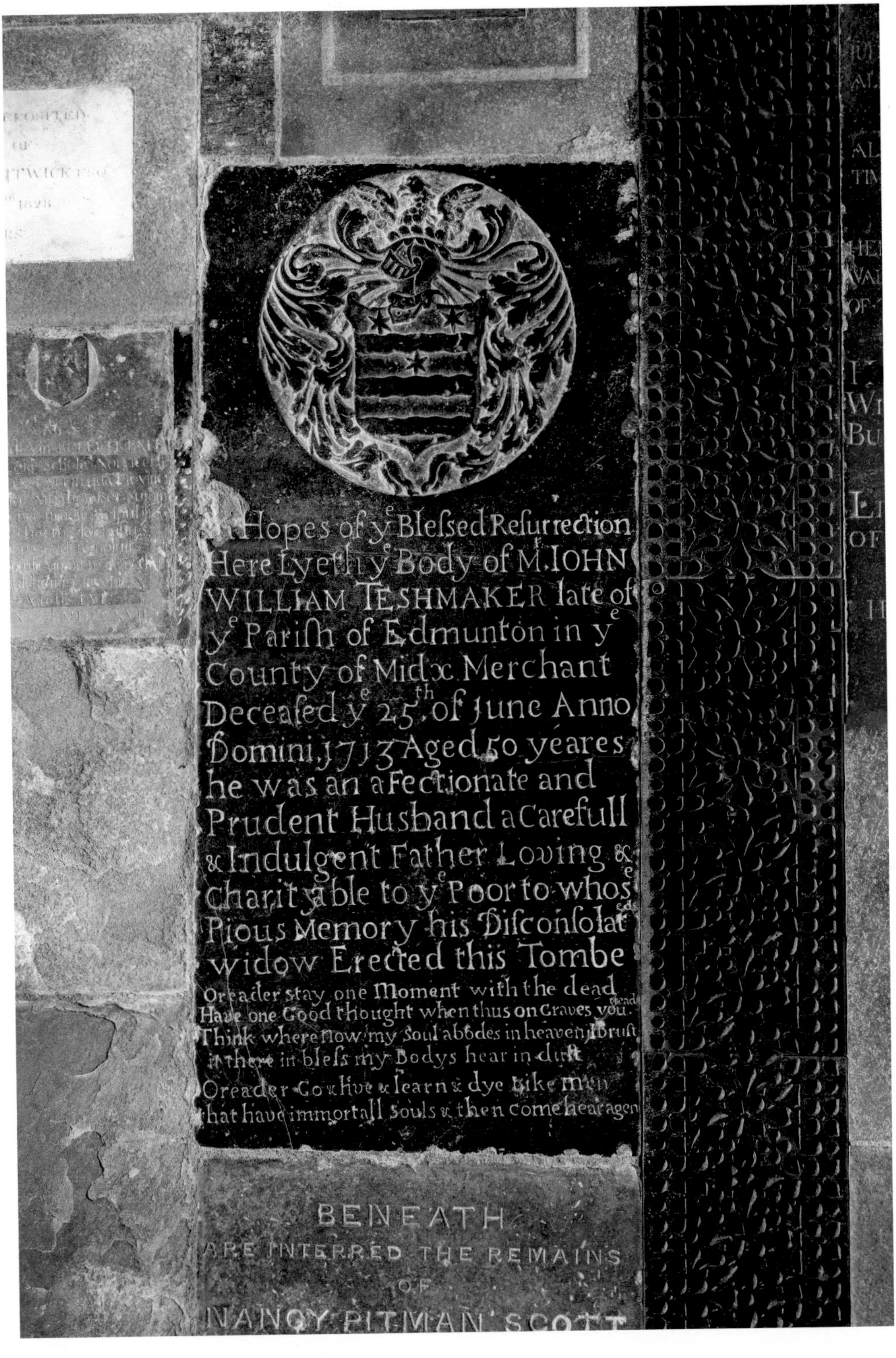

Hopes of ye Blessed Resurrection
Here Lyeth ye Body of Mr IOHN
WILLIAM TESHMAKER late of
ye Parish of Edmunton in ye
County of Midx. Merchant
Deceased ye 25th of June Anno
Domini 1713 Aged 50 yeares
he was an aFectionate and
Prudent Husband a Carefull
& Indulgent Father Loving &
Charitable to ye Poor to whose
Pious Memory his Disconsolated
widow Erected this Tombe
O reader stay one Moment with the dead
Have one Good thought when thus on Graves you tread
Think where now my Soul abodes in heaven I trust
it there in bless my Bodys hear in dust
O reader Go & live & learn & dye like men
that have immortall Souls & then come hear agen
BENEATH
ARE INTERRED THE REMAINS
OF
NANCY PITMAN SCOTT

Colour Plate M: Early eighteenth-century ledgerstone to John William Teshmaker (d. 1713) at the west end of the Nave. Like many monuments in the Abbey, it addresses the reader, asking them to 'Have one Good thought when thus on Graves you tread'. © Bath Abbey.

Colour Plate N: Monument to Jacob Bosanquet (d. 1767) by Thomas Carter the Younger, centre, in its present location on the east wall of the South Transept. The large monuments to Josiah Thomas (d. 1820), by Gahagan, and Joseph Sill (d. 1824) can be seen on the right and left, respectively. © Bath Abbey.

Detail of the carving of the story of the Good Samaritan on the monument to Jacob Bosanquet (d. 1767) by Thomas Carter the Younger. © Bath Abbey.

Colour Plate O: Inscription tablet to C.M. (Catherine Malone, d. 1765) in the North Aisle. It is all that remains on the Abbey's walls of the larger monument that was erected to her in the North Aisle c.1765–67. *© Bath Abbey.*

*Colour Plate P: Relief carving from Catherine Malone's monument (*c.1765–67*). It depicts 'a boy sleeping by an urn, with a branch of cyprus in his left hand, resting his head on an hour-glass'. The carving was removed in the nineteenth century and discovered by archaeologists beneath the Abbey floor in 2020. © Bath Abbey.*

Colour Plate Q: Monument to Leonard (d. 1761) and Elizabeth Coward (d. 1759) erected in 1764. It was probably carved by a Bath sculptor and is similar in design to that to Catherine Malone erected in the Abbey c.*1765–67 (shown in Colour Plate P). © Bath Abbey.*

Colour Plate R: Monument to James Quin (d. 1766) created by Thomas King between April 1766 and April 1769. © Bath Abbey.

who died at Bath March 11th
1808.
Adeſte ô Cives, adeſte lugentes!
Hic ſilent Leges
RICARDI NASH Armig:
Nihil amplius imperantis:
Qui diu et utiliſſime
aſſumptus Bathoniæ,
Elegantiæ Arbiter,
Eheu!
Morti (ultimo deſignatori)
haud indecore ſuccubuit;
Ann: Dom: 1761 Æt: ſuæ 87.
Beatus ille qui ſibi imperioſus!
If ſocial Virtues make remembrance dear,
Or Manners pure, on decent rule depend;
To His remains conſign one gratefull Tear,
Of Youth the Guardian, and of All the Friend.
Now ſleeps Dominion; Here no Bounty flows;
Nor more avails, the Feſtive Scene to grace;
Beneath that Hand which no diſcernment ſhows,
Untaught to honour, or diſtinguiſh place.
HH
Sacred to the Memory of
ROBERT BROFF Esqr

Colour Plate S: Detail of the figures of Liberality (left) and Genius (right) either side of the 'Batheaston Vase' and a medallion portrait of Lady Anna Miller (d. 1781) from her monument created by John Bacon. © Bath Abbey.

Colour Plate T: Monument to Richard 'Beau' Nash (d. 1761) by John Ford. It was erected in 1791 after Dr Henry Harington invited subscriptions from the Bath public. © Bath Abbey.

Colour Plate U: Group of ledgerstones to members of the Harvey family of sculptors, including 'The Very Ingenious' John Harvey (d. 1742) and his sisters, Sarah (d. 1691/2) and Ann (d. 1696) to the left of it. © Bath Abbey.

Colour Plate V: Tablet to botanist Dr John Sibthorp (d. 1796), centre, by John Flaxman. Sibthorp's Flora Graeca *introduced the plants of Greece to British readers. Consequently, Flaxman's monument alludes to Greek mythology, depicting Sibthorp crossing the River Styx, stepping from Charon's ferry into the underworld. © Bath Abbey.*

Colour Plate W: Detail of monument to Colonel Alexander Champion (d. 1793) by Joseph Nollekens, showing 'Fame *on a pedestal, with her trumpet inverted, holding a medallion of the deceased. A coat of mail, cannon, battle-axe, & warlike trophies, surround the pedestal.' © The author.*

Colour Plate X: Monument to Sir William Baker (d. 1770), centre, by John Francis Moore, erected in the Abbey at the end of August 1776. Its form was altered in the nineteenth century. Notably, the original black marble pyramid has been removed from the background and its pedestal. © Bath Abbey.

Colour Plate Y: John Francis Moore's original design for the monument to Sir William Baker (d. 1770). In the top right of the watercolour is written 'Erected in Walcot Church at Bath'. It seems that it was ultimately decided that Bath Abbey was a more fitting location for the monument. © Victoria and Albert Museum, London.

Colour Plate Z: South wall of the Gethsemane Chapel, South-East Choir. What remains of the monuments with busts to Mary Frampton (d. 1698) and Dorothy Hobart (d. 1722), left and centre, respectively, after the nineteenth-century works. The inscription to Elizabeth Winkley (d. 1756) sits between Frampton and Hobart, her portrait to the right of Hobart. © Bath Abbey.

Opposite:

Colour Plate Z(ii): Inscription tablet from the monument to Mary Frampton (d. 1698) where the text 'by Mr. Dryden' appeared before it was printed as the poem 'The Monument of a Fair Maiden Lady'. © Bath Abbey.

Colour Plate Z(iii): Details of the monument and bust of Dorothy Hobart (d. 1722) by the 'Very Ingenious' Bath sculptor Mr John Harvey. © Bath Abbey.

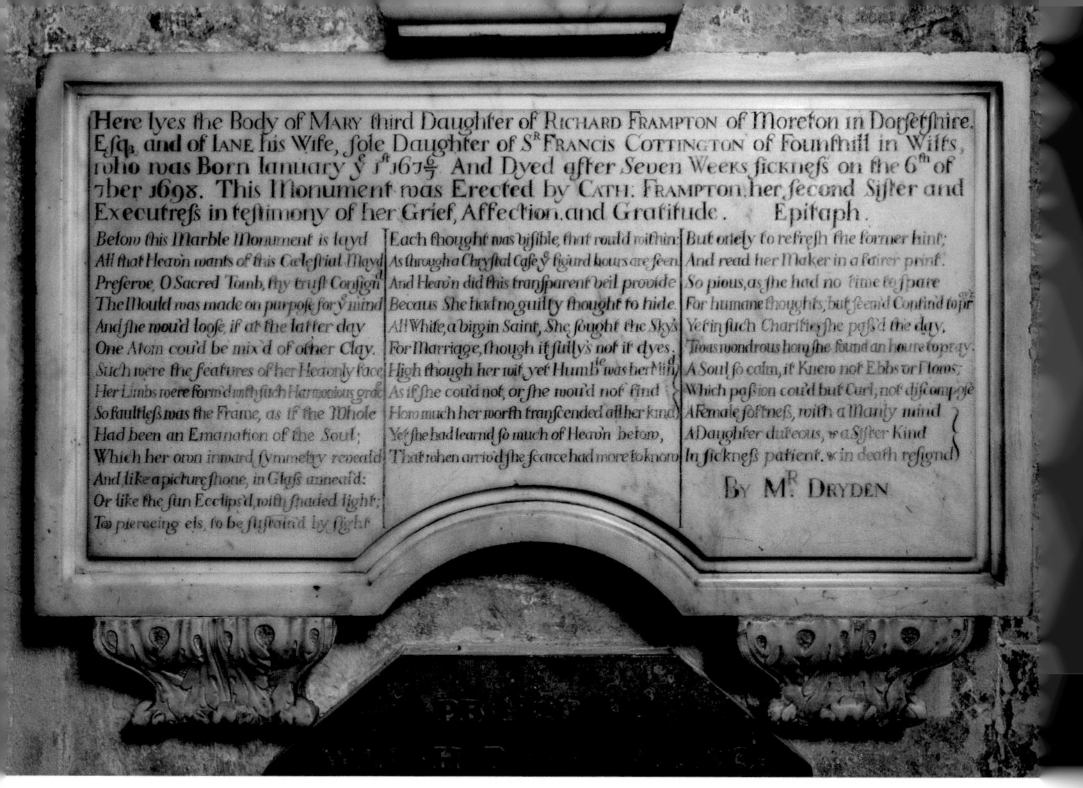
Here lyes the Body of MARY third Daughter of RICHARD FRAMPTON of Moreton in Dorsetshire,
Esqr. and of IANE his Wife, sole Daughter of Sr FRANCIS COTTINGTON of Founthill in Wilts,
who was Born January ye 1st 1676/7 And Dyed after Seven Weeks sickness on the 6th of
7ber 1698. This Monument was Erected by CATH: FRAMPTON her second Sister and
Executress in testimony of her Grief, Affection and Gratitude. Epitaph.
Below this Marble Monument is layd
All that Heav'n wants of this Cælestial Mayd
Preserve, O Sacred Tomb, thy trust Consign'd
The Mould was made on purpose for ye mind
And she wou'd loose, if at the latter day
One Atom cou'd be mix'd of other Clay.
Such were the features of her Heavnly face
Her Limbs were form'd with such Harmonious grace
So faultless was the Frame, as if the Whole
Had been an Emanation of the Soul;
Which her own inward symmetry reveal'd
And like a picture shone, in Glass anneal'd:
Or like the sun Ecclips'd, with shaded light;
Too piercing els, to be sustain'd by sight
Each thought was visible, that would within:
As through a Chrystal Case ye figurd hours are seen
And Heav'n did this transparent veil provide
Becaus She had no guilty thought to hide.
All White, a virgin Saint, She sought the Sky's
For Marriage, though it sully's not it dyes.
High though her wit, yet Humble was her Mind
As if she cou'd not, or she wou'd not find
How much her worth transcended all her kind
Yet she had learnd so much of Heav'n below,
That when arriv'd she scarce had more to know
But onely to refresh the former hint;
And read her Maker in a fairer print.
So pious, as she had no time to spare
For humane thoughts, but seem'd Confin'd to prayr
Yet in such Charities she pass'd the day,
Twas wondrous how she found an houre to pray.
A Soul so calm, it Knew not Ebbs or Flows;
Which passion cou'd but Curl, not discompose
A Female softness, with a Manly mind
A Daughter duteous, & a Sister Kind
In sickness patient, & in death resignd
BY MR DRYDEN

SACRED TO THE MEMORY OF
BENJAMIN ALLEYNE COX OF THE ISLAND
OF BARBADOES ESQre WHO DIED IN THIS CITY
DECr 11TH 1802, AGED 74.
THIS TABLET IS ERECTED TO HIS MEMORY
AS A MARK OF ESTEEM AND GRATITUDE
BY HIS NEPHEW THOMAS YARD ESQre

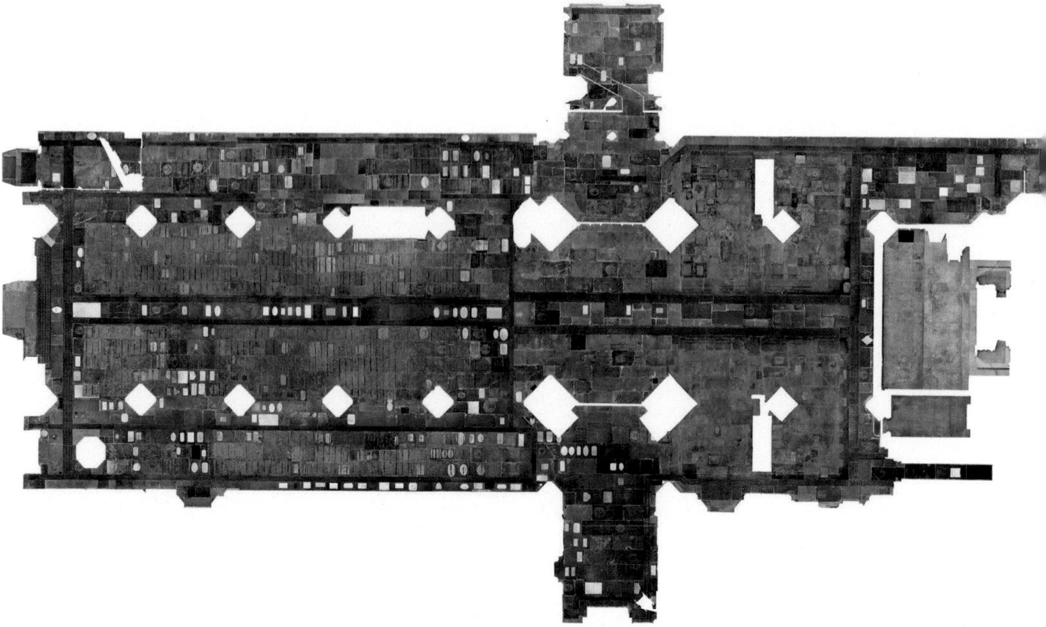

Colour Plate AA: Photogrammetric survey of the Abbey floor after the removal of the Victorian furniture in 2018. It shows the arrangement of the ledgerstones and heating grates after George Gilbert Scott's work 1864–74. Small white marbles can be seen inset into the floor, concentrated in the Nave. © Bath Abbey.

Colour Plate AB: Monument to Henry Harington (d. 1816) by Thomas King (centre). Beneath is the tablet to his daughter-in-law Esther Harington (d. 1829), the only tablet beneath the bench seating in the Choir. This helps to illustrate the different approaches to the Victorian rearrangement of the tablets in the Nave and Choir. © Bath Abbey.

Colour Plate AC: Interior of the Abbey *by J.C. Nattes (1805) showing the Choir looking west. On the left, buildings south of the Abbey block light from the windows. The size, arrangement and placement of monuments under the organ gallery before 1835 can all be seen. © Bath Abbey.*

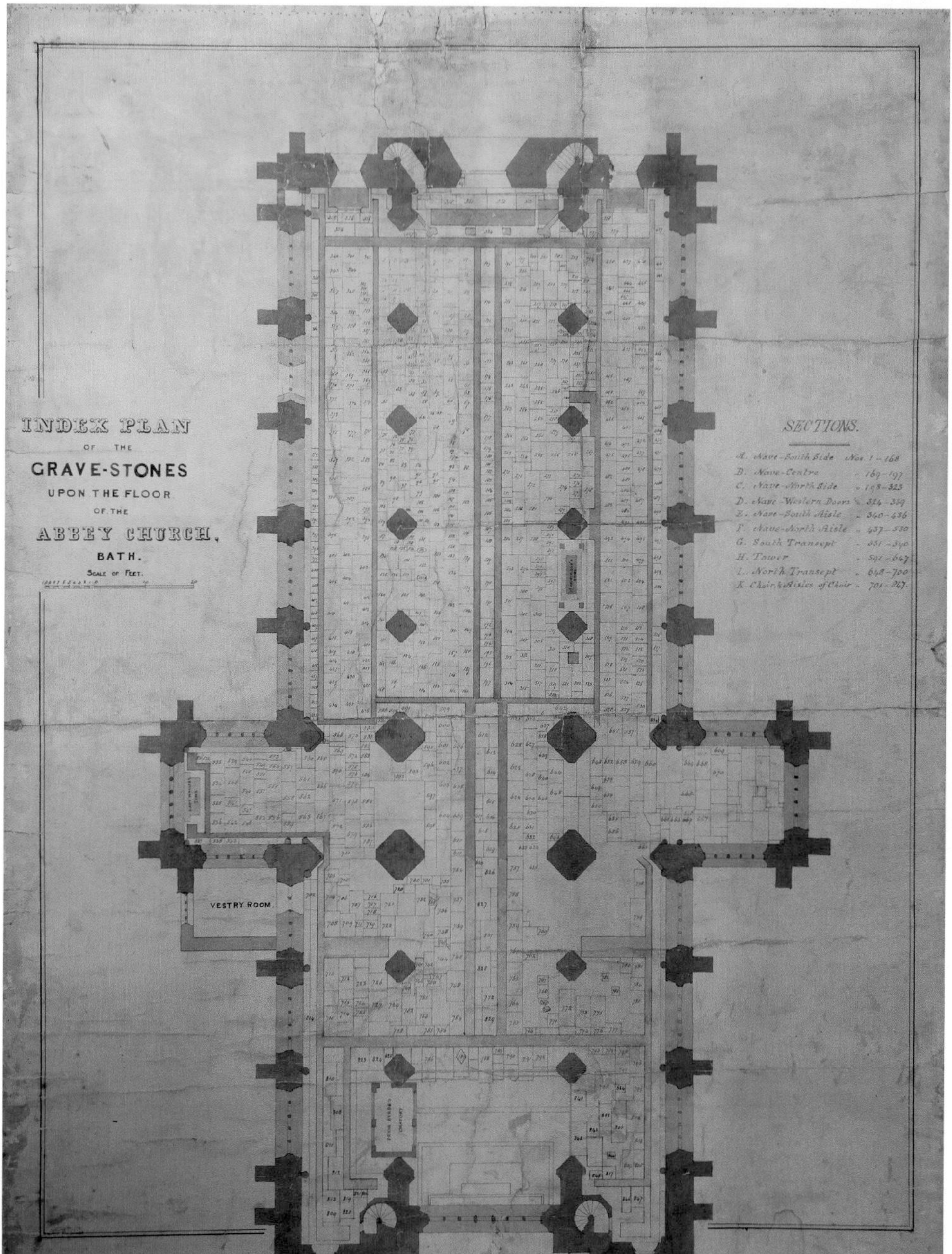

Colour Plate AD: Index Plan of the Grave-Stones upon the Floor of the Abbey Church, Bath *by Charles P. Russell (1872). The blank area on the right, in the North-East Choir, was found to have been paved with many marble backing stones from wall monuments when the Corporation Stalls were removed in 2018. © Bath Abbey.*

Colour Plate AE: The floor of the North-East Choir paved with marble backing stones removed from wall tablets between 1868 and 1872. The outlines of urns, foliage and oval-shaped marbles keyed to receive carvings that originally comprised the tablets can be seen and compared with the designs on the wall behind. © The author.

Colour Plate AF: Arrangement of monuments in the middle bay of the North Nave Aisle. The tablet to Robert Walsh (d. 1788) can be seen in the centre of the bay, with its black marble backing intact, around which the others, which have had their backings removed, have been arranged symmetrically. © Bath Abbey.

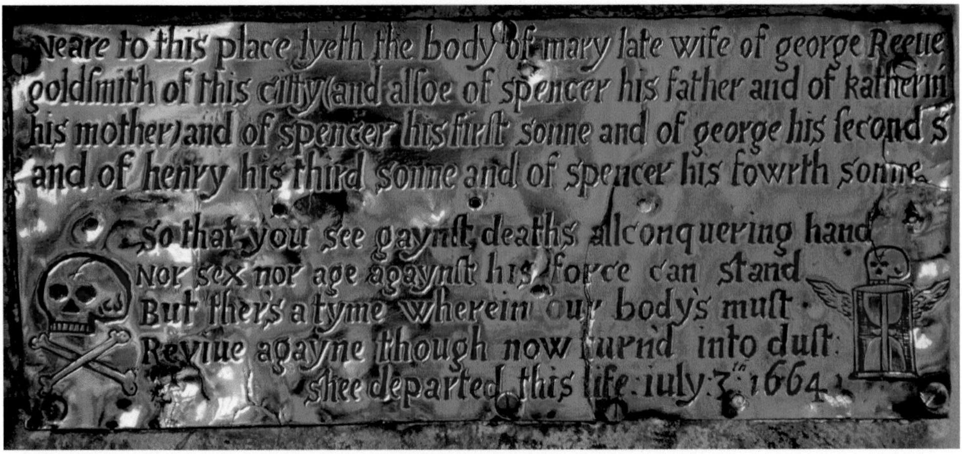

Colour Plate AG: Brass plaque to Mary Reeve (d. 1664) and four of her sons, possibly executed by her husband George Reeve, Bath's city goldsmith. It is all that remains of a larger monument originally erected on a pillar on the south side of the Nave. © Bath Abbey.

Colour Plate AH: Monument to the painter William Hoare (d. 1792). Francis Chantrey was commissioned to make it in 1828 by his son Prince Hoare, who directed that it be 'cleaned with pure water only' annually. This appears to have lapsed. It was specially cleaned in 1902. © Bath Abbey.

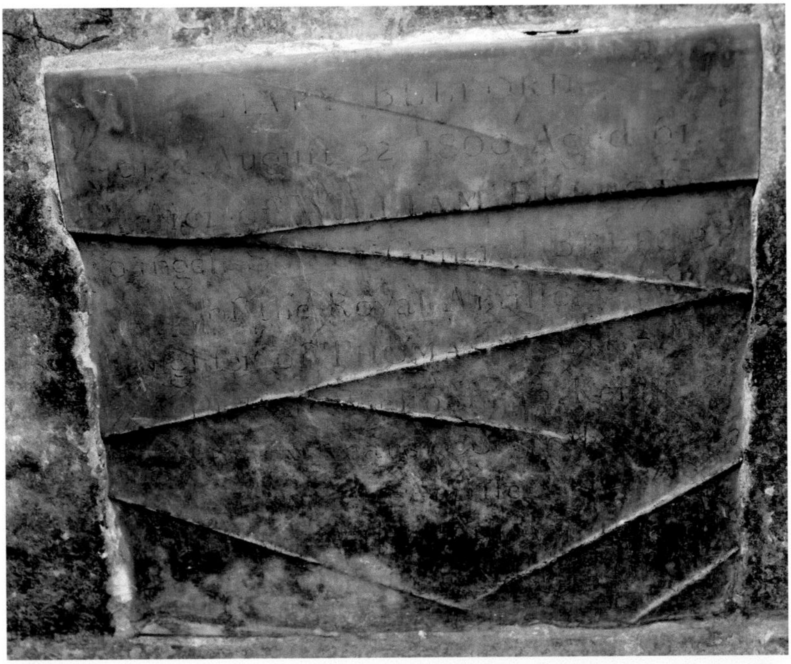

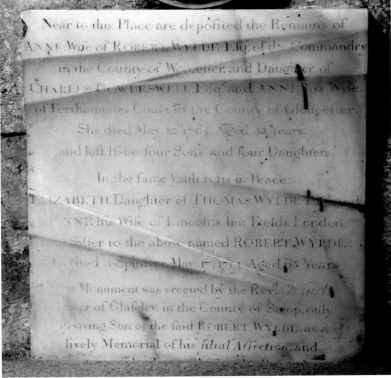

Colour Plate AI: Tablets of similar design to Anne Wylde (d. 1764) and Mary Belford (d. 1800). Mary Belford's tablet was one of six to be 'left dirty, in order to show what some of the monuments were like before the cleaning and conservation work in 1997'. © Bath Abbey.

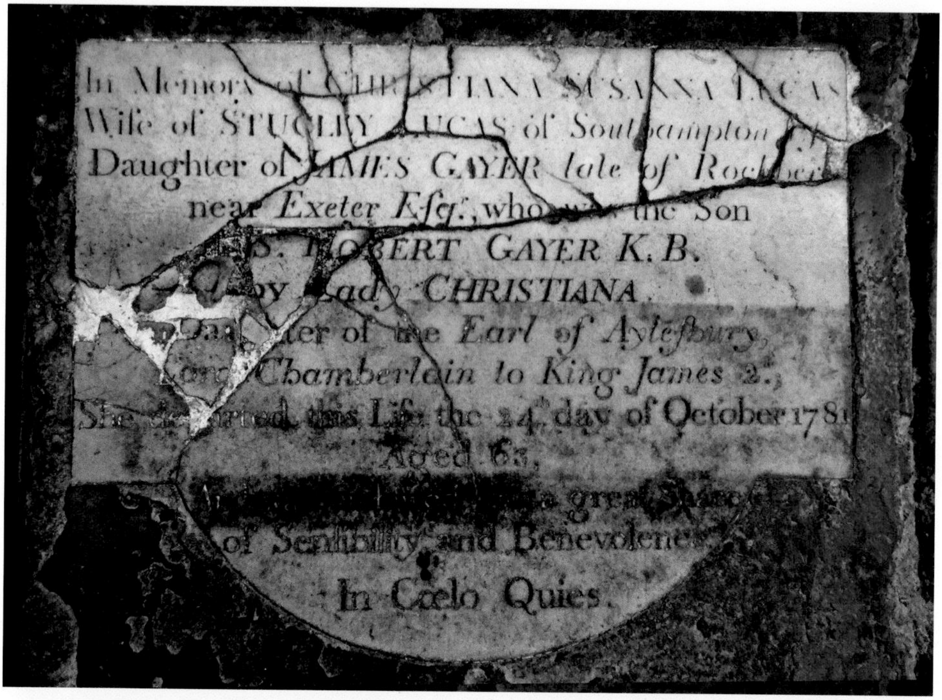

In Memory of
Wife of STUCLEY
of Southampton
Daughter of
late of
near Exeter Efq.,
the Son
ROBERT GAYER K.B.
CHRISTIANA
of the Earl of Aylefbury,
Chamberlain to King James 2.
She departed this Life the 24th day of October 1781
Aged 63.
a great Share
of Senfibility and Benevolence
In Cœlo Quies.

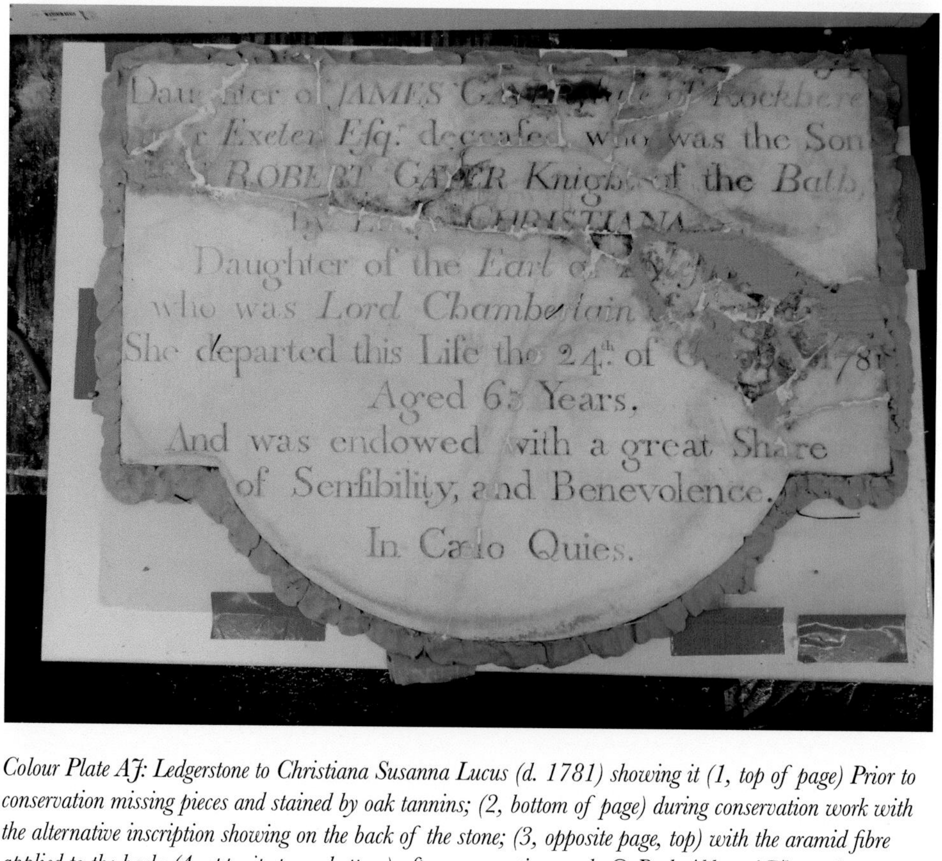

Colour Plate AJ: Ledgerstone to Christiana Susanna Lucus (d. 1781) showing it (1, top of page) Prior to conservation missing pieces and stained by oak tannins; (2, bottom of page) during conservation work with the alternative inscription showing on the back of the stone; (3, opposite page, top) with the aramid fibre applied to the back; (4, opposite page, bottom) after conservation work. © Bath Abbey / The author.

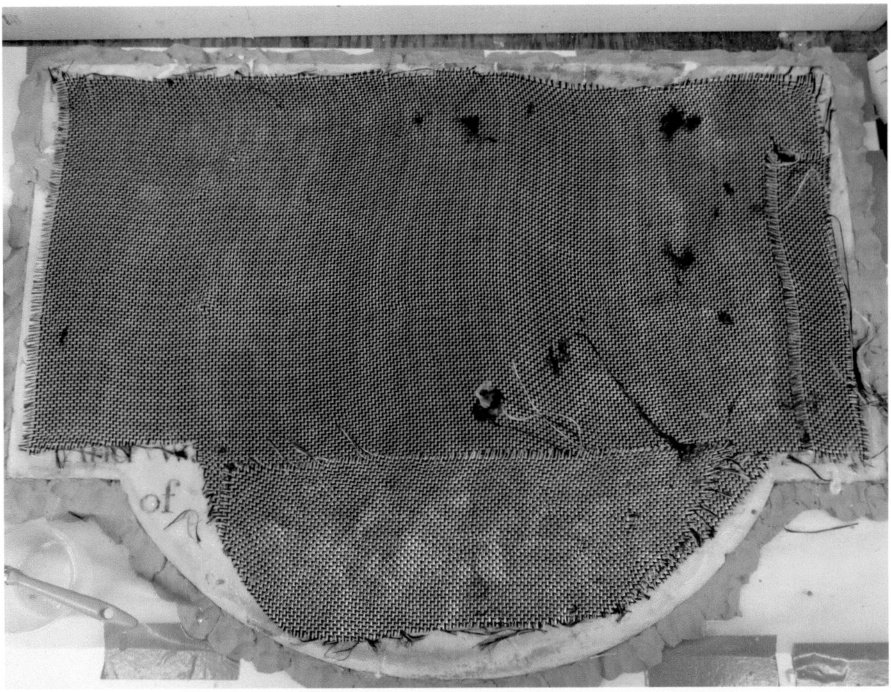
of

In Memory of
Wife of STUC LUCAS of South
Daughter of MES GAYER late of Roc
near Exeter Esq., who the Son
St. ERT GAYER K.B.
by CHRISTIANA
ter of the Earl of Aylesbury,
Chamberlain to King James 2d.;
She rted this Life the 24th day of October 1781
Aged 63,
And was endowed with a great Share
of Sensibility, and Benevolence.
In Cœlo Quies.

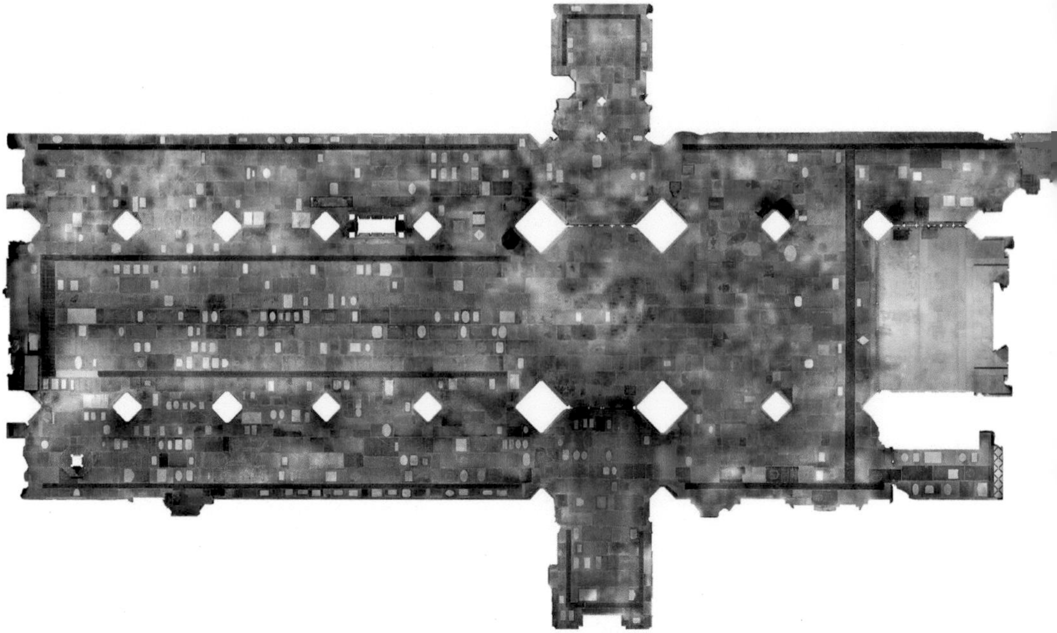

Colour Plate AK: Photogrammetric survey of the Abbey floor in 2021. The image shows the new positions of the ledgerstones and of the heating grates, which may be compared with the arrangement of them in photogrammetric survey of the 1872 arrangement in Colour Plate AA. © Bath Abbey.

Colour Plate AK (ii): Bath Abbey looking east from the west end showing the ledgerstones in the Nave. © Bath Abb

'Honesty, faithfulness, and assiduity': Bath Abbey's sextons, 1700–1807

The installation of a finished monument or ledgerstone in the Abbey was the end of a process involving a number of people. As we have seen, sculptors, both from Bath and London, acted as go-betweens for the families commissioning monuments and the church to arrange the Abbey's fees. The Abbey's sextons played pivotal roles in receiving these fees on behalf of the church and coordinating the installation of monuments. In the most practical sense, they were the men who stood thigh-deep in grave-earth, preparing the ground for corpses to be interred and ensuring that ledgerstones were (re)placed respectfully over them. However, they were also authorities on and guides to the monuments for the Abbey's increasing number of tourists, as well as discharging a number of other duties on behalf of the parish. Who were the Abbey's sextons, how did one become one, what did they do, and how were they regarded in the eighteenth century?

We have seen that writers such as Pepys and Fuller passed fleeting comment on the Abbey's seventeenth-century sextons. However, it is not until the middle of the eighteenth century that a rounded picture of the sextons begins to emerge. Early eighteenth-century records concerning the Abbey's sextons are patchy. After the death of the sexton 'John Davice' in 1700, the records are silent on the role until 1711. Whilst sidesmen and churchwardens were elected to their offices annually, this does not seem to have been the case for sextons, who appear to have held their posts for years, sometimes without being formally elected. Such was the case for Isaac Warren, whose displacement from and re-election to the office took place at a meeting of the Abbey's vestry on 27 December 1711. The minutes record that Warren, 'having officiated as Sexton of this Church without being duly Elected and contrary to ye Consent of the Parishoners [sic] of this Parish', was 'displaced from being Sexton' by unanimous vote of twenty to none. The only other item of business recorded at the meeting was an agreement, by the same margin, to officially elect Isaac Warren to 'be Sexton of this Parish'.[167] Warren was therefore the likely recipient of the payment of the 4*s* 'Pd the Sexton by Mr. Mayors order' in the city's Chamberlain's Accounts in 1720–21. This is probably an occasional payment rather than a reflection of a salary. Warren was buried in the Abbey on 25 January 1728 and appears to have held the office continuously until his death.

The following week the vestry met to appoint Warren's successor, 'John Blatchly of the sd. City Pastry Cook', who was elected sexton 'by a great Majority of Votes'.[168] Blatchly appears to have held the office for even longer than Warren, as shown by the burial register, which records the burial of 'John Blatchly, sexstone' on 21 October 1749. In the early eighteenth century, the Abbey looked after its own. Blatchly's son, John, who was also a pastry cook, was buried at the Abbey at night 'after which a Funeral Peal was rang, with the Bells muffled'[169] on 17 June 1761. Two funerals took place in the Abbey on 17 June, for which only one payment of 1*s* was made.[170] These accounts suggest that the usually substantial fees for burial at night and bell-ringing were waved for the former sexton's son. In March 1778, Mr John Hay was buried under 'Jno [sic] Blatchley's Stone in ye South Isle'. No fees were paid for Blatchley's stone in 1761, and Elizabeth Blatchley's burial in October 1774 was marked 'Poor' in the register, indicating that no fee was paid. As we will see, in the nineteenth century, the parish did not always take such good care of its sextons' families.

Blatchly was probably succeeded by John Bretton, a cooper. Although there is no extant record of Bretton's election, he witnessed at least seven marriages per year at the Abbey from 1754–58, many with James Davis, a clerk whose son was apprenticed to him. Like his predecessors, the entry in the register recording Bretton's burial in the Abbey on 22 July 1765 is dignified with his title: 'John Bretton, sexton of this parish'. Three days later, the following advertisement was placed in *The Bath Chronicle*:

> To the Inhabitants of the Parish of St. PETER and PAUL, in the City of BATH.
>
> THE Office of SEXTON of the said Parish being now vacant, by the Death of Mr. BRETTON; at the Desire of many of my Friends, I take this Opportunity (having a large Family to provide for) to offer myself a Candidate for the same. Shou'd I be so fortunate as to succeed, it will be my constant Study to give entire Satisfaction in the said Office; and I shall always have a grateful Remembrance of the Favours conferr'd on, Your much oblig'd, And most obedient humble Servant, MATHIAS WALTER.[171]

By the 1780s and 1790s, other prospective sextons of Bath's parish churches would follow Walter's example of using the newspaper to canvas support from parishioners. Like Bretton, Mathias Walter, a cabinetmaker, would have been a competent woodworker whose skills may have been helpful when wooden coffins were required. Walter's successor, William Handcock, was also a cabinetmaker. They would all certainly have been handy men, ones able to fulfil the manual duties of the sexton, such as digging graves, lifting and replacing ledgerstones, and helping to erect monuments. However, the Abbey delayed in

Walter's appointment. On 24 October, over three months after Bretton's death, Walter took out another advertisement in *The Bath Chronicle*:

> It being determined, at a Vestry held on Friday last, that there shou'd be more than one Person employed to execute the Office of SEXTON of the Parish of St. Peter and Paul in the City of Bath; MATHIAS WALTER, of the said Parish, humbly begs Leave to offer himself for such Part of it as the Gentlemen of the Parish shall think him capable of; and should he be so fortunate as to succeed, he will use his most Endeavours to merit their Approbation.[172]

Having more than one person acting as sexton was not a new practice for the Abbey (we have seen that Edward Wright was only 'one of ye sextons' in 1620). But as with Isaac Warren's election above, perhaps it was one the vestry wanted to formalise. Even so, it was not until 11 March 1766 that Mathias Walter was elected sexton 'by a very great Majority'. Naturally, Walter took to the newspaper again to 'take the earliest Opportunity of returning (in this public Manner)' his 'most grateful Thanks'. At the same time, he assured them once again, that he would use his 'utmost Endeavours to give entire Satisfaction'.[173] Certainly, John Penrose was impressed with the skill with which Walter managed to bury Ann Parker Wynter in May 1766, only needing to lift two existing ledgerstones from the floor to make her grave: 'not above two Stone's cast off'.[174]

Walter's advertisements reveal how desirable the office of sexton was as a way of supplementing a parishioner's regular income, the extremely public nature of the role, and that, for the Abbey, the amount of work necessitated two people to carry it out by the end of the eighteenth century. It seems that, from this time, the duties of the role at the Abbey were often shared between husbands and their wives. This was not uncommon, and as Wanda Henry observes, during 'the eighteenth and nineteenth centuries, women sextons were ubiquitous in England'.[175] Whilst some female sextons, such as Hester Hammerton, did dig graves, at the Abbey it seems that traditional gender roles generally prevailed: the men did the more physically demanding parts of the job; the women cleaned the church, opened the pews, kept the doors. That being said, *Gye's Bath Directory* for 1819 shows that by the early nineteenth century a number of sextons in Bath were women, although not at the Abbey, St James', or St Michael's.[176] The Abbey sexton also kept a set of keys to the fire 'Engine-House' in Orange Grove.

Elizabeth Walter (nee Bishop), Matthias's wife, was, according to Reverend John Penrose, a refined if slightly unreliable sexton. She was probably the 'Sexton-Woman' who, wearing 'a Silk Cardinal and Bonnet', Penrose described as 'very genteel', a good quality for someone opening pews for visitors to the city like Penrose.[177] However, writing to his daughter Peggy on 1 May 1766, Penrose told her of 'a singular adventure':

> When I came to the Abbey this Afternoon to read Prayers, the Vestry was locked, and Miss Sexton gone away, no body knew where, with the Key: so that after waiting, and keeping the Congregation waiting, a Quarter of an Hour, I was forced to desire the Clark to go to a neighbouring Church to borrow a Surplice.[178]

Complaints about the sextons were not uncommon (and generally reveal more about the snobbery of the plaintiffs than the conduct of the sextons). The Walters' successors were publicly reprimanded in the newspaper after 'the Sexton and the Pew-Women' were 'negligent in opening the Pew Doors for receiving the People, and keeping good Order in the Church'. They were 'ordered by the Churchwardens to be more diligent for the future'.[179] Such complaints smack of a disdain for working-class people by certain impious and pompous visitors to the city and Abbey. Whether such people even desired for pews to be opened for them might not have always been clear-cut: Penrose himself observed on more than one occasion a lady brought into the Abbey 'in a Sedan, and placed before the Reading Desk in the Alley, and remained in it all Service Time'. This was, he wrote, 'no uncommon thing'.[180] Certainly, Matthias Walter's obituary in 1771 speaks of him as 'a man much respected for his honesty, faithfulness, and assiduity' as sexton. By then the large family he had provided for had grown to 'a widow and seven children, four of them unprovided for' at his death. Like her late husband, Elizabeth Walter took to the newspaper to implore the parishioners to consider 'her diligent attendance on the duties of the church during her husband's long illness' and permit her 'to continue in the office of keeping the church clean' to 'enable her to provide for her family'.[181] Upon the death of Mr William Handcock (sometimes Hancock), the Walters' successor as Abbey sexton, on 16 August 1792, aged 68, a similar plea was made on behalf of his widow by the newspaper: 'His widow, by whom the office of Sexton has been conducted with great propriety during a very long and expensive illness of her husband, will, it is hoped, be continued in that station by the benevolence of the parishioners.'[182]

The Abbey sexton was, amongst other things, a guide to strangers to the Abbey, especially to its monuments. Whilst William Handcock is only named as the seller rather than the author of the guide to the Abbey and monuments published in 1778, his knowledge of the latter, especially those added after the first edition was published, must have helped to inform and probably to compile it. After all, it is consciously structured as a tour around the monuments, perhaps similar to those Handcock gave to visitors in person. It would be easy to think of Handcock as a simple cabinetmaker, but he seems to have come from an educated family able to interpret Latin inscriptions. In 1788, possibly during William Handcock's 'very long and expensive illness', his father, Thomas, appears to have assumed the role of sexton, as can be seen from the piece signed 'T.H. Sexton', which was published in *The Bath Chronicle* on 15 May:

> The *Sexton of the Abbey* presents his compliments to the public, and finding many wagers depending upon the meaning of the following inscription, and variety of conjectures among the learned, humbly offers *his own*, upon the authority of *Gruterus*, well skilled in classical antiquities.
>
> Although the Sexton acknowledges himself much favoured by the *opinions* of the *Sons of Aesculapius*, and under the *greatest obligations*, yet is inclined to think that the *Daughter* is rather alluded to on the present occasion. T. H. Sexton.
>
> HYGEIAE
> AESCULAPII FILIAE,
> THERMULAE VOTIVAE;
> A.C. 1788.
> SUB
> LEONARDO COWARD,
> PRAETORE URBANO,
> PUBLICO SUMPTU CURATAE.
> T. BALDWIN, extruxit.
> Translated.
> Private Warm Baths
> Devoted to Hygeia,
> Daughter of AEsculapius,
> A.C. 1788,
> Provided at the Public Expence,
> In the time of LEONARD COWARD,
> Mayor of the City.
> T. BALDWIN, Architect.[183]

The piece is obviously tongue-in-cheek, but it also illustrates the Handcocks' standing, education, confidence and wherewithal to take to the public stage to interpret a recent public inscription (the above appeared on the foundation stone laid by Leonard Coward of the Baths in Stall Street). Such self-assurance must have come, in part, from the experience and facility of interpreting the Abbey's church monuments. As we can see, James Tunstall was right to say the inscription 'caused much mirth to the wits of the day'[184] and we must count the Abbey's sexton, Handcock, amongst those wits of late eighteenth-century Bath. Handcock's piece attracted a response from the anonymous 'AE', who only half-jokingly took issue with his interpretation:

> *To the* SEXTON *of the* ABBEY.
>
> Mr. SEXTON,
>
> AS I take it for granted you are a good Christian, as well as a good Antiquary, I should be glad to be informed, with what propriety these New Baths are dedicated to an Heathen Goddess, in a Christian country, and in the year of Christ 1788.
>
> Modern Poets often allude to Hygeia, as an allegorical deity; but in plain prose, the Baths might as well as have been inscribed to the Virgin Mary, as to the nymph Hygeia.[185]

AE's response is obviously as much a critique of the absurdity of the inscription itself as it is a dig at Handcock's piece the week earlier. But it also cannot be disentangled entirely from the slightly supercilious attitude towards sextons by Penrose and others writing in the newspaper at the end of the eighteenth century.

Whilst many of the Abbey's sextons were intelligent men and genteel women, part of their job required nothing less than a strong stomach. In the same year that William Handcock began to sell the guide to the Abbey's monuments, Philip Thicknesse published *The New Prose Guide to Bath for the Year 1778.*[186] In it, Thicknesse doubted 'whether the *Abbey Church* [was] not, on many Accounts, a very improper Place (except to People in full Health) to attend Divine Service at'. One reason for this was, according to Thicknesse, the 'vast Number of Bodies buried within the Church, and *near the Surface*, and the Frequency of the Ground being opened, before the Effect of Putrefaction [was] over'. Neither were the doors or windows kept sufficiently open, rendering 'the confined Air perceptibly disagreeable at first entering the Church'. An opening or 'Ventilator' in the roof seems not to have helped. If anyone should 'place their

Nose' over it, Thicknesse claimed, 'they will meet, at *all Times*, a Stench scarce to be imagined'. Thicknesse even insinuated that the 'malignant, sore Throat' then 'not very uncommon at BATH' might have been caused by that 'Source of Corruption'. St James', St Michael's and the chapels were, Thicknesse urged his readers, 'certainly preferable to the *Abbey*'.[187] Anxieties about the length of time burials were left undisturbed and the judgement of the sexton were felt by Dr Robert Peirce a century earlier. Thicknesse's passage suggests that the increase in the numbers of visitors to the city had not eased either the anxiety or the pressure on space for intramural burial.

The reputation that the Abbey had for being crowded with burials at the end of the eighteenth century was also recorded by Richard Sheridan in his play *The Rivals* (1775), set in Bath, in which the character Sir Lucius O'Trigger is told 'there is very snug lying in the Abbey' should he be killed in a duel. The frequency with which gravedigging took place in the Abbey meant that both earlier burials and archaeology were disturbed: 'A chalice was found in the North transept of the abbey church of Bath, in a stone coffin, wherein were also leather soles of shoes, and what the sexton called short tobacco pipes.'[188] For Thomas Handcock, the 'good Antiquary', such discoveries must have been one of the only occasional perks of an otherwise grim, almost everyday job.

Looking again at the Abbey's burial register for 1774–92, which overlaps entirely with the period in which the Handcocks were sextons, we can see the often pragmatic decisions made by them when approaching burials in the Abbey. The entries for November 1775 illustrate the frequency with which disparate areas of the floor were being taken up for burials: on the 5th 'ye white Stones at ye foot of Mr Ryder's Stone in the Middle Isle by the Bishop's Monument' on the north side of the Nave, the following day (the 6th) 'ye white Stones at the head of Mr Veasey's [Vesey's] Stone by ye Christning Vaunt' in the South Transept, on the 19th 'the foot of Mr Matthew's Stone Opposite ye Abbey House Garden door' on the south side of what the register called the 'Middle Isle', two days later (the 21st) 'Mr. Flood's Stone' in the 'N.[orth] Isle', on the 26th 'ye blue Stone at ye right side of Dr. Butt's Stone in ye South Isle', and finally on the last day of the month (the 30th) 'under Mr Reddall's Stone between ye Pillars opposite Dr Oliver's Monument'.[189] Raising the stones, preparing the grave, and replacing the stones for six burials would have been back-breaking work in the cold days of freezing ground at the year's end. As far as possible, it seems that the sextons tried to spread burials out in the church to minimise the disturbance of recent burials (and the consequent effect on those who usually worshipped in those areas), as can be seen in the alternation between the North and South Aisles in 1776 and many subsequent years. However, where family members died within days or weeks of each other, the same stone would be lifted to accommodate their burial together, even when the burials did not take place beneath a family stone, as can be seen from the burial of the Ralls' children, James and Ann, who were each 'Buried in ye Church under Mr. Deverel's Stone in the South Isle' on 6 and 17 March respectively.

Certain stones, such as that to Captain Edward Arlond in the middle of the Nave, were used repeatedly by the Handocks, even where there was no obvious familial connection between the deceased. This may have had as much to do with the position and size of the stone being easier to raise as anything. Even when the same stone wasn't used to cover multiple interments, the fact that it had been raised obviously made it easier to raise others next to it, such as in May 1778 when Osborne Ewing was buried 'under their own Stone in ye Cross Isle by ye Engins' on the 19th, making it easier for Benjamin Vassas to be buried 'under ye blue Stone by the side of Mr Ewing's in ye Cross Isle by ye Engins' the following day. A recently replaced stone would also have been easier to lift again, as can be seen by the lifting of Mr James Fisher's stone in the South Aisle to cover two different burials a week apart in November 1786.

From the middle of 1787, the burial register shows the sexton beginning to work in particular zones for increasing amounts of time. The reason for this is obscure but may be related to a direction from the new rector, James Phillott, or to Thomas Handcock taking on his son's duties when William's health prevented him from discharging them. In May and June 1787, burials took place in the North Aisle and North Transept (a pattern repeated from May to September 1789). From January to May 1788, burials took place almost exclusively in the Middle and North Aisles, whereas between October 1789 and March 1790 burials almost exclusively took place in the Middle and South Aisles. Between June and December 1790, burials took place almost exclusively in the Middle Aisle, then from December 1790 to March 1791 they took place on the south side of the church, before returning to the pattern of alternating between the north, south and centre of the Nave common in the late 1770s.

Given this work and the working conditions, it is hard to imagine any of the Abbey's sextons carrying out their duties with anything less than 'honesty, faithfulness, and assiduity'. In the midst of the 'irreverence that prevail[ed] throughout a large part of this venerable House of God'[190] by 1801, the sextons brought an air of decorum and welcome as best they could. The anonymous author of the critical tract on Bath's public worship found the pew opener (probably the sexton or his wife) one of the few redeeming aspects of a service at the Abbey: 'I can quietly take my seat there unannoyed by the extortion and rudeness of a pew opener.'[191] The income that the office provided was an important supplement to their professional income as coopers, cabinetmakers and pastry chefs. But they must be seen, first and foremost, as practical men and women who served the Abbey and supplemented their professional incomes through their sense of vocation to their parish church.

In 1802, 'the Sexton of the Abbey-church, Bath, by trade a taylor' won a share of the £20,000 prize in the English State Lottery.[192] There can have been few more deserving of a stroke of luck. With the exception of the pastry chef, these coopers, cabinetmakers and tailors would have brought desirable practical skills to a role that dealt with wooden coffins and battens to lift ledgerstones and well-used funeral silks in need of repair. St James' Church also had sextons who were carpenters by the 1790s. Although in 1801, the 22-year-old Peter Lidiard, the third member of his family to hold the role, blemished their reputation by eloping, leaving his family chargeable to the parish. A reward of two guineas for his arrest was issued by the overseers for this curly-haired, smooth-faced scoundrel, of decent appearance.[193] Whilst the Abbey's sextons appear to have been generally well-respected, the scrutiny of those in the role, a slight disdain for their intelligence and criticism of their work when it was wanting was never far away. We will see in the following chapter the dedicated service of William Skrine and Samuel Rogers as Abbey sextons, and what the records they have left behind tell us about the role and the Abbey's monuments in the nineteenth century.

'The gloomy mansions of the dead': Conclusion

On 16 July 1770, a poem written by 'The INVALID', 'On a ROBIN, which strayed into the Abbey, during Divine Service', appeared in *The Bath Chronicle*. Its opening quatrain is indicative of the how the volume of monuments had caused the Abbey to be characterised in literature by the end of the eighteenth century: 'Sweet Bird, which in this melancholy shade, / Where many a trav'ller rests his weary head, / Serenely twits thy tranquil hour away, / Amid this cool retreat, at blaze of day'. Cold and melancholy like the white statuary marble covering its walls, the Abbey was a place where many visitors to the city rested for eternity. By the end of the century such euphemisms were dispensed with by the author of another poem, 'On viewing the Monuments in the Abbey Church at Bath', which appeared in the *Weekly Entertainer* in August 1799:

Now I tread, or seem to tread,
The gloomy mansions of the dead;
Silent and still the sleeper lies,
Clos'd, for ever clos'd his eyes!

Moulders here the lovely face,
Ere while array'd with winning grace;
The pow'rful limb, the stately form,
The prey, ah me! of the devouring worm.

Hither turn thee, lofty pride,
Turn, and for a moment deign
To lay thy witless scorn aside,
And glance oblique of insolent disdain.

Here the high-born and the brave,
The wife, the beauteous, and the strong,
(An undistinguish'd throng)
Are laid together in the peaceful grave.

Closed, for ever closed their eyes,
'Till the day-spring shall arise,
'Till the final morn unfold
Her orient portal bright with gold.

Usher the beams of everlasting light,
Annihilate the power of night,
Burst the fetters of the tomb,
And summon all that sleep to their eternal doom.

The poet's description of the burials and ledgerstones ('An undistinguish'd throng') might be equally applied to the monuments by the end of the century: 'Moulders' captures perfectly the Abbey's atmosphere described by Thicknesse, Smollett and others. Whereas Mary Chandler would pick out Montagu and Frampton for special celebration in verse at the beginning of the century, the overwhelming number of monuments led writers by the end of the century to either describe the Abbey, as this poet did, as a sombre mausoleum, or simply note, as John Penrose did, the 'innumerable Monuments, the Walls and

Pillars being lined with them'.[194] The eighteenth-century surveys, guides, lists and newspaper reports of the Abbey's monuments that had lauded them gave way to critical assessments of the monuments' tastefulness, arrangement and negative effect on the worship space and visitors in the nineteenth century. None more strongly, at the beginning of the century at least, than in Feltham's *Guide to all the Watering and Sea-Bathing Places* (1806), which warned its readers that 'a walk in the Abbey, must fill every reflecting mind with the most serious thoughts, even in the enjoyment of the highest health; and, on invalids, it must have a very injurious effect. Not a pillar, a portion of the wall, or a yard of the floor, but records mortality'.[195] It is tempting to see the 'mat' that had been placed over the ledgerstones where the congregation sat 'in the chancel' (but not in the Nave)[196] by 1801 not only as a response to the frequent comments about the coldness of the Abbey and its smells, but also as an attempt to conceal at least some of the scale of the interments.

The history of the monuments to Beau Nash and Sir William Baker and the celebration of new monumental sculptures (often from London) by *The Bath Chronicle* suggest a conscious and intentional approach by the Abbey and city to create a desirable interior and identity for the church through its monuments. The intention seems to have been for it to appeal to the city's often unwell visitors who might, in turn, be buried and commemorated there. The narrative that monuments like those to Nash and Baker told to its visitors were ones that amplified eighteenth-century values of decorum (Nash), patriotism (Baker) and, as with many other monuments throughout the country, implored visitors not only to shed tears for the deceased but to emulate their charitable acts, often to the benefit of the parish or city. The guides to the monuments sold by the sextons and the way in which the Abbey's rectors increased their fees throughout the century, worked with the city's undertakers and cloth dealers to maximise profit from funerals, and positioned monuments in the church (e.g. Bosanquet) illustrate this approach.

The monuments had come to define the appearance of the interior, having become a tourist attraction in their own right, as much as the sculpture of the West Front defined the exterior. The Abbey's 'monstrous high' fees for burial gained it a reputation for being the place of rest and commemoration for the city's wealthiest visitors, and with that came their monuments. The pride taken in the work to create and install these monuments, by the sextons and local sculptors, like King and Harvey, is clear. Their work, as much as the celebrated London sculptors, helped to create the character of the space, the civic pride in which was registered by Warner in 1801 in his description of the 'elegant

Sacred to the Memory of
ANDREW BARKLEY Esq.r late a
Post Captain in his Majesty's Royal Navy
who departed this Life January 30th 1790:
Aged 49 Years.
He Married ELIZABETH WILLIS.
one of the Daughters of RICHARD WILLIS of Digswell
in the County of Hertford Esq.r deceased:
who out of respect to the Memory of her most
affectionate Husband has caused this Monument
to be erected.
Also of ELIZABETH Relict of the above named
ANDREW BARKLEY Esq.r
who died 17th December 1800.
Also of JOHN BARKLEY Esq.r his Nephew
who died 16th December 1822, Aged 74 Years
MARTHA CAROLINE

Fig.18: The 'elegant' monument to Andrew Barkley (d. 1790) by Thomas King. © Bath Abbey.

monument' to Captain Barkley (d. 1790) of the Royal Navy: 'It does great credit to the skill of Mr. King, sculptor, of this city, whose art has contributed greatly to ornament this venerable pile' (Fig. 18).[197] As a group, the Abbey's monuments were therefore a statement about the sophistication of Bath, a collection of monuments to rival those of the churches of London, and an echo of the local pride in the ability of the city's masons to define and beautify the city's church, just as they had done a century before. However, as we will see, this view of the effect of local sculpture on the aesthetics of the Abbey was not shared by all.

HARVEY
Near this place lies buried DOROTHY
sixth Daughter of Sr HENRY HOBART of Blick
inge in the County of Norfolk, Bar: deceas'd.
She was born the second day of April 1697.
And died the day of October 1722.
To whose memory this is erected by her affec-
tionate Sister CATHARINE CHURCHILL

3

RENOVATION

'SUCH UNDISTINGUISHING ACCUMULATIONS OF SEPULCHRAL TRIFLING', 1807–1885

One of the most often-quoted (and misquoted) descriptions of the Abbey's monuments in the nineteenth century was made by the doctor, composer and writer Henry Harington (d. 1816). The summer before his death, Harington, like many other authors, took a walk in the Abbey. Turning to his son-in-law, who accompanied him: '"Come," said he, "let us choose a spot for my old bones".' Such a response to the Abbey's monuments was not unusual, as we have seen from Fanny Burney and others in the previous chapter. Gathering himself, he said, suddenly:

> These ancient walls, with many a mouldering bust,
> But show how well Bath waters lay the dust.[1]

Harington's own tablet is an exception to his rule. Along with the tablet that he helped raise to Beau Nash, as well as many others installed in the two centuries before his death, the Abbey's monuments show that commemorating the civic elite was just as important as enabling those who visited Bath for the waters to be remembered. As we will see, Harington's own monument was as well-regarded as its subject, and indeed, as complimented as any tablet in the Abbey in the early nineteenth century. However, by the end of the century opinion had

Opposite: Details of the monument and bust of Dorothy Hobart (d. 1722) by the 'Very Ingenious' Bath sculptor Mr John Harvey. © Bath Abbey.

changed. Harington, in Reverend George Wright's opinion, was 'honoured with a tomb, unequal in all respects to his worth. The grotesque organ at the top, suggests an equivoque – the leaves of music, the less of his great acquirements – the books, nothing definite' (Colour Plate AB).[2] In line with the national trend, by the middle of the nineteenth century marble monuments were beginning to fall out of fashion, with a 'sharp decline' after the 1840s:

> After 1850 more and more people agreed that it was more suitable to erect a window or to even a church to someone's memory, than to block a window by a large monument or to turn a church into a family mortuary chapel. Also with the opening of the new suburban garden cemeteries, burial in church vaults became less essential for the upper-classes.[3]

This is especially true of the Abbey's monuments, in particular the ongoing conflict between the amount of light able to enter the Abbey's windows and the wall tablets. The effect of this in the 1840s was threefold. First, it reignited and intensified the already heated and largely negative assessments of the Abbey's monuments only a few years after George Philips Manners's rearrangement of them as part of his works to the interior from 1835. Secondly, Bath's monumental masons for whom intramural tablets had been a stock-in-trade suffered: Reeves & Son, who have more signed monuments in Bath churches than any other firm, went bankrupt in 1849. *The Bath Chronicle* announced that on 21 February their stock would be auctioned, including '2 Specimen Tables; 1 Pier ditto; 10 Monumental Tablets of chaste design' and 'About 600 Original Designs of Chimney Pieces, Monuments, Tablets, Tombs, &c., adapted for Cemeteries; several valuable Books of Designs'.[4] Thirdly, the Abbey's revenue from monuments declined, placing greater importance on other streams of income, such as offerings and pew rents, to keep the building (and the monuments) in a good state of repair. Between 1801 and 1845, 390 ledgerstones and 293 tablets had been installed in the Abbey, contributing £2,012 9*s* 2½*d* to its income.

On 12 February 1844, the first burial took place in the Abbey's new garden cemetery designed by J.C. Loudon. Burial in the Abbey ceased the following year. By then, the smell of and subsidence caused by the burials was no longer tolerable. However, early in the nineteenth century, the floor was not as badly regarded as it would be after 1825. A year before Harington's death, a fellow Bath doctor, William Bowen (d. 1815), Jane Austen's apothecary and Bath City Council member, was buried in the Abbey. The inscription on his ledgerstone, although slightly conventional in its address to the reader, is noteworthy for the way in which it is tailored to a typical visitor to Bath (who would visit the city for the waters and the Abbey for its monuments) and for its description of the Abbey's entire pavement (not simply Bowen's own stone) as 'this sacred floor':

> Here Bowen lies! whose health restoring art
> Was but inferior to his feeling heart;
> Perchance you now who tread this sacred floor
> Breathe by his skill who breathes alas! no more.
> Think oh how soon! his noble spirit fled,
> Think he who sav'd the dying here lies dead;
> Moisten with grateful tears his Mournful Stone
> And with a widow's sorrows blend your own.
> Tho' cold the hand that cured, the hand that gave
> His genial bounty reach'd beyond the grave;
> The liberal current of his generous mind
> Flowed in a boundless stream to all mankind.

With the Abbey cemetery open, intramural burial ceased in the church in January 1845, fittingly, with interments from two local families, the Prests (William Prest was a churchwarden from 1843) and the Helicars (from Bristol). Robert Brooke's double ledgerstone shows that the church intended to honour the burial of others in family vaults. The left-hand side commemorates Robert's death on 10 December 1843; the right-hand side was left blank for his widow, Elizabeth. However, the 1852 Burial Act would have made any such intentions and assurances void, stopping burial inside churches altogether.[5] This and the opening of the Abbey's cemetery brought the laying of ledgerstones in the Abbey to an end (and in the case of the Brookes, the placement of the Corporation Stalls over the ledgerstones in the Choir in 1873 prevented the stone being further inscribed with Elizabeth's name).

Insofar as the wall tablets were concerned, the impact of J.H. Markland's highly influential *Remarks on English Churches: and on the expediency of rendering sepulchral memorials subservient to pious and Christian uses* (1843) was amplified by the author living in Bath. Looking back to the early 1860s, Frederick Shum, one of the secretaries of the Restoration Committee who oversaw George Gilbert Scott's work to the Abbey and its monuments in the 1860s and 1870s, recalled that, on the death of Charles Empson in 1861 (a man of similar standing in the city as Harington was earlier in the century), he 'invited a number of friends together and suggested the idea of placing a stained-glass window in the Abbey

Church, to his memory; carrying out the proposal by the late Dr. Markland [...] to substitute stained-glass windows for stone monuments'.[6]

That is not to say that interest in seeing the monuments diminished, but at the end of the century they were in competition with fashionable stained glass. The monuments continued to be tourist attractions, although less so than during the late eighteenth century. However, interest in George Gilbert Scott's work to the interior rejuvenated comment on them at the end of the century. For example, Herbert Russell, at the end of the century found, 'many monuments to linger over' on the 'dim grey walls'. However, he remarked at how the sexton was interpreting the windows for a party of people, including an American gentleman. Looking up and around, the American whispered, 'I guess the 'Mericans would be very glad to swap the State of Ohio, ay, and perhaps Illinois too, for such a church as *this*!'[7] Scott's works had imposed an order to the monuments and reduced their impressive size, decoration and sculpture. The monuments gained a reputation for exclusivity, they became the preserve of the sextons, who (some said) knew them by heart and who were the gatekeepers of them (sometimes literally). Undesirable visitors wishing to see them were quietly 'shepherded' out of the Abbey by the sexton and his wife.[8] The tablets always had been affordable only to the upper-middle classes and above. In removing their decoration, leaving their coats of arms and inscriptions, Scott's works damaged the monuments' effect and their value as sculptural artworks in their own right, emphasising class and pedigree rather than artistry or piety. The form they are in today is largely the result of his work to and rearrangement of them.

This chapter will tell the story of how the Abbey's tablets came to be in the form and locations we experience them today (with the exception of those in the North Transept and above the string course, which were arranged in the twentieth century). It will begin with an account of how the monuments were described and arranged in the early nineteenth century, before looking in detail at the work of the architects George Philips Manners and George Gilbert Scott to the interior. By the nineteenth century, the monuments were so all pervasive in the Abbey that they dominated the aesthetic of the interior and became inextricable from its architecture. The chapter will show how thinking on the interior and the works by Manners and Scott were both part of a general turn against 'stone monuments' within churches and, in particular, related to the desire to bring order to the arrangement of the monuments, light through the windows, and to situate the organ other than in the centre of the building. From Manners's work in the 1830s to Thomas Jackson's works in

1915, the position of the Abbey's monuments and its organ became interlinked problems. The Abbey's sextons continued to play a central role in managing burial and monuments in the church, especially the work to repair, relocate monuments, and carve the stone organ screen within which some tablets were placed in the 1830s. As both a sculptor and Abbey sexton, Samuel Rogers was the best man for this job, although he could be held in equally low regard as his predecessors. Local sculptors, like Rogers, largely created the works for this gallery of sculpture. Although by the end of the century their work came to be thought of as undistinguished and paltry.

'The whole looks like a gallery of sculpture': Descriptions and drawings of the monuments, 1800–28

Perhaps unsurprisingly for the man who succeeded in placing a monument to Beau Nash in the Abbey, Henry Harington's monument received more comment in *The Bath Chronicle* than any other. The day after Harington's burial in the family vault at Kelston, the newspaper informed its readers that an 'admirable cast' had been taken since his death and that 'from it the artist (Mr. Harris, jun. of New Sydney-buildings) [was] now preparing a bust'. The correspondent went on to mention that 'The erection of a monument at the public cost' had also 'been suggested as a proper testimony of respect and veneration to the memory of this amiable and accomplished gentleman'.[9] Early in the century, marble monuments continued to be thought of as both fitting and tasteful. A month later, the 'friends of the late venerable DR. HARINGTON [...] resolved to raise a plain and elegant MONUMENT to his memory in the ABBEY CHURCH'. The list of thirty-five subscribers, including both the rector and mayor of Bath, all but one of whom had contributed a guinea (£1 1*s*), had by then raised £37 15*s* towards the monument.[10] The newspaper was an effective way of canvassing support for such a monument: a fortnight later, the list of the subscribers had increased to sixty-one and the total raised to £64 19*s*. By 4 April 1816, a further nine contributors, including the MP, had brought the total to £78 11*s* (approximately £4,500 in today's money).[11] The contributors and the amount raised show what a civic project erecting monuments in the Abbey could be. On 5 March 1817, the 'chaste and elegant Monument' was erected in the South Choir of the Abbey. The following day *The Bath Chronicle* informed its readers of the event and interpreted its relief carvings. 'The execution of the monument,' it continued, 'reflects the highest credit on the artist Mr. T. King, sculptor, of this city.'[12]

In the early nineteenth century, other monuments, such as that to Josiah Thomas (d. 1821), the Archdeacon of Bath, were raised through similar subscription schemes via *The Bath Chronicle*. The scheme towards Thomas's monument made clear what was tacit in the subscription scheme for Harington's monument, namely, that contributions should 'not exceed one guinea each [£1 1*s*]'.[13] Two years later, the newspaper was pleased to report that Thomas's monument had been erected in the church, doing 'great credit' to 'the talents of the sculptor, Mr. Gahagan, of London'.[14] *The Bath Chronicle* frequently covered the erection of other monuments to scientific and medical practitioners (Henry Harington, John Mervin Nooth and Caleb Hillier Parry) local philanthropists (Harington, John Parish), local artists (William Hoare, Venanzio Rauzzini), as well as national celebrities (Sir Richard Hussey Bickerton, Sir Alexander Thomson) in the Abbey. What is striking about the reports of these monuments is that, with the exception of those to Thomas, Bickerton and Hoare (which were executed by London sculptors Gahagan and Chantrey) and John Parish, all of them were sculpted by Thomas King of Bath (Parish's was completed by Joseph Harris of Bath in 1829, which coincides with a period 1826–44 when there is an absence of known commissions by King's studio). All of the descriptions of these monuments by King celebrate the tastefulness of the design and the quality of the carving.[15] The sense that civic pride should be taken in these objects and their display in the Abbey is best conveyed in the piece on Lt Colonel John Mervin Nooth's monument, which *The Bath Chronicle* described as 'a very superb monument, classically and beautifully executed by *our townsman* Mr. King'.[16] Collectively, these reports helped to sustain the idea, conceived at the end of the eighteenth century through the placement of monuments to Sir William Baker and Beau Nash, that Bath Abbey was the most appropriate place in the city for tasteful (and sometimes even artistically significant) monuments by Bath's sculptors to be displayed, artworks that celebrated local social virtues and achievements, as well as those on the national stage.

In 1801, Reverend Richard Warner in his *History of Bath* had praised 'the skill of Mr. King, sculptor, of this city, whose art has contributed greatly to ornament this venerable pile'.[17] Warner's views influenced other early nineteenth-century writers on the Abbey and its monuments and the civic pride in them. As curate of St James' from 1795 to 1817 (and candidate for rector of Bath in 1815) he would have known the Abbey's monuments better than most and understood the financial benefits to Bath's churches that arose from them. The monuments selected by Warner for comment do not diverge greatly from those noted by eighteenth-century writers (and like early eighteenth-century writers, he emphasises the concentration of 'Numerous monuments ornament[ing] the transepts and nave'[18]). Consequently, Warner's account of the monuments is almost entirely approving, the one lengthy criticism being of the 'lamentable' ornamentation of Sir William Draper's monument:

> (emblems of his temporal distinctions) stuck upon a marble urn, which surmounts the tablet. Trifles like these, at best but splendid gewgaws, should find no room on the stone which designates man's mortality and corruption, and whispers to the observer, that all the pride, and pomp, and parade of life, is but vanity and a lie![19]

Pierce Egan's *Walks through Bath* (1819) echoed Warner's assessment that the monuments: 'numerous, and, in general, admirably executed; and many of them, for beauty of design and elegance of sculpture, reflect great credit upon the different artists under whose particular care they have been executed'.[20] Naturally, monuments created by 'the chisels of NOLLEKENS and BACON' were those that were said to display 'exquisite touches of sculptural excellence'.[21] Like early eighteenth-century writers, Egan also contrasted the collection of monuments and their effect on the viewer favourably to the Tudor carving of the West Front: 'If the eye is charmed with the superior architecture of the exterior and the grand appearance it displays, how much more is the mind gratified on entering this sacred repository of the dead, in wandering amidst the tombs of so many departed great characters?'[22]

For Egan, not only were the Abbey's monuments collectively gratifying, the 'solemnity of the scene' was also instructive, conveying 'a sublime and wholesome truth', which, if properly applied by the observer, would operate 'as a useful lesson towards the improvement of life'.[23] Like Warner's critical assessment of Draper's monument, the general lesson was 'that all our consequence and pretensions are in an instant lost sight of by that awful monitor – DEATH!'[24] However, Egan also picked out a number of a monuments that he supposed would have had specific appeal, and be particularly instructive to certain visitors. 'TO THE LADIES', Rebecca Leyborne's monument, with its inscription to a clergyman's wife who was 'Always caring how to please her husband', was, he wrote, 'of the most interesting nature'.[25] Although 'it may fall to the lot of but few of the fair sex to realize such perfections as are described on this inscription,' Egan continued, 'it nevertheless offers a most laudable stimulus to them, to "*go and do likewise*," in order to obtain a similar superior character'.[26] Beau Nash's 'plain neat monument' recording 'his exertions in favour of the city of Bath' was also perceived by Egan as having 'rescued' Nash from 'total oblivion'.[27] Egan's other selections celebrate, on the one hand, the city's celebrities (including the 'highly respected public character' Lady Anna Miller, the actor James Quin, authoress Sarah Fielding, and musician Venanzio Rauzzini) and, on the other, nationally recognised figures, sometimes with monuments by celebrated sculptors (including Dr John Sibthorpe's monument by John Flaxman and Herman Katencamp's monument by John Bacon Jr). In one sense, through a combination of the Corporation's patronage and public's subscriptions, the Abbey's monuments were a gallery of Bath's civic achievements, as well as the nation's. A visit to the Abbey's monuments, for Egan at least, was an opportunity not only for edification but also for education and emulation: 'The ABBEY, whenever leisure offers, may be again visited with increased attention and profit.'[28]

As we have seen, responses to the Abbey's monuments were documented by a variety of writers in a variety of genres. These were predominantly in histories of and guidebooks to the city. However, creative writers continued to respond to the monuments in the nineteenth century, notably Maria Gertrude Cooper's poems 'On a Skeleton in a Stone Coffin, found under the Abbey Church, Bath, 1869' and 'On the Abbey Bells of Bath' from her 1870 *Thoughts in Ideal Hours: Poems*, the latter locating her grandmother's ledgerstone 'in centre aisle'[29] prior to George Gilbert Scott's rearrangement of the floor (discussed below). The most evocative and powerful prose on the monuments in the nineteenth century was written by Hermann Ludwig Heinrich von Pückler-Muskau, the 'German Prince', who recorded his *Tour in England, Ireland and France 1826–29* in a series of letters. The Abbey made a 'great impression' upon him and he struck up a friendship with the sexton, William Skrine.[30] On the following evening, Pückler-Muskau also asked Skrine for 'permission to see the church by moonlight'. Skrine unlocked the church for him (a regular job for the sexton and easy for Skrine as, by then, he was probably living in Orange Grove, just behind the Abbey itself). However, as soon as he had let him in, Skrine was 'dismissed'[31] by Pückler-Muskau, leaving the latter to wander 'like a solitary ghost among the pillars and tombs'. Pückler-Muskau wrote that he had 'often remarked that almost all the ancient churches of England are disfigured by scattered modern monuments'. However, the fact that, in the Abbey, there were 'so many, and they are placed with such an odd kind of symmetry, that the complete contrast they present to the simple and sublime architecture produce[d] a new and peculiar kind of picturesque effect'. The floor presented, for Pückler-Muskau, 'a continual mosaic of grave-stones with inscriptions'. The walls, he wrote:

> are inlaid in the same manner up to a certain height, where a horizontal line divides them without any intervening space, from the busts, statues, tablets and monuments of every kind, of polished black or white marble, or of porphyry, granite, or other coloured stone, which are ranged above: – the whole looks like a gallery of sculpture.[32]

The description is extremely important for what it tells us about the arrangement of the monuments at the end of 1828. As we will see, from the mid-1820s the lack of 'symmetry' in the arrangement was a motivating factor in the case for the reordering of the monuments in the 1830s and 1860s. Those renovations make it difficult for us to know precisely how the monuments were arranged when Pückler-Muskau visited. However, the side aisles of the Nave in Samuel Grimm's 1788 drawing and Henry Storer's drawing and the engraving of the 'S[outh] Transept, Bath Cathedral' for his father, James Storer's *History and Antiquities of the Cathedral Churches of Great Britain* (1814,) are instructive of the 'horizontal line' described by Pückler-Muskau (Fig. 19). Grimm's drawing suggests that this 'horizontal line' ran just below the string course of the Nave aisle windows, since Grimm depicts the monuments erected in a line level with this in both the north and south Nave aisles.

Grimm's drawing also suggests that there was, of course, a very practical reason for wall space below this level to be free from monuments; namely, that before the introduction of fixed seating in the Nave, the bench seating around the wall was used during services by worshippers and for prayer. Storer's drawing appears to confirm this: the only monuments below this line in his depiction of the South Transept are located where there is no bench seating (e.g. on the pillars and at the end of Nave wall where the transept arch is formed). The family group, with two men sitting on a bench, helps to give a sense of scale. The monuments around and behind these characters in Storer's drawing also illustrate well Pückler-Muskau's sense that the more elaborate, three-dimensional wall tablets were situated higher up the walls than the plainer tablets. This may also have been in consideration of those using the bench seating around the walls, although probably has more to do with families wanting their prestigious monuments to have pride of place higher up the walls.

Drawn & Engd. by H.S. Storer.
Pl. 8.
S. Transept, Bath Cathedral.
Published Oct.1 1816, by Sherwood, Neely & Jones, Paternoster Row.

Fig.19: Henry Storer's drawing and the engraving of the S[outh] Transept, Bath Cathedral *for his father, James Storer's* History and Antiquities of the Cathedral Churches of Great Britain *(1814). © The author.*

Fig.20: View, looking S.W. of Nave, &c. *(1820) engraved by John Le Keux from a drawing by Frederick Mackenzie, published in John Britton's* History and Antiquities of Bath Abbey Church *(1825). © The author.*

An inspection of the *View, looking S.W. of Nave, &c.* (1820) engraved by John Le Keux from a drawing by Frederick Mackenzie, which was published in John Britton's *History and Antiquities of Bath Abbey Church* (1825), is also instructive of this kind of arrangement (Fig. 20). In the background of the drawing, a line of small monuments can be seen along the horizontal line of the string course of the windows in the South Aisle, with larger, more elaborate monuments above this level, especially in the south-west corner of the church, where the large monuments appear to obscure at least half of the window (a point discussed fully below). It is also worth noting in this engraving, in regard to the 'symmetry' described by Pückler-Muskau, that the lowest monument on the pillars, in both the foreground and the background, all appear to be designed on an oval background, giving an indication of the thought given to the placement of these tablets and their effect on the aesthetic and symmetry of the building.

It is also worth comparing James Storer's etching of the *Interior of Bath Cathedral* (from Henry Gastineau's drawing) (Fig. 21) with James Vertue's 1750 etching in this respect (Colour Plate H). Both show the Abbey Nave looking east from the Great West Doors. The perspective of Storer's etching obscures the Nave aisles (and the westerly pillars on the north side in particular). However, the monuments he does depict on the west faces of the Nave pillars show that, on the south side, the large monuments first erected on them in the late seventeenth and early eighteenth centuries necessitated the arrangement of small monuments above and below them, which effectively created 'an odd kind of symmetry'. The large monuments in the centre of two pillars closest to the Great West Door on the right-hand side of Storer's 1814 etching are obviously those of Mary Reeve (1676) and Granville Pyper (1717). Reeve's is unchanged after almost a century and a half. Pyper's has lost the coat of arms on the top and the urn and figures shown in the centre of the monument by Vertue in 1750 (this is unlikely to be a simplification for the engraving, given that Storer details the figures in the Reeve monument). It is possible that the coat of arms at the top of the monument (shown by Vertue in 1750) was removed to make room for the monument to be erected above Pyper's (shown by Storer in 1814). Whatever the reason, the coat of arms was kept and present when Wright described Pyper's monument in the South Transept in 1864 (four years before Scott's works to the monuments began): 'a rich specimen [...] two columns support a broad tablet, having a shield of arms in the centre'.[33]

Fig.21: James Storer's etching of the Interior of Bath Cathedral *(from Henry Gastineau's drawing). © The author.*

Another detail confirmed by Storer's engraving of the *Interior of Bath Cathedral* is that by 1814, the Wakeman family's hatchment (shown on the pillar west of the Montagu Tomb by Vertue in 1750) had been removed. Peter Chapman's wooden monument originally in the North Choir was removed to the vestry in the nineteenth century. These older monuments were slowly removed from the church to make room for more fashionable, marble tablets on the pillars. This process took place fully under Manners in the 1830s (see below).

Looking at the arrangement of the monuments in these early nineteenth-century depictions indicates the care given to their placement by the Abbey. Whilst writing on the monuments in the first quarter of the nineteenth century tended to appraise their designs and arrangement in broadly positive terms, from 1825 critical voices became louder and their cry for change more forceful. The volume of monuments in the Abbey by the nineteenth century was a blessing and a curse. On the one hand, the Abbey became a gallery of sculpture unrivalled outside of London. On the other, many of the monuments were generic tablets. By 1814, James Storer wrote that the monuments 'which abound in all parts of this sacred edifice, have justly attracted general attention, and a kind of traditional celebrity has been acquired by the sculptor's art and muse's praise'. However, he complained, it would have 'been as becoming had reason always prevailed over feeling in these mortuary records, and urnal tablets to infants given place to the monuments of divines, philosophers, statesmen, or heroes'.[34]

Writing three years after Storer, John Britton, in his *History and Antiquities of the See and Cathedral Church of Winchester* (1817), criticised the monuments he found in Winchester Cathedral, and applied his criticism especially to Bath and Westminster Abbeys:

> It is much to be regretted that our venerable and noble Cathedrals should, for so many ages, have been disgraced and disfigured by petty and pretty monumental tablets. The white, black, and variegated colours, of which they are formed, are not only inimical to all harmony and beauty; but the manner in which they are usually inserted in the wall and columns, is ruinous to the stability of the buildings. If the proper officers of the church are regardless of such shameless proceedings, there should be committees of taste, or a general public surveyor appointed, to watch over and direct all the monumental erections, as well as the reparations of each edifice. It is a lamentable fact, that we scarcely ever see a new monument raised with any analogy, or regard to the building in which it is placed. The sculptor and director seem only

> ostentatious of themselves. To render it showy, imposing, and even obtrusive, is their chief solicitude; and the trustees of a Cathedral are too generally regardless of every thing but handsome fees. Hence Westminster Abbey Church, and Bath Abbey Church, are become mere show rooms of sculpture, and warehouses of marble.[35]

Britton was therefore familiar with Bath Abbey and convinced of the problems its monuments presented aesthetically before writing his history of it (published in 1825). His was the first book-length history of Bath Abbey. Continued and edited by R.E. Peach in 1887, it was the only dedicated history of the Abbey until E.M. Hick's *Bath Abbey: Its History and Architecture* in 1913. Britton's views on the Abbey therefore influenced thinking and subsequent writing on the Abbey more than any other book. Just as Harington's 'epigrammatic distich' (quoted by Britton) about the Abbey's mouldering monuments and busts has been the enduring sense of the character and raison d'etre of the monuments, Britton's uncritical comparison of (the numbers of) monuments in Westminster and Bath has been unquestioningly repeated, accepted, and acted as a terminus for thought on the monuments ever since: 'Perhaps there is not a Church in England, not excepting that national mausoleum, Westminster Abbey, so crowded with sepulchral memorials as the sacred edifice now under notice.'[36] One distinguishing factor between the two, and indeed between Bath and Winchester, was the floor, Britton remarking that 'the pavement' was 'wholly formed of inscribed slabs'.[37] This feature was remarked on more than once by Britton, who noted that the floor was paved almost in its entirety with 'slabs'. In addition, there were, he noted, 'at least 450 tablets, &c., of all descriptions, affixed to the side walls and pillars of the building':

> Nearly the whole interior surface of the walls, floor, and columns, is lined or covered with slabs and tablets, of all sizes, forms, colours, and materials. Brass, copper, stone, slate, marble, and wood, are distributed over the surface; to attract the eye of the visitor. From their number and diversified forms and colours, they may be said to counteract the destined purpose of each,– sympathy and awe. Instead of solemnity and repose, they produce fritter and confusion. The eye cannot rest, nor can the mind be serene, where such distraction and incongruousness prevail. Here is neither order nor symmetry; nor has there been any attempt at systematic arrangement. In excuse it may be said that it would be impracticable, if not impossible, to remedy such a defect, where the fancies of so many persons are allowed to prevail. The beginning

> of the evil is not of the present day or present age; and few have the courage and good taste to commence a reform, where so much is to be undone, as well as done.[38]

The problem wasn't unique to Bath. Britton noted that such remarks were equally 'applicable to Westminster Abbey, to St. Paul's Cathedral, and to many other ancient and modern fabrics'. In passing through these metropolitan churches:

> as well as that at Bath, every person of sensibility and real taste must be more offended than delighted. Monstrous masses of marble, with broken-backed horses, rampant and tame lions, figures of Time, Fame, Angels, and Cherubim, are the component parts of most of the great monuments; whilst weeping Cupids, inverted torches, and urns *ad infinitum*, are the prevailing characteristics of the smaller tablets. It is high time that this common-place mode of sculpture was abandoned; and it is equally to be wished that the inappropriate and absurd practice of clothing British generals and statesmen in Roman togas was avoided.[39]

A year before the publication of Britton's history of the Abbey, 'An Abstract Account of the Register Books Belonging to the Rectory of Bath' was taken. This manuscript includes 'An Alphabetical List of the Monuments in the Abbey Church' up to 1824, and the list is possibly related to Britton's history, although it has not been possible to establish this for certain. Like the late eighteenth-century lists of monuments, the list in this manuscript must be read carefully since, from the beginning, its author conflates a list of people named on monuments with its purported aim to list the monuments themselves: the first two entries on the list are Ann Amory and Benjamin Amory, but after Benjamin's entry the author notes that he is named on the 'same Mont. [monument]'. Whilst the manuscript's author occasionally notes where multiple entries of names relate to the same monument (for example, the Chapmans and the Enyses) he does not always do so (for example, in the entries for the Fords and the Throckmortons). There are also a number of duplicated entries of the same name and monument. Comparison of the manuscript with the eighteenth-century surveys and the surviving monuments in the church is essential, and even then the number of monuments listed cannot be taken as completely definitive. For example, it is likely that the monuments listed to Bramston and Tryme, not named as such in earlier surveys, are in fact duplications of the monuments to

Turnor and Leman (the inscription to Diana Bramston is discussed in Chapter 2). With those caveats, the list records 451 monuments in the church in 1824. These are all tablets on the walls and pillars, with the exception of the tombs of Montagu, Waller and Lichfield. The list records 175 monuments dating between 1800 and 1824, with five undated in the manuscript. This suggests that list omits twenty nineteenth-century monuments, since 195 payments for wall tablets erected in the church are recorded in the Churchwardens' Accounts between 1800 and 1824.

Whilst the 1824 list of monuments cannot, therefore, be taken as a comprehensive list of all the wall tablets in the Abbey, its value lies in its detailed description of the monuments' locations in the Abbey, as shown in the table below:

Location of Monuments as recorded in 1824 in MS BA/2/BMD/7/1, Bath Abbey Archives		
Location	**Number tablets**	**Subtotals**
Middle Aisle[40]	54	82
Middle Aisle, South Side	9	
Middle Aisle, North Side	2	
Middle Aisle, West End	17	
North Aisle[41]	102	125
North Aisle, North Wall	1	
North Aisle, East End	11	
North Aisle, West End	11	
North Cross Aisle	23	24
North Cross Aisle, East End	1	
South Aisle[42]	103	130
South Aisle, East End	3	
South Aisle, West End	24	
South Cross Aisle[43]	52	52

Choir, 'Under the Organ'	8	
Choir[44]	17	38
Chancel	13	
Total	**451**	**451**

The 1824 list shows that the trends in the arrangement of the monuments in the eighteenth century continued into the nineteenth century. The majority of the monuments continued to be erected in the Nave, evenly distributed between the north and south sides, with the minority of monuments located in the Choir. That said, the 1824 list shows that almost half of the monuments in the Choir (12/25) were erected between 1802 and 1822. Fees for the erection of monuments in the Choir were more expensive than those in the Nave (see below). Given that regular services were held in the Choir, the infrequency with which monuments were erected and burials took place there was advantageous practically for the church. The South Cross Aisle (Transept) was also an area where many monuments were erected in the early nineteenth century: twenty of the fifty-two monuments recorded there in 1824 were erected within 1800–24. In comparison, only seven of the twenty-four monuments recorded in the North Cross Aisle (Transept) in 1824 were erected in the same period.

The number of monuments described in the 1824 list as located at the 'West End' of either the Middle, North and South Aisles is interesting (especially the number in the South Aisle). Of the fifty-two monuments described as being at the 'West End' of these locations, nineteen were erected within 1800–24 and all but Frances Allen's, at the west of the North Aisle in 1816, were erected at the west end of either Middle or South Aisles. This would suggest the continuation of the trend we saw emerging in the eighteenth century, namely, that the south side of the Abbey, particularly the west end, was used to accommodate the volume of monuments erected in the early nineteenth century. The volume of monuments shown in the south-west corner of the Nave can be seen in plate VIII of John Britton's *History and Antiquities of Bath Abbey Church* (1825) (Fig. 20). The location is, perhaps unsurprisingly, that chosen by the artist to place the couple viewing the monuments in the church. In his description of this plate, Britton noted that the 'archway seen in the distance, formed what is still called the Prior's Entrance, but it has long been closed up'.[45] The additional surface area may have afforded extra space on which to erect monuments. Another reason why the monuments could be erected in quantities here, which elsewhere would have obscured the light, is that 'the window [shown in the south west corner in Britton's Plate VIII] has been closed up, a private house abutting against the wall'.[46] Britton's plate appears to show that the majority of the window in the Abbey is covered by monuments.

The list also notes the material of a number of monuments. Four are marked as 'Brass' (three dating to the early seventeenth and one to the early eighteenth century). Five of the monuments are described as wooden or 'wood and painted', Grace Gethin's (d. 1697) is described as 'a Painting', and John Duncombe's as a 'Painted Coat of Arms in a Frame' (a hatchment). Five of these seven monuments are in the North Aisle. All but two date to the seventeenth century, John Duncombe's being the latest, dated 1747. It is a mark of the care given to these monuments and the enduring importance of the Chapmans' legacy to the story of the Abbey that Peter Chapman's wooden monument was still in place in 1824, over 200 years after his death in 1602. However, other wooden monuments, such as those to Hester Barnes and William Child, had been removed by 1824. The remainder of the wooden memorials, hatchments and paintings in the church would be removed by George Philips Manners during his works 1835–36 (see below).[47]

An 'Addenda' to the list records a 'Curious Inscription' (unrecorded elsewhere) over John White's grave in the Chancel ('Earth take my Earth, Satan take my Sin, I leave / the World my Substance, Heaven my Soul receive'), as well as the following inscription on 'a defaced Monument' on 'the outside of the East Wall of the Abbey': 'In Memory of Thomas Guidot, M.D. by whose authority drinking the Bath Waters was revived A.D. MDCLXXIII. and who died MDCCVI. This Inscription was here placed MDCCXXVII. by John Winter, M.D.'[48] The manuscript concludes with a 'Brief Account of Celebrated Individuals interred in the Abbey'.[49] In this part of the manuscript, its unidentified author expresses many of the prevailing attitudes towards the monuments in early nineteenth-century Bath. For example, the author describes Sarah Currer's (d. 1759) monument by Benjamin and Thomas Carter as 'the best finished in the church' and the decorations as 'specimens of excellence in Carving not often met with'.[50] This is almost verbatim from *The Original Bath Guide for 1811*, which described Currer's monument as 'universally allowed to be the best sculpture in the church; the foliage is admirably executed'.[51] Many of the monuments selected for special praise in the 1824 manuscript are the same as those selected for the same treatment in Pierce Egan's *Walks through Bath* (1819) and *The Original Bath Guide*, which, unsurprisingly, are also those commemorating local celebrities, virtues and values, discussed in Chapter 2.

'Servants of the church': The Skrine family and managing the monuments, 1807–33

Keeping the monuments in a good state of repair was overseen by the Abbey's sexton. We have seen that from 1620, the role of sexton was often held by at least two people concurrently, and that from 1765 husbands and wives shared the roles of sexton, cleaner and pew keeper. In the nineteenth century, that was continued by William and Elizabeth Skrine. William served as sexton 1807–36. Like John Bretton, Matthias Walter and William Handcock, who had held the office of sexton before him, Skrine was initially a woodworker, apprenticed to a cabinet-maker in 1770. As with the Handcocks at the end of the eighteenth century, the way in which family members stepped in for one another to fulfil the office can be seen from an entry in *Gye's Bath Directory* for 1819, which contained the entry: 'Skrine, J[ames]. sexton of the Abbey-church, 8 Orange-grove'. By 1833, William and Elizabeth Skrine were living at 7 Orange Grove, just behind the Abbey to the east; Elizabeth was described as a 'Milliner' and William as 'Verger of the Cathedral Church of Ss Peter and Paul'. William Skrine's Sexton's Accounts (1810–36) are a meticulous record of what was required of the sexton during the first three decades of the nineteenth century (in addition to showing visitors the monuments). The Churchwardens' Accounts (discussed below) are the most comprehensive record of (the fees for) burial and memorialisation at the Abbey in the nineteenth century. But the Sexton's Accounts reveal both the variety and monotony of a job that impacted the Abbey from its highest heights to its subterranean vaults, as well as providing a fascinating insight into the maintenance of the Abbey and its monuments in 1810–36.

Skrine co-ordinated and paid the bell ringers, bought the oil and sometimes 'lard' to lubricate the bells, and paid the man when the clock was being worked on in the tower. He employed his family's skills to wash and repair surplices, mend cushions, and dye 'ye blk pulpit Curtains'. He bought wood for the fires, soap for the vestry, even the biscuits for the meetings there. In the winter of 1811, Skrine paid 'The men for throwing ye snow from ye Church Roofs'.[52]

Co-ordinating workmen and ensuring the church was in a good state of repair and cleanliness was an important part of the Skrines' job. Late eighteenth-century perceptions of the negative effects of the 'stench' and the burials on the health of those entering the building continued into the nineteenth century. The Skrines had worked to 'resolutions' agreed to on 27 March 1815 (now lost). Certainly to 'sweep and cleanse' the church, including specifically the monuments and the floor, was part of the sexton's duties. Skrine's accounts suggest the Abbey interior was deep cleaned once a year, with the men sweeping and fetching water and the women washing and cleaning. A payment in 1827 to 'ye man at ye Bath for Water for ye use of ye Church cleaning' suggests the water the men fetched for the cleaning the Abbey was the warm water from the thermal springs. In addition, specialist cleaning appears to have taken place to treat the graves, in order to make the church more hospitable. On 3 July 1810, Skrine paid 7*s* 'for girl Webb for ye Graves'. Mr Webb supplied 'oil and turpentine' throughout the decade. The oil, the payment in 1818 tells us, was 'for ye Bells'. Given the 1810 payment above and another mysterious one in 1829, linking the payments to the Webbs with the graves ('Paid for Grave Webbs for ye Church'), the turpentine may have been used in some way to help ensure that the floor where graves had been created and ledgerstones raised was as clean and smelled as little as possible. Additionally, the *New Prose Bath Guide for 1778* reported that the Abbey had a ventilator in the roof to help with the smell. It was still in use in July 1814, when the Abbey paid 10*s* for 'Oil Cloth for Ventilator'.[53]

On a number of occasions between 1811 and 1813, Skrine paid masons for mending the 'pavement' (floor) of the church. This was in addition to the weekly raising and replacing of ledgerstones for intramural burials, the result of which was a smelly and uneven floor surface. In June 1813, Skrine paid 7*s* 7*d* for 'Beer for ye Men when levelling ye Church pavement'. An entry in the vestry minutes for 1824 gives an indication of the cost of materials. On 23 September, the vestry agreed to 'the necessity of repairing and raising part of the pavement in the Abbey Churchyard' and to a tender 'from John Long to do the same and to put what new stone would be wanted at 2s 10d per yard'.[54] The total cost amounted to £26 12*s*.[55] Skrine also liaised with sculptors to install and repair the monuments. On 14 November 1823, Skrine paid 'Mr. Reeves Bill for repairing a monument £1 12s 6d'. Having such a number of monuments in the church obviously came with a cost when they needed to be repaired. The Abbey's Churchwardens' Accounts show the frequency with which masonry work was required. From 1819, the sculptor, Samuel Rogers, was paid annually for 'Mason's Work'. Before 1836, Rogers's work is not usually described in detail, often noted simply as 'Masonry repairs'. However, his work could be both structurally and aesthetically significant, not to mention lucrative, as was his work on the foundations, walls and four 'Gothic Pillars under the church gallery' in 1825–26, for which he was paid over £400 (approximately £27,000 today). From 1836 he was frequently paid for his work to the Abbey floor.

The business of burial and commemoration was bread and butter for the sextons. William Skrine dug graves on a weekly basis and made, on average, four walled graves a year, to say nothing of the '8ft by 5ft wide' walled grave Skrine made for John Bathoe in the Choir in January 1814. Digging through the cold, hard ground in winter must have been back-breaking work. During his time as sexton (1807–36), Skrine arranged for the installation of 500 monuments in the Abbey – 294 ledgerstones laid over graves and 206 tablets on the walls and pillars.[56] In the most tragic circumstances, Skrine had to bury members of his own family, notably W.W. Skrine on 1 May 1819, Nathaniel Skrine on 4 October 1822, and his wife, Elizabeth Skrine, on 28 February 1833. No charges were made for these burials, nor the £5 fee paid for the walled grave for Elizabeth, which Skrine would have built himself. Such fees were seldom waived, and when they were it seems to have been discretionary,[57] the most notable occasion for one individual being the waiving of the fees for the burial, walled grave, and overmeasure of the monument for the Archdeacon of Bath, Josiah Thomas. Given his position, it is unsurprising Thomas's fee should have been waived. However, that the fees for William and George Lockyer were 'given up' (waived) illustrates that working-class craftspeople – especially those working on the monuments – who worked on the Abbey were equally looked after: in 1814, George Lockyer was paid £21 10*s* for 'Repairing Pavement in the [Orange] Grove, raising & relaying Pavement [in the Abbey] & fixing Christening Font &c in the Church'.[58] However, the expectation was that parishioners paid. Even when they were poor and the full fee couldn't be met, some payment was taken from them.[59] So when the parishioners heard of how Elizabeth's burial fees had been waived, complaints were made. The vestry had intended 'not to charge' for Elizabeth's fees as she had 'for thirty years been a servant of the Church'.[60] But public pressure appears to have prevailed and in September 1833, almost half a year after Elizabeth's burial, William Skrine was ordered to 'pay 25s as the burial fees for his late wife'.

It is hard to imagine both the shame and the sorrow that this must have caused him. It must have been salt in an already painful wound when, a week later, he buried and paid the burial fees (£1 5*s* 6*d*) for his daughter, Constantia.[61] As with his predecessors as sextons, the way in which he was regarded and treated by the parishioners and public, was much less than he deserved. Skrine had had to fight to recover substantial income (£12 12*s*) he had lost in 1809 when the church was closed for repairs. The way in which this 'supposed loss' is recorded in the Churchwardens Accounts (27 June 1809) and the 'question of [the] regulation of the office [of] Sexton & Pew opener' (in the vestry minutes for 27 March 1826) hint at the slightly fractious relationship between the parish and its sexton in the early nineteenth century. The embarrassment and lack of compassion over Elizabeth's fees must have been the last straw. William Skrine 'resigned through age and infirmity' in 1836. On 25 February 1838, the fees for the burial of the late rector's wife in the Chancel were waived without question.

'A reform in the monuments': The work of G.P. Manners, 1833–36

By the early 1830s, the Abbey had undergone major work in 1814 and 1825. The expense, aesthetics and practicalities of the latter had dissatisfied some parishioners, especially the screen between the Nave and Choir.[62] Moreover, neither restoration project had addressed the monuments (although the sharp drop in income from ledgerstones and tablets in 1825 show how building work could affect the ability or desire to erect monuments in the Abbey). On 30 September 1833, the city council minuted that 'cracks and other defects' had appeared 'in the tower of the Abbey Church in consequence of the great consequence of the great weight and projection of the Clock'. A committee was appointed to consider and report on the expense of removing the clock and replacing one on the North Transept, and the city architect, George Phillips Manners (1789–1866), was called upon to estimate for the repairs. Manners had acted as the architect for the work at the Abbey in 1825 when the roofs were repaired, so was the natural choice.[63] The need for the work to the clock and tower led to Manners's wider work to the exterior and interior, which would define the appearance of the Abbey for three decades. Hitherto, historians have ignored Manners's reorganisation of the Abbey's monuments, choosing instead to write about the controversial works to the exterior and the 'warfare' that took place in newspaper columns over the appropriateness (or otherwise) of the pinnacles.[64]

The reorganisation of the monuments must be seen in the wider context of the works between 1833 and 1836. This was the intention at the time. At the end of 1833, the former mayor, William Clark, wrote a long piece in *The Bath Chronicle and Weekly Gazette* putting the works proposed and undertaken in the context of the Abbey's history. The conclusion of the article encouraged readers to give a 'sovereign or two' towards the works (it was also said that 'the names of all the contributors' would 'be inserted in the manuscript Codex Parochianus of benefactors to the Church', although this turned out to be an empty promise). By then, work had begun on the restoration of Prior Birde's Chantry chapel, including the repair of 'the effects of the Vandalism of the erectors of monuments against the beautiful mullions of the windows of this oratory'. Clark hoped that similar improvements would take place throughout the interior, hinting at a plan to re-pew, remove the 'disgraceful galleries', and effect 'a reform in the monuments, by reducing them to something like symmetrical order, by cropping off their ridiculous exuberances and excrescences in like manner as been effect in Winchester Cathedral'. Clark claimed that such work had taken at place at Winchester 'so judiciously, that not one family connected with the monuments [had] made the slightest complaint'.[65]

It is also important to understand the wider context of works around the Abbey in the early nineteenth century. From the end of October 1819, Bath Corporation had planned the removal of the houses on the north side of the Abbey (Wade's Passage), which reflected poorly on their town planning, piety and taste:

> Where shops have sprung up to shut out all the light
> Of a fine gothic church, day converting to night;
> The outside of the temple devoted to prayer
> Decked with *ham, tongues,* and *sausages,* rabbit and hare
> While its long lancet windows in darkness remain
> to the taste of the city and churchmen a *stain!*[66]

From 25 March 1826, 'the removal of the houses against the church commenced'.[67] There was a suggestion that the ground on the north side of the Abbey might be used as a burial ground, although this came to nothing.[68] However, the houses on the south side of the Abbey belonging to Earl Manvers remained:

> the *Abbey Church* its splendour rears,
> The sacred monument of former years;
> Behold its sculpture – and mark, whilst you view it,
> The pretty little houses sticking to it;
> The Citizens of Bath, with vast delight,
> To hide their noble Church from vulgar sight,
> Surround its venerable sides with shops,
> And decorate its walls with chimney tops!
> Surely from these designs, so pure, so chaste,

Bath has been called emporium of taste:
Oh! men of classic judgment! bear them hence
To Grecian relics of magnificence;
There let them deck (to prove their polished minds)
Athenian temples with Venetian blinds![69]

Both poets criticised the effect on the amount of light that could enter the church through its windows (a problem that had been acknowledged since the seventeenth century, and was compounded by the building around the Abbey in the eighteenth century). The extent to which the houses on the south side of the Abbey blocked the light from the Abbey's south-facing windows can be seen, at the lower level, in F. Mackenzie's *View of the Nave looking East* in Britton's *History* and, at clerestory level, in J.C. Nattes's *Interior of the Abbey* (1805) (Colour Plate Ac). On 18 July 1834, the Abbey's Sexton's Accounts record a payment of £1 1*s* to the bell 'Ringers on Lord Manvers giving up ye Ground on ye South side of ye Church'. By August 1834, these houses on the south side of the Abbey belonging to Earl Manvers had been demolished.[70]

Manners's thinking on the monuments was interconnected with that on the (newly revealed) windows and screen dividing the church, too. On 27 September 1834, Manners wrote to the mayor, Johnson Phillott, with his plan for the alterations to the interior of the church. This largely concerned Manners's plans for the seating and screen. However, he also wished to direct Johnson's attention to 'another subject in connexion with the improvement of the interior of the Church', namely, 'the removal of those monuments, to make room for which the Architecture of the Church has been mutilated and obscured'. The problem, for Manners, was that the monuments were:

> so numerous, that even if divested of their ornaments and the tablets containing the inscriptions only refixed, it is doubtful if the walls would afford space enough for them; should this upon a deliberate survey be found to be the case, it has occurred to me that a great number may be disposed of between the pillars of the Nave where they may be build up in pyramidal and other groups, without destroying the symetry [sic] of the building.[71]

On 14 October 1834, the Corporation resolved to follow 'Mr Manners Plan No.2', and by 20 November Manners's 'Specification of work and General Conditions' had been drafted. None of this work concerned the monuments. However, the specification stipulated that, 'The Tables of donations are to be refixed where directed by the architect and any damage done to them in taking down is to be made good.' These are the two marble shields listing the 'Benefactors to this Church' and 'Benefactors to the Poor' now fixed to the left and right of the door to the Abbey shop respectively. That Manners had made a proposal concerning the treatment of the monuments under Plan No.2 is clear from the Corporation's resolution on 20 January 1835, that 'the Estimate for taking down and refixing the Monuments and for warming the Church be approved and confirmed'.[72] The substance of this proposal is not known. In the same month, the Corporation also 'abandoned' their decision to follow 'Plan No.2' and resolved that 'Plan No.1 be substituted and carried into execution'.[73] One minor but important practical difference between the plans was that a 'Sexton's closet' was included in the screen. This housed the tools needed to create graves and work on monuments, including a 'Pick axe & Shovell',[74] as was common elsewhere.

On 24 February 1835, Manners submitted his 'Report and estimate as to the removal of monuments and repairing the Windows'. As a record of both the arrangement of the monuments and the work proposed in the mid-1830s, it is worth quoting in full:

> There are 68 monuments against the walls in the ailes [sic] of the Nave, which obstruct the light and interfere with the drip mouldings of the windows and the shafts between the windows – To take down these and such others as may be necessary for a rearrangement of them, so as to leave the windows drips and shafts free, is estimated to cost including restoration of the Masonry £120.
>
> There are 19 monuments now remaining on the Pillars of the Choir it would be desirable that these should be removed and placed in other situations – the cost £14 14s 6d.
>
> There are 120 monuments on the Pillars of the Nave – The walls will not afford room enough for these; if therefore they are to be taken down and refix'd, I know not at present how better to dispose of them, than by erecting skreens between the pillars; against which they may be placed, selecting those most worthy of notice for such conspicuous situations.
>
> But any arrangement of this description will require more time for consideration – The expence [sic] may be roughly estimated at from £300 to £400.[75]

The following day, 25 February 1835, the Corporation resolved to remove the sixty-eight monuments 'from the Walls in Ailes [sic] of the Nave' and the 'nineteen monuments from the Pillars of the Choir'.[76] At the same meeting, the council, 'Resolved that the works now in progress in the Interior of the Abbey Church be stopped, and that the opinion of Mr Blore, Architect of London by immediately taken on the General Plan now in execution.'[77] Blore visited Bath on 13 March and submitted a report on the plans, after which the Corporation resolved to continue with the works to the interior of the Abbey. One caveat being that Manners's proposed 'Plan of the Screens and for finishing of Prior Birds Chapel [sic]' be 'submitted for Mr Blore's approbation'.[78] This helps to date a 'Plan of the Screens' signed by Blore. Blore's plan view marks the 'Front of [the] Gallery' above which, adjoining two pillars, are marked 'Recesses for Monuments' (Fig. 22). The precise nature of these 'recesses' is not known. However, given that Manners did not know how room for the monuments would be afforded elsewhere, the Corporation's confidence in Blore's oversight of Manners's plans for the screens, and the later description of the number of tablets displaced when the organ screen was dismantled by George Gilbert Scott, they must have been executed. The scale on the plan shows each recess was approximately 10ft by 5ft (3m by 1.5m) either side of the central door in the screen. They were certainly large enough to accommodate a monument like Robert Walsh's (d. 1788), although perhaps not one of the size of Jacob Bosanquet's (d. 1767), which, even after it was cut down, takes up the full height from the floor to the string course on the east wall of the South Transept. Height would have been a limiting factor in terms of which monuments might have been placed in the recesses. What is certain is that 'the removal of the Monuments from the Pillars of the Nave of the Abbey Church' took place after 11 July 1835, when the Corporation resolved to indemnify the committee overseeing the work against the cost, which was £127 6*s* 6*d*.[79] It would make sense for the recesses to have been constructed in the screen by then, so that those monuments removed from pillars, like Walsh's, that were placed there, could be moved straight into them.

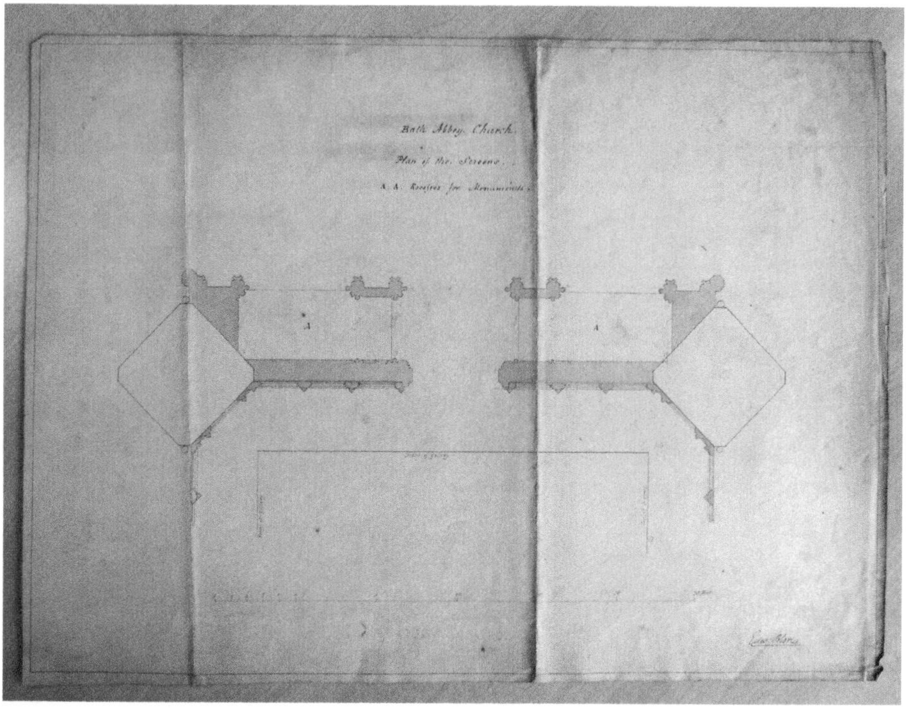

*Fig.22: Plan of the new Choir Screen signed by Edward Blore (*c.*1835) showing 'Recesses for Monuments' marked on the north and south side of its central door. © Bath Abbey.*

Because of the lack of records concerning Manners's work, as well as Scott's reorganisation of the monuments later in the century, it is impossible to say how Manners treated or relocated the majority of the tablets. One general principle was noted in G.N. Wright's *Historic Guide to Bath* (1864): 'Monuments, or other memorials to the dead, are very properly refused a place upon the clustered columns of the Abbey, and several have been removed thence to the galleries at the north-east end of the choir.'[80] Wright's book and Tunstall's *Rambles about Bath* (1848) include sometimes detailed descriptions of the locations of some monuments in the church. Written before Scott's work to the Abbey, comparison of the locations of certain monuments mentioned with the locations in the 1824 manuscript enable us to understand further how Manners accommodated the monuments. The table below uses these sources. It illustrates how the transepts and the space within the new organ gallery were used by Manners as out-of-the-way locations to place monuments, which had either been removed from the pillars (e.g. Pyper) or which were moved to make way for other, more modern, monuments (e.g. Bosanquet, Sill). It is interesting that, whilst the Abbey was closed for 'cleaning and rebeautifying the interior'[81] in the middle of August 1834, Sir Richard Hussey Bickerton's monument by Chantrey should be installed in the North Transept. Perhaps by then thought was already being given to the relocation of the monuments. Certainly, in 1868, the North Transept was noted as an area of the Abbey that contained 'several well-executed examples of sepulchral statuary'.[82]

Monument	**1824 Location**	**Location in 1848/1864**	**Present location**
Peter Chapman	North Aisle [Choir]	Vestry	Missing
Henry Harington	Choir	'South side of the choir' (1848)	North Choir Aisle
Jacob Bosanquet	Middle Aisle West End	'Opposite' to Waller Tomb [East wall South Transept] (1848)	East Wall South Transept
Mrs Elizabeth Grieve	North Aisle	'North Transept [...] Against the organ gallery' (1848)	North Aisle
Fletcher Partis	Middle Aisle	'on the eastern aspect of this [North] transept' (1848)	North Choir Aisle
John Sibthorpe	North Aisle	North Transept (1848)	South Choir Aisle
Granville Pyper	South Aisle [Pillar]	North Transept (1848)	Gethsemane Chapel
Robert Walsh	South Aisle	'by the centre door, under organ gallery' (1848)	North Aisle
Joseph Sill	Middle Aisle West End	'by the centre door, under organ gallery' (1848)	South Transept East Wall

Joseph Ewart	North Aisle	'Near to the [Robert] Walsh monument [by the centre door, under organ gallery]' (1864)	North Aisle
Peter Capper	South Aisle	'The choir' (1868)	North Choir Aisle
George Gordon	South Cross Aisle	'The choir' (1868)	Gethsemane Chapel
William Meyler	North Cross Aisle	South Transept (1868)	South Aisle

As well as the practical need to denude the pillars of the monuments and prevent the monuments obscuring the light from the windows, propriety, patriotism and popularity appear to have been behind some of Manners's rearrangements (for example, removing the busts of Hobart and Winkley to the south-east corner out of view of the worshipping space or moving Herman Katencamp's (d. 1807) and Alexander Champion's (d. 1795) monuments prominently either side of the Great West Doors to show off large sculptures by Joseph Nollekens and John Bacon Jr to worshippers and visitors. Similar thematic or typical groupings of monuments can be found to have been created by the nineteenth-century works, although it is often impossible to determine whether these are the work of Manners or Scott. For example, the concentration of monuments with connections to the West Indies and the Royal Navy on the walls of the South Nave Aisle. Historic groupings of monuments with local significance, dating back to the seventeenth century, such as those in the South Transept commemorating Bath's mayors and members of the corporation and the collection of monuments commemorating the Chapman family in the North-East Choir Aisle, survived the nineteenth-century works.

Another solution to the problem of space for the monuments removed from the pillars appears to have been to set their inscription tablets into the floor of the Abbey. This was not without its problems. On 3 November 1835, the Abbey's churchwardens, James Lea and John Stokes, wrote to the mayor, criticising the decision not to reinstate the curtains from the old screen that had kept out the draughts into the new screen. Another thing they felt it 'proper' on their parts to mention was 'the present state of the pavements in the Nave of the Church'. In consequence of 'the pressure of the heavy stones which have been taken over and laid on them, have sunk to that degree, that

Fig.23: Marbles removed from wall monuments set into distinctive striated stone c.*1835–36 in the south-west Nave.* © *The author.*

in many places it is extremely dangerous'. Besides, they continued, 'many of the marble tablets inserted in such pavements have been broken into pieces, which in the event of a dispute we should be called onto [sic] restore'. They trusted that the mayor would deal with the matter so that they may be 'exonerated' from claims on them and blame 'from the Parish, for not taking proper Security for the due restoration of the Parish Property'. The mayor did just that. On 10 November, he and the committee overseeing the works at the Abbey resolved that Manners should 'make a written report of the State of the Works executed and in progress, and take into consid[eration] the state of the pavements and who is bound to replace them & to confer with Mr. Lewis [the contractor] & the Churchwardens thereon'.[83] The result of this is not known. Prior to the Footprint Project works to the Abbey floor (2018–21) it was possible to see the way in which all of these marble tablets had been set into the floor. Two and sometimes three marbles had sometimes been set into a distinctive pattern of light-grey stones with fine horizontal striations. Some of these backing stones remain in the floor with the marbles that were removed from the pillars; other marbles have been removed from these backing stones and reset in new stone backings into the floor. It is not possible to identify all of the marble inscription tablets that had formerly been on the pillars before Manners's work. However, the shapes of many of the marble tablets, in particular those whose designs obviously show where they sat on larger marble structures on the walls, makes those that were originally mural monuments recognisable in many cases (Fig. 23).

It is also telling that almost all of the marble tablets set into the floor of the Abbey are dated before 1835. Manners's work obviously increased the pressure, both in weight and available space, on further floor stones. At the end of the nineteenth century, the verger and acting clerk, Thomas Basey, used the pages at the back of his predecessor Charles Russell's 'Index to the Monuments and Tablets in the Abbey Church Bath' (1876) to list twenty-six 'Monuments & Tablets' he thought were 'formerly in the Abbey Church, Bath' but 'removed in 1834'.[84] To compile the list, Basey appears to have compared the monuments he found in the Abbey with those listed in Richard Rawlinson's 1719 survey. Basey appears to have been unaware of the 1824 manuscript List of Monuments. If he had been, he would have found that four of the monuments he suggested had been removed under Manners were, in fact, no longer present in the church by 1824.[85] With such a small number of tablets removed from the church by Manners in 1835–36, it emphasises just how many tablets must have been set into the floor, relocated from the pillars to the organ gallery and beneath the galleries in the north-east of the church, and replaced in other locations on the walls of the church. In 1867, a year before George Gilbert Scott's work on Bath Abbey's monuments began, John Gough Nichols lamented that the 'storied walls' of Bath Abbey had 'been denuded'. It was to be 'feared', said Gough, that 'many records belonging to families in all parts of England have been obliterated and lost'.[86] Nichols's writing is uniquely sympathetic towards the Abbey's monuments at the end of the century and is indicative of the extent and impact of Manners's work to them. Many more monuments would be lost and damaged under Scott.

'Monuments principally exhibited to the study and inspection of the sexton': Works and woes, 1836–58

William Skrine's successor as sexton, Samuel Rogers, picked up the pieces. He was one half of another husband-and-wife team, with his wife Charlotte, who fulfilled the offices of sexton and pew opener in the middle of the nineteenth century. Although this had been a convention since 1765, the Abbey formalised the arrangement at the vestry meeting on 1 April 1839: 'That the Office of Sexton and Pew keeper shall be divided, and given to two persons, a Man and a Woman.'[87] As has been noted above, Samuel had been employed by the Abbey as a mason since 1819. He was a skilled monumental sculptor in his own right and monuments created by him can be seen in the Abbey today. In the late 1700s, the woodworking skills of John Bretton (a cooper) and Mathias Walter (a cabinetmaker) and their ability to supply the Abbey with wooden coffins would have been valuable. Now, having a sexton on the books with Rogers's skills was even more advantageous to the Abbey and its ever-growing number of monuments.

Rogers was paid a shilling to attend the vestry meeting that was held on 4 February 1836, at which the outcome of Manners's report and the state of the church floor must have been discussed. His work in 1836–37 must have been a direct consequence of the decisions taken at this meeting and the aftermath and completion of Manners's work to the monuments. On 25 June 1836, he was paid 'for removing a monument to make room for Dottin Maycocks Monument 9s'.[88] The rector's notebook for parochial fees records that Rogers's work took place in the North Aisle, where Maycock's monument still stands, although his ledgerstone has since been moved to the North Transept, presumably during Scott's work.[89] In October, Rogers was paid again 'for raising [the] Pavement of Church &c. £7 14s 1½ d'. On 13 April 1837 there is a further payment to 'Rogers for moving Monuments & repairing Pavement £3 18s 6d'. This kind of work would appear to have been part of completing Manners's work, rearranging the tablets, setting some into the floor, and making good the pavement afterwards. The day before, the churchwardens had also paid the sculptor Charles Reeves £3 14*s* 2*d* 'for repairing Monuments &c'.[90] As with the erection of monuments, the rearrangement of them was a collaboration between the sexton and sculptors. Since Skrine's time, the sexton's salary had been £10. In 1839, the salary rose to £15 per annum: the church knew it was onto a good thing with Rogers.

Assessments of the work on the monuments were as mixed as the reception of Manners's work to the exterior. Sir Stephen Glynne, who visited after Manners's works but before 1840, remarked in his Church Notes that 'the whole edifice' was 'light and neat, but the nave is much disfigured by paltry modern monuments'.[91] For *Gibbs's Bath Visitant* (1835):

> Latterly a very large sum has been expended by the corporation in remodelling the arrangement of the pews, and beautifying the interior [...] A window on the south side, long blocked up, is re-opened, and a good many of the monuments have been taken down, cleaned, and in some instances differently replaced. The superior lightness of the building over most similar structures has been made more apparent.

Whereas the monuments had helped to create a new identity for the building for seventeenth- and eighteenth-century writers, the final sentence emphasises the point that, from the 1820s, the monuments were increasingly seen to be at odds with the church's architecture. The poetry of the 'lapidary inscriptions' was not generally pleasing: 'of nearly five hundred mortuary records, scarcely a dozen are worthy of a place in the note book or album'. And the people they commemorated were also not the role models and household names they had been: 'Nabobs and buffoons, the gay, the self assuming, and the titled, here mingle with the modest, the beautiful, and the gifted, and have alike passed into oblivion.' Where earlier, monuments to the plantocracy and colonial administrators would have been celebrated, now that 'Persons of all climes' should 'mingle their dust' beneath the Abbey floor was of dubious value for Gibbs. It is the first sense of derogatory description of monuments commemorating those coming back from the colonies. Previously, writing in Bath on the monuments was proud of the way they conspicuously commemorated 'heroes' of the Empire such as Baker, Champion, Stibbs and others. Now, it was said that the monuments' inscriptions were incongruous with the character of the church: 'This church is filled with inscriptions, the records of human vanity: most of them of little value.' Where earlier, monuments to local celebrities in the Abbey had been a source of local pride, now their monuments began to feel a little provincial: the 'host of medical men', for example, had only 'some claims to be remembered in their locality'. Although the Abbey's monuments would continue to be a feature of the city that guidebooks would highlight, this attitude was a long way from the late eighteenth century and the printing of the inscriptions for visitors. Gibbs's visitant to the Abbey would 'not fail to find in the inscriptions a task in reading them which will draw heavily upon his time'. They might not be 'useless to his philosophy, nor without religious effect' but neither were they seen as the exemplars or artworks they had been.[92]

In terms of the ledgerstones, Gibbs's assessment was that 'Ecclesiastical cupidity' had 'caused the pavements literally to be laid in human dust, and the health of the living runs the risk of suffering, that the senseless ashes of the dead may be turned over and over to make room for new deposits, to be served in their turn in the same manner'.[93] The view was echoed by John Britton and others. But it was not just the effect on the health and feelings of visitors to the Abbey. Britton 'deplored' the practice of intramural burial, pointing to how 'injurious' it was 'to the stability of buildings'.[94] Certainly the amount of work undertaken by Rogers on the pavement in the 1840s shows how Manners's works and burials continued to affect the Abbey floor. Manners's placement of the marble inscription tablets into the floor appears not to have helped its stability. Indeed, frequent payments for repair to the pavement begin to be made in the Churchwardens' Accounts from 1836, coinciding with the completion of Manners's work to the monuments.[95] Prior to 1836, Rogers's work is simply described as 'Mason's Worke' or 'Masonry Repairs'. Manners's work and its aftermath appears to have brought the problems with the floor sharply into focus from 1836. The condition of the ledgerstones and the burial layer underneath them were clearly badly in need of repair. The problems the church faced simultaneously with its heating and lighting and Rogers's work 'Opening Ground for Gas pipes'[96] and their repair cannot have helped the situation either. Against the backdrop of these general repairs to the ledgerstones, the Parish Records show that, in Rogers, the Abbey had a sexton under whom the re-arrangement, repair and disposal[97] of monuments was carried out on an organised, regular, if small scale, prior to the systematic re-arrangement and cutting down of monuments during George Gilbert Scott's reordering. The large payment of £11 15*s* 3*d* to him for 'repy pavement' on 25 March 1845 coincided with the cessation of burials within the Abbey. Perhaps it was hoped this would be a final act of tidying up and that the floor would then remain in good order when it wasn't opened so frequently for burials.

Rogers's involvement in moving and removing monuments can be seen again in 1847, when he and two of the Abbey's monuments formed part of the evidence in a high-profile peerage case. On 23 March 1847, Rogers gave evidence before the House of Lords' Committee for Privileges who were hearing the petition of James Tracy Esquire, who claimed the right to be Viscount and Baron Tracy of Rathcoole. Naturally the inscriptions on the monuments preoccupied the Lords' enquiries; however, other details in Rogers's evidence illuminate his work on the monuments and intimate knowledge of the ledgerstones. When asked about the monuments to Ann Wylde (d. 1761), Rogers stated that the 'flat Stone' (ledgerstone) was in the church where it was originally laid but 'the Monument is removed'. When asked about a different monument, this time to Anne Wylde (d. 1764), Rogers stated that whilst the monument itself had 'not been altered; it has been moved from one Part of the Church to another Part of the Church'.[98] The monument was recorded in the 1824 manuscript as being in the 'Middle Aisle'. This almost certainly meant on a pillar at the east end of the Nave, given Rogers's statement that the 'flat stone' was located 'Before the Screen' (e.g. near to the screen dividing the Nave from the Choir) and that the first line of the tablet reads: 'Near to this place are deposited the remains of'. The date is wrongly recorded in the manuscript as '1784' rather than '1764', suggesting perhaps that its elevated position on the pillar may have hampered the inscription's legibility. Wylde's monument is not given in the 1778 guidebook, 1783 *Gentleman's Magazine*, nor Collinson's list in 1791, so there is no way of knowing its precise position. However, if, as is likely, the tablet was on a pillar, it would have been 'removed' in the 1830s and Rogers was also probably personally involved in its removal. Its present location in the St Alphege Chapel, in the north-east corner of the Abbey, suggests it may have been moved under 'galleries at the north-east end of the choir' with other tablets by Manners, and then not moved far from that location by George Gilbert Scott. Ann Wylde's ledgerstone was relocated, by quite some distance, like so many others, by George Gilbert Scott's work and was moved to the south-west of the central nave.

By the time that the Abbey's new cemetery, near Prior Park, was consecrated in 1844, the Abbey was an example of the country's 'already overgorged burying places'. It was 'so full of bodies that it [was] a work of the greatest difficulty to make fresh graves'.[99] This, the state of the Abbey floor and Rogers's works to it must have struck the new rector, William Brodrick, when he took up the incumbency in 1839. The problem wasn't unique to Bath or the Abbey, although the Abbey had always lacked (space around it for) a burial ground. In an age of 'phenomenal urban growth, when the land that may have been available for cemeteries within towns and cities, as at Bath, was rapidly and fully filled with housing and other buildings, the 'only way to provide sufficient burial places for the increasing number of dead was to utilize sites outside and beyond the town centre'.[100] Brodrick used his personal wealth to purchase 'the land from the Catholic Bishop Baines'[101] and the cemetery, designed by John Claudius Loudon (1783–1843), is one of 'the earliest well-planned cemeteries' and 'the best surviving example of a cemetery' by Loudon.[102] James Tunstall wrote approvingly in 1848 that although the cemetery were only 'lately opened', it had already begun to assume 'the air of a Necropolis'.[103]

George Phillips Manners designed the chapel, which was built 1843–44. Manners's original design for the chapel 'comprehend cloisters for the erection of monuments', which were not executed. Had they been, James Tunstall thought, 'it would have produced a most picturesque effect'.[104] It is interesting that Manners's approach to the monuments at the new Abbey cemetery was originally similar to the recesses he designed into the organ screen to accommodate the monuments in the Abbey. Without the cloisters, monuments could either be erected in the open ground over graves or on the walls of the chapel. If the walls of the chapel were used, permission for tablets on the outside walls 'not exceeding 5 superficial feet' cost £3 13*s* 6*d*, whereas inside the chapel tablets 'below the Window-table, agreeable to specified design, 27 inches by 13 inches' cost £5 5*s*, and tablets 'above the Window-table, not exceeding 5 Superficial Feet' cost £7 7*s*.[105] The specifications are interesting and show a clear desire for uniformity and control of monuments' design, size and location from the outset at the chapel. The use of the string course of the window as a dividing line for the size of the monuments is interesting in the context of how the string course of the windows in the Abbey had been used to reorganise those in the Abbey by Manners. The Abbey clearly didn't want to repeat the problems it was suffering from in the Abbey at the chapel.

However, at the Abbey the problems were not only aesthetic ones. Mid-nineteenth-century writers were concerned that the health of visitors and structural stability of church buildings were jeopardised by intramural burial. To make their point, they often used metaphors of illness to describe how the aesthetic and architecture of church buildings were also being injured by monuments. For example, visitors need only walk into Bristol Cathedral to see 'how the lower portion of its piers [had] been eaten into as with a marble leprosy'.[106] Whilst some writers thought that the 'Monuments of St. Paul's and Westminster Abbey [were] the largest and most tasteless of all', Bath Abbey's monuments were more often than not used to make this point: 'what a miserable mutilation and disfigurement it is to turn them [church walls] into monumental Mosaic [...] Look at the Abbey Church of Bath, whose walls form a dull biography, every part except the roof being plastered over with mementos of the forgotten!'[107] Prior Birde's Chantry had been 'cut into, and injured by monumental slabs affixed to the surface'.[108] The North Transept was a 'striking illustration' of 'marble excresences;– sepulchral fungi;– stone tumours'.[109]

Such was the opinion of J.H. Markland in his *Remarks on English Churches.* Markland had retired to Bath in 1841, and would influence the Abbey's brief for George Gilbert Scott's work on the Abbey's monuments in the 1860s. His comments on Bath echo and amplify his friend John Britton's assessment of the hundreds of monuments in the Abbey. What value did these monuments have, Markland wondered:

> If any one could have the patience to go through them, how small would be the proportion of those who merit posthumous notice! From such undistinguishing accumulations of sepulchral trifling, taste, and we may add, both piety and good feeling, revolt. On the other hand, was it necessary to inscribe, on petty and perishable tablets, the names of Melmoth, Anstey, and Malthus?[110]

In his appraisal of epitaphs, Markland selected Catherine Malone's ('C.M.'s) for especially savage criticism. The monument and the inscription were 'worthy of each other', wrote Markland, 'the former being of almost unrivalled ugliness'.[111] The 'representation' of Catherine Malone's monument by the artist James Cross, included by Markland, appears to have been intentionally distorted to support Markland's point (Fig. 24).

Fig.24: Drawing of Catherine Malone's (d. 1765) monument by James Cross for James Hayward Markland's Remarks on English Churches *(1843). Cross's depiction appears intentionally distorted to support Markland's description of the monument's 'unrivalled ugliness'. © The author.*

NORTH TRANSEPT,
BATH ABBEY CHURCH.

Fig.25: North Transept, Bath Abbey Church *by James Cross for James Hayward Markland's* Remarks on English Churches *(1843). © The author.*

However, Cross's depiction of the North Transept (Fig. 25) is much more accurate and is arguably the most important nineteenth-century drawing of the monuments for what it tells us about the detail of the work carried out on them under Manners. Markland included the plate 'not to ridicule whatever the hand of affection may have placed there' but as a striking example of how 'the fair proportions, symmetry, and effect of a fine Church may be diminished, and injured by the indiscriminate accumulation of monuments and tablets'.[112] The plate shows the east wall and window of the North Transept and several unique and easily-identifiable monuments, including the 'beautiful Monument, of exquisite workmanship, by Chantrey, in memory of the late Sir Richard Hussey Bickerton' (Fig. 16),[113] John Sibthorp's monument by Flaxman (Colour Plate V), and the monument to Elizabeth and Joseph Lowe.

Cross's drawing is best read in conjunction with James Tunstall's *Rambles about Bath* (1848), the first chapter of which ('A Ramble about Old Bath') includes a walk 'round the church' to 'note its more remarkable epitaphs'.[114] Tunstall's tour of the North Transept confirms the location of many monuments depicted by Cross. However, surprisingly, Tunstall describes Granville Pyper's monument ('of the later or debased style of the seventeenth century') next to Flaxman's, where Elizabeth Lowe's monument can be seen in Cross's 1843 drawing. Lowe's monument can now be found in the south-west porch, likely moved there by Scott after his main works in the Nave (see below).

That large monuments were still being moved after Manners's reorganisation of them illustrates how the Abbey continued to wrestle with the aesthetic problems, and others that the monuments presented the building with. It also helps us to understand just how substantial some of Rogers's work in moving the monuments was during his time as sexton. Flaxman's monument to Sibthorp is a case in point. Cross's drawing helps us to understand how this smaller monument was moved more than once in the nineteenth century. Sibthorp's monument was installed in the Abbey in 1802. Both Richard Warner's *New Guide Through Bath and Its Environs* (1811) and the 1824 List of Monuments locate it in the North Aisle. *The Original Bath Guide* for 1841 then described that it had moved to 'the pillar leading to the North Transept',[115] before it appeared in the North Transept in Cross's drawing in 1843. Sibthorp's monument may now be found in the South Choir Aisle, having been moved there during George Gilbert Scott's works.

Fig.26: George Philipps Manners's arrangement of the tablets on the South Nave Aisle wall, seen in the Illustrated London News, *7 January 1854. © The author.*

Cross's 1843 drawing of the North Transept and other mid-century depictions of the Abbey interior help us to understand Manners's arrangement of the monuments and some of the principles behind it. The view of 'The Procession in Bath Abbey Church' on the 'Tercentenary Festival of the Bath Grammar School', published in the *Illustrated London News* (*ILN*) for 7 January 1854, shows the Nave pillars free from monuments, the South Aisle windows unobscured by them, and monuments on the walls of the South Aisle up to the top of the mullions of the windows (Fig. 26). Cross's drawing shows the same kind of arrangement, with the exception of Bickerton's monument, which obscures the bottom right of the transept's east window. It seems this slight incursion onto the window in the transept was acceptable for Manners (the size, location, recent installation, quality and reception of Bickerton's monument may have meant Manners decided to leave it be in 1835). It is striking that Bickerton's and Lowe's are the only very large monuments in either Cross's or the *ILN*'s depictions that do not conform to the regular-sized rectangular, pyramidal or oval tablets, and that they are located in the transept. Other large and uniquely shaped monuments originally installed in the Nave, such as Joseph Bosanquet's and Granville Pyper's, were moved to the transepts during or shortly after Manners's work. This seems to have been another way in which an order was achieved. The *ILN* and Cross's drawings also appear to show that some of the black slate or marble backing slabs were removed from the monuments during Manners's work. There appears to have been no systematic approach to this. For example, the pyramidal monument to the right of the window mullion in Cross's drawing – probably the monument to the Stibbs family, moved from the North Choir Aisle – has retained its black backing (but not the coat of arms at the top of it), whereas the pyramidal monument to the left of the window mullion appears to have had its backing removed. The same approach seems to have been taken in the Choir too, as shown by John Charles Maggs's view of the Choir, which post-dates Manners's work and pre-dates Scott's.

The appearance and position of the monuments mattered. But Manners's work, although successful in ensuring the monuments didn't obscure the light from the windows, and allowing the Tudor arcades to be seen unencumbered by tablets for the first time in almost two centuries, did not create an entirely satisfactory aesthetic, nor did it stop what Britton had called the 'the fancies of so many persons', both commissioners of monuments who continued to want monuments to their loved ones to be erected in the Abbey and those giving permission for them to be installed in the Abbey. It seems that it was occasionally unclear who had authority to give permission for the erection of monuments. On 20 April 1840, the rector, William Brodrick, ordered that:

> In future the placing of Monuments – the fees for the same – charges for making walled Graves – inscriptions on Monuments or Stones – Mortuaries and all other matters connected with Internments be under the sole direction and management of the Churchwardens. That no charge of any kind be made or bill delivered for any such objects, except by the churchwardens, whose receipt alone shall be a proper discharge.
>
> It is also ordered that all fees for Churchings, Baptisms, and Burials, Marriages and Banns, and all other fees whatsoever, be received by the Clerk, and that the Sum received be entered by him at the time of receiving it, in a Book provided for that purpose.[116]

Reading between the lines, one wonders if one of the implications of Brodrick's 'orders' about permissions for monuments above was that perhaps Samuel Rogers, the sculptor-cum-sexton, had allowed himself to be caught up in conflicts of interest. An entry in the diary of Brodrick's successor as rector, Thomas Carr, also suggests how the Abbey had gained a reputation for permissiveness insofar as monuments were concerned. Those commissioning monuments expected their fancies to be accommodated, even taking the liberty of commissioning first and asking permission to install them second, as Carr recalls on 28 December 1854, for this monument (presumably intended for the Abbey's cemetery, where Margaret Dalrymple was buried, rather than its walls):

> Mr. C. G. Stuart Montieth called to ask permission to erect as a monument to a Mr[s]. Dalrymple, of Lord Camperdown's Family, a large stone cross about six feet high, and on my refusing, requested to have it laid down – to which I also objected; he urged that the Cross was actually prepared. I expressed my regret at not having had the opportunity to decline it earlier, but that it could not be allowed. Afterwards at the Vestry I learned that Mr. Brodrick had received the application and refused permission: They expected, it is said, that the new Rector, would allow it.[117]

Those commissioning monuments could be persistent, too: 'Thursday March 15th 1855 Mr. Dickson called about the laying flat the cross over Mrs Dalrymple's grave to which I objected and Mr. D. seemed to agree in my objection.'[118] Although the Abbey cemetery was consecrated in 1844, monuments continued to be erected in the Abbey itself throughout the 1850s.[119] That Carr was less permissive of monuments is perhaps no surprise, given that he dined occasionally with James Markland when in Bath and the two may have shared views on what might best be done in regard to the Abbey and its monuments.[120]

The Abbey remained a desirable place to admire the monuments. Showing visitors the monuments was a source of income for Samuel Rogers, the sexton, his wife Charlotte, and the Abbey. Despite the 'uniform urbanity', which gained Samuel Rogers 'the esteem of the parishioners and the numerous worshippers at the Abbey',[121] the relationship between the Rogers and would-be inspectors of the monuments was not always harmonious. An incident on Friday, 17 October 1856 caused 'very considerable mortification to those who witnessed it' and was reported in the following week's newspaper:

> Shortly after one o' clock, Madame Grisi, Signor Mario, and Monsieur Gassier, presented themselves at one of the east gates of the Abbey. As they were desirous of inspecting its noble architectural beauties, and the numerous interesting monuments which it contains. After ringing the bell, an old woman [Charlotte Rogers] came forward, and, on being politely requested to open the gate said, 'No, I haven't got the keys; besides, it's dinner time, and you must wait.' A gentleman, who was passing, observed the occurrence, and, feeling mortified at the proceeding, interposed, and begged her to open the gate, observing that there were some visitors at that moment going round the church. The woman admitted that there were, but said she would not let any one else in until her master came back. Every remonstrance was used to persuade her into compliance, but without success, and, eventually, she cut the colloquy short, by abruptly shutting the inner door, saying, 'We've dinner hours as well as you.' The applicants were, consequently, obliged to pass on, without being gratified by an inspection of the Abbey.[122]

The newspaper had 'no doubt' that the circumstances would be 'fully inquired into by the churchwardens, and steps taken to prevent a recurrence'. Samuel Rogers expressed, in both the *Bath and Cheltenham Gazette* and *The Bath Chronicle*, 'his regret' at the 'unfortunate incident' and assured readers that 'had he been summoned on the occasion he should have been proud to show the distinguished strangers every attention'. The incident was no doubt in Thomas Carr's mind when he chastised Rogers at the vestry meeting on Monday, 13 April 1857, when Rogers was re-elected as sexton. There had been, Carr said, 'some complaints' of 'inattention at the Abbey' and 'he sincerely hoped that Mr. Rogers would be careful in showing every civility and attention to visitors, and that it would not be necessary to make any further complaints'.[123] No further complaints appear to have been made, and Carr's fondness for Rogers appears to have been unchanged. Carr compassionately visited Rogers during his last illness that lasted for most of 1858.[124] Unable to fulfil his duties, his brother, James Rogers, stepped into the role of sexton. Samuel Rogers died on 8 November 1858, having been 'for about 40 years sexton at the Abbey Church'.[125] However, even at the end of the century, the impression of the Abbey during Rogers's time was that 'the beauty of the interior [was] hermetically sealed from the vulgar eye, and its mural monuments principally exhibited to the study and inspection of the sexton' (Fig. 27).[126]

Fig.27: Samuel Rogers Jr, mason, Canal Bridge, Widcombe, Bath c.*1864. A cabinet photograph by J. & J. Dutton, photographers, Bath. Samuel Rogers's firm carved a number of monuments for the Abbey and its cemetery here in the mid-nineteenth century. © Bath & North East Somerset Council.*

'Customary Fees': The costs of burial and monuments, 1801–45

Rogers had been paid as sculptor but was not necessarily remunerated as he should have been in his work as sexton. Whilst an official set of Sexton's Accounts do not exist for his period in office (perhaps, in part, because of Brodrick's directives that the churchwardens and clerk should account for burial fees from 1840), we get a sense of the profitability of showing the church and monuments from the vestry minutes for 1856 and 1857 and the newspaper's reports of the first meeting. The 'regulations' of the sexton were rarely written down and updated. Prior to Rogers's time, those being used in 1834 were still those that had been agreed in 1815.[127] They were updated in 1849,[128] and again on 24 March 1856. Covering nine points across three handwritten pages, they are too lengthy to quote in full. For our purposes, it is sufficient to see that in points three and four that Rogers agreed to the following:

3rd. That the duties of the Sexton shall be to Ring and knell the Bells for Divine Services, Funerals, and Vestries, to open and shut all the Church Doors and Gates before and after Service. To attend in the Church the during the whole time of Service, to open the Pews at the time of daily prayers, to keep the Church free from noise and disturbance, to wait on the Minister to the Communion Table and Pulpit, to attend the coming in of the Mayor and open his Pew, the Chancel and the Pews in the south Aisle of the Choir, to attend Weddings, Christenings, Churchings, and Vestries, to cleanse and sweep all round the outside of the Church, Church doors, Vestry Room and Window, Window Sills of the Nave and Choir, Monuments, Tower Steps, Mayor's Seat, Chapel, Communion Table, Chairs, Rails and steps, Bishop's Throne, and all the Pews and Seats in the Choir, Aisles Chancel, Galleries, Organ Gallery, Pulpit, Reading Desk, Clerk's Desk, Churchwarden's Seat, and every other part of the Choir and Chancel, the walls of the Chapel and Chancel, Fronts of the Galleries, Organ, Pulpit and Desks, Floor of the Nave, Choir, Aisles, galleries, Chancel and Vestry; to clean the Communion Plate and to lay it in a decent manner upon the Table on Sacrament days; to have the keeping of the Surplices Table Cloths, Pulpit Cushions and Curtains; to light the Vestry fire; and to attend particularly to the closing of the outward lobby and Gallery doors during the time of Divine Service and to pay every attention to all persons frequenting the Church at all times.

4th. That in consideration of duly performing all these offices he shall over and above the usual stipend paid him by the Churchwardens receive all the profits belonging to the Sexton arising from Bells, Weddings, Churchings, Christenings and Monuments, and all voluntary contributions from Strangers inspecting the Church and Monuments.[129]

It is interesting that the clause concerning the receipt of the profits from 'all voluntary contributions from Strangers inspecting the Church and Monuments' is not present in earlier versions of the sexton's regulations. The newspaper report of the vestry that appeared in *The Bath Chronicle* the following Thursday is extremely interesting in relation to this, in that it illuminates how showing of the monuments and the remuneration of the sexton had become inextricably linked by the 1850s, and the difficult position the Abbey found itself in in regard to maintaining the building. Rogers was called in to 'give an account of his salary and the fees he received'. His account showed receipts of £50, 'including his salary (£20), and gratuities from visitors, to the sum of £28.

The expenditure, amount to £27, was for cleaning the church, which cost £27, and the bell tolling, thus making Mr. Rogers's actual remuneration about £23'. The sum was 'much too small for the duties which Mr. Rogers had to perform' but the churchwardens themselves acknowledged they had 'no funds to increase' it. With 'no rate' on the parishioners and 'only the income of many village churches', the problem was one, some thought, that was not only the parish's but the city's: 'The church was an ornament to the city of Bath, and if the person who had the care of the church was not sufficiently remunerated for exhibiting it to the visitors who came here, it was a question for the city to consider.'[130] The following year, the clause was struck from the rules and it appears that Rogers was remunerated 20*s* a week for showing the monuments and 13*s* a week for cleaning.[131]

The Churchwardens' Accounts for the period 1801–45 and the table of 'Customary Fees' help us to understand the costs of ledgerstones and tablets, and the extent to which the income from the permission to erect them contributed to the overall income of the Abbey in the early nineteenth century. In this period, 390 ledgerstones and 293 tablets were paid for in the Abbey (after burial ceased in the Abbey in 1845 a small number of tablets continued to be erected, two in 1846–47 and the same number in 1847–48, compared with about eight per year at the beginning of the nineteenth century). In comparison, there were only 'more than 300 monuments' in total in Westminster Abbey by the 1820s.[132] The large table of 'Customary Fees To be paid by Order of Vestry for Burials and erecting of Monuments in this Church' written on paper backed on linen was probably displayed in the Vestry Room. It is undated but the locations where it is possible to erect a monument are limited to 'Chancel', 'Choir' and 'the Aisles', suggesting that it possibly post-dates Manners's reorganisation (erecting monuments on the pillars not being an option). A pocket book, that possibly pre-dates the table of Customary Fees, allows for the erection of monuments in the 'Chancel', 'Choir' or 'Nave & Transepts'. However, the costs for the erection of monuments in the Abbey is the same in both documents.

Customary Fees to be paid by Order of Vestry for Burials and erecting of Monuments in this Church (D/P/ba.ab/23/1/3/22)

Monument / ***Ledgerstone***	**Aisles**	**Choir**	**Chancel**
Parishioner	£4 4*s* 0*d*	£5 5*s* 0*d*	£8 8*s* 0*d*
	£1 11s 6d (£1 1s 0d)	*£1 11s 6d*	*£2 2s 0d*
Stranger	£10 10*s* 0*d*	£12 12*s* 0*d*	£16 16*s* 0*d*
	£3 3s 0d (£2 2s 0d)	*£3 3s 0d*	*£4 4s 0d*

As was common practice elsewhere, fees for burial and monuments were higher (approximately double) for non-parishioners ('strangers') than parishioners.[133] Burial fees ranged from £3 5*s* 8*d* for a parishioner in the Nave to £11 2*s* 2*d* for a stranger's burial in the Chancel. There were also a range of optional extras for burial, including £10 to the rector for permission for a walled grave, £2 2*s* if buried in a lead coffin, £2 2*s* if buried before nine o'clock in the morning. A 'full size' ledgerstone was '6 feet by 2 feet 6 [inches]'. 'Small size' stones were an option in the Nave at slightly lower costs (£2 2*s* 0*d* for strangers and £1 1*s* 0*d* for parishioners).

Despite the table of 'Customary Fees', in practice the vast majority of payments received for permission to erect tablets from 1801–17 were £4 4*s*. From 1818–45, the majority of such payments rose to £5 5*s*.[134] The reason for this rise is obscure; however, it may relate to a review of the fees by Reverend Charles Crook (rector 1815–38). The sexton, William Skrine, began a new, separate 'Account of Fees due to Revd. Charles Crook from the Abbey' on 29 April 1816.[135] The other plausible explanation is that a note on the 'Customary Fees' reading 'A person tho' not resident, but having an Estate in the Parish to be deem'd and pay the same as a Parishioner (viz.) Monument' was applied to those in Bath for the season, or to those who had taken rooms in the city during their medical treatment. There was no equivalent rise in the standard payment for a ledgerstone, which remained between £1 1*s* and £1 11*s* 6*d* throughout 1801–45.

Whatever the reason for the rise in the fee for permission to erect tablets, Crook was certainly engaged in the business of fees for the monuments in the Abbey. The Churchwardens' Accounts in 1822 include an entry noting that they had received cash 'of the Revd. C. Crook in part Fees of Dr. Fordyces's

Monumet. [sic] £20'.[136] He and the churchwardens occasionally adjusted fees on a discretionary basis where a monument was being erected to a parish officer (or their one of their family members), or where a parishioner was buried in the Abbey but was too poor to afford the full published fees. Generally, the fee for tablets commemorating parishioners and parish officers was £2 2*s*. Surviving examples of tablets in the Abbey erected at this lower fee include those to John Stokes (d. 1816), the bookseller William Meyler (d. 1821) and the brass to James Lea (d. 1841), who had been churchwarden for a decade, among others. In comparison, the fees in St James' parish were as follows: 'For a Monument in the Church: Parishioner £6 16s 6d; Stranger £9 19s 6d'.[137]

One of the most interesting aspects of the 'Customary Fees' are the 'overmeasures'. Overmeasures were additional payments for large marble monuments that exceeded the standard size. The fees for standard tablets were based on the expectation that they not exceed '12 square feet' measuring 'from the outside of the Ornaments'. An overmeasure was charged for 'every square foot exceeding that dimension'. Like the charges for the monuments themselves, the overmeasure charges were a sliding scale based on the location of the monument in the Abbey and whether it commemorated a parishioner or a non-parishioner. They ranged from '7s for every square foot exceeding 12 feet' for a parishioner's monument in 'the Aisles' (the Nave) to '28s for every square foot exceeding that dimension' in 'the Chancel'. This was presumably devised to try to control the 'fancies' (either of the commissioner or sculptor) and to profit from those for whom money was no object. However, those who could afford to pay hundreds of pounds for monuments were unlikely to be deterred by these small sums. The Churchwardens' Accounts indicate a payment of £8 8*s* for permission to erect the monument to William Bingham by John Flaxman in 1806 (when it was commissioned), followed by a further £1 1*s* for the 'over measure of Mr Bingham's Mt.' in 1808 when it was installed in the Abbey. The Abbey's total fee of £9 9*s* for permission to erect it was less than 5 per cent of the £206 19*s* 2*d* paid to Flaxman for the monument and its installation. Likewise, the Churchwardens' Accounts record receipts of £10 15*s* 3*d* for permission to erect William Hoare's monument in 1828, and £22 15*s* 0*d* for permission to erect Sir Richard Hussey Bickerton's monument in 1834, compared with Chantrey's costs of £522 16*s* 0*d* and £527 1*s* 0*d* for them, respectively. The fee for the permission to erect Bickerton's monument was the joint largest receipt for permission to erect one in the Abbey with the £22 15*s* 0*d* received for permission to erect Herman Katencamp's monument in 1809.[138]

From 1818, a greater number of 'overmeasures' paid for tablets start to be recorded in the Churchwardens' Accounts. With the exception of Herman Katencamp's monument, the overmeasure payments to 1818 only increased the overall payments for tablets above £4 4*s* by relatively small amounts. From 1819 onwards, the Churchwardens' Accounts show how important overmeasures were to boost the income from monuments. This coincided with the increase in the standard fee charged. Overmeasures could easily double and sometimes almost triple the standard £5 5*s* payment expected from monuments. These payments peak in the late 1820s and then tend to be smaller in the 1830s, coinciding with Manners's work and church monuments (especially excessive ones) beginning to fall out of fashion. Building work in 1825 and 1834–35 had a negative impact on the revenue from monuments (only two payments for ledgerstones were made in 1834–35). It is perhaps telling that although charges for reinscribing stones were nominally part of the 'Customary Fees', they were seldom charged. The two instances of this recorded in the Churchwardens' Accounts occur in the 1830s and 1840s, perhaps suggesting that such payments were insisted upon when income from monuments dropped noticeably.

In the first decade of the nineteenth century, fees from burial and monuments contributed to at least half of the church's income, with monuments contributing approximately a quarter of this sum. In the 1810s, fees from burial monuments contribute to approximately a third of the church's income, with monuments contributing approximately a third of the income from burial and monuments. As the century progressed, the income from burial and monuments continued to decline in importance. In the 1820s, less than a quarter of the overall income of the church was from burial and monuments, and monuments continued to contribute between a third and a quarter of this income stream. In the 1830s, there is a sharp decline in importance of money from monuments and burial. Money from this source was less than a sixth of overall income, with the fees from monuments contributing between about a third to a half of this. A full table showing the income from fees for ledgerstones and tablets can be found below. By the middle of the century, the Abbey's monuments had diminished in importance both in terms of their aesthetic and financial contribution to the Abbey. The end of burial and regular commemoration in the church in 1845 was the beginning of a new financial world for the Abbey: between May 1845 and April 1846, the 'Sexton's Salary', 'Lautier for Winding Clock 7 Repairs' and 'Rogers for Cleaning Church & Repairs' in the Choir of the Abbey were noted as being set against the 'pew rent a/c', rather than the burial fees as they usually had been.[139] The amount of light able to enter the Abbey, known as

'The Lantern of England', was important, and stained-glass memorial windows came into fashion. The floor was also badly in need of repair. George Gilbert Scott's work to the interior would reveal its windows, address the problems with the floor and heating system, and redefine the monuments' place in the building as never before.

Summary of numbers of payments for ledgerstones and tablets from 1801–45 from Bath Abbey Churchwardens' Accounts, D\P\ba.ab/4/1/1

Year	No. of payments for ledgerstones	Subtotal of payments for ledgerstones	No. of payments for tablets	Subtotal of payments for tablets	Total payments from permission for monuments
1801	2	£2 2s 0d	4	£16 16s 0d	£18 18s 0d
1802	6	£6 6s 0d	8	£33 12s 0d	£39 18s 0d
1803	9	£9 8s 6d	11	£48 6s 0d	£57 14s 6d
1804	11	£11 0s 6d	11	£44 9s 0d	£55 9s 6d
1805	19	£21 5s 3d	7	£31 10s 0d	£52 15s 3d
1806	10	£9 19s 6d	11	£52 6s 6d	£62 6s 0d
1807	8	£8 8s 0d	10	£42 17s 6d	£51 5s 6d
1808	16	£21 15s 9d	6	£31 10s 0d[140]	£53 5s 9d
1809	14	£15 15s 0d	6	£39 11s 0d	£55 6s 0d
1810	14	£19 19s 0d	6	£24 3s 0d	£44 2s 0d
1811	10	£11 5s 9d	7	£33 15s 6d	£45 1s 3d
1812	15	£21 17s 6d	10	£48 2s 6d	£70 0s 0d
1813	17	£22 1s 0d	12	£47 5s 0d	£69 6s 0d
1814	16	£20 9s 6d	9	£38 17s 0d	£59 6s 6d
1815	14	£16 5s 6d	9	£38 10s 0d	£54 15s 6d
1816	12	£11 11s 0d	7	£25 4s 0d	£36 15s 0d

1817	12	£13 18s 3d	6	£26 5s 0d	£40 3s 3d
1818	12	£12 12s 0d	14	£72 12s 6d	£85 4s 6d
1819	6	£6 16s 6d	8	£49 0s 0d	£55 16s 6d
1820	12	£15 15s 0d	4	£23 12s 6d	£39 7s 6d
1821	9	£12 6s 9d	7	£43 18s 6d	£56 5s 3d
1822	5[141]	£7 1s 9d	9	£47 8s 6d	£54 10s 3d
1823	8	£10 9s 0d	3	£15 15s 0d	£26 4s 0d
1824	11	£11 11s 0d	8	£52 6s 6d	£63 17s 6d
1825	4	£3 18s 9d	3	£17 0s 4½d	£20 19s 1½d
1826	13	£15 4s 6d	10	£56 0s 0d	£71 4s 6d
1827	4	£4 4s 0d	4	£21 0s 0d	£25 4s 0d
1828	7	£9 3s 9d	8	£58 18s 7d	£68 2s 4d
1829	8	£11 5s 6d	8	£48 11s 3d	£59 16s 9d
1830	15	£17 17s 0d	6	£32 11s 0d	£50 8s 0d
1831	6	£5 15s 6d	5	£41 6s 0d	£47 1s 6d
1832	8	£7 17s 6d	4	£21 0s 0d	£28 17s 6d
1833	7	£8 8s 0d[142]	4	£26 5s 0d	£34 13s 0d
1834	1	£1 1s 0d	6	£49 0s 0d	£50 1s 0d
1835	1	£1 1s 0d	2	£18 4s 0d	£19 5s 0d
1836	7	£7 17s 6d	5	£26 5s 0d	£34 3s 6d
1837	5	£5 10s 3d	2	£14 10s 0d	£20 0s 0d
1838	4	£4 19s 9d	7	£37 16s 0d	£42 15s 9d
1839	2	£1 16s 9d	3	£20 9s 6d	£22 6s 3d
1840	8	£7 1s 9d	4	£25 4s 0d	£33 5s 9d
1841	8	£8 18s 3d	3	£13 13s 0d	£22 11s 3d
1842	1	£1 1s 0d	4	£24 3s 0d	£25 4s 0d

1843	6	£6 6s 0d	3	£15 15s 0d	£22 1s 0d
1844	6	£7 1s 3d	6	£42 12s 9d	£49 14s 0d
1845	1	£1 1s 0d	3	£17 1s 3d	£18 2s 3d
Total	**390**	**£457 10s 0d**	**293**	**£1,554 19s 2½d**	**£2,012 9s 2½d**

'Untasteful monuments to disgust the good sense of the spectator': George Gilbert Scott's Major Changes, 1860–74

Looking back to the 1860s, R.E.M. Peach recalled the monuments and the fixings, modifications, and brackets that had had to be made in the fabric of the Abbey to accommodate them:

> The cenotaphs, with their ungainly and vulgar surroundings, were affixed against pillars or window jambs in every direction, and in the most heterogeneous and unsymmetrical manner. Pillars and mouldings were cut away for them, window openings and door jambs built up in any fashion. Untasteful monuments, for the most part filled with fulsome and debasing epitaphs, were hung up or bracketed out to disgust the good sense of the spectator.[143]

However, as Peach recalled, on the appointment of the new rector, Charles Kemble, 'the old order was completely changed'. Early in 1860, Kemble engaged George Gilbert Scott to make 'a minute examination of the Abbey'. Scott's report proposed alterations that would increase the seating capacity (which potentially meant increased revenues from pew rents and offerings), remove all the galleries and the screen dividing the Nave from the Choir, move the organ to the North Transept and the pulpit against the north-west column of the tower, where it is positioned today.[144] Scott also proposed to carry out what he saw as the 'original design of the stone-groined ceiling', by creating one in the Nave that was 'similar to that over the choir'. Together, those improvements, with the heating and lighting of the building with gas, were estimated to cost £12,000 (about £710,000 in today's money). Kemble revealed to the vestry on 12 April 1860 that, before he came to Bath, conversations had arisen 'with respect to certain alterations which seemed desirable in the Abbey Church'.[145] However, circumstances 'prevented the work being then commenced'. Between April 1860 and April 1864, 'further decay in the roofs of the Nave and Ailses' had become apparent and in 1863 portions of the mullions from the clerestory windows on the north side of the Choir had had to be replaced.

As with Manners's renovations earlier in the century, the late nineteenth-century work to the monuments appears to have been neither unimportant nor unthought of, but nonetheless secondary to Scott's wider changes to the building. On 20 February 1868, the vestry made a decisive move, one which changed the arrangement of the ledgerstones and tablets forever. It drew up and agreed a scope of work for a Faculty that would form the brief for George Gilbert Scott, who had been commissioned to reorder the interior and install central heating. Some twenty-first-century writers on the Abbey's ledgerstones have blamed Scott for how they were treated, but it is clear that the terms of the rearrangement were formalised and 'resolved unanimously' at this vestry meeting. The minutes record the detail of the proposed Faculty for the 'alterations within the parish Church', namely:

> To take down and remove the Organ from the present Gallery and re-erect the same in the North Transept – To take down and remove the pulpit, reading Desk, Clerks Desk, Galleries, Pews and sittings in the Nave and relay the floor of the Choir with the same stones.
>
> To remove the Stone Screen from the middle of the said Church and re-erect the same at the West end thereof or some other convenient place or otherwise.
>
> To take up the flooring of the Nave and relay the same with the Stones taken up.
>
> To erect Pews and Sittings in the Choir, Nave, and Transept.
>
> To use and employ any of the materials removed in the refitting of the said Choir and Nave or otherwise to sell the same and apply the proceeds in and towards the expenses of such refittings.
>
> To remove all Tombs Monuments and Tablets now erected and being in and against the walls of the said Church and (without destroying or defacing any inscriptions thereon) to reduce the same in size and reerect and fix the said Tombs, Monuments and Tablets in some other appropriate and convenient place or places within the said Church and to remove alter and re-erect the Rails of the Chancel of the said Church.[146]

Such works were resolved upon 'unanimously' by those present at the meeting. The following day (21 February 1868) Richard Stothert wrote to Henry Bernard (chapter clerk at Wells Cathedral) enclosing a copy of the resolutions. He observed that 'it is a rare instance of so important a Faculty being asked for without exciting either more interest or more opposition but the Parishioners have full confidence that the Rector will do nothing in opposition to their views or disabuse their confidence'. Enquiring whether Bernard would require 'a ground plan' showing the works, he wrote, pragmatically, that 'much of the detail has yet to be decided upon by Mr Scott when the work is more advanced & cannot be correctly laid down til the organ & screen are cleared away which is likely to be two years first presuming the money asked for comes in'.[147]

On 29 April, Stothert wrote to Bernard again, informing him that 'Mr. Scott has been here [the Abbey] and arranged the plan of the interior of the church as intended to be furnished.' Once the plan had been 'copied', Stothert would send it 'to be deposited in the Registry'. The citation was fixed to the door of the Abbey on 3 May and a copy of the 'Faculty to restore and improve the Abbey Church' dated 12 May 1868 sent to the Abbey. The plan was then sent to Wells on 7 July. The report on 'Bath Abbey Restoration', reprinted from *The Bath Chronicle* in 17 December 1868, only alluded to the monuments, 'a faculty has been obtained for the alteration in the internal arrangements'. By the end of 1868, 'the new vaulting of the nave and aisles was nearly complete; the roof and windows had been repaired; and the organ, which had been rebuilt, was now placed in the north transept'.[148] Clearly, the monuments and the works to them had been considered. But naturally the focus of the works was elsewhere.

In 1869, 'the choir screen was removed to the west end'. The screen became a new porch around the inside of the Great West Door. These works would have been a fulcrum for the work to the monuments. Edwin Morcombe Hick's summary of these events makes this point, and reveals that Manners's screen had accommodated numerous tablets:

> Owing to the great number of tablets attached to it [the choir screen], for which new places had to be found, an entire rearrangement of these memorials took place throughout the church. The piers, which had not been repaired when the tablets were removed in the previous restoration [*c.* 1835], were also taken in hand, and the whole nave floor was levelled and concreted.[149]

At the vestry meeting held at the end of March 1869, it was reported that, 'Tenders had been sent in and the contracts taken for the paving of the whole of the Abbey choir as well as the nave, and also for heating the building.'[150] By then, the 'works had been commenced, and in consequence of that it had become necessary entirely to close the nave from the ingress of the public for paving the nave and concreting the whole surface'. The newspaper noted that the work would probably take 'a few months'. Then, the congregation could return to the Nave and 'the workpeople [take] possession of the choir'. By the end of 1871, the works in the Nave and its aisles, including the 'cleansing' of the walls and pillars and the 'mural tablets rearranged', was complete and the Choir was 'in the hands of the contractors'. It was hoped that 'in the course of twelve months it [the Choir] may be opened'. Not only does this sequence of events show the monuments in the Nave were worked on first, but also helps to explain the different approaches taken to the arrangement of the wall tablets in the Nave and Choir respectively.

The repair of the floor and the alterations to the monuments were 'the third portion' of Scott's sequence of works (after the repairs to the roofs and windows and the stone fan vaulting in the Nave). These third works involved 'first, concreting the nave, second, the repewing of the nave, third, the removal and re-arrangement of the mural tablets, fourth, the construction of channels and laying down grating for the warming of the building, and last, though by no means least, the lighting'. All these works combined was estimated to cost £6,000 (about £375,000 today).[151] Funding such major works was a constant concern. Insofar as the works to the monuments were concerned, numerous applications were made to the descendants of those who had monuments in the Abbey for their repair, and (in some cases) for permission for their removal, and 'considerable sums were received'.[152] The Abbey also capitalised on the renewed interested in the monuments and interior caused by the works and the closure of the building. In 1856, the vestry had revised the sexton's 'Rules and Orders' at the vestry to make provision for the sculptor-cum-sexton Samuel Rogers to receive 'all the profits belonging to the Sexton' arising from 'all voluntary contributions from Strangers inspecting the Church and Monuments'[153] (a clause not present in earlier versions of the rules and one struck from the rules the following year).[154] It was reinstated, in an amended form, at the vestry meeting held on 1 April 1872 to incentivise Rogers's replacement as sexton, Josiah Cook. It was agreed that Cook would receive 'a commission of 5 per cent on all sums paid to the Restoration Fund by Visitors'.[155] The Abbey would have used these sums to help fund the completion of the works to the monuments and ledgerstones in the Choir.

In terms of how the works to the monuments were carried out, records are scant. According to Frederick Shum, one of the secretaries of the Restoration Committee, 'great difficulty arose in removing and locating' the monuments in their new positions. Shum, George Gilbert Scott and the rector Charles Kemble discussed the problem in the church on more than one occasion, judging from an article by Shum in *The Bath Chronicle* in 1903. Recalling one such occasion when the trio were in the church discussing the works to the monuments in the

Fig.28: Photograph of the North Nave Aisle looking west by Dawson & Dutton, c.*1860.*
© *The author.*

1860s, it was suggested that Quin's monument should move 'higher up in the nave'; that is, further east. Kemble 'protested that he could not preach with that humorous face before him' so 'another place was found for it'.[156] It is obvious from the repositioning of the monuments to Dorothy Hobart, Mary Frampton and Elizabeth Winkley in the south-east corner of the church that female busts were also positioned out of the preacher's and congregation's general view.

Photography of the Abbey interior prior to Scott's rearrangement of the monuments illustrates the different effects of Manners's and Scott's work on the monuments. The photographs also reveal the state of the floor and the unevenness of floor level and ledger stones. A number of images by photographers J. & J. Dutton show this, especially their pictures of the South Transept and North Aisle (Fig. 28), where stones can be seen set at angles, protruding from the general floor level in one corner and sinking beneath it at another. The number of smaller marbles set into the floor can be seen in Dawson & Dutton's photograph of the Nave looking east (Fig. 29), as well as the North Aisle looking west, showing some of the marbles originally on the walls placed into the floor by Manners. The most striking changes made by Scott, revealed in comparing the North Aisle today with the pre-1868 photography by Dutton, are the removal of the black backings of the monuments, the lowering of the monuments to sit below the string course of the window, and placement of marble inscription tablets below the bench seating in the Nave.

The removal of the backings and the placement of marble inscription tablets beneath the bench seating were ways of Scott making the wall space he needed for all the tablets (especially those that would have been displaced when the Choir screen was dismantled) and working within the terms of the Faculty. An undated article, which must be from the early 1870s and written by someone from Bath who knew the works, stated that the 'demolition of the galleries and screens displaced many of the tablets' and in order 'to find room for so large a number of tablets, it was needful to do away with the black margins, urns and other extraneous ornaments, where it could be done without interfering with the inscriptions or armorial bearings'.[157] Makers' nameplates were obviously also considered 'extraneous' and repurposed. Attributing tablets one finds in the Abbey today to a sculptor based on a nameplate placed beneath them (i.e. not integral to them) must be done with care. These nameplates were removed and replaced sometimes at random, sometimes to hide iron bars used to support the main body of the tablets when they were refixed to the walls of the Abbey. Some have been placed upside down (as in the north-west corner of the Abbey). In the strangest juxtaposition, the monument to Marie Nicolls (d. 1614),

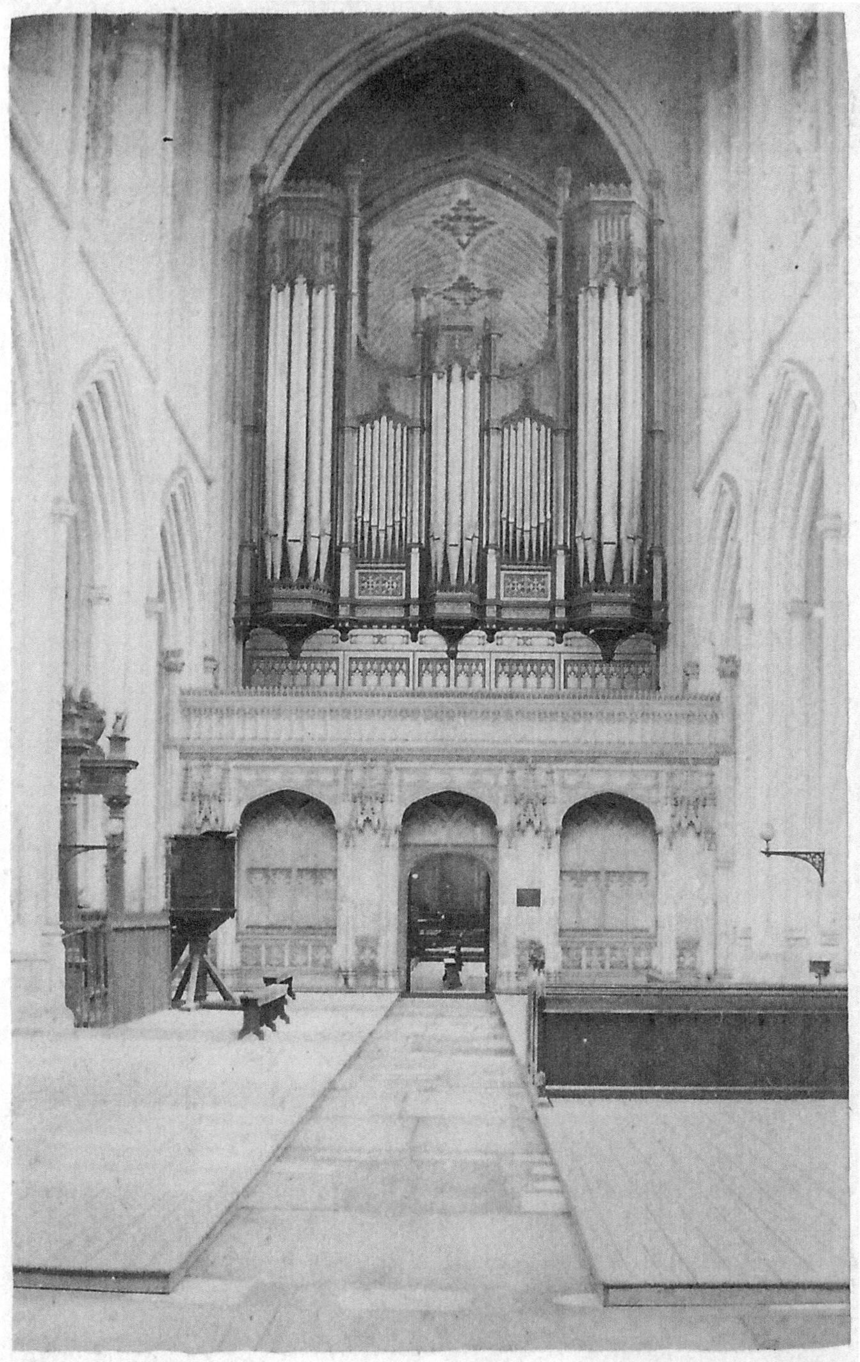

Fig.29: Photograph of the Nave looking east by J. Dutton, c.1860. © The author.

Fig.30: Tablet in the Abbey Church, Bath *to John Bowles (d. 1819) published on p.305 of the* Gentleman's Magazine *for October 1820. © The author.*

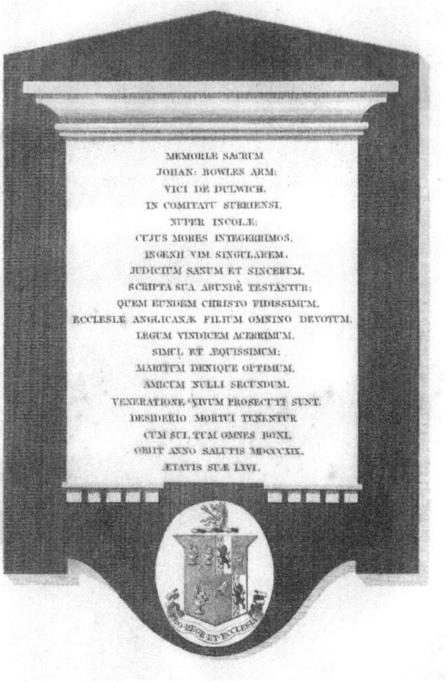
MEMORIÆ SACRUM
JOHAN: BOWLES ARM:
VICI DE DULWICH.
IN COMITATU SURRIENSI.
NUPER INCOLÆ:
CUJUS MORES INTEGERRIMOS,
INGENII VIM SINGULAREM,
JUDICIUM SANUM ET SINCERUM,
SCRIPTA SUA ABUNDÈ TESTANTUR:
QUEM EUNDEM CHRISTO FIDISSIMUM,
ECCLESIÆ ANGLICANÆ FILIUM OMNINO DEVOTUM,
LEGUM VINDICEM ACERRIMUM,
SIMUL ET ÆQUISSIMUM:
MARITUM DENIQUE OPTIMUM,
AMICUM NULLI SECUNDUM.
VENERATIONE VIVUM PROSECUTI SUNT.
DESIDERIO MORTUI TENENTUR
CUM SUI, TUM OMNES BONI.
OBIIT ANNO SALUTIS MDCCCXIX.
ÆTATIS SUÆ LXVI.

originally erected in the North Transept, was moved to the south wall of the South Transept and a nameplate reading 'T. King Ft.' placed beneath it. Thomas King wasn't born until 1741 and his studio did not flourish in Bath until the 1760s, over 150 years after Nicolls's monument was made, possibly by Nicholas Stone the Elder, who made her husband's monument *c.*1616.[158]

The same might be said of the monument to John Bowles (d. 1819), which has had the nameplate 'T: King F[eci]t.' placed beneath it. Thomas King died in 1804 and it would be odd for the monument therefore not to be signed 'T King & Sons'. King's nameplate was not originally part of the monument, a print of which was published in the *Gentleman's Magazine* for October 1820 (Fig. 30) from a 'correct Drawing' submitted to the magazine. The tablet was originally erected 'in the South-west aile' in 1820. It remains in the South Aisle today. However, comparison of the monument's original form with its form today (Fig. 31) illustrates how even simple tablets were altered radically and now appear out of proportion once their backings were removed by Scott. It also illustrates that the decision to keep the inscriptions and coats of arms and to dispense with the other elements of the monuments irreparably damaged their original aesthetics. This is perhaps unsurprising given the late nineteenth-century narrative about the value of the Abbey's monuments being more historical than artistic.

MEMORIÆ SACRUM
JOHAN: BOWLES ARM:
VICI DE DULWICH,
IN COMITATU SURRIENSI,
NUPER INCOLÆ;
CUJUS MORES INTEGERRIMOS,
INGENII VIM SINGULAREM,
JUDICIUM SANUM ET SINCERUM,
SCRIPTA SUA ABUNDÈ TESTANTUR;
QUEM EUNDEM CHRISTO FIDISSIMUM;
ECCLESIÆ ANGLICANÆ FILIUM OMNINO DEVOTUM;
LEGUM VINDICEM ACERRIMUM,
SIMUL ET ÆQUISSIMUM;
MARITUM DENIQUE OPTIMUM,
AMICUM NULLI SECUNDUM,
VENERATIONE VIVUM PROSECUTI SUNT
DESIDERIO MORTUI TENENTUR
CUM SUI, TUM OMNES BONI.
OBIIT ANNO SALUTIS MDCCCXIX,
ÆTATIS SUÆ LXVI.
T. KING

Fig.31: Tablet to John Bowles (d. 1819) in the South Aisle today. The tablet has been reduced to its inscription and coat of arms. It is therefore representative of the way in which George Gilbert Scott treated such simple tablets and applied the terms of the 1868 Faculty to his work on them. © Bath Abbey.

Archaeological works in the Abbey between 2018–21, as part of the Abbey's Footprint Project (discussed in the following chapter), revealed the extent to which 'extraneous ornaments' were removed. Wessex Archaeology recovered 'Approximately 4000 large fragments of eighteenth and early nineteenth century marble funerary monuments [...] within the 1860s disturbance layer within Abbey'.[159] These included marble carvings of a pistol, a sword, an angel's wing, a bishop's mitre, a candlestick, a flame with its gilding intact and other unique pieces, as well as numerous generic urns, drapery, borders, volutes, sculptors' nameplates, etcetera. In a few instances the marble pieces contained pencil markings, the names of those whom the monument was commissioned for on the back of some pieces and crosses on the front of some pieces, possibly drawn on the monuments by J.T. Irvine (Scott's clerk of works) to indicate to workmen which parts of certain monuments should be removed. These pieces were generally broken up and used as construction material (hardcore).

However, others, such as the cherub from Catherine Malone's monument, were treated with care (Colour Plate P). According to Cai Mason, Senior Project Officer for Wessex Archaeology, the cherub 'is a delicate object that had clearly been placed face down with some care. We can only speculate as to why this care was taken, but perhaps the workmen tasked with dismantling the monument appreciated its artistry and decided to place it in a way that ensured its survival for future generations.'[160]

The black marble backing stones were used similarly beneath the floor, sometimes unbroken and stacked on top of each other to provide structure. They were also used in the Choir (especially in the North Choir) as a new floor surface. Their concentrated use in the North Choir was not marked by the parish clerk, Charles Russell, on his 'Index Plan of the Grave-Stones upon the Floor of the Abbey Church, Bath' 1872 plan of the Abbey floor after Scott's works (Colour Plate AD). This area of the floor was covered by the new Corporation Stalls in 1873, and the use of the marble backings of wall monuments as floor surface not discovered there until 2018 (Colour Plate AE). The Corporation Stalls were replaced in 2021, after the works to the floor. However, a number of other examples of this use of backing stones as flooring can be seen in the Choir. Together, these examples of Victorian reuse of materials illustrate how Scott and his clerk of works, James T. Irvine, applied the clause in the Faculty 'To use and employ any of the materials removed in the refitting of the said Choir and Nave' to their work to the monuments and ledgerstones. Archaeological works beneath the floor in 2018–21 also found 'Prior Bird's chantry chapel, and James Montague and Lady Waller's tombs (which were originally erected in the sixteenth and early seventeenth centuries), were founded on a bed of 1860s limecrete, indicating that these structures were completely dismantled and rebuilt during Gilbert Scott's refurbishment.'[161]

The wall monuments are largely in the forms and locations that Scott's works put them in. His rearrangement of the wall monuments illustrates an overt curation of them, which achieved the order and symmetry found wanting by Britton and other nineteenth-century writers. As per the Faculty, the individual tablets were reduced in size, their backings and decoration removed, their inscriptions and coats of arms retained. A large monument appears to have been selected for each bay and other, smaller monuments arranged symmetrically around it, all below the window level. The same attempt at symmetry can be seen beneath the bench seating in the Nave. This arrangement can be found in every bay of the Nave, with the exception of the south bay of the South

Transept (because of the location of Lady Waller's tomb) and in the south-west corner next to the Font (where three large memorials are located in the left, centre and right of the bay). To achieve this arrangement, Scott must first have removed all the monuments from the walls, selected the large monument for the centre of each bay, carried out the work to reduce all the monuments in size (including the centrepieces of each bay), and finally reattached the monuments to the walls, beginning from with the centrepiece of each bay and working outwards.

Some of the large wall monuments placed in the centre of each bay of the Nave had already been moved into the positions they kept under Scott by Manners in 1835–36. For example, Jacob Bosanquet's monument had moved from the left of the Great West Door to the centre of the east wall of the South Transept. Some of these monuments, like Sir William Baker's (d. 1770), remained in the locations where they had originally been erected, unmoved by either Manners or Scott, albeit reduced in size by the latter. However, some of these large monuments moved radically from their original locations to the bays where they were placed centrally by Scott. For example, the central monument with the broken column commemorating Robert Walsh (d. 1788) is now located in the North Aisle of the Nave (Colour Plate AF). Walsh was buried on 25 September 'under Betty Villers's Stone'.[162] Elizabeth Villers was Walsh's aunt, and his Will and the burial register confirm that these burials took place in the 'middle aisle'. The inscription on his celebrated monument, one of the earliest to use the symbol of the broken column, begins 'Near this Place'. Both Warner (1801) and the 1824 List of Monuments confirm that Walsh's monument was originally erected 'against a pillar in the south aile [sic]'.[163] Walsh's monument was removed from the South Aisle pillar when Manners cleared them of the monuments in 1835–36 and placed 'Underneath the organ gallery'.[164] His monument was then moved again by Scott to the wall of the North Nave Aisle when he dismantled the Choir Screen and organ gallery. The screen had provided Manners with much-needed space for large monuments that he needed to remove from the pillars and wanted to keep intact.

Another example is Joseph Sill's (d. 1824) monument, which was moved from the west end of the Middle Aisle by Manners near to Walsh's under the organ, before, in a twist of fate, being moved to the east wall of the South Transept by Scott next to Joseph Bosanquet's monument, next to which Sill's was originally erected. Manners succeeded in removing the monuments from the pillars by using the space beneath the choir screen, the height of the walls (up to the height of the aisle windows), setting marble inscription tablets into the floor, and cutting down a number of monuments in size. Mary Reeve's monument being a case in point: removed from the pillar in the south of the Nave (Fig. 8) by Manners, only the 'ancient brass' (the dimensions of which were noted as being 'unusually limited' in 1864)[165] retained and placed on the south-west wall of the Nave (another instance of busts and effigies of women being moved out of the main worshipping space by Manners, Sill's being another example of this) (Colour Plate AG). Scott had neither the option of space beneath a central organ screen nor room above the string course of the window, hence he reduced the monuments' size and ornamentation more than Manners. The 'two weeping female figures'[166] on Joseph Sill's monument reduced to one when it was moved from beneath the organ gallery to the east wall of the South Transept by Scott (Colour Plate N).

It is probable that the tablets in the North Transept were moved after the arrangement of the tablets in the bays in the Nave was decided. The quality of the sculpture of those in the North Transept was remarked upon in the nineteenth century. However, it did not find a place in the arrangement in the Nave, perhaps due to works to install the organ in the North Transept, perhaps precisely because its quality was felt best suited to the Choir. The monuments identifiable in Cross's 1843 drawing of the North Transept (such as Sir Richard Hussey Bickerton's and John Sibthorpe's) and others known to be either originally erected there (such as Dorothy Frampton's and Sir Philip Frowde), or moved there by Manners (such as Granville Pyper's), all moved to the wall of the South Choir, towards its east end.

Elizabeth's Lowe's monument moved to the south-west porch of the Nave, perhaps the only space remaining (in the Nave) that could accommodate the size of such a monument; the symmetry in the Nave having already been created and therefore unable to accommodate either physically or aesthetically these large monuments. On the other hand, Captain Bartholomew Stibbs's monument moved only a few metres from the east to the west wall of the North Transept. Clearly the original grouping of these monuments was not a consideration, as they were dispersed. Since Scott's works took place in the Choir after those in the Nave, the Choir would have been the natural place to move the monuments in the North Transept. Fletcher Partis's (d. 1820) was another monument noted on the east wall of the North Transept by Tunstall in 1848 but not depicted by Cross. Partis's monument moved to the wall of the North Choir, as did Henry Harington's from the wall of the South Choir, having perhaps been displaced by the monuments moved from the North Transept named above. This in itself shows a great deal of consideration and historical sensitivity to move memorials to two local philanthropists (Harington, Partis) to the North Choir, the so-called 'Chapman Aisle', traditionally the place where such Bathonians were commemorated since monuments began to be erected in the Abbey, whilst the South Choir had traditionally been the place where well-to-do visitors to the city had erected spectacular monuments. These moves shed light on both the sequence of the works to the monuments and the consideration given to their eventual positions under George Gilbert Scott and James T. Irvine.

However, the order and symmetry the Abbey felt it could gain by rearranging the whole collection of monuments was to the detriment of each as an individual work of art. The loss of the 'extraneous ornaments' has, arguably, resulted in an even stranger patchwork where coats of arms, busts and inscriptions have been retained but at the loss of the monuments' original designs and proportions. On the south wall of the Gethsemane Chapel (in the South-East Choir): Granville Pyper's coat of arms now sits awkwardly in the middle of the monument; Dorothy Hobart's bust totters precariously on the top of the plinth and is laughably out of proportion; Mary Frampton's bust sits starkly on top of Dryden's inscription, no longer under the 'curtain [and] between [the] two Urnes'[167] it had when it was recorded in the North Transept in 1719; worst of all, Elizabeth Winkley's bust sits several feet away from her inscription, the 'lozenge shield with the family arms [...] large urn adorned with Laurel leaves and branches of Palm'[168] noted when it was recorded in the 'Middle Isle' in 1778 all removed. It was suggested in the survey of the Abbey's monuments by Nimbus Conservation in 2003 that the Bath stone frame for the likeness of Winkley may have been created during the nineteenth-century works. The south wall of the Gethsemane Chapel, then, is one of the clearest examples of an area where monuments have been moved large distances to be curated by type (monuments of women that have busts) (Colour Plate Z).

These monuments on the south wall of the Gethsemane Chapel also draw attention to the relatively poor treatment of monuments to women by the Victorians. The removal of the ornamentation has diminished the way in which these memorials convey the stories of those whom they commemorate. In the case of the monument to Mary Reeve (d. 1664), for example, the two children and the woman kneeling between them (now lost) were integral to the story of generational loss told by the inscription. However, it is not just monuments that moved a great distance in which this is seen. The same might be said of the monument to C.M. (Catherine Malone, d. 1 January 1765), which consisted of 'a Pyramid of Dove Marble, and an Oval Tablet. Over which are two branches of Palm, beneath, in a Basso Relivo, is a boy sleeping by an urn, with a branch of cyprus in his left hand, resting his head on an hour-glass, with other statuary ornaments.' We have seen the low regard it was held in by the time of Scott's works, and so the treatment it received is unsurprisingly insensitive. In addition to the removal of the carving, it was relegated to a supporting role on the wall of the North Nave Aisle in the fourth bay from the west.

Sadly, the same trend can be seen in the treatment of portions of ledgerstones containing inscriptions to women. Whilst the inscription to John Vavasour was retained on stone 735, the part containing the four lines of inscription to Katharine 'his beloved Wife' has been lost, no doubt when the stone was raised and moved from the North Choir Aisle, its approximate location in 1719,[169] to the south side of the Choir by Scott. Likewise, portions of ledgerstone 652 near the North Transept commemorating the female members of the Willis family were lost when the stone was cut to accommodate the heating grilles.

After the works to the floor, the 'Inscriptions on the Flat Grave-Stones in the Bath Abbey Church' were copied by the parish clerk, Charles P. Russell, 'at the time of the Restoration of the Church in 1872'. In spite of Scott's desire for the ledger stones to be recorded prior to the works, no such record is extant. Consequently, their original positions are not known. Russell's copy of the inscriptions was unfinished at his death in February 1887. According to a handwritten note at the beginning of Russell's manuscript, Russell completed the copy of the first 427 inscriptions with the remainder (to number 847) completed posthumously by his son by September 1889. Very 'few' coats of arms on the ledgerstones had been drawn by Russell and they were also finished by his son, 'though with draughtsmanship greatly inferior' to his father's. The accompanying numbered plan gave the positions of all the ledgerstones' positions on the floor, with the exception of those beneath the organ (numbers 671–700) and fifteen others. Pages 287–88 also gave a list of forty-seven inscriptions 'not found' by Russell but which were recorded in Rawlinson's *History and Antiquities of the Cathedral Church of Salisbury, and the Abbey Church of Bath* (1719). Russell also created an 'Index to the Monuments and Tablets in the Abbey Church Bath' in a separate volume in 1876. He counted 578 monuments and tablets (including 'Bishop Montague', which he numbered separately).

Whilst Scott's rearrangement sometimes imposed a new thematic and aesthetic coherence, it compromised the commemorative function of the majority of the Abbey's monuments. When Scott's workmen broke up the burial layer, disarticulated the remains beneath, and rearranged the ledgerstones, inscriptions reading 'Here [lieth or resteth]', 'Underneath', even 'Near this Place' became empty signifiers. Individual monuments lost their original forms and thereby their power to communicate the lives of and solicit sympathy for their subjects. Pairs of ledgerstones and wall tablets originally arranged together lost their ability to speak in dialogue about their subjects. For example, John Taylor's ledgerstone (number 475), reading 'This Stone and Monument Agst: Ye Pillar', is now far away from the monument to which it draws its reader's attention. Groups of monuments, such as those to Dr Pierce and his family, had their combined coherence broken: the resonance of their mutual quotation from the Psalms lost when encountering the single quote on the remaining ledgerstone; the significance of the original location of Elizabeth Pierce's monument in the South Transept lost in its move to the North Nave Aisle. In 1750, the architect John Wood described the Abbey's monuments as a 'miscellaneous apotheca of mortality'. It is an even better description of them at the end of the nineteenth century.

Conclusion

Despite the rearrangement of the monuments, late nineteenth-century assessments of them were mixed. The centuries-old description of the Abbey's architecture as 'ancient grace' compared with the 'modern deformity' of the monuments continued.[170] On the other hand, Scott's unfinished work to the exterior naturally led writers to compare the 'awe and solemnity' of his interior and arrangement of the monuments with the 'dilapidated' West Front.[171] Although its walls were still 'crowded', the monuments were described as 'graceful', even 'wonderfully interesting'.

Ironically, such debates also surrounded the design and positioning of the monument to the rector, Charles Kemble, major funder of Scott's works and credited with restoring an 'ugly interior' to 'perfection'.[172] On Kemble's death, proposals for a monument to him in the Abbey began to be put forward. The idea of a 'statue' or something 'conspicuous'[173] near the tower pillars was objected to by Kemble's family and a 'handsome brass'[174] preferred. However, the positioning of such a monument was problematic after Scott's work. Scott advised that 'no monument should again be permitted to deface the columns' and 'great difficulty and anxiety' had been experienced in obtaining the removal of the monuments from the pillars.[175] The committee appointed to oversee Kemble's memorial pointed out that the only available space after Scott's work was on the pillars, and given the 'great cost' and 'considerable difficulty' with which these 'monumental defacements' had been removed from them, 'strong objections were raised against the projected renewal of this distasteful work (however beautiful the design)'. After all, the monuments on the pillars 'for past generations had been a by-word and disgrace'. Furthermore, a monument, like the font given in recognition of Kemble in 1874, that would 'embrace some useful purpose rather than a mere ornamental work in brass or marble', was also desirable.

The alternative was an oak screen from the west end of Prior Birde's Chantry to the south wall of the church, designed by Sir George Gilbert Scott's son, John Oldrid Scott, which created a vestry space for the church (Fig. 32).[176] The oak screen, which had 'two handsome brasses' (one giving the history of the Abbey, the other 'stating the object of the erection of the screen') set into it, met with 'unanimous approval' in 1885. However, a decade later, 'A Parishioner' writing

Fig.32: Kemble Memorial Screen, Bath Abbey Church, *designed by John Oldrid Scott and executed by Harry Hems, published in* The Builder, *24 April 1886. © The author.*

Fig.33: Tablet to Jesse and William Mead by Bath masons Turvey and Perrin, erected in 1929. Like the tablet to William Siddons (d. 1808), it was placed above the string course in the South Nave Aisle. The Faculty paperwork shows that the lettering of the Mead tablet was to be 'like the "Siddons" Tablet'. © Bath Abbey.

to *The Bath Chronicle* asked 'if it is true that there is no nobler memorial to the late Rev. Prebendary Kemble than a miserable tablet in the Abbey?'[177] The low regard for marble and brass memorials in the Abbey, the pride in a Gilbert Scott-designed interior and the desire to keep it intact, and the memory of the previously disordered arrangement of the monuments and the embarrassment that it had caused all informed the writing on the Abbey monuments at the end of the century.

In the late nineteenth and early twentieth century, a small number of cenotaphs were installed in the Abbey (discussed in detail in the following chapter). *The Bath Chronicle* covered those with a local connection, notably the Mayor Charles Simpson (1915), Lieutenant Roy Box (1918), Jesse Mead and Donnett Mary Paynter (both 1929), Thomas William Dunn (1932), as well as that to Sir Isaac Pitman (1960) in the second half of the century. The monuments to Mead and Paynter in particular were noted as being 'above the string course' but positioned 'appropriately'. The monument to the Meads was positioned above Flaxman's monument to another American, William Bingham. Paynter's was positioned close to her great-great-grandfather's (Rev. Thomas Haweis's) monument in the North Choir Aisle. The Mead monument was executed by the monumental masons Turvey and Perrin at a cost of £17 10*s* in the 'Best quality Statuary Marble Tablet with Cut and Painted Inscription', including the fixing in the church. The lettering was to be 'like the "Siddons" Tablet' referring to the tablet to William Siddons (d. 1808), whose tablet is also above the string course at the opposite end of the South Nave Aisle (Fig. 33).[178] Another example of how the detail of the monuments was intended to be controlled and coherent after Scott's work.

Prior to Scott's works, the Nave 'was used as an ambulatory and meeting place. Frowsy mats, broken settles, and irregular-toothed hat-rails, lay huddled together in all corners, and decency and order had no abiding place in this, even then, beautiful old building.'[179] After them, the former 'waste' of the Nave was transformed, and it was even said that church attendance from those living in North and South Parades increased. Scott's works transformed the arrangement of the Abbey's monuments from 'admired disorder' into an order that was of 'less detriment to architectural effect' of the building as a whole.[180] It is largely the arrangement we experience today. However, it would not be until the relocations of the organ in the early twentieth century under Thomas Jackson were complete that the tablets in the North Transept would settle. Even then, the cenotaphs to the city's war dead and the need for the city and individuals to honour past luminaries resulted in additions to Scott's arrangement of the tablets and conservation of them. Perhaps most importantly, the twentieth century would present the need for major conservation work, first of the wall tablets and then of the ledgerstones. In 2018, the Abbey would begin its Footprint Project, a programme of conservation work to the ledgerstones on the scale of George Gilbert Scott's work to the interior 150 years earlier.

4

CONSERVATION

'TO RESTORE THOSE WHICH HAVE HISTORIC INTEREST OR ARTISTIC MERIT', 1895–2021

In 1878, Mary Deane made Bath in the time of George II the setting of her novel *Seen in an Old Mirror* (republished as *Mr Zinzan* in 1891). The novel tells the story of visitors from Hampshire and satirises Bath society in the time of Beau Nash. Deane's descriptions of the Abbey, its curate (the eponymous Mr Zinzan) and its monuments both reflect attitudes of the period in which the novel is set and hold up a mirror to certain attitudes still prevalent towards them in the late nineteenth century. As Bath is introduced, the 'old Abbey' comes into view, its West Front 'so blocked up with houses, that Oliver King's headless angels, tumbling recklessly down the dream ladders, had been more than once mistaken for toads'[1] (recalling John Wood's description of the angels as like 'so many bats clinging to the wall'). In Chapter VI, the characters meet in the churchyard before Mr Zinzan shows them the interior of the Abbey, pointing out 'such tombs and tablets as were likely to interest them'.[2] After a ball and a trip to the Pump Room, the fashionable party – including the protagonist Dolly – are unimpressed:

> Lady Di did her best to improvise remarks suitable to the occasion, and Camilla yawned repeatedly, and uttered cynical levities aside to Dolly, who thought it all so tiresome that she was ready to smile at them. Having satisfied her curiosity

Opposite: Detail of the pediment of Lady Jane Waller's tomb (d. 1633) attributed to Epiphanius Evesham. The paint dates to April 1948 when the restorer Pearl Blencowe carried out her 'experiment in cleaning' the monument. © Bath Abbey.

> in seeing 'How well Bath waters serve to lay the dust,' [...] Lady Chesney made her parting salutation to her new acquaintance, and took Dolly home.[3]

Deane uses the monuments at two key points in the novel as metaphors for Dolly's feelings of love. First, using the Abbey's monuments in Chapter XVIII, titled 'In the Abbey'. 'Heartsick' with life at Lady Di's, Dolly wakes one Sunday morning 'with a strong desire to hear Mr. Bernard Zinzan preach'. Entering the Abbey: 'She passed into the gray old nave, whose sole attraction was supposed to lie in the monstrous tablets – semi-classic, wholly heathen – which obtruded their ugliness on every side. Passing these with respectful admiration, Dolly made her way into the chancel, which was well filled by the congregation.'[4] The lack of improvement in the condition of the neglected church since the seventeenth century is noted. Zinzan's voice and sermon move Dolly and she is 'smitten to her soul'.[5] The narrator says that 'Never in future years, when the preacher's graven name on a tablet in the old Abbey had long been all earth's visible witness of him, should that sermon be forgotten by Dolly Chesney',[6] foreshadowing the marriage of Dolly and Zinzan and the implying that it is Dolly who erects a tablet in the Abbey to Zinzan's memory.

Before Zinzan's proposal at the end of the novel, the emptiness of her love for Sir Piers Ludlow and growth of that for Zinzan are given through two more metaphors using monuments. Dolly feels that '"Died of a broken heart" would not be written by shadowy fingers over the epitaph on [her] tomb.'[7] She buries 'her dead love [for Ludlow], and roses and heart's-ease grew over the grave'[8] and in the spring the following sentence stands as a metaphor for her underlying feelings for Zinzan:

> The stone in the little country churchyard, engraven with a foreign name, after lying in the sunshine and frost hidden by a rich russet pall of leaves in autumn, and by a pitiful mantle of snow in winter, now emerged gray and old-looking, with lichen creeping stealthily about it, as if that too would hide the story from all eyes.[9]

The denouement on the following page is that Ludlow has married Lady Blunt (whom he thinks of as 'the rose among flowers', an opinion 'destined to go with her to the grave').[10] Another contemporary novel, Emma Marshall's *Her Season in Bath: A Story of Bygone Days* (1889), also used the Abbey's monuments to dramatic effect, contrasting a moment of peace in Prior Birde's Chantry Chapel for the protagonist, Griselda, with the appearance of the dreaded figure of her antagonist from behind the Waller tomb.

Despite Scott's rearrangement of the Abbey interior, by the time of the novel's republication in the 1890s, commentators like Dolly had a 'respectful admiration' for the monuments at best. Over the previous two centuries, they had become part of the Abbey's identity, as much so as the West Front. Generally, the collection of monuments had been the poor relation of the West Front and paled in comparison with it (their modern deformity contrasted with the ancient architectural grace of the building). However, Gilbert Scott's hand behind their reordering rejuvenated the way in which the monuments and the interior were written about. For one correspondent to *The Bath Chronicle* in 1895, the monuments were comparable to the fan-vaulted ceiling in creating a feeling of 'awe and solemnity'. This was in contrast to the 'ragged', 'unsightly' and 'dilapidated' West Front. To commentators who wished that 'touches of fancy' would 'lighten' the 'mostly ponderous' monuments, it might have been said that those touches had been removed in the late 1860s.[11]

With the 400th anniversary of the building of the Tudor Abbey in 1899, the twentieth century on the horizon, and the work to the West Front begun by Scott incomplete, the attention of the Abbey naturally turned to the exterior. Equally, Scott's renovation of the interior led the monuments to be cared for in ways they hadn't been before, in part because they were much more accessible (closer to the ground), smaller and less elaborately shaped. That being said, it was the historically 'important' monuments that were considered for additional work. In 1877, *The Bath Chronicle* reported that steps were being taken to 'restore the monument of Quin, the actor, in the north-east corner of Bath Abbey' because the epitaph could 'scarcely be read, so many of the letters having become indistinct'.[12] The following year (1878), the town clerk, John Stone, paid for the 'thorough' restoration of the Montagu Tomb, although the proposal that the tomb 'be removed from its present position [where it was originally erected in the North Nave], and placed in the chancel, near Prior Birde's chapel' came to nothing.[13] The Montagu Tomb, originally 'well layde in oyle colours', had been 'rebeautified' by the Duke of Montagu in 1767, and was 'denuded of the paint with which it was originally covered' by 1841 when it was recorded by Matthew Bloxam. According to Bloxam, this was a 'great mistake' because 'in removing the paint, that episcopal habit, the chimere, which ought to have been sculptured, but was scamped, and only painted in' had 'entirely disappeared'. Bloxam seems to imply that the paint of the chimere was 'then visible' in 1841, and certainly recorded that 'the mantle appeared of a black or purple colour'.[14] When the tomb was assessed in 2014, 'small traces of polychromy' were 'still visible in deep recesses' of the effigy, 'particularly beneath the pillow and between the ear and the ruff of the cloak'.[15] Early in 1881, the 'handsome monument to the memory of Lady Jane Waller in the south transept' was 'restored, the alabaster figures re-polished, and the armorial bearings re-emblazoned, by Mr. W. E. Reeves of James-street'.[16]

In this chapter we will look at the legacy of George Gilbert Scott's arrangement of the Abbey's monuments and how the Abbey has arranged and cared for them since. Beginning with the rearrangement of the tablets in the North Transept (the last large area of wall tablets to be rearranged after Scott) by Sir Thomas Jackson, it will go on to look at the careful placement and narrative created by the tablets added to Scott's arrangement in the twentieth century. The role of the rector, Sydney Adolphus Boyd, his enthusiasm for the wall tablets, their conservation, and willingness to accommodate new additions to Scott's scheme to confirm the Abbey and tablets there as an important aspect of civic commemoration in the twentieth century will be described. Boyd's successors continued his spirit of care, if not his passion for the monuments. The Friends of Bath Abbey and Bath Heraldic Society, both founded in 1948, collaborated to conserve the monuments after the Second World War. A former curate of the Abbey, Everhard Rowe, was one of the latter's founding members. The chapter will conclude by describing the conservation work to the monuments in the late twentieth and early twenty-first centuries. The National Lottery Heritage Funded Footprint Project, which repaired the entire Abbey floor and conserved its ledgerstones in 2018–21, was, at the time, the most ambitious conservation project then being delivered in the Church of England.

'Refixed on the transept walls': Arranging the monuments in the North Transept, 1895–1918

The works to the organ in the late nineteenth and early twentieth centuries had an impact on the location of a small number of monuments. The Smith-Hill organ, installed in the North Transept as part of George Gilbert Scott's renovations, was described as 'a crazy collection of pipes which had so long done a make-believe duty',[17] and by 1892 the 'mechanism was worn out' and the need to replace it had become 'critical'.[18] By March 1893, a scheme for 'dividing the organ [...] below the north and south transept arches'[19] was approved by the Abbey's Organ Committee and the organ builders Norman Bros. & Beard. This scheme had previously 'been rejected because the view of both transept windows would have been blocked'.[20] The 'Swell and Choir organs were placed on a platform supported by steel girders under the north arch of the tower, while the Great and Solo organs occupied a similar position opposite, under the south arch. The Pedal organ, divided into two halves, was placed in the north transept.'[21]

The organ was officially opened on 11 October 1895, and was 'both unsightly and an acoustical failure'.[22] Its installation necessitated the removal of thirty-five monuments listed by the long-serving acting clerk and head verger of the Abbey, Thomas Basey (d. 1908), as an appendix to Charles Russell's 'Index to the Monuments and Tablets in the Abbey Church Bath' (1876).[23] Basey's list of 'Tablets removed in 1895 "for New Organ" and refixed in sections as marked' is revealing of the impact and displacement of the tablets. There is no way of knowing where the tablets moved from precisely, since no record of Scott's arrangement of them is extant. But the locations they were moved to reveal the lack of space left for them and the reluctance to alter Scott's arrangement of the tablets, either in the Nave or Choir, to accommodate them. The areas around the north-east and south-east doors of the church were used in the same way that the porches were used by Scott to accommodate monuments in the Nave: Basey indicates that four tablets were moved to section I (near the south-east door) and five to section XXVI (near the north-east door). Eight tablets were set into the floor of sections XXIV–XXVI (what is now the St Alphege Chapel in the North-East Choir) and one to section VII (the South Transept). Sixteen of the tablets on Basey's list moved to section XXI (the north wall of the North Transept). These monuments are still arranged there as they were in 1895.

Whilst it seems that the locations the tablets were moved to were chosen so as not to interfere with Scott's arrangement of the wall tablets, the arrangement of the tablets on the north wall of the North Transept did not follow the aesthetic principles of Scott's arrangement of the tablets in each bay. Theirs was a functional move. It seems that the north wall of the North Transept was clear of monuments before the tablets were fixed there in 1895 (probably because of Scott's installation of the Smith-Hill organ in the North Transept). Basey does not record that any tablets were moved from there to accommodate those on the north wall of the North Transept. However, generally some thought does appear to have been given to the placement of the tablets and a knowledge of where Scott located certain tablets. For example, one tablet, that to Esther Harington (d. 1829), was moved to section XXIII (Colour Plate AB). This appears to have been in the North Choir, and the tablet is sensitively placed there beneath the tablet to her father-in-law, Dr Henry Harington (d. 1816), although the tablets were originally erected in different locations, Esther's in the Nave and Henry's in the Choir. Esther's tablet is the only tablet beneath the bench seating in the Choir, and it is important to note that this was a move made after Scott's reordering. Scott only placed tablets beneath bench seating in the Nave. It seems that bringing together the Harington tablets superseded Scott's aesthetic principles and coherence in the Choir as well as the Nave.

As early as 1904, it became apparent that removing the organ from the North Transept and dividing it had been a costly mistake.[24] The architect Sir Thomas Jackson was approached. Jackson's sensitivity to the needs of the Abbey had been appreciated in his work to the West Front: 'We did not want an architect that would make the Abbey "Smick, smack, smooth," but one who would say, "Lightly touch, tis hallowed stone"'. Such an one we have found in Mr Jackson.'[25] A number of options were considered, including the Organ Committee's suggestion of 'placing the organ in a gallery at the west end of the church. But Jackson was opposed to such a move pointing out that "a gallery large enough for both choir and organ would project very much into the nave, and the organ would block the fine west window".'[26] In the end, the erection of the organ in a gallery in the North Transept was unanimously recommended by the Church Council in June 1912.[27] Jackson drafted an 'Abstract of specification for a Faculty' on 22 July 1913. It is worth quoting in full, as it conveys the consideration given to the monuments:

> The organs resting on girders & partly blocking the two arches N. & S. of the central tower, are to be removed, & the masonry made good.
>
> A new organ loft of concrete & iron is to be formed in the North transept, with iron supports, to be Encased in oak, with carved work of crockets & angels in front, & with a winding stair of oak.
>
> Proper foundations to be formed for the supports on a firm bottom. Any human remains disturbed will be carefully shifted out of the way & reinterred close by.
>
> A certain number of memorial tablets will be removed to make way for the new loft, and refixed on the transept walls which will be exposed by the removal of the great pipes, & other woodwork.
>
> An airtrunk for blowing the organ will be formed in continuation of the existing trunk in order to reach the new position of the organ.
>
> It is also proposed to remove the modern screen-work, now in front of the West door which was once at the East End of the Nave & was placed in its present position about 40 or 50 years ago.[28]

As in the 1830s and 1860s, the monuments, the organ, aesthetics and keeping the windows clear of obstructions to let light into the building were interrelated matters. Unlike Scott, Jackson seems not to have been concerned about the ledgerstones in the works. The treatment of human remains was a consideration, but not the impact of the works on the floor. The fact that Russell had shown the locations of Scott's arrangement in his 1872 plan of the ledgerstones, and Jackson's relatively small intervention into the floor compared with Scott's (inserting tablets into the floor of the North-East Choir in 1895), would have made the ledgerstones even more of a peripheral concern than they already were by the early twentieth century compared to the wall tablets.

The Abbey's resolutions, based on Jackson's thinking, carried unanimously at the vestry meeting on 3 October 1913, make clear Jackson's further thinking about the removal and placement of the monuments because of the Abbey's desire to remove the stone screen at the west end. As well as the works to the organ and alterations to 'the positions of a few Monumental tablets' outlined above, the typescript resolutions record the terms in which the Abbey considered the stone screen and how it had continued to be a place where tablets were fixed. The vestry resolved to:

> ask for the removal and disposal of the modern stone screen, now forming the Lobby to the Great West Door of the Church, which darkens the end of the Church, which is of no utility and is an addition of some forty or fifty years ago quite out of character with the strength and solidity of the Abbey structure and unworthy of it. As there are a certain number of monumental Tablets affixed to this screen on each side, permission is asked for the removal of these Tablets, that they may be affixed in other suitable places upon the walls of the Church.[29]

The Faculty papers include two sheets of tracing paper on which Jackson drew the east and west elevations of the North Transept and the new organ screen. Stuck to these sheets are scale outline drawings of the monuments on white paper, which Jackson obviously created to try out different arrangements of the tablets that were being removed to the east and west walls of the transept. On each paper version of the tablet, Jackson wrote the name of the person commemorated by it and where it had moved from, helping us to understand where Scott had placed these tablets during his arrangement of them. On the east wall of the North Transept, Jackson proposed the following tablets be installed: Richard Crowe's, Andrew and Alexander Sutherland's, and William Fraser's (all from the old stone screen at the west end), and Lady Pennington's (moved from elsewhere in the North Transept). On the west wall of the North

Transept, Jackson proposed the following tablets: Thomas March Phillips's, Duglass Sherwen's, and Elizabeth Webb's (all from the old stone screen at the west end) and John Stibbs's, James Dottin Maycock's, Alexander Haig's, and Theophilus Clive's (moved from elsewhere in the North Transept). Assuming Jackson's drawings represent all the tablets removed from the screen at the west end (and there is no reason why he wouldn't be comprehensive in the Faculty paperwork), six tablets were removed from Manners's old stone screen at the west end of the Nave.

The arrangement of the tablets in the North Transept remains broadly that which Jackson created in 1895–1918. His drawings show that room was available and this space was used to erect new tablets before the final meeting of the Organ Committee and completion of the work in March 1918.[30] For example, in September 1917, the tablet to Richard England Brooke (rector of the Abbey, 1875–95) was installed on the east wall of the North Transept. The position 'close to the staircase leading to the organ loft' was chosen 'in order that the interest of Canon Brooke in the music at the Abbey may be more definitely commemorated'. *The Bath Chronicle* reported that the 'prevailing impression' of the 'simple design' of the 'white marble, oval in shape, on a rectangular black marble base' was 'distinctly severe'.[31] It is also worth noting that Brooke's tablet was executed by Turvey and Perrin of Bath, the same monumental masons who carried out a similar oval tablet to Jesse Mead in 1929.

In comparison to his work on the West Front in the early 1900s, Sir Thomas Jackson's modifications to the interior were modest. However, after the First World War, Jackson was architect of the Memorial Chapel in the south-east corner of the Choir (1923),[32] the War Memorial 'Cloister' (1927),[33] as well as 'a simple shelf to go under the 4th Somersets' memorial brass in the north transept of the Abbey, which will be found useful for the depositing of chaplets and wreaths'.[34]

Jackson also designed the cenotaph tablet to Captain Aubrey Reilly (d. 1917) that was unveiled on Saturday, 26 April 1919 (Fig. 34). It was installed at the very east end of the North Nave Aisle and, as with the other First and Second World War Memorials, installed above the string course. It was executed by Farmer and Brindley, who were responsible for the organ loft carving, next to which the tablet is placed. *The Bath Chronicle* described it as a 'very handsome addition to the many mural memorial tablets in the Abbey Church', the patriotic, approving tone for reports of these kinds of tablets differ from the reporting on other types of tablet. Reilly's father, who became a churchwarden of the Abbey in the same week his son's tablet was unveiled, sat 'near the tablet' during the memorial service held for

Fig.34: Tablet to Captain Aubrey Reilly (d. 1917) by Farmer and Brindley, installed above the string course at the east end of the North Nave Aisle.
© Bath Abbey.

those who died in the First World War. In his obituary, in 1936, it was said that 'never a day passed on which he failed to visit the church'. It is easy to imagine him drawing near to his son's memorial daily.

The memorials to those who died in the First World War naturally renewed the civic focus on the Abbey's monuments, and the relevance of the Abbey as an historic place of memorialisation for the city beyond draping the Union Jack over Admiral William Hargood's tablet on the centenary of Trafalgar. Tablets such as that to Brooke (discussed above, erected 1917), and especially that to three-times mayor Major Charles Henry Simpson (erected 1915), illustrate how the installation of a monument in the Abbey was still a major source of pride and galvanisation for Bath (especially when considered in the context of the memorial windows and colours of the Somerset Light Infantry that were installed in the period) during the First World War. *The Bath Chronicle* covered the service at which Simpson's tablet was unveiled on 10 November 1915 in unusual detail. The mayor, H.T. Hatt, addressed the Abbey congregation as follows:

> This old Abbey Church is the church to which the Mayor and Corporation and citizens of Bath have brought all their joys and sorrows. In times of great national anxiety and danger and sadness, such as that we are passing through in the present time, we have brought our sorrows here, and we have interceded with Almighty God for help and for protection. In times of national thanksgiving we have come here to offer our praise and our thanksgiving to Almighty God. And it seems a strange thing that in a church like this, associated through the centuries with the civic life, I am unable to find, amongst all the hundreds of tablets upon its walls, any tablet to the memory of a Mayor of the city of Bath. [...]
>
> I am very glad that this memorial has found a place in this old Abbey, and I think it is a very fortunate thing also that it should have found a place so near the chair which his reserved for the Mayors of Bath when they attend these services. I hope that succeeding Mayors as they pass up the aisle will cast more than a passing glance at the reproduction of those features which we knew so well, and will find from that face and from the memories of all that he has done an inspiration, a guidance and a help through their year of office.[35]

The position of the monument on the east wall of the South Transept, near the Mayor's Seat in the Corporation Stalls, was obviously considered, in the same way that the position of Brooke's tablet near the organ was. These tablets are examples of a continuation of the tradition, begun in the eighteenth century, of the city and Abbey cooperating to mutual benefit towards the creation of an arrangement of monuments in the Abbey that were beneficial as objects of reflection – inspiration, even – to the worshippers, citizens and visitors alike.

'Most fitting': Sydney Adolphus Boyd and the tablets, 1902–38

On the unveiling of Thomas William Dunn's cenotaph in 1932, the Abbey's rector and Archdeacon of Bath, Sydney Adolphus Boyd, remarked on 'how welcome in Bath Abbey was a memorial such as that to such a man' (Fig. 35). Dunn had been a distinguished headmaster of Bath College for almost twenty years: an original, vivacious, intimate and inspirational teacher of Latin and Greek, he had shaped the lives of hundreds of pupils, and caused the city's college to become known as 'the honours-winning establishment'. In reply to Boyd, the barrister Mr Cecil Carr, one of the 'energetic secretaries' of Dunn's 'Memorial Committee', 'testified to the very sympathetic assistance' that had 'from the first been forthcoming' from him. The tablet was the work of Thomas Baylis Huxley-Jones (1908–68) who was recommended for the commission by William Rothenstein (1872–1945), principal of the Royal College of Art. The cost of the tablet was met 'by the subscriptions of nearly 200 old boys of the College' and its unveiling had a whole page devoted to the 'Bath Abbey

Fig.35: Tablet to Thomas William Dunn by Thomas Baylis Huxley-Jones, erected above the string course on the south wall of the East Choir in 1932, opposite the monument to William Hoare and the memorial to those from Bath College who lost their lives in the First World War. © Bath Abbey.

Memorial to Mr. T. W. Dunn' in *The Bath Chronicle*. Not since Henry Harington's (d. 1816) tablet over a century earlier had there been such support for a tablet in the Abbey to such a worthy citizen.[36]

Boyd was crucial to the resurgence of the importance of the Abbey as a place where civic monuments were installed and cared for. Boyd balanced a curiosity and enquiry about the monuments with an erudite, scholarly mind, a compassion for the individuals and families to whom the monuments were meaningful, with an understanding of the value of installing new monuments in the Abbey and conserving the monuments that had been there for centuries. Boyd came to be known as an expert on the monuments, and he studied and conserved them during his incumbency. Less than a year into his incumbency,

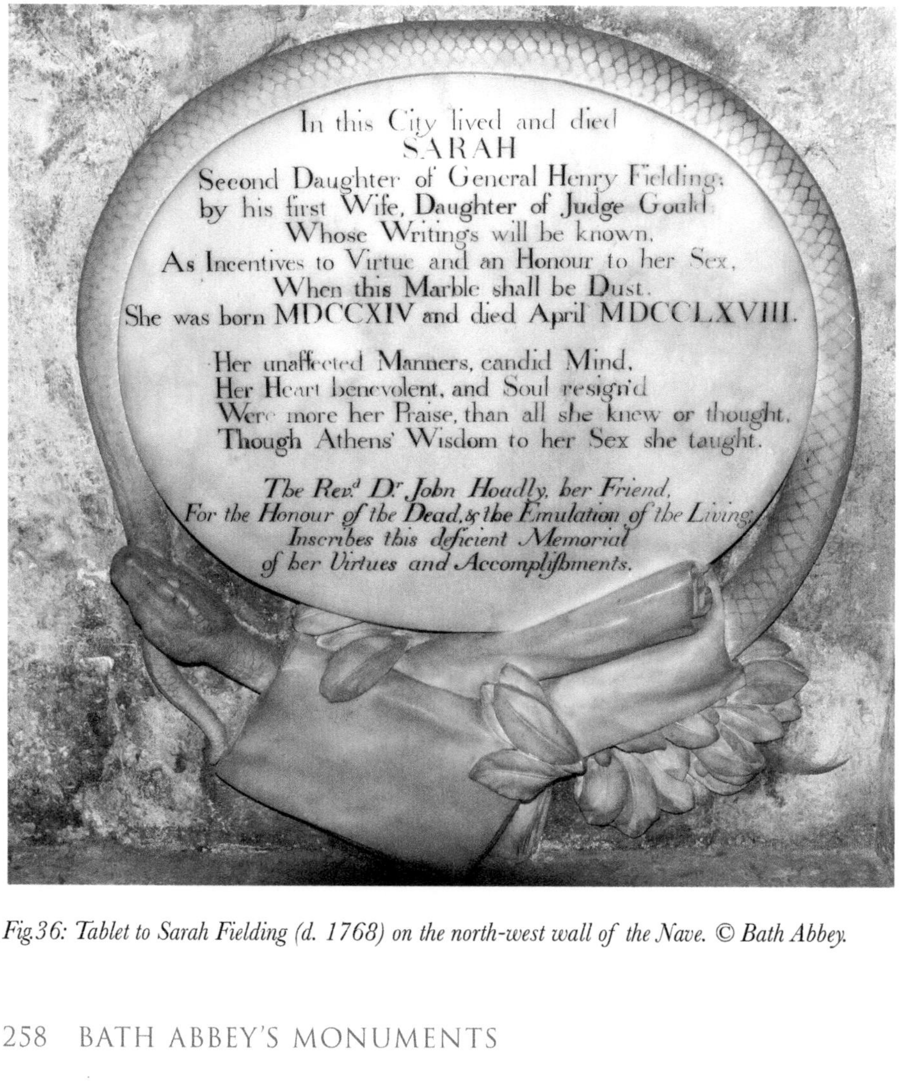

Fig.36: Tablet to Sarah Fielding (d. 1768) on the north-west wall of the Nave. © Bath Abbey.

the Montagu and Waller tombs were 'carefully overhauled and everything done to them, short of being repainted and gilded'. Boyd noted in September 1902 that the effect had been 'marked, and endeavours will be made to keep them in this improved condition', directing those 'who are curious to see what cleaning in these cases can do' to also 'inspect Chantrey's Monument to William Hoare' (Colour Plate AH), which was to be 'found in the Choir Vestry on the north side'. Boyd also remarked that Bartholomew Barnes's (d. 1606) monument in the sanctuary was in 'very fair order, but if it were painted and gilded in the places originally so treated it would look a very different thing, and be an attraction and an ornament'.[37] Boyd also encouraged others' curiosity about the tablets and their history, removing a 'seventeenth century palimpsest' brass from the wall of the Abbey so that R.G. Naish could study the back of it.[38]

Members of families commemorated in the Abbey continued to travel to Bath, and were occasionally unhappy at the state or treatment of their loved one's memorial. The novelist Mary Forrester (Elsie Mary Humphries, b. 1905) had a family connection with Bath through the Fieldings, her ancestor being the novelist Henry Fielding, whose sister, the novelist Sarah Fielding, has a marble tablet in the north-west corner of the Abbey (Fig. 36). One of Forrester's early recollections of her childhood was a 'feud' between her mother and the Abbey authorities 'because they persisted in placing a ladder in front of Sarah Fielding's monument'. Forrester humorously recalled that:

> It was an unequal contest because my mother only visited Bath once a year, and the perpetrator of the desecration was on the spot. Last summer I was motoring through Bath, and seized the opportunity of turning into the Abbey to make sure that the Sarah Fielding monument was no longer obscured behind the caretaker's ladder. I was glad to find everything in order.[39]

Five years later, Forrester had had another opportunity to inspect the tablet and wrote to *The Bath Chronicle* again. While the others in her party ate Bath buns, she:

> slipped into the Abbey to see if the ladder was still kept in front of the monument, but, either my memory of its location was faulty, or the monument or the ladder [had] been moved. In the few minutes at my disposal I failed to find either the ladder or the monument.

F.G. Warwick, the head verger, had no recollection of the 'feud', suggesting that 'the incident referred to may have been due to the progress of repairs or restoration in the building at the time',[40] presumably referring to the works to the organs in the early twentieth century.

It would be easy to think of the monuments as declining in importance in the late nineteenth and early twentieth century. But Forrester's accounts of her visits are one of many reported in *The Bath Chronicle* to inspect the monuments in the early twentieth century. People 'from all parts of the country and from the colonies come to the Abbey and wish to be told the whereabouts of the grave of an ancestor or distinguished persons. It is surprising how many are the inquiries of this nature.'[41] Charles Russell's late nineteenth-century record of the ledgerstones, combined with the completion of Reverend Dr Dunn's typescript of all the 'inscriptions appearing on the walls of the Abbey, or in the porches'[42] in August 1915, helped to satisfy their curiosity. In 1935, Boyd gave a lecture on 'Bath Abbey's 614 Tablets' at the AGM of the Somerset Archaeological Association. Referring to the burial of Francisco Antonio Zea (d. 1822) in the Abbey, Boyd concluded it by saying that 'the interest aroused by [the Abbey's] tablets' had 'repercussions, not only here, but elsewhere, and even on the other side of the globe'.[43]

In his preface to the lecture, Boyd explained that he would be dealing with 'less celebrated persons whose tablets were in the Abbey' rather than the 'principal tablets' covered in Britton's history. Boyd's approach to the tablets, like Britton's and the overwhelming majority of writers on the monuments, was biographical. At its conclusion, Boyd discussed the 'more recent tablets' in the Abbey. It illustrates Boyd's engagement with the memorials and the families of those memorialised, the way in which the renovations and furniture in the Abbey obscured many of the monuments, and Boyd's historically informed and sensitive approach to placing new tablets in the church. When the Abbey was visited by the 'Chief of Clan Mackinnon' from Inverness, who expressed 'concern' at the fact that the 'tombstone' of his ancestor was 'now almost entirely covered by the seating in the nave', Boyd arranged for a new tablet 'with an exact copy of the inscription on the tombstone' to be placed where it could be 'easily read' in the south-west of the Nave. Likewise, a new brass commemorating Aeneas Mackay (d. 1697) was placed on the south wall of the Sanctuary in 1925. Mackay had been buried in the Chancel, and the location of the brass acknowledges this. Boyd's approach to placing new tablets was similarly sympathetic in placing the cenotaph tablet to Thomas William Dunn at the east end of the 'Memorial Chapel' (now 'Gethsemane Chapel') in the south-east of the Choir in 1932. Dunn had been headmaster of Bath College (1878–97), and Boyd located his memorial 'opposite' and 'at the same level' as another twentieth-century cenotaph, namely the 'sadly long list of his pupils who fell in the Great War'. The journalist and author John Alfred Spender (1862–1942), a former pupil of Dunn's, who was present at the unveiling of Dunn's tablet, wrote poignantly about how the sensitive location of Dunn's tablet near the cenotaph to the Bath College fallen shed light on both tablets:

> The memorial which stands opposite the tablet we are unveiling to-day is its own witness to the fruit of [Dunn's] teaching, but in many a humbler sphere it has been a sheet-anchor to his old pupils when, as happens to most at some time or other in their lives, they have had to make the choice between self-interest and their sense of right. Dunn himself was uncompromising in this choice.[44]

Boyd himself thought the tablet's place 'most fitting'[45] to one who 'exerted, through the pupils he taught' so 'remarkable an influence'.[46]

Perhaps the best example of Boyd's championing of memorial tablets and sensitively placing them is the 1912 brass plaque to Michael and John Mallet (d. 1630/44). On a visit to the Abbey, Colonel Harold Mallet, a descendent, informed Boyd that there 'had been a window' commemorating his ancestors in the North Aisle but that 'it had been taken away'. Harold Mallet 'did not resent this' but 'he was anxious to have something to preserve the memory of his ancestors' in the Abbey. As a result of Boyd's conversation with him, Mallet designed what Boyd described as the 'interesting little brass tablet' himself and Boyd arranged for it to be 'placed on the wall near where the window had been'.[47] The placement of Jesse Mead's (d. 1929) tablet to create a group of marbles commemorating Americans is also characteristic of Boyd's thoughtfulness in selecting positions for monuments in the Abbey. Being a student of the history of the Abbey's monuments, Boyd would have been acutely aware of the need for the rector to take an interest in the monuments, their prospective design, placement and raison d'etre in the Abbey. For Boyd, however, this last consideration seems to have been of greater importance than in previous generations. Far from thinking about revenue, with so few tablets being erected in the Abbey in the twentieth century, the purpose and meaning of each for the Abbey, and more widely Bath, appears to have been utmost in Boyd's mind. Like other rectors since the mid-nineteenth century, Boyd faced public suggestions that 'Bath Abbey would be considerably improved aesthetically were its interior walls not covered by memorial tablets'.[48] But his incumbency was marked by a period in which the tablets were appreciated in a way that they hadn't been since the end of the eighteenth century.

In his mind, the monuments and their condition reflected on the dignity of the Abbey itself.

'The gaping hole in the floor': The ledgerstones and subsidence, 1947–77

It is testimony to Boyd's care for the tablets that, in the same column in *The Bath Chronicle* reporting his resignation as rector and archdeacon, notice was also given of the cleaning of the 'two large monuments at the west end of the nave of Bath Abbey' to Champion and Katencamp. The short piece on the monuments included a quote from Boyd's 'Abbey Notes' for the week: 'The cleaning has done justice to each work, and the effect is undoubtedly good, adding to the dignity of the church.' Thanks to many of the friends of the Abbey, 'a vacuum cleaner' had also been purchased and had 'already been put into operation with good results'.[49] Boyd was a keen reader of Richard Rawlinson's 1719 account of the Abbey's monuments. But, unlike Rawlinson, Boyd's focus appears to have been exclusively on the wall tablets. The ledgerstones, after Scott's work and Russell's record of their locations, seem to have been forgotten. Sir Thomas Jackson's description of Manners's stone screen as 'quite out of character with the strength and solidity of the Abbey structure' suggests that he had observed or intuited the problem of subsidence. However, trust in Scott's 50cm limecrete floor slab to solve the problem of subsidence, first highlighted by Britton in 1825, perhaps led to complacency. By the middle of the twentieth century the problem could not be ignored.

On 1 March 1947, 'Abbey Floor Subsidence' was reported and a 'large heap of earth blocking the West door, and a gaping hole in the floor of Bath Abbey, at the West end of the centre aisle' could be seen. Weeks before that, part of the floor 'had sunk to some extent' particularly where the heating water pipes 'run underneath the floor'. The 'gratings' covering the trenches and pipes 'sloped at a considerable angle'. Investigations showed that part of the floor had sunk '2½ inches' and that the subsidence had 'been going on for some time'. To prevent it from getting worse, Haywood and Wooster, the building firm of Walcot Street, Bath, were commissioned. They excavated the central aisle and laid down a bed of concrete. From this 'foundation', 'brick walls' were built 'to take the weight of the floors' before the ledgerstones were 'replaced as before'.[50]

Haywood and Wooster were also contracted for the post-war repairs to the Abbey between 1948 and 1960, which sought to address problems in the building, principally in the roof timbers (dry rot and death-watch beetle) and external stonework (mainly of the tower, parapets, pinnacles and West Front). Although no significant or equivalent work took place to the floor, it is clear that problems there were also beginning to be identified and addressed. The repairs to the organ in 1949 seem to have involved some investigative work to the 'under-ground "wind breach" [the organ's iron blower-pipe] which ran beneath the Abbey floor', which 'was found to have decayed'.[51] In the same year, it was suggested that cracks in the masonry of the piers and near the west wall were, in certain cases, 'due to the settlement of the foundations'.[52]

The North Transept seems to have been an especially problematic area, possibly due to the weight of the organ. In 1952 a 'subsidence occurred in the filling near the north transept, caused partly by a leakage in the hot water system'. The structure of the building was not affected but it was recommended that 'the area of paving slabs [ledgerstones]' which had sunken 'should be lifted, levels made up and the paving slabs re-set'.[53] By the end of the following year, the 'floor near the North Transept had settled leaving the paving uneven'. It was 'adjusted to provide an even, although not level surface'.[54] By October 1955, there was 'a hole in the floor by the door to the Blower Chamber [in the North Transept]' and 'one paving slab' was 'loose'[55] there. The scale of the ongoing problems in the North Transept and the interventions there can be judged from the report for 1959, which found 'a variation in depth of six inches, owing to irregular sinking'.[56] To enable the then recently donated screen to the transept to be level, 'the paving at the entrance to the North Transept' was 'lifted, the floor levelled and the paving replaced'.[57]

After the main post-war works were completed between 1948 and 1960, attention returned to the floor in the 1960s. In 1961, the central Nave Aisle west of the Crossing had begun to sink again. It was decided to carry out the necessary excavations to provide proper supports for the 'paving slabs in the Aisles' beginning with the central aisle.[58] The following year, subsidence at the east end 'had become distinctly worse'[59] and was 'interfering' with services. Repairs took place in August 1962 (on a similar scale to the 'considerable work' at the west of the Nave in 1947) at a cost of £500.[60] In 1963, the Abbey architect, Frank Beresford-Smith, finished a 'Report on the problem of subsidence of the floor'. He concluded that 'a slow but continuous settlement of the floor of Bath Abbey will no doubt continue for many years.'[61] Beresford-Smith had considered a number of ways to deal with the settlements, obtaining a quotation from the Cementation Company Ltd to pressure grout under the floor to fill voids left by the collapse of lead coffins to reduce settlement to a minimum.[62] After studying the report, the Fabric Committee accepted Beresford-Smith's advice 'that the floor should be dealt with as and when it subsided by lifting paving slabs, packing the space below with gravel and then replacing the paving slabs'.[63] The Parochial Church Council (PCC) 'unanimously' agreed with this approach and the minutes also record that when the floor was opened up for repair 'a modern type of heating pipe be substituted for the old cast-iron pipes'.[64]

This decision was really only a continuation of a need from the early nineteenth century, when Samuel Rogers frequently repaired the floor, especially around the heating pipes. Thinking of a solution to the problems of subsidence and heating the Abbey as one would ultimately inform the Footprint Project and the eco-friendly, underfloor heating laid on top of the new reinforced concrete. In the twentieth century, however, the significance of the ledgerstones comprising the Abbey floor was very much secondary to their function as paving. It is rare for the stones to be described as anything other than paving, the dangerous breaking up of Richard Morgan's 'memorial paving stone'[65] in the South Transept in 1967 being one exception. However, when concrete 'floated in above the paving stones' during repairs near the North Transept (which was 'very uneven') in 1968, it was noted that it had 'disfigured some of the carved paving stones' and that this was 'considered a most unsatisfactory and undesirable form of repair'.[66]

'Cared for and interesting': Wall tablets and their conservation, 1948–97

During the Second World War, the Abbey was visited by a number of overseas troops, as well as those from Bath and the UK. At the beginning of May 1943, the head verger, Mr A. Marquiss, said that during the previous four weeks there had been 'a steady stream of visitors from the time we open til we close'. The monuments remained an attraction, albeit not to the extent they were in the eighteenth century. Members of the Australian forces, Marquiss continued, were 'very interested in a tablet to the memory of Admiral Phillip, who was the first Governor of Australia'. Marquiss quipped that he thought 'members of the American and Colonial Forces [took] a keener interest in the Abbey than our own people, perhaps because their countries are comparatively new'.[67] As head verger, Marquiss would have been the visitors' guide to the monuments, just as the sextons were in the eighteenth and nineteenth centuries before him. What Marquiss didn't see when his back was turned to show ANZAC personnel

Arthur Phillips's monument was a number of visitors making their marks on the tomb of Lady Jane Waller in the South Transept. The soft alabaster of her effigy is covered with graffiti, much of it dating to the Second World War. The Abbey's monuments were not only objects of reflection – it seems they could also be a place to think about one's own commemoration, a record of one's life, in a precarious world in the middle of war. The 300th anniversary of the English Civil War's Battle of Lansdown, fought just to the north of Bath in July 1643, may also have drawn visitors from the city to the tomb.

Like the ledgerstones, although the monuments were not the focus of the post-war restoration of the Abbey (1948–60), conservation work took place to them and they continued to be more highly thought of than the 'paving'. On 10 April 1948, *The Bath Chronicle* reported that Miss Pearl Blencowe, a restorer from Weston-super-Mare, intended to carry out her week-long 'experiment in cleaning at least one of the monuments in the Abbey'[68] on Monday, 12 April. Blencowe worked on two monuments in the South Transept: Jacob Bosanquet's large tablet in the centre of the east wall and the tomb of Lady Jane Waller. Blencowe returned three years later, when she worked intensively 'for five or six hours a day' for at least 'three weeks' on the tomb of Bishop James Montagu. Working 'under the auspices of the Central Church Council for the Care of Churches', Blencowe cleaned the tomb, aiming to restore it to its 'former glory'. By 28 August 1951, 'the results of her efforts [were] apparent'. The gilding done by a Mr Field in 1878 was 'gleaming again'. Blencowe 'found the names and initials of Mr Field and a Mr Davis [Charles Edward Davis, Bath City Architect], who last cleaned the monument, cut into the top ledge as she removed the dirt and grime'. Much of it was 'deposited there during the [Second World] war, when the large aisle windows were blown in by a bomb blast'. Nevertheless, Blencowe was 'surprised' to find the tomb in 'such good condition'. It was, in her opinion, 'very fine and important, and one of the best of its kind',[69] an opinion shared by Katherine Esdaile.[70]

Pearl Blencowe worked on at least one other monument in the 1950s.[71] In January 1954, John Hatton, the chairman of the Abbey's Fabric Committee, wrote to her asking her to look at Bartholomew Barnes's and Lady Anna Miller's monuments in the Sanctuary. The latter, Hatton thought, 'could certainly be cleaned up, but this is white or, at any rate, mostly white'. The reinstallation of the stained glass in the East Window was taking place and must have been progressing well for Hatton to make such an invitation. With the first tier complete in April 1953, Harry and Ron Kirk, Clayton and Bell's glaziers, would have been working on the middle tiers throughout the week, before returning to their studio in London at weekends. However, some combination of Pearl Blencowe's illness, the discovery (in October 1954) that the stonework in the tracery of the East Window was damaged and in need of repair before the window could be fully installed, and the intensive installation of the glass in time for Easter in March 1955, must have been factors in delaying Blencowe's work to Barnes's and Miller's monuments. On 21 December 1955, Blencowe wrote to Hatton, remarking that Barnes's monument was 'rather ugly looking alabaster marble' and that if it were 're-coloured' it would be 'very conjectural' unless she could find 'very definite traces of colour'. Given the complexities, a decision was made to only clean the monument and retouch the painted shields (although the shield in the left niche is now unpainted and that in the right-hand niche is now missing).

Blencowe was working on Barnes's monument in February 1956, and consulted with Hatton over the cleaning of further monuments in conjunction with Bath Heraldic Society. By the summer, a 'Miss Lloyd and her helpers' from the society had begun cleaning some monuments. In a letter to John Hatton, dated 30 July 1956, M. Hughes of the Bath Heraldic Society recommended that five tablets – Sarah Scriven (in the South Transept) and Frances Lowther, Johan Bowles, Anne Cocks and William Wharton (on the south wall of the Nave) – needed 'to be touched up with colours in the shields'. He regretted that 'we cannot touch up the gold as that would mean gold leaf and special treatment'. Their work was complete by 10 May 1957, when Hatton wrote to Miss Lloyd, Honorary Secretary of Bath Heraldic Society, thanking her as follows:

> The Fabric Committee is most grateful to the Bath Heraldic Society for the work its members have done in cleaning memorials on the south side of the Abbey and for the restoration of the many arms on which colour was worn, and in many cases almost lost. This side of the church now looks cared for and interesting and the Fabric Committee wondered whether your Society would be so kind as to undertake the north side in the same way.

Blencowe's and Bath Heraldic Society's cleaning and retouching of the monuments can be seen as complementary to Hayward and Wooster's works to them in the interior. Between 5 August and 16 September 1950, a mason and labourer from the building firm 're-fixed loose memorial tablets on inside walls repairing where required'. When the winter weather prevented the main Hayward and Wooster works to the tower and exterior stonework in the mid-1950s, their masons carried out work to the interior, including work on Prior Birde's Chantry and repaving the Sanctuary.

Members of The Friends of Bath Abbey, formed as major funders of the post-war restoration of the Abbey, also worked on the monuments in the 1950s. In May 1949, Bryan Little, author of *The Building of Bath*, gave a talk on 'Bath Abbey' at the invitation and residence of Lady Noble at 23 Royal Crescent. During the talk, Little 'made the practical suggestion that the Friends of Bath Abbey might with advantage devote themselves to the task of cataloguing and co-operating in the preservation of the many memorials in the Abbey which commemorated officers in the Navy'. The monuments occupied a third of Little's 'sketchy little talk' and, he suggested, those that had been 'erected in the eighteenth and nineteenth centuries might be classified for their artistic importance, and for the historic interest of the people commemorated'. Although, for Little, 'not many more than 24 of the memorials were either of great artistic value or commemorated really famous people'. Jacob Bosanquet's monument was 'right in the top flight of artistic memorials' and Little also drew the Friends' attention to Alderman Henshaw's memorial in the North Aisle, which had been 'recently cleaned'.[72] The terms of Little's talk clearly made an impression on Gerald Deacon, a Friend of Bath Abbey, member of the Fabric Committee, and later a churchwarden. On 15 January 1952, the newspaper photographed Deacon holding a shoe brush cleaning the carving on the tablet to Henry Harington in the North Choir Aisle. The discolouration of the marble is obvious, as is the loss to the painted lettering of the inscription. The caption stated that Deacon had made restoring the monuments in the church 'his hobby' and, repeating Little's terms (which must have been given by Deacon), that it was 'intended to restore those which have historic interest or artistic merit'.[73]

The papers of John Hatton OBE (Director of the Spa 1909–46 and Chair of the Abbey's Fabric Committee 1948–65) in Bath Abbey Archives contain further correspondence and notes about the restoration of monuments in the late 1950s and 1960s, representing a continuation of the work by Blencowe, Bath Heraldic Society, and Haywood and Wooster in the 1950s. Restoration of the paint on the monuments to General Sir Manley-Powers in 1958 and George Bolton Eyres in 1962–63 was proposed, but proved problematic and does not appear to have been carried out.[74] Likewise, Hayward and Wooster quoted to carry out the cleaning of the north-west and south-west porches on 6 February 1961 as follows:

> Brush down ceilings and walls. Apply special cleaning paste as recommended by the Building Research Station to all the marble memorial tablets. Cover with a coating of whiting paste and clean off with chamois leather and water. Clean and treat both sides of the oak swing doors and the oak ceilings with wax. Approximate cost seventy-three pounds.

There is no record of the work being carried out, but 'it may be possible that the method [was] used elsewhere'. Perhaps the necessary and pressing problems of the floor in the centre of the Nave in the 1960s took precedence. The one exception to this was the erection and unveiling of the cenotaph to Sir Isaac Pitman in January 1960. By then it was said that there was 'an unwritten law that no more [monuments]' could be 'erected' in the Abbey. However, the rector, E.A. Cook, made an 'exception' for Pitman because his 'name and invention were known in every corner of the world. No other Bath man had been so well known.'[75] Cook's terms echo those of his predecessor, Boyd, in identifying that the Abbey's monuments were both a source of civic pride and had relevance 'even on the other side of the globe'.

In 1990, the new rector, Richard Askew, decided that 'the Abbey should not tinker with minor works of first aid, but should attempt major surgery on the extremely grubby patient' that was the church building. These major works were carried out under a project called 'Bath Abbey 2000', which took place almost a century after Sir Thomas Jackson's works to the West Front, and in time for the 500th anniversary of the building of the Tudor church and the millennium. Six projects were identified: 'continuation of the restoration work on the west front; the cleaning and conservation of the interior; the rebuilding of the organ; the creation of the Heritage Vaults Museum; the lighting of the aisles; and the cleaning and conservation of the exterior of the building'.

In 1997, the wall tablets were cleaned as part of the cleaning and conservation works that took place in the interior in 1996–97. In June 1996, the sculptor Laurence Tindall compiled a condition report on the monuments. There had 'never been a report of this kind before' and Tindall 'fixed the present state of the monuments to a date', allowing their condition to be monitored over time and problems to be assessed and rectified. As he wrote the report, 'bay 3 in the north aisle' was being 'cleaned as a trial', and one tablet had 'been retouched with paint to help its legibility'. Prior to Tindall's report, it had already been decided that 'all the monuments should be cleaned and the inscriptions should be legible'. Tindall therefore paid special attention to the lettering of the inscriptions, noting 'a strange practice on many of the monuments of almost scratching the letters into the stone and then over painting them as if they were only a guide to the painter'. Further study of those monuments that Tindall identified this technique had been used on would contribute to future studies on Bath's sculptors' style and techniques.

Tindall's report informed the 'Bath Abbey Monument Survey' completed by Jenny Jacobs of Nimbus Conservation. Jacobs's report, compiled in 2003, documented the work carried out on each tablet in 1997 and made additional notes on the condition of thirty-four tablets in 2003. English Heritage 'were concerned that no unnecessary invasive work or over-cleaning should take place. This would spoil the patina of age of this remarkable collection of monuments.' Cleaning methods therefore 'had to be gentle and required the most restraint in how contact was made with the surfaces. Very mild poultices were devised for those monuments with the most engrained dirt and some were steam cleaned.' The cleaning and conservation of each tablet required different stages. Jacobs explained that:

> More often than not, the variations in construction materials and their stability, the nature of the dirt and environmental conditions had an influence on the type of work required. This resulted in each monument having its own tailor-made cleaning system.
>
> As a general rule, the least aggressive system of cleaning was adopted with which a '*satisfactory result*' could be achieved. The definition of this term was understood to mean an improvement in the appearance of the monument, together with the removal of harmful surface coatings and atmospheric pollutants, without causing damage, or to create conditions to accelerate future decay.

The report also identified six tablets on the north wall of the Nave in the first bay from the west end that were 'left dirty, in order to show what some of the monuments were like before the cleaning and conservation work in 1997': that to Roger Gee (d. 1788), above the bench seating, and those below the bench seating to Eleanora Walsh (n.d.), John Horsford (d. 1795), Mary Belford (d. 1800), Mary Webb (d. 1786) and Edward Woolmer (d. 1721) (Colour Plate AI, showing tablets to Belford and Wylde side-by-side).

The cleaning of the tablets was a 'significant' part of the overall conservation cleaning of the interior. The fact that the contrast between Sir George Gilbert Scott's copy in the Nave of the Tudor fan-vaulted ceiling in the Choir would have been stark in the 1870s, the new Victorian stonework jarring with the blackened stonework of the rest of the Abbey's stonework, has not previously been considered. These conservation works illustrate how the installation of new monuments in the Abbey, and especially white marble tablets, would have appeared in the eighteenth and nineteenth centuries. New, polished, white marble shining for a time in the candlelight; the gilding fresh, the painted coats of arms colourful; the black epitaphs stark, legible. The conservation works also perhaps help us to understand how monuments could be so carelessly treated by the Victorians when they were dirty and dilapidated. By the early 2000s, therefore, the stonework of the Abbey, inside and out, and its monuments, could be seen almost as new, albeit the tablets significantly cut down from their original designs. Seeing the clean marble and alabaster next to the golden Bath stone gives us a glimpse of the effect that the early tablets must have had in the church, and how attractive a proposition commemorating a loved one in the Abbey had been, especially in the seventeenth and eighteenth centuries.

Conserving the ledgerstones: The Footprint Project, 2018–21

In 1990, Gerald Deacon was chairman of Bath Abbey's Fabric Committee (the committee responsible for the care of the church building). In November of that year, Deacon wrote to Jane Fawcett, who was then writing the *Cathedral Floor Damage Survey* (1991) for the International Council on Monuments and Sites (ICOMOS), saying that personally he did not think:

> that any of the visible ledgers is of great importance; many of them have been defaced and damaged. A few years ago I had the tablet on the nave floor marking the burial place of James Quin the actor recut. The fine James Quin memorial tablet is now in the north choir aisle.

Deacon's view is perhaps unsurprising given his care of the wall tablets over decades. He was not alone in valuing them over the ledgerstones. However, Fawcett noted in her report that a decision, one that Deacon himself would have been central to, had:

> not yet been taken [at Bath Abbey] as to whether to regard the ledgers as expendable, as at [St George's Chapel] Windsor, or whether they should be recut. Many are no longer identifiable but records do exist […] A decision

would also have to be made as to whether recutting should be confined to stones of historic interest, or of artistic importance [...] Nevertheless, they form an important link in the social history of the area, and the texture they give to the floor adds significantly to the interest of the building.

We have seen that in the 1990s attention was focused on the cleaning of the interior and the wall tablets. However, the Abbey's neglect of the floor would force a decision to be taken about the ledgerstones.

The piecemeal repair of the floor in the late twentieth century did not address the underlying and ongoing problem of subsidence caused by the decomposition of the approximately 6,500 burials beneath it. Deterioration of the burial layer and the thick slab of lime Scott laid over it was causing historic ledgerstones to crack and the floor to sink. Over the course of a decade, the Footprint Project was devised. In the Abbey, Footprint would: permanently remove the fixed Victorian pews and the pew plinth, allowing the ledgerstones to be seen; lift the stones and address the structural problems beneath the floor; conserve the ledgerstones and relay them; and install underfloor heating beneath the ledgerstones using the heat-energy from the one million litres of water flowing out of the Roman baths every day. The threefold benefits of Footprint were in creating a more accessible interior, conserving and representing the highly significant ledgerstones, and reducing the Abbey's carbon footprint by 50 per cent. The £20 million project was funded with £10.7 million from the National Lottery Heritage Fund.

Trial repairs to the North Aisle took place in 2013, informing the conservation and repair methodologies. Archaeological investigations revealed that George Gilbert Scott's works 'had only disturbed the ground 1m beneath the Abbey floor. The planned floor works for the Footprint Project restricted activity to the zone of previously disturbed soil, thus allowing the undisturbed archaeology beneath to be protected.' The removal of the pews revealed 'very serious fracturing' to some ledgerstones, as well as:

> Heavy surface deterioration was also evident with the resultant loss of inscriptions on carved stones. This was a particular problem with the Welsh blue pennant floor stones. Some of these had delaminated to a point where their integrity was compromised, making them unfit for use in the Abbey floor. There was also heavy staining to some of the stones caused by tannins from the timber pew supports. This was particularly evident on the white marble stones that are a notable and striking feature of the Abbey floor.[76]

These white marble stones are almost exclusively inscription tablets removed from monuments on the pillars by Manners and set into the floor in 1835–36.

In August 2015, David Odgers, formerly of Nimbus Conservation (the company who carried out the 'Bath Abbey 2000' conservation works described above), carried out trial repairs to a small number of ledgerstones that had been removed from and not relayed in the North Aisle in 2013. Five stones were worked on by Odgers to trial different repair methods. Odgers noted that 'previous attempts at joining broken stones have been [made] by inserting mortar or resin into the joint'. However, the 'presence of any material in the joints has the disadvantage of widening tightly fitting breaks and distracting from the aesthetics of the ledger'. Before consolidation work, the ledgers had 'Very thorough removal of all old mortar from broken faces using chisels and brushes'.[77] Larger ledgerstones were repaired using carbon fibre or stainless steel dowels perpendicular to the break, with thicker ledgers (over 10cm depth) repaired with stainless steel bars inserted at right angles to the face of the stone, close to perpendicular to the break, and the bars not parallel to each other. A repair method using Aramid fibre, 'a weave of carbon fibre and Kevlar', laid on the back of the stone was also trialled. The 'back face of the stone was treated with layering resin and then Aramid fibre laid and further resin applied. Once cured, this formed a very stable, reversible reinforcing plate across the joint.'[78] This repair method was especially useful for 'providing additional strength across breaks and particularly useful for thinner ledgers'.[79] The thin marbles inset into the floor, either originally as ledgerstones or when they were removed from the walls, were stones that could benefit from this method because they were too thin for dowels. Elizabeth Ravenscroft's (d.1801) was successfully repaired using this method. After the repairs, Ravenscroft's marble and the ledgerstone to the Hayward family (repaired using a combination of carbon fibre dowels and Aramid fibre) were displayed in the South Transept.

In September, in situ repairs to the ledgerstones took place by the Font. Two marble inlays – those commemorating Captain Henry Haynes (d. 1838) and Christiana Susanna Lucas (d. 1781) – were repaired, Lucas's using the Aramid fibre and resin technique, Haynes's not using Aramid. Deep undercut joints between the ledgerstones in the trial area were grouted, pointing the joints with an approved lime/ash mortar, and further consolidation to protect laminations and vulnerable edges was carried out. Lucas's marble was considerably fragmented, missing pieces, with plaster of Paris (on which the stone was bedded) between the breaks, dirty, and had a strip of tannin staining from an oak support for the pews. Having used tracing paper to outline the marble fragments in situ, it was taped upside down onto a flat board. The marble fragments were then lifted, cleaned of the plaster, and placed upside down on the board. During the work an almost identical inscription was found on the reverse of the stone, which had presumably been rejected by either the commissioner or sculptor. The stone's inscription reads:

> In Memory of CHRISTIANA SUSANNA LUCAS
> Wife of STUCLEY LUCAS of *Southampton Esq*
> Daughter of JAMES GAYER late of Rockbere
> near *Exeter Esqr.,* who was the Son
> Sr. ROBERT GAYER K.B.,
> by Lady CHRISTIANA
> Daughter of the Earl of Aylesbury,
> Lord Chamberlain to King James 2d.;
> She departed this Life the 24th day of October 1781
> Aged 63,
> And was endowed with a great Share
> of Sensibility, and Benevolence
> In Coelo Quies.

The inscription on the reverse of the marble omits the crucial first two lines that commemorate and name Christiana, as well as the following minor textural differences: the addition of the word 'deceased' after '*Esqr.*' in line four; K.B. given in full as '*Knight* of the *Bath*' in line five; the addition of 'who was' at the beginning of line eight; the omission of the word 'day' after '24th' in line nine; and the addition of the word 'Years' after '63' in line ten. Clearly, the omission of Christiana's name was unacceptable. The history of the commissioning of this inscription is not known, but the omission of the first two lines in the rejected version is indicative of how monuments are so often more about those commissioning them than those commemorated by them. This is especially true of monuments to women, which, like the first version of the above, sometimes became genealogies more to do with male lines (often the commissioners) than with the lives and virtues of the women they ostensibly commemorate. Once the inscription on the reverse of the stone had been recorded, the cracks and joints of Lucas's ledgerstone were grouted with dispersed lime mortar. When dry, a two-part epoxy resin was applied with a brush, the Aramid fibre mat cut to size and pushed onto the resin. A second coat of resin was then applied over the fibre. Once cured, the consolidated marble was reset into its backing stone in the floor (Colour Plates AJ 1, 2, 3, 4).

The trials resulted in a suite of repair methodologies for the floor and the ledgerstones themselves. Permission for the pews in the Nave to be removed was given by the diocese following a Consistory Court case (heard in the Abbey itself) between the Abbey and the Victorian Society on 4 and 5 October 2017. During the case, the Abbey argued successfully for the permanent removal of the Victorian pews in the Nave. Although the platform the pews were on had protected the concealed ledgerstones from footfall (erosion), it had consequently concentrated wear of others (limiting the areas where the floor was walked over). Contact with the wood of the pews had caused the ledgerstones to become stained through exposure to oak tannins. The voids beneath the pew platforms had their own levels of moisture, which potentially contributed to the delamination of some ledgerstones. The weight of the platforms themselves may also have contributed to the cracking of some ledgerstones.

The judgement in favour of the Abbey enabled three years of work from 2018–21, in which all the floor stones were lifted and conserved by conservators from Sally Strachey Historic Conservation, using the repair methods identified in the trial. New blue lias stone quarried at Ashen Cross Quarry, Somerton, was used to create backings for marbles that needed resetting into new stone. These stones were given a patina by agitating the surface in troughs filled with pebbles and water. It is beyond the scope and purpose of this book to document the movement and conservation process of every stone. However, certain key alterations to the historic arrangement of the ledgerstones are worth noting. In Phase 1 (2018–19), the floor at the east end was repaired, including the removal of the wooden parquet floor in the Gethsemane Chapel, introduced by Sir Thomas Jackson when he altered George Gilbert Scott's floor layout when the chapel was created as a War Memorial Chapel in 1923. The areas either side of the central aisle, where Jackson's parquet was, were replaced with new blue lias stones into which repaired marbles were set.

Other stones, such as Julian Penny's late seventeenth-century ledgerstone, were consolidated after being laid into the floor in disparate pieces during George Gilbert Scott's work (Fig. 37), thus allowing the viewer to read the stone's beautifully carved decoration as originally intended. In the case of Joseph Philips's (d. 1703) ledgerstone (laid in the south-west corner of the Abbey near the door to the Abbey shop), the pieces of stone necessary to put the inscription back together were missing. In 1872, Charles Russell had noted in his entry on this stone on p.128 of his transcriptions of the ledgerstones that 'A large portion of this stone has been cut away & removed' (probably discarded by George Gilbert Scott's workmen). Russell, as with some other stones missing

Fig.37: The pieces of the Julian Penny's (d. 1657) ledgerstone undergoing consolidation and conservation work in June 2019. © The author.

their inscriptions (such as John Vavasour's), recomposed the inscription using the record of it in Richard Rawlinson's 1719 survey. In 2020, a new piece of stone was therefore carved with the missing piece of the inscription using that recorded in Charles Russell's book of ledgerstone inscriptions (1872) (Fig. 38). The crest on Theodore Luders's ledgerstone that was beyond reasonable repair was modelled using photogrammetry by David Littlefield at the University of the West of England to allow the re-carving of this crest on the new piece of stone in the future.

The stabilisation of the burial layer 1m beneath the ledgerstones ensured the ledgerstones would not be at risk of cracking because of the subsidence. The cast-iron grilles covering George Gilbert Scott's heating trenches were replaced in the floor. However, the position of the trenches for the heating system was altered from Scott's original layout (Colour Plate AK). The grilles running down the centre of the Nave (which were formerly dictated by the placement of the aisle formed by Scott's pew plinths) were widened, and in the Choir removed entirely. Those running along the walls were moved further out from it to accommodate the size of new backing stones. This required the position of some ledgerstones to be adjusted. However, using the historical records

Fig.38: Ledgerstone to Joseph Philips (d. 1703). The portion on the left (with the crest) was all that remained after George Gilbert Scott's work in 1872. Charles Russell's 1872 and Richard Rawlinson's 1719 record of the ledgerstones were used to newly carve the missing inscription. © The author.

to inform the placement of certain stones enabled them to be repositioned sensitively (e.g. the ledgerstone to the 'carver' John Harvey, d. 1675, grandfather of 'The Very Ingenious Mr. Harvey', was moved from the North Aisle to be reunited with the Harvey family group in the South Aisle) and moved closer to their original positions (e.g. Susanna Pierce and Mary a Court's ledgerstone moved closer to the South Transept, where it was originally laid).

Before the ledgerstones were relaid on top of the new reinforced concrete slab, underfloor heating was laid beneath the entire Abbey floor, insulated with Glapor (100 per cent recycled glass). The system is connected to heat exchangers in the Great Roman Drain, harnessing the heat energy in the 1 million litres of 40 degrees centigrade spring water flowing out of the Roman baths every day. Therefore, the Footprint Project not only repaired and conserved the Abbey's unique historic ledgerstones, it also made the entire pavement more accessible, and engineered a solution that would reduce the Abbey's carbon footprint.

CONCLUSION

On the evening of 1 April 1925, two young men loitered outside Bath Abbey. They were Norman Staples, a former painter's labourer, and Lawrence Pow, an apprentice chef. At about 7.30 p.m., the pair entered the Abbey and tried to steal a number of donation boxes in the church. The pair were caught and brought before Bath's magistrates. Both Staples and Pow said they had gone 'to look at the inscriptions on the walls'. The following exchange was recorded in the court:

> Pow said they went into the church to read the tablets on the walls.
>
> The Clerk (Mr. E. Newton Fuller): Mr. Warwick [acting clerk and head verger] said there are none there?
>
> Prisoner: Yes there are, thousands of them.
>
> The Clerk: Can you repeat what you read?
>
> Prisoner: Old English.
>
> The Clerk: You could not make it out?
>
> Prisoner: That is what we are studying.

The monuments made bad alibis. Both men were found guilty of 'one of the meanest crimes', the robbing of a church. The magistrates took a long time to decide what to do with them. They were nearly sent to jail. But that, it was said, would have meant 'the ruination of their lives'. Pow and Staples escaped the sentence Lockey Hill had received for a similar crime two centuries earlier. Perhaps fittingly, given their supposed interest in the inscriptions, which speak so much of redemption, they were put on probation and given 'another chance'.[1]

Whilst tastes in and criticism on the monuments have changed over the centuries, their value as genealogical records and as expressions of faith and redemption have been enduring. These final two qualities were amongst those appreciated in Georgian headstones by John Betjeman in his poem 'Churchyards'. His observations on them are also equally applicable to the Abbey's monuments, the majority of which were carved and inscribed by Bath's sculptors:

Notice the lettering of that age
Spaced like a noble title-page,
The parish names cut deep and strong
To hold the shades of evening long,
The quaint and sometimes touching rhymes
By parish poets of the times,
Bellows, or reaping hook or spade
To show, perhaps, the dead man's trade,
And cherubs in the corner spaces
With wings and English ploughboy faces.
Engraved on slate or carved in stone
These Georgian headstones hold their own.
With craftsmanship of earlier days
Men gave in their Creator's praise.
More homely are they than the white
Italian marbles which were quite
The rage in Good King Edward's reign,
With ugly lettering, hard and plain.[2]

Historically, much of the writing on the monuments has either described their subjects' biographies or the value (or otherwise) of their designs. However, studies of the Abbey's monuments' epitaphs, letter forms, relief carvings, materials and many other aspects would make fine thematic studies in the future, and further enhance the understanding of the Abbey's unique collection of monuments.[3] As demonstrated in Chapter 2, using the Abbey's accounts to date the creation of monuments and appraise groups of them chronologically would shed further light on the development of local idioms, the styles of Bath's studios, and would help understanding of the makers' plates sometimes wrongly misplaced and misattributed to monuments moved by the Victorians. Further study of the fragments of marble removed from the monuments and used as packing around the heating trenches by the Victorians would shed light on the history of the monuments and Bath's sculptors, and their provincial styles and working methods. For example, a number of the fragments reveal that some of the monuments were constructed in Bath stone and veneered with marble, especially the expensive Sienna marble popular in the 1770s. The study of these fragments and the pencil markings and names written on them would also shed further light on James T. Irvine's direction of the works to the monuments under George Gilbert Scott. It is hoped that this book provides a general history of the Abbey's monuments that will help future appreciation of and criticism on them, as well as that of the Abbey's and Bath's history. As Betjeman said: 'Our churches are our history shown / In wood and glass and iron and stone'.[4] Future historians of Bath would do well to consider the Abbey's and city's monuments in conjunction with the social history of the city that is written on the walls and floors of its churches.

The monuments today define the identity of the Abbey's interior as much as they did in the eighteenth century. With the Tudor fan vaulting, and the Victorian stained glass, they are objects that attract comment, curiosity and empathy. Yet, as we saw in Chapter 2, monuments that were simple and unproblematic expressions of nationalism, colonial trade and slavery in the eighteenth and nineteenth centuries are now 'contested heritage' and the subjects of interrogation by the Church of England.[5] Certainly, the rhetoric, ideals and symbolism of those monuments are now the 'crumbling anachronisms of societies and ambitions long past'. However, that is not necessarily to say that church monuments per se have 'outlived their rationale for existence'.[6] It is true that 'thousands' of monuments in churches in the Church of England's 16,000 churches and forty-two cathedrals 'are in some way associated with the eighteenth century British Empire'. As we have seen, only those with the means to pay the sculptors' and churches' fees could afford to commission and erect such artworks, and 'virtually anyone involved in trade or in the military or navy in the eighteenth century – and this was just about anyone who was making any significant money at all – had a personal stake in the emergent empire'.[7] In that sense, the Abbey's monuments are a 'shrine of the Empire'.[8] The monuments we encounter today are multifaceted. Some are still beautifully carved artworks that should be appreciated, as such, more so than they are. They are also sometimes uncomfortable and paradoxical: their inscriptions and relief carvings simultaneously glorifying colonial exploits and exploitation (or altogether silent on it), and celebrating their subjects' faithful Christian virtues.

As Betjeman's poem also concludes, one of the purposes of church monuments is to express the Christian faith. The Abbey's monuments' symbolism and inscriptions frequently testify to their subjects' belief in new life after death. William Savage's (d. 1777) ledgerstone is a good example:

Sacred to the Memory of
William Savage Esq.
Late of Charlestown S Carolina
Merchant
who departed this life February 8th. 1777
Aged 46.
He died in this City to which he came for
the recovery of his health.
He was an affectionate tender Husband.
A loving Father and kind Master
Ever ready to relieve the distresses of the poor.
Beloved by all who knew him whilst living
And at his death generally lamented

God my Redeemer lives
And ever from the skies
Looks down and watches all my dust
Till he shall bid me rise.

Arrayed in glorious grace
Shall then vile bodies shine
And every shape and every face
Look heavenly and divine.

The epitaph is highly conventional, with the exception of the verses at the end of it, which are taken from the second and third stanzas of Isaac Watts's hymn 'Triumph over Death in hope of the Resurrection'. Watts's hymn was included in an 'altered form' in John Wesley's *Psalms and Hymns*, which was published at Charlestown, South Carolina, in 1736–37,[9] which is presumably how the young William Savage first came to hear and love it. His ledgerstone is also slightly unusual in that it is a cenotaph. There is no record of William being buried in the Abbey, or indeed in Bath. Savage's ledgerstone is typical in that his health brought him to Bath in the late eighteenth century. The Savage family's mercantile success meant William could travel to England. Unsurprisingly, given Savage's birthplace and class, that success was partly based on the slave trade. William Savage was the owner of the 70-ton brigantine *Charming Betsey*, built in Boston in 1763.[10] On 15 March 1769, Savage's ship landed in Charleston from St Eustatius, carrying enslaved people.[11] Another brig owned by Savage, the *Hercules*,[12] carried enslaved people from Dominica to Charleston on 20 July 1769.[13] A third ship, the sloop *Kendall*, co-owned by Savage, was 'condemned for illicit trade by vice-admiralty court' in New Providence on 12 November 1761.[14] Other members of the Savage family, perhaps those who paid for the ledgerstone to be carved and laid in the Abbey floor in William's memory, appear to have been involved in the transatlantic slave trade.

The monument, therefore, illustrates well the paradox sometimes encountered in the Abbey's monuments: that they are statements and symbols of profound Christian faith paid for and about people who, in life, did things that were inhumane and unchristian. The monuments are salutary reminders that their very existence as objects is often because of their subjects' ability to pay for them. Those commissioning monuments controlled their designs and narratives. For us to fully appreciate the monuments it is necessary to get beneath their inscriptions, titles, professions and place names to understand their subjects and the means by which they were commemorated in the Abbey. It is hoped that this book will help others to approach the monuments questioningly and curiously, to enquire about their original designs and locations in the Abbey, and to understand better the people they commemorate, rather than taking them at face value. This book has shown that original designs and intentions behind the locations of the monuments reveal much about the values the city and Abbey wished to express over the centuries.

In his Easter sermon in the Abbey in 1881, the Reverend R. Hayes Robinson invited the congregation to 'look around upon these walls'. It is, strangely, one of the few times in the records that the monuments are drawn attention to from the pulpit. Even John Chapman, in his sermon on the qualities of churches, referred to the 'magnificent' interior of the Abbey in passing.[15] Robinson asked the congregation to think of 'the men who first planned this great Abbey, of the workmen who dug its foundations and reared its walls', even of 'the first congregation that ever assembled here!' For him, 'along the walls' one could find 'no inscription so mournful or so eloquent as the eye of fancy reads in the grey old masonry itself'.[16] In this sense, Robinson used the enduring structure of the Tudor church itself as a metaphor for the Christian hope in resurrection: 'in the midst of this great panorama of glory and change and decay stands one figure who cries, "I am the Resurrection and the Life"'. The monuments around the walls, and indeed on the floor, are filled with expressions of that Christian hope. In their different forms, designs, inscriptions, materials and locations they also tell the story of the Abbey, its people, and the city which it has been at the heart of for over 500 years. Their very number expresses the importance of commemoration in the Abbey since the late sixteenth century, and the way in which monuments have been part of the changing identity and role of the Abbey in the city.

Benefactors to the Abbey raised monuments to loved ones, whom they buried in the church under repair in the late sixteenth and early seventeenth centuries. Such monuments are therefore also expressions of faith in the vision for the Abbey as the parish church for the city and its visitors. Their examples, and especially that of Bishop James Montagu, pointed the way for the Abbey to accommodate monuments in its glorious and grand architectural space, to the benefit of the church building and its parishioners. The vestry's decision not to expand its capacity for extramural burial in 1722 coincided with the rise of Bath as the country's most fashionable spa under Richard 'Beau' Nash. The 'gallery' of seventeenth- and eighteenth-century sculpture that visitors from across Britain and its colonies could experience in Bath Abbey was unrivalled outside of Westminster Abbey until the end of the eighteenth century. It wasn't until 1796 that 'the first modern monument was erected on the cathedral floor' of St Paul's Cathedral, 'followed by 77 further large monuments before 1913'.[17] Church monuments were by far the most accessible artworks for the general public until the late eighteenth century and the founding of the Royal Academy (1768), opening of the British Museum (1759), Dulwich Picture Gallery (1817) and the National Gallery (1824).

The Abbey's Georgian monuments have been forgotten as one of the attractions for the city's visitors. The refined examples of sculpture that could be experienced there and the complimentary terms in which new sculpture was reported made commemoration and tourism in the Abbey desirable to the city and visitors alike. Even when the English church monument as an artform began to fall out of fashion in the early nineteenth century, hundreds of monuments continued to be erected in the Abbey. An indication that whilst the detrimental effects of monuments on the structure and aesthetic of churches were problematic for writers like Britton and Markland, that for those wanting to commemorate a loved one, the collection of monuments caused them to consider Bath, like Westminster Abbey, a worthy and desirable place for them to erect a monument amongst those of equivalent social status.

The thousands that came to Bath for the season certainly guaranteed that a monument in Bath Abbey would be a public spectacle. The Abbey's authorities were influenced by Britton and Markland, although by the time they came to brief George Gilbert Scott in 1868 to treat the monuments as those writers might have wished, burial in the Abbey had ceased and the fashion for marble monuments was over. Scott's and George Phillips Manners's rearrangement of the monuments earlier in the nineteenth century mean that today we can only glimpse the original impact, design and arrangement of the monuments through depictions and accounts of the interior of the Abbey from the eighteenth and nineteenth centuries. They and the archival record speak of the important contribution made by the monuments to the Abbey and the city and vice-versa. Despite the damage done to individual monuments in the nineteenth century, they continue to have been recognised and cared for as a special and unique collection. Important, if undervalued and under-researched, tangible objects (largely) from Bath's Georgian heyday.

Despite the low ebb in the reputation of Bath Abbey's monuments in the mid-to-late nineteenth century, the twentieth and twenty-first centuries have seen their importance as objects and records of individuals, the history of the Abbey, and the city, recovering. Unlike those grandest of monuments in Westminster Abbey or St Paul's Cathedral, perhaps it is the combination of their number, their comparative and provincial ordinariness, and that the nineteenth-century works have removed most elements that would otherwise have distracted from their inscriptions, that have helped Bath Abbey's monuments to speak to readers of them over the centuries. Certainly, the large volume of them in the relatively small interior of the Abbey has captured visitors' attention, imagination and hearts. In 1925, a writer in the *Sunday Times*, referring to Bath Abbey, remarked that they knew nothing that brought more 'peace and calm than an hour in a cathedral', especially reading the monuments, picking out the brass listing the priors and rectors of the Abbey erected in 1911 by the rector Sydney Adolphus Boyd and the tablet to Catherine Malone for special treatment. Of Malone's tablet, the author wrote:

> I love the tablet [...] There is a very human touch in the words, and one likes to know that it was in unbounded affection and tenderness that her husband and children 200 years ago raised the monument, longing that all who passed by should have their attention called to so amiable a character.[18]

As we have seen, this is perhaps a slightly romanticised reading of the monument, but the writer does read the 'human touch' in Edmond Malone's words well. The inscription for his mother is as personal and considered as the selection of the bas relief carving on her monument was. Through the book we have looked at the changing fortunes of and opinions on Catherine's monument. The enduring power of its epitaph to intrigue and move visitors illustrates well how these objects abide in and with the sacred space of the church.

The 'Romance of the Tablets' has also continued to capture visitors' imaginations, as Bishop James Montagu intended them to 400 years ago. Such was the subtitle of a piece in *The Bath Chronicle* in October 1931. The local correspondent began their 'half-an-hour' in the Abbey by wondering 'how many Bath people ever go in and "have a look round?" Very few I am afraid.' However, on walking round and studying the tablets, they found 'romance in those quiet walls, stories of adventure and braveness hidden in the writings of the tablets'. Closing their eyes at Admiral Sir William Hargood's monument (d. 1839), they wrote, "Twas no difficult matter to imagine that great battle [Trafalgar] – the roar of guns, the smoke, the crash of falling spars, the screams of the wounded and the clash of cutlasses as a boarding party fights its way to the poop of a French frigate.'[19] They noted the continuation of the tradition, begun in the nineteenth century, of draping Hargood's monument with a Union Jack on the anniversary of the Battle of Trafalgar. The columnist uncritically and patriotically picked out other monuments that glorified heroes of the Empire. Historians today would not take such glib and one-sided views of the subjects of the monuments as the author of the 1931 article, as Miranda Carter's recent appraisal of the 'Dudes in Drapes' at Westminster Abbey shows.[20] As we have seen, the monuments to Stibbs, Baker, Savage (above) and others require writers on the monuments to fully consider their subjects' histories and the historical context in which the monuments as objects were created. The 1931 column does remind us that creative writing and imaginative and creative responses to the monuments have been sadly lacking since the early twentieth century. Other monuments, such as that to Erasmus Philipps mentioned in the Introduction, were picked out by the author of the piece, who went so far as to say that there were 'many other interesting tablets, as interesting as the history of the Abbey itself'.

Certainly, as this book has shown, the history of the Abbey has always been inextricably bound up with its monuments: some the relics of those who shared in the original vision for the Abbey as a magnificent parish church for the growing spa resort; some the monuments of the 'nobilitie' (and the ignoble) who visited it; some the records of parishioners, citizens and craftspeople who worked on the Abbey, even sculptors who created monuments for it; some the records of those who gave their lives in life and death to the city and its people. It is hoped that readers of this book, both from Bath and beyond, will find their half an hour to visit the monuments, to walk on the Abbey's 'sacred floor', experience the peace, awe and solemnity of being amongst so many monuments in such a majestic interior, be inspired by the faith expressed in their inscriptions, even moved by their designs and artistry, and be curious to read beyond the inscriptions to discover the stories of those commemorated in this unique and significant collection of church monuments.

ENDNOTES

Introduction

1 *Morning Herald* (London), Wednesday, 21 July 1819, p.2. See also: *Bath Chronicle and Weekly Gazette*, 15 July 1819, p.3.
2 *Autobiography, Letters, and Literary Remains of Mrs. Piozzi* (Thrale), ed. and introd. A. Hayward, Volume II (London: Longman, 1861) p.141.
3 John Britton, *The History and Antiquities of Bath Abbey Church: Including Biographical Anecdotes of the Most Distinguished Persons Interred in that Edifice; with an Essay on Epitaphs, in which its Principal Monumental Inscriptions are Recorded. Illustrated in a Series of Engravings* (London: Longman, 1825) pp.95–96.
4 See: www.westminster-abbey.org/about-the-abbey/history/the-nations-memory; www.british-history.ac.uk/rchme/london/vol1/pp101-110.
5 It has been beyond the scope of this book to definitively determine the number of monuments in Westminster Abbey today and in the different periods considered by this book. In 1989, John Physick wrote that there were 'about 450 monuments' in Westminster Abbey, that was excluding the ledgerstones, which Physick described as 'the many grave-slabs, a large number of which have been worn smooth and are now unidentifiable'. See: *Westminster Abbey: The Monuments*, introd. John Physick (London: Murray, 1989) p.9.
6 www.westminster-abbey.org/about-the-abbey/history/the-nations-memory.
7 historicengland.org.uk/listing/the-list/list-entry/1394015?section=official-list-entry.
8 The National Archives; Kew, Surrey, England; *Records of the Prerogative Court of Canterbury*, Series PROB 11; Class: PROB 11; Piece: 132.
9 Charles Dickens, 'English Cathedrals. Bath' in *All the Year Round. A Weekly Journal*, Saturday, 5 June 1875. No. 340 (New Series), p.226.
10 In 1876, the *Drogheda Argus and Leinster Journal*, for Saturday, 9 September, reported that 'In Bath (England) Abbey is to be seen the following: "Here lies Ann Mann, / She lived an old maid and died an old Mann."' (p.6). This was repeated in the 'Amusing Epitaphs' section of the *Canvan Weekly News* and *General Advertiser* for 11 July 1890 (p.4), and the *Hamilton Advertiser* for 4 December 1920 (p.3). The source of the misattribution has not been identified. No ledgerstone to Ann Mann was recorded by the Parish Clerk, Charles Russell, in 1872, in his 'Index to the Flat Grave-Stones' in the Abbey. Neither was there a wall tablet to her found by Mark Hudson in his comprehensive list of the 'Tablets, Memorials and Flags' in 2017.
11 For example, Ken Hylson-Smith's *Bath Abbey: A History* (Bath: Friends of Bath Abbey, 2002) p.157: 'Here are those who found Bath to be socially congenial in its halcyon days of Palladian splendour, and who regarded it, and more particularly the Abbey, as a fitting final place, where they might be duly commemorated. Many wanted to be honoured after death as they had been in life; and where better to ensure this than in the most magnificent and respected shrine for the dead in the city.'

12 All references to the cost of monuments in this paragraph taken from the House of Commons debate on 20 May 1881 (Vol. 261 cc.949–50): api.parliament.uk/historic-hansard/commons/1881/may/20/westminster-abbey-monuments.

13 Alex Morris, 'Bath Abbey Footprint Project: An architect's view of the project objectives and the works' in *Journal of Building Survey, Appraisal & Valuation* (Vol. 10, No. 2, 2021) p.146.

14 Sebastian Gahagan carved the monument to Rev. Dr Charles Burney in Westminster Abbey and that to Archdeacon Josiah Thomas D.D. in Bath Abbey; Francis Leggatt Chantrey carved the monuments to Col. Charles Herries and Granville Sharp in Westminster Abbey and those to Admiral Sir Richard Hussey Bickerton and William Hoare in Bath Abbey; John Flaxman carved the monuments to The Earl of Mansfield William Murray, George Lindsay Johnstone, Captain James Montagu and Pasquale de Paoli in Westminster Abbey, and those to Senator William Bingham and Dr John Sibthorp in Bath Abbey; John Francis Moore carved the monuments to John Earl Legonier and Jonas Hanway in Westminster Abbey and that to Sir William Baker in Bath Abbey. Numbers of monuments in Westminster Abbey are taken from the list of the 'Names of Sculptors and Designers of Monuments in the Abbey Church [Westminster]; with References to their Respective Works' in Edward Wedlake Brayley, *The History and Antiquities of the Abbey Church of St. Peter, Westminster*. In Two Volumes. Vol. II. (London: Hurst, 1823).

15 Nicholas Penny, *Church Monuments in Romantic England*. Paul Mellon Centre for Studies in British Art. (New Haven: Yale UP, 1977) p.3.

16 *Bath Chronicle and Weekly Gazette*, 4 November 1950, p.13.

17 See Roger Morriss, *Naval Power and British Culture, 1760–1850: Public Trust and Government Ideology* (London: Routledge, 2004).

18 *Westminster Abbey: The Monuments*, introd. John Physick (London: Murray, 1989) p.14.

19 Jason Edwards, Amy Harris and Greg Sullivan, *Monuments of St. Paul's Cathedral 1796–1916* (London: Scala, 2021) p.6.

20 Ibid.

21 Ernest R. Suffling, *English Church Brasses: From the 13th to the 17th Century: A Manual for Antiquaries, Archaeologists and Collectors* (London: Gill, 1910) p.13.

22 www.batharchives.co.uk/burial-index.

23 The same is true of Westminster Abbey, which, from the late seventeenth century, 'faced mounting bills for the maintenance of the building, and an admirable source of revenue was found in the fees for both interments and monuments' (Physick, *Westminster Abbey: The Monuments*, pp.11–12).

1. Creation: 'What else doth arise by breaking Ground for Burial Places, and for Monuments', 1569–1712

1 See: www.pepysdiary.com/diary/1668/06/14/.

2 Kenneth Hylson-Smith, *Bath Abbey: A History* (Bath: Friends of Bath Abbey, 2003) pp.119–20.

3 Hylson-Smith, *Bath Abbey: A History*, p.121.

4 Bath Abbey Archives, Benefactors' Book, n.p.

5 *Somerset Medieval Wills* (Third Series) 1531–1558 ed. Rev. F.W. Weaver (Somersetshire Archaeological and Natural History Society: 1905) p.24.

6 *The Itinerary of John Leland in or about the Years* 1535–1543, Parts I to III, ed. Lucy Toulmin Smith (London: George Bell and Sons, 1907) p.143.

7 Ibid. p.144.

8 *Somerset Medieval Wills (Second Series) 1501–1530 with some Somerset Wills Preserved at Lambeth*, ed. Rev. F. W. Weaver (Somersetshire Archaeological and Natural History Society: 1903) p.30.

9 Ibid. p.64.

10 See 'Vita beate Katarine' in MS. Longleat 55 ff. 55r-65r ('libello Rubro de Bath'). The life of St Katherine written in the manuscript ends: 'Kateryn of maydes martyr & flour / we prayeth thee be oure socour / In alle maner greuaunce / In worschupp of thee ys oure chapelle'. This text quoted from the transcript of the 'Vita beate Katarine' in Jacqueline Jenkins, 'Such people As Be Not Letterd In Scripture': Popular Devotion and the Legend of St Katherine of Alexandria in Late Medieval England' (The University of Western Ontario, PhD Thesis, 1996) p.275.

11 *The Accounts of the Chamberlains of the City of Bath 1568–1602*, ed. F.D. Wardle (Somerset Record Society Vol. XXXVIII, 1923) p.14.

12 Jean Manco, 'The Buildings of Bath Priory' in *Somerset Archaeology and Natural History* (1993) p.101.

13 Amy E. Bush and John Hatton, *Thomas Bellott 1534–1611: Steward of the Household of William Cecil, First Lord Burghley, Friend of Bath Abbey, Founder of Bellott's Hospital* (Bath: Friends of Bath Abbey, 1966) p.6.

14 *A Copy of the Chamberlains' Accounts of the City of Bath with a List of Freemen and Other Interesting Matter*, ed. C.W. Shickle (Bath Record Office Unpublished Typescript, 1904) 6.2.

15 *The Registers of the Abbey Church of SS. Peter and Paul, Bath.* Vol. II, ed. Arthur J. Jewers (London: Harleian Society, 1901) p.329.

16 Peter Davenport, 'The Church of St. Mary Northgate, Bath' in *Bath History* (2011, Vol. 12) ed. Graham Davis, p.15.

17 Peter Davenport, *Medieval Bath Uncovered* (Stroud: Tempus, 2002) p.171.

18 Peter Davenport, 'The Church of St. Mary de Stall, Bath' in *Bath History* (2019, Vol. 15) ed. Graham Davis, p.98.

19 The date ostensibly carved onto the monument is 1572. However, no Richard Chapman was buried in the Abbey in that year. It has been plausibly suggested that the monument commemorates the 'Richard Chapman, alderman' who was buried in the 'Abby' on 5 February 1579. See: Elizabeth Holland, 'This Famous City The Story of the Chapmans of Bath 470 Years of History: The Chapmans and Bath Abbey' in *The Survey of Bath and District: The Magazine of the Survey of Old Bath and Its Associates*, ed. Mike Chapman and Elizabeth Holland (No. 7, June 1997) p.23. A further consideration is that the inscription commemorates both Richard Chapman (d. 1572) who was buried 'Neere unto this place' and his son Richard Chapman (d. 1627) who was buried 'heere' (presumably in the Abbey), and the letter forms for both epitaphs are almost identical.
It is plausible, therefore, that the monument was created *c.*1627 and the earlier date 1572 misremembered or miscarved for 1579.

20 The anonymous author of the 'An Abstract Account of the Register Books Belonging to the Rectory of Bath Taken down to 1824' (Bath Abbey Archives: BA/2/BMD/7/1) shared the sense that the registers from 1569–1600 were copies. However, he draws short of suggesting that they are copied from the registers of St Mary de Stalls. In the opening 'Remarks and References to particular Entries in Register No. 1, Parish of St Peter and St Paul' the author writes: 'The writing in 1569 to 1600 being in the same character, or manner, and all in the same coloured ink, it is not improbable that these Entries are only Copies from other Memorandums' (p. 2). It is probable that the author of this document was John Britton, author of *The History and Antiquities of Bath Abbey Church* (1825). The document BA/2/BMD/7/1 will be discussed at greater length in Chapter 3.

21 Robert Rich, first Earl of Warwick (1559–1619), was only one of two individual donors to contribute to the fundraising for the bell (the other being Thomas Bellott (1534–1611)). In 1596, Rich helped to finance and sailed with the expedition to Cadiz, 'but left it early. He abandoned the Islands voyage in [June–August] 1597 because of seasickness' (ODNB). Perhaps to recuperate, Rich seems to have been in Bath in 1597, as shown by two gifts of wine and sugar given to him recorded in the city's Chamberlain's Accounts for that year: 'gave unto the Lord Ritch a pottle of Canara & a pottle of Clarett iii. s iiii. d / gave to him also on loafe of Suger of vj pounde & a halfe at xviij d the pounde ix. s ix. d' (36.3).

22 'John Harington to the Lorde Treasurer Burleigh' in *Nugae Antiquae: Being a Miscellaneous Collection of Original Papers, in Prose and Verse; Written During the Reigns of Henry VIII, Edward VI, Queen Mary, Elizabeth, and King James by Sir John Harington, Knt. And by others who lived in those Times*, ed. Henry Harington (Vol. I) (London: Vernor and Hood, 1804) p.185.

23 Davenport, 'The Church of St. Mary de Stall, Bath', p.109. Davenport also goes on to note that 'burial for the elite took place in the church, and there are likely to have been tombs and memorials, some plain, some elaborate, but all now lost.'

24 Inscription taken from the monument to Peter Chapman in the North-East Choir Aisle. The inscription also declares itself to be a 'copy of the original epitaph'.

25 Henry Harington and Thomas Park, N*ugae Antiquae: Being a Miscellaneous Collection of Original Papers, in Prose and Verse; Written During the Reigns of Henry VIII, Edward VI, Queen Mary, Elizabeth, and King James by Sir John Harington, Knt. And by others who lived in those Times*, ed. Henry Harington (Vol. II) (London: J. Wright, 1804) p.143.

26 Stow, John, Anthony Munday and Humphrey Dyson. 'Survey of London (1633): Walbrook Ward', *The Map of Early Modern London, Edition 6.6*, ed. Janelle Jenstad, U of Victoria, 30 Jun. 2021, mapoflondon.uvic.ca/edition/6.6/stow_1633_WALB2.htm. Draft.

27 Bath Abbey Archives, Benefactors' Book, p.5.

28 Edmond Smith, 'The Social Networks of Investment in Early Modern England' in *The Historical Journal*, 64 (4), pp.912–39.

29 'In memory of the departed / Bartholomew Barnes, / a most loved man of true faith, lately a / London merchant and now a citizen of the / heavenly kingdom above. / Christian belief, elegant wit, with strength of / character, attractiveness with a simple life style, / a generous hand, a noble heart, a steadfast love. / Lastly, he has whatever Nature can add, he has / whatever graciousness can add. All these attributes / belonged to Barnes whilst he was alive. Hateful / death destroyed them all at one time. It is allowed / that savage death, with its sad tomb, may destroy / such things, but his fame will be everlasting.'

30 Smith, 'The Social Networks of Investment in Early Modern England'. For references to Bartholomew Barnes as the late father-in-law of Rowland Backhouse see 'Backhouse's Will': The National Archives; Kew, Surrey, England; *Records of the Prerogative Court of Canterbury*, Series PROB 11; Class: PROB 11; Piece: 205.

31 In 1544–46, Barnes's namesake and likely ancestor, Bartholomew Barnes, Mercer, served as a Common Councillor, as did one Robert Chapman, Draper, possibly of the London branch of the Chapman family. One of Peter Chapman's older brothers was called Robert and another known as 'John of London' (Elizabeth Holland, 'This Famous City The Story of the Chapmans of Bath 470 Years of History: The Chapmans and Bath Abbey' in *The Survey of Bath and District: The Magazine of the Survey of Old Bath and Its Associates*, ed. Mike Chapman and Elizabeth Holland (No. 7, June 1997) p.23). In 1576, Backhouse's ancestor, Alderman Nicholas Backhouse, left funds for poor scholars at the universities of Oxford and Cambridge. At Cambridge, the bequest was to be

administrated by John Whitgift, the Master of Trinity College and 'John Still, Master of St. John's College, Canon of Westminster, and future Bishop of Bath and Wells' (David J. Hickman, *The Religious Allegiance of London's Ruling Elite 1520–1603* (London: University College, Unpub. PhD Thesis, 1995) p.247).

32 Hickman, *The Religious Allegiance of London's Ruling Elite* 1520–1603, pp.248–49.

33 Henry Chapman, *Thermae Redivivae; or, The City of Bath described, &c.* (1673) in Thomas Guidott, ed. Henry Chapman (Bath: Leake, 1725) p.420.

34 D/P/ba.ab/2/1/1 Baptisms , marriages & burials 1569–1743, n.p.

35 Davenport, *Medieval Bath Uncovered*, p.171.

36 *A Copy of the Chamberlains' Accounts of the City of Bath*, ed. Shickle, 47.2.

37 *A Copy of the Chamberlains' Accounts of the City of Bath*, ed. Shickle, 47.3.

38 D/P/ba.ja/4/1/1, n.p. In 1676, John Farr was named as one of the Overseers of the Poor at a Vestry held at St James' Church.

39 D/P/ba.ja/4/1/1 [37].

40 On 23 January 1676, the Abbey's burial register records the burial of 'John Bartlett which was drowned at the weirs' (Jewers, *The Registers*, Vol. II, p.383). However, given the high cost of the payment for the one who 'drouned' in the Chamberlain's Accounts, the payment is more likely to relate to the burial of 'Doctor Stubbs', who, according to the burial register, was buried in the Abbey on 13 July 1676. According to Anthony a Wood, Stubbs 'was drowned neare Bath' and when Wood visited his ledgerstone had been laid; however, the 'epitaph' that had 'been made for him by Tho. Guydott' was 'intended' but had yet to be carved into it (Anthony a Wood, *Monumental Inscriptions*, p.10).

41 *A Copy of the Chamberlains' Accounts of the City of Bath*, ed. Shickle, 137.5.

42 Bath Abbey Archives, Benefactors' Book, p.3.

43 *Nugae Antiquae*, Vol. 2, ed. Harington and Park, pp.162–63.

44 Henry Harington and Thomas Park, *Nugae Antiquae: Being a Miscellaneous Collection of Original Papers, in Prose and Verse; Written During the Reigns of Henry VIII, Edward VI, Queen Mary, Elizabeth, and King James: by Sir John Harington, Knt. And by others who lived in those Times*, ed. Henry Harington, Vol. I (London: J. Wright, 1804) pp.xvi–xvii.

45 Henry Chapman, *A Collection of Treatises relating to the City and Waters of Bath* (Bath: J. Leake, 1725) p.102.

46 *A Copy of the Chamberlains' Accounts of the City of Bath*, ed. Shickle, 53.3.

47 Bath Abbey Archives, Benefactors' Book, p.17.

48 What remains of Marie Nicols's (d. 1614) monument is now on the south wall of the South Transept. Only the inscription tablet survives and it is has obviously been heavily cut down. A maker's plate made by Thomas King has been placed anachronistically beneath it in the nineteenth century. Thomas King and Sons' studio flourished between 1760 and 1860.

49 The lack or nature of the records makes it impossible to date the other gifts to the Abbey's floor in the early 1600s. Even where records exist, they don't help to clarify the dates of the donations or work. For instance, John Tayler the 'Clerke Parson of Colaston, Gloucester' who gave £1 2*s* to the paving of the South Nave Aisle held the post of rector of Cold Ashton from 1581–1624.

50 *A Copy of the Chamberlains' Accounts of the City of Bath*, ed. Shickle, 41.5.

51 Ibid. 41.8.

52 Ibid. 54.3.

53 Ibid. 56.3.

54 The National Archives; Kew, Surrey, England; *Records of the Prerogative Court of Canterbury*, Series PROB 11; Class: PROB 11; Piece: 155.

55 The National Archives; Kew, Surrey, England; *Records of the Prerogative Court of Canterbury*, Series PROB 11; Class: PROB 11; Piece: 132.

56 Evelyn Philip Shirley, 'The Will, Inventories, and Funeral Expenses of James Montagu, Bishop of Winchester, anno 1618. From the original in the possession of the Baroness North' in *Archaeologia* 44 (02), pp.393–421.

57 Thomas Fuller, *The Church History of Britain, from the Birth of Jesus Christ until the Year MDCXLVIII*, Vol. 3 (London, 1837) p.286.

58 *Bath Chronicle and Weekly Gazette*, Thursday, 7 November 1907, p.5.

59 Chapman, *Thermae Redivivae; or, The City of Bath described, &c.*, p.419.

60 Timothy Baldwin, 'Transcript of several Coates of armes belonging to several Noble Familyes their plaices of Buriall together wth the Epitaphes and Inscriptions upon their several Tablets & Grave Stones' (Unpub. Ms. Society of Antiquaries, MS 434).

61 Chapman, *Thermae Redivivae; or, The City of Bath described, &c.*, p.416.

62 *An Historical Description of the Church Dedicated to St. Peter and St. Paul, in Bath (Commonly called The Abbey) with its Monuments and Curiosities. Designed as a Guide to Strangers, in viewing this Venerable Pile, And, to point out to them the most valuable Remains of Antiquity, contained therein, as well as the Beauties of Modern Statuaries* (Bath: Salmon, 1778) p.30.

63 For biography of Robert Mason see: www.histparl.ac.uk/volume/1604-1629/member/mason-robert-ii-1590-1662.

64 Chapman, *Thermae Redivivae; or, The City of Bath described, &c.*, pp.417–18.

65 Anthony a Wood, *Monumental Inscriptions in the Churches of Bath, taken in July 1676* (London, 1881) p.6.

66 The date of 1646 is obscure: Waller's contribution was in 1635, Lady Booth died and was buried in the Abbey in 1628 and an Edward Sturridge was buried in the Abbey in 1632.

67 *A Copy of the Chamberlains' Accounts of the City of Bath*, ed. Shickle, 86.4 and 86.8.

68 The monument would not be properly restored until the 1881, when 'the alabaster figures [were] re-polished, and the armorial bearings re-emblazoned, by Mr. W.E. Reeves, of James-street' *Bath Chronicle and Weekly Gazette*, Thursday, 24 February 1881.

69 D/P/ba.ja/4/1/1 [45]. He obviously distinguished himself, as in 1686 and 1687, now 'Mr. John Sugar', he was elected as one of the sidesman for the church [69, 71]. In 1688, 'Mr. John Suger' was elected one of the churchwardens. This is the last time either John Sugar or the role of sexton is mentioned in these accounts. A Tobias Shugar, probably John's son, is named as a member of the vestry in 1702 [137].

70 *A Copy of the Chamberlains' Accounts of the City of Bath*, ed. Shickle, 134.4 and 135.5.

71 Ibid. 136.5.

72 The only suggestion of the resumption of these payments occurs in 1720–21, when Thomas Clement was paid £2 for 'On years Salary'. The same payment is made in 1721–22. What possibly suggests these are for the sexton is the sum and the fact that both payments come directly after payments for the Abbey organist's salary in the Chamberlain's Accounts. See *A Copy of the Chamberlains' Accounts of the City of Bath*, ed. Shickle, 162.2.

73 See Somerset Heritage Centre: DD/PO/50 and DD/Pot/135.

74 The National Archives; Kew, Surrey, England; *Records of the Prerogative Court of Canterbury*, Series PROB 11; Class: PROB 11; Piece: 517.

75 Peirce's memoirs record the date as 'October 1666' but this must either be an error or a typo for 1665.

76 Robert Peirce, *The History and Memoirs of the Bath* (London: n.p., 1723) pp.27–30.

77 Anthony a Wood, *Monumental Inscriptions in the Churches of Bath, taken in July 1676* (London, 1881) p.5.

78 Ibid. pp.4–5.
79 In comparison, in 1683 the vestry of St James' ordered that 'whosoever will have ye fourth or ye fifth bells rung shall pay if a stranger two shillings, if an inhabitant but one' (D/P/ba.ja/4/1/1 [57]).
80 The vestry of St James' Church made a similar stipulation in 1707 (D/P/ba.ja/4/1/1 [167]).
81 Jewers, *The Registers*, Vol. II, p.394.
82 Ibid. p.394.
83 Ibid. p.401.
84 Ibid. p.397.
85 Ibid. p.400.
86 Richard Rawlinson, *History and Antiquities of the Cathedral Church of Salisbury, And the Abbey Church of Bath* (London, 1719) p.205.
87 Bath Abbey Archives, Benefactors' Book, p.44.
88 D/P/ba.ja/4/1/1 [167].
89 Bath Abbey Archives, BA-MS/12/1.
90 Bath Abbey Archives, Benefactors' Book, p.42.
91 Edward Ward, 'A Step to Bath' (1700) reprinted in *The Reformer*, 3rd ed. (London: How, 1708) p.164.

2. Identity: 'As much Speculation as can be met with, perhaps, in any Parochial Church', 1712–1807

1 Mary Chandler, *The Description of Bath. Humbly Inscribed to Her Royal Highness the Princess Amelia. With several other Poems.* (London: Leake, 1733; 7th ed. 1755) pp.8–9.
2 Daniel Defoe, *A Tour Thro' the Whole Island of Great Britain*, Vol. II, (London: Birt, 1748) p.294.
3 John Wood, *A Description of Bath*, Vol. 2 (London, 1765) pp.310–11.
4 A similar position is taken by Rev. John Penrose in 1766, who described the West Front as 'wretchedly executed, and atop of all is the Image of a venerable old man, designed (I am told) to represent God the Father, an execrable Design!' He took no such issue with the carving of Abbey's 'innumerable Monuments'. See Reverend John Penrose, *Letters from Bath 1776-1777*, introd. and notes by Brigitte Mitchell and Hubert Penrose (Gloucester: Alan Sutton, 1983) p.45.
5 *Bath: A Glance at its Public Worship, Style of Dress, Cotillons Masquerades, &c. &c.* (Bath: Meyler, 1814, 2nd edition) p.10.
6 Bath Record Office, '[A Cambridge Undergraduate] A Tour from Cambridge to Halifax and Wakefield, returning via Oxford, Bath, and Bristol', 1725. MS in bound vol. Access. No. 38.43, Class: 914.238b. The manuscript is accompanied by an email to the Bath Record Office, dated 2 January 2019, from the researcher who identified the author of the manuscript as Charles Perry.
7 Anthony a Wood, *Monumental Inscriptions in the Churches of Bath, taken in July 1676* (London, 1881) p.5, hereafter *Monumental Inscriptions*.
8 Richard Rawlinson, *History and Antiquities of the Cathedral Church of Salisbury, And the Abbey Church of Bath* (London, 1719) p.222, hereafter History and Antiquities.
9 *An Historical Description of the Church Dedicated to St. Peter and St. Paul, in Bath; (Commonly called the Abbey) with its Monuments and Curiosities. Designed as a Guide to Strangers, in viewing this Venerable Pile, And, to point out to them the most valuable Remains of Antiquity, contained therein, As well as the Beauties of Modern Statuaries* (Bath: Salmon, 1778) p.55, hereafter *An Historical Description*.

10 Rawlinson, *History and Antiquities*, p.229.
11 *An Historical Description*, p.52.
12 Wood, *Monumental Inscriptions*, p.10.
13 Rawlinson, *History and Antiquities*, p.240.
14 Ibid. p.231.
15 *An Historical Description*, p.39.
16 Ibid. p.34.
17 The National Archives, Kew, England. Prerogative Court of Canterbury and Related Probate Jurisdictions: Will Registers. Digitized images. *Records of the Prerogative Court of Canterbury*, Series PROB 11. Piece Description: Piece 534: Leeds, Quire Numbers 139–180 (1713) passim.
18 The National Archives; Kew, Surrey, England; *Records of the Prerogative Court of Canterbury*, Series PROB 11; Class: PROB 11; Piece: 537.
19 John Thomas Smith, 'Near Mrs Teshmaker's, Edmonton' (1793) from *Twenty Rural Landscapes from Nature* (London: Nathaniel Smith). British Museum. Object Number: 1865,0610.991.
20 *An Historical Description*, p.71.
21 Ibid. p.42.
22 Ibid. p.46.
23 Ibid. p.20.
24 This figure includes the Montagu Tomb.
25 This figure includes the Montagu Tomb.
26 *Bath Chronicle*, 30 October 1794, p.3.
27 *Westminster Abbey: The Monuments*, introd. John Physick (London: Murray, 1989) p.12.
28 *An Historical Description*, p.41.
29 Penny, *Church Monuments in Romantic England*, p.136.
30 Ibid. p.140.
31 Ibid. p.137.
32 Rev. Edward Bayly, *A Sermon Preach'd at the Abbey-Church at Bath, on SUNDAY, April 23, 1749, For the SUPPORT of the GOVERNORS of the said HOSPITAL* (Bath: Boddely, 1749) p.21.
33 *An Historical Description*, p.29.
34 Rev. Richard Warner, *A New Guide Through Bath, and its Environs* (Bath: Cruttwell, 1811) p.75.
35 The same is true of the monuments commemorating interments at Walcot. For example, the monument to Anne (d. 1793) and Major General Hugh Henry Magan (1805) whose cenotaph, now in the North Choir Aisle, commemorates them 'Both being interred in Walcot Burying Ground'.
36 *An Historical Description*, p.45.
37 In his unpublished PhD thesis, Clive James Easter 'attributed' the Fry monument to Harvey largely because of the similarity of the two busts (See: Clive James Easter, 'Church Monuments of Devon and Cornwall *c.*1660–*c.*1730', PhD thesis (University of Plymouth: Unpub., 2006) Vol. 1, pp. 191–92). Easter did not consider Samuel Grimm's drawing. However, comparison of the original appearance of the monument, as shown by Grimm's depiction of it in 1788, with the extant Fry monument confirms that the two monuments were, originally, identical. Furthermore, it must also be concluded from the comparison that the elements now missing from the Fry monument were those described in 1778 and drawn in 1788, e.g. the 'cherubims heads, a crown of glory and festoons of flowers' surrounding the bust.

38 James Storer, *The History and Antiquities of the Cathedral Churches of Great Britain*, Vol. 1 (London: Rivingtons; Murray; et. al, 1814) n.p. [q.].

39 In 1670, 'there were 461 houses in the parish' but by 1796 'the number was 752, an increase of three-fifths; the total population was then 4,123'. British History Online: www.british-history.ac.uk/vch/essex/vol5/pp184-190 [accessed 3 July 2020].

40 'The ancient parish of Barking: Introduction', in *A History of the County of Essex: Volume 5*, ed. W.R. Powell (London, 1966), pp.184–90. British History Online: www.british-history.ac.uk/vch/essex/vol5/pp184-190 [accessed 3 July 2020].

41 Stephen Roberts, 'Malone, Edmund (1704–1774), barrister and politician.' *Oxford Dictionary of National Biography*. 04. Oxford University Press: www.oxforddnb.com/view/10.1093/ref:odnb/9780198614128.001.0001/odnb-9780198614128-e-17895 [accessed 28 February 2022].

42 Sir James Prior, *Life of Edmond Malone, Editor of Shakespeare. With Selections from his Manuscript Anecdotes* (London: Smith, Elder & Co., 1860) p.4.

43 Peter Martin, 'Malone, Edmond (1741–1812), literary scholar and biographer.' *Oxford Dictionary of National Biography*. 25. Oxford University Press: www.oxforddnb.com/view/10.1093/ref:odnb/9780198614128.001.0001/odnb-9780198614128-e-17896 [accessed 28 February 2022].

44 Peter Martin, *Edmond Malone, Shakespearean Scholar* (Cambridge: Cambridge UP, 1995) pp.3–4.

45 Ibid. p.5.

46 Ibid. p.8.

47 Ibid. p.8.

48 The Abbey's earliest extant financial records cover the period 1756–65. The next set of accounts date cover 1768–83. Entries in the later set of accounts for monuments erected in the Nave from 1768 always give the name of the subject for whom the monument was commissioned. This suggests that the monument was not erected within 1768–83 (the period covered by this early set of accounts). It would be highly unusual for the monument to be erected after 1783, so long after Catherine's death. It was therefore probably erected in the two years following Catherine's death, sometime in 1765–67.

49 *An Historical Description*, p.32.

50 James Hayward Markland, *Remarks on English Churches, and on the Expediency of Rendering Sepulchral Memorials Subserviant to Pious and Christian Uses* (Oxford: Parker, 1843, 3rd Edition, Enlarged) p.162.

51 *Bath Chronicle*, 24 April 1766, p.2 and 20 April 1769, p.2.

52 *Bath Chronicle*, 27 April 1769, p.2.

53 *Diary and Letters of Madame D'Arblay, Author of 'Evelina,' 'Cecilia,' &c. Edited by Her Niece.* Vol. I. (Philadelphia: Carey and Hart, 1842) p.191.

54 *An Historical Description*, p.38.

55 Further examples that might be given are the repetition of the Chapmans' names but the omission of the Fords' names on the monument to Richard Ford, or the separate listing of Diana Bramston and John Turnor when the former appeared on the latter's monument.

56 See: www.batharchives.co.uk/sites/bath_record_office/files/heritage/Rack%20Journal.pdf.

57 Somerset Heritage Centre, D/P/ba/ab/9/1/1 Bath Abbey Vestry Minutes 1684–1732 n.p.

58 The manuscript version of the list is held at Bristol Record Office, AC/Unlisted/box 32c.

59 Gresley and Boothby.

60 This figure has been calculated by including inscriptions dated earlier than 1787 where they appear on a single family monument. The assumption being that the monument was

created after the latest date of death given, e.g. the inscriptions to George Throckmorton Esq. (d. 1762) and his children Mary (1763), Robert (1779), Anne (1783) and Francis (1788) are all absent from the manuscript list but all present in the printed list and on a single monument in the Abbey.

61 Reverend John Penrose, *Letters from Bath 1776–1777*, introd. and notes by Brigitte Mitchell and Hubert Penrose (Gloucester: Alan Sutton, 1983) p.99.

62 Ibid. p.45.

63 Ibid. p.73. This suggests that the rule, recorded by Warner, that 'No monuments [were] permitted to be placed in this church [St James']' must have been made after St James' was rebuilt.

64 Ibid. p.199.

65 Ibid. p.140.

66 Ibid. p.155. Penrose made no such comment on the Abbey's paving, although he was complimentary about the paving of Bath's streets.

67 Ibid. p.166.

68 The National Archives; Kew, England; *Prerogative Court of Canterbury and Related Probate Jurisdictions: Will Registers*; Class: PROB 11; Piece: 1842.

69 Penrose, *Letters from Bath 1776–1777*, p.81. Penrose was informed by 'Mr. Roberts, Minister of this Parish, St. James' that 'there is now such a Resort of People to Bath, that in some Seasons here are ten thousand Persons Strangers', pp.76, 73.

70 Ibid. p.81.

71 Somerset Heritage Centre, D/P/ba/ab/9/1/1 Bath Abbey Vestry Minutes 1684–1732 n.p.

72 John Wood, *A Description of Bath*, Vol. 2 (London, 1765), p.311.

73 See: Somerset Heritage Centre, D/P/ba/ab/9/1/1 *Bath Abbey Vestry Minutes 1684–1732* n.p; and L. Hill, *An Appeal to Justice, and the Impartial World. Being a True and faithful Narrative, and just Complaint, of the unparallel'd and unjustifiable Barbarity and hellish Cruelty exercis'd on L. Hill, Esq; a Prisoner in the County Goal [sic] of Somerset, at Ilchester, by the Keeper thereof and his Adherents (*Exon: Andre Brice, 1726).

74 Somerset Heritage Centre, D/P/ba/ab/9/1/1 *Bath Abbey Vestry Minutes 1684–1732* n.p.

75 Somerset Heritage Centre, D/P/ba/ab/9/1/1 *Bath Abbey Vestry Minutes 1684–1732* n.p.

76 Bath Record Office, *Council Minute Book* 1711–1728, p.214.

77 The incident appears to have caused Bath's Corporation to stipulate clauses concerning the height of prospective buildings around the Abbey, especially that they should not obscure windows, although not necessarily those of the Abbey, from this date. For example, in 1721 when Mr Thomas Sheyler wished to build on his newly leased tenement in the Upper Walks, the Corporation agreed on the proviso that it did not exceed 'the same height and depth as Mr. Alderman Collibee's house next to it'. Then, in 1724, when 'Mr. Alderman Atwood' wanted to 'inclose with a Stone wall' a piece of ground between his house in Wade's Passage (north of the Abbey) and Robert Saxon's tenement, the Corporation agreed provided that the building was not 'above Seven feet high' nor would it 'obstruct or darken the lights of any house ajoyning', although the Abbey is not mentioned (Bath Record Office, *Council Minute Book 1711–1728*, n.p.).

78 James Storer, *History and Antiquities of the Cathedral Churches of Great Britain*, Vol. 1, (London: Rivingtons, etc., 1814) n.p. [Description of Plate 5].

79 Somerset Heritage Centre, D/P/ba/ab/9/1/1 *Bath Abbey Vestry Minutes 1684–1732* n.p.

80 Somerset Heritage Centre, D/P/ba/ab/9/1/1 *Bath Abbey Vestry Minutes 1684–1732* n.p.

81 This figure includes fees for funerals, burials, mortuaries, breaking ground in the Choir, burying after ten o'clock at night and before nine o'clock in the morning at the Abbey.

82 See: Shakespeare Birthplace Trust, ER 3/2189 'Certificate of Burial of William Ingram in the Abbey Church, Bath; Thomas Coney, rector and James Davis, clerk. 29 April 1737'. This can also be seen in the nineteenth century when such certificates were used in litigation concerning inheritances. On 27 February 1841, the rector of Bath Abbey, William Brodrick, certified a copy of the entry in the Abbey's burial register concerning the burial of Thomas Bunter Williams, the son of a Bristol shoemaker, on 23 December 1830, aged 17. This was appended to a statement made by Thomas Bunter Williams's cousin, Joseph, for the Chancery in 1845 stating that he had attended his funeral in the Abbey. See: Bristol Record Office, 5535/53/d 'Declaration of Joseph William of facts concerning life and death of Thomas Williams, Mary his wife and Thomas Bunter Williams, his son'.

83 John Nichols, *Illustrations of the Literary History of the Eighteenth Century. Consisting of Authentic Memoirs and Original Letters of Eminent Persons; and Intended as a Sequel to The Literary Anecdotes*, Vol. III, (London: Nichols, 1818) p.585.

84 See British Library Add MS 36379, John Buckler Drawings, p.101.

85 Miranda Carter, 'Dudes in Drapes' in *London Review of Books* (Vol. 44, No. 19) 6 October 2022.

86 *The Bath Chronicle*, 12 November 1778, p.3.

87 Ibid.

88 Bath Record Office, *Council Minute Book 1751–1761*, p.26.

89 Penrose, *Letters from Bath 1776–1777*, p.180.

90 Ibid. p.199.

91 Somerset Heritage Centre, D/P/ba/ab/2/9/3 'Proffitts arising from the Rectory of Bath', n.p.

92 Penrose, *Letters from Bath 1776–1777*, p.189.

93 Somerset Heritage Centre, D/P/ba/ab/2/9/3 'Proffitts arising from the Rectory of Bath', n.p.

94 Ibid. This set of accounts is the basis of discussion for the remainder of this section. The pages of the accounts are not numbered and references may be found by consulting the relevant page(s) described for each year given.

95 From 1774, payments of 1*s* were also made for burial in the 'skullhouse', five in 1774 and twelve in 1775. There are two payments of 2*s* for this in 1775.

96 This figure includes the payment of £1 11*s* 6*d* on 19 October 1782 for the burial of Mr Welch in the Choir.

97 In 1772–77, there were seven payments of £1 8*s* for burials before nine o' clock in the morning and two payments of the same amount for burials after ten o' clock at night. Payments of the lower sum of £1 4*s* were occasionally made for burial before nine o' clock in the morning, once in 1768, once in 1770, and twice in 1775. In comparison, the accounts record two payments of £1 (1778), one of £1 4*s* (1771), and one of £1 8*s* (1781) for burials before nine o' clock in the morning at St James'.

98 The figure of seven ledgerstones for the Abbey includes entries for a 'flat stone' and for 'laying a stone' and includes the payment of £5 5*s* on 28 March 1783 for Mrs Scriven's monument and flat stone.

99 John Wood, *A Description of Bath*, Vol. II (London: Bathoe, 1765, 2nd Edition, Corrected and Enlarged) p.308.

100 The National Archives; Kew, Surrey, England; *Records of the Prerogative Court of Canterbury*, Series PROB 11; Class: PROB 11; Piece: 1145. Piece Description: Piece 1145: Norfolk, Quire Numbers 423–479 (1786).

101 Unless otherwise noted, these dates refer to burials in the Abbey.

102 The *Oxford Dictionary of National Biography* entry for Sarah Fielding states that she 'was buried at St. Mary's, Charlcombe, Bath'.

103 John Chapman's book reads 'Mr Clement'. Given the rank of the others recorded in the accounts, it has been assumed that this refers to Mr William Clement, Esquire.

104 John Chapman's book reads 'Dr Saunders'. It has been assumed that this refers to Erasmus Saunders, Doctor of Divinity.
105 Sir William Baker was buried at St Swithin's, Walcot, Bath.
106 John Chapman's book reads 'Mr Ward'. It has been assumed that this refers to Edward Ward, Esq.
107 John Chapman's book reads 'Mr Gordon'. It has been assumed that this refers to George Gordon, Esq.
108 John Chapman's book reads 'For Governor Ellison's monument at Abby'. There is an extant monument to H. Ellison in the Abbey, although he cannot be the man meant by Chapman since he died in 1795. It has been assumed that Chapman is referring to Roger Hope Elletson, the Governor of Jamaica.
109 John Chapman's book reads 'Mr Gee'. It has been assumed that this refers to Mr Roger Gee, Esq.
110 I am indebted to Kim Jordan, for making his research data on 'Makers of Monuments in Bath Churches 1700–1900' available, and to his paper on 'Monumental Masons in Bath in the 18th and 19th centuries' in the *Proceedings of the History of Bath Research Group* No. 8 (2019–20) pp.24–32.
111 *An Historical Description*, p.47.
112 Wiltshire and Swindon History Centre 161/125/2.
113 Ibid.
114 At the end of the accounts for 'the Sale of cut Silks 1778' is a 'memorandum' that reads 'Mr Page indebted for a W[hite] Sattin Suit at two Guineas – taken in May 1779 £2 2*s* 0*d*'. This sum has been included in that of £27 12*s* 0*d* for Silks in 1779 and has not been counted in the sums for 1778.
115 In 1782, where a payment is marked in 'Goods & Cash' (e.g. 20 June 1782), for the purposes of quantifying the amounts, the payment has been counted as Goods.
116 The entry in the burial register for 10 June 1780 reads: 'Judith Russell was Buried in ye Church under Mr Russell Stone between ye 2 pillers [sic] in ye South Isle[.] Paid to hire.' This probably refers to the practice of hiring palls established in 1705, but possibly refers to the hire of other funeral silks.
117 Mr Pettingall (22 October 1787), Mr Woodford (21 May 1790), and Mr William (8 March 1791) are undertakers named in the Abbey's burial register.
118 *Bath Chronicle and Weekly Gazette*, 16 February 1786, p.3.
119 The monument is number 120 in the manuscript and the text quoted from Gordon Priest, *The Paty Family: Makers of Eighteenth-century Bristol* (Bristol: Redcliffe Press, 2003).
120 *Records of the Prerogative Court of Canterbury*, Series PROB 11. The National Archives, Kew, England. Piece Description: Piece 1427: Nelson, Quire Numbers 426–483 (1805).
121 Philip Carter, 'Nash, Richard [known as Beau Nash] (1674–1761), master of ceremonies and social celebrity.' *Oxford Dictionary of National Biography*. 24. Oxford University Press: www.oxforddnb.com/view/10.1093/ref:odnb/9780198614128.001.0001/odnb-9780198614128-e-19789 [accessed on 28 February 2022].
122 The only other monument with such a long gap between its subject's death and the erection of the monument being Chantrey's monument for William Hoare, who died in 1792 and whose monument was commissioned in 1828.
123 James Tunstall, M.D., *Rambles About Bath, And Its Neighbourhood*, (London: Simpkin, Marshall, & Co.; Bath: M. Pocock, 1848, 2nd Ed., With Map and Illustrations) p.29.
124 *Bath Chronicle and Weekly Gazette*, 10 December 1789, p.1.
125 *Bath Chronicle and Weekly Gazette*, 14 April 1791, p.3.
126 *The Diary of a West Country Physician* [Claver Morris], A.D. 1684–1726, ed. E. Hobhouse (London: Simpkin Marshall, 1934) p.69.

127 James Tunstall, M.D., *Rambles About Bath, And Its Neighbourhood*, 2nd Ed., With Map and Illustrations (London: Simpkin, Marshall, & Co.; Bath: M. Pocock, 1848) 36.
128 Penrose, *Letters from Bath 1776–1777*, p.99.
129 The National Archives; Kew, Surrey, England; *Records of the Prerogative Court of Canterbury*, Series PROB 11; Class: PROB 11; Piece: 795 Description Piece Description: Piece 795: Bettesworth, Quire Numbers 133–179 (1752).
130 *Bath Chronicle and Weekly Gazette*, Thursday, 17 June 1773, p.3.
131 Edward Croft-Murray, 'An Account Book of John Flaxman, R.A. (British Museum Add. MSS. 39,784 B.B.)', *The Volume of the Walpole Society*, Vol. 28 (The Walpole Society, 1939) p.64. www.jstor.org/stable/41830880.
132 From an album of original drawings by John Flaxman held at The British Museum 1926,1115.25.1–59.
133 Edward Croft-Murray, 'An Account Book of John Flaxman, R.A. (British Museum Add. MSS. 39,784 B.B.)' *The Volume of the Walpole Society*, Vol. 28 (The Walpole Society, 1939) p. 8. www.jstor.org/stable/41830880.
134 Alison, Yarrington, et al. 'An Edition of the Ledger of Sir Francis Chantrey R.A., at the Royal Academy, 1809–1841.' *The Volume of the Walpole Society*, Vol. 56 (The Walpole Society, 1991) p.285.
135 *Robson's 1839–40 Directory*, p.51.
136 Alison, Yarrington, et al. 'An Edition of the Ledger of Sir Francis Chantrey R.A., at the Royal Academy, 1809–1841.' *The Volume of the Walpole Society*, Vol. 56 (The Walpole Society, 1991) p.284. www.jstor.org/stable/41829570.
137 Chantry's charges for William Hoare's monument were as follows: 'To executing the Monument according to an approved design £500; Mens time packing mont. &c. £2 16s 0d; Mans wages erecting do £4 5s 0d; Mans travelling & other expenses £5 6d 0d; Strong Copper cramps [blank]; Two strong packing Cases & fittings £10 9s 0d: [Total] £522 16s 0d'. See: Alison, Yarrington, et al. 'An Edition of the Ledger of Sir Francis Chantrey R.A., at the Royal Academy, 1809–1841.' *The Volume of the Walpole Society*, Vol. 56 (The Walpole Society, 1991) p.199. www.jstor.org/stable/41829570.
138 *Bath Chronicle and Weekly Gazette*, 6 November 1828, p.3.
139 *Bath Chronicle and Weekly Gazette*, 1 September 1785, p.3.
140 *Bath Chronicle and Weekly Gazette*, 15 October 1795, p.3.
141 James Storer, *History and Antiquities of the Cathedral Churches of Great Britain*, Vol. 1, (London: Rivingtons, etc., 1814) n.p.
142 William Dalrymple, *The Anarchy: The Relentless Rise of the East India Company* (London: Bloomsbury, 2019) p.64.
143 Ibid. pp.xxvi–ii.
144 Penny, p.179.
145 James Gordon Paker, 'The Directors of the East India Company 1754–1790', PhD thesis (University of Edinburgh, 1977) pp.34–35.
146 John Stibbs attended meetings of the Abbey's Vestry in 1686 (Mayor), 1687, 1689, 1698, 1699 (Mayor), 1700, 1701, 1704, 1705, 1707, and 1708 (Mayor).
147 The National Archives, HCA 32/55/28, 'Ship: Cornwall Galley (master Bartholomew Stibbs). History: An English vessel with a letter of marque. Ship's papers: letter of marque and undertaking for bail, 1718'.
148 Bartholomew Stibbs's 'Journal of a Voyage up the Gambia' (1723/4) was published in Francis Moore's *Travels into the Inland Parts of Africa* (London: Cave, 1738) pp.235–97.
149 The National Archives, C 217/123, 'Bill for burial of Bartholomew Stibbs, 1735'.

150 Bath Abbey Archives, *Churchwardens Accounts 1801–48*, pp.184–85.

151 Joan Coutu, *Persuasion and Propaganda: Monuments and the Eighteenth-Century British Empire* (Montreal: McGill-Queen's UP, 2006) pp.90–91.

152 *Bath Chronicle and Weekly Gazette*, 8 March 1792, p.1.

153 See: *Heraldic church notes from Cornwall: Containing all the heraldry and genealogical particulars on every memorial in ten churches in the deanery of East, with copious extracts from the parish registers, annotated with notes from wills, etc.* (London: Mitchell and Hughes [1889]); *Wells Cathedral: its monumental inscriptions and heraldry: together with the heraldry of the palace, deanery, and vicar's close: with annotations from wills, registers, etc., and illustrations of arms* (London: Mitchell and Hughes, 1892); 'The monumental inscriptions and armorial bearings in the churches within the City of London', a five-volume work by Arthur Jewers, compiled for the Library Committee of the City of London, 1910–19, London Metropolitan Archives, CLC/256.

154 Somerset Heritage Centre, D\P\ba.ab/2/1/2 Bath Abbey Register of Marriages Baptisms and Burials 1742–1792, p.269.

155 Somerset Heritage Centre, D\P\ba.ab/2/1/2, p.271.

156 Somerset Heritage Centre, D\P\ba.ab/2/1/2, p.273.

157 Somerset Heritage Centre, D\P\ba.ab/2/1/2, p.274.

158 Somerset Heritage Centre, D\P\ba.ab/2/1/2, p.267.

159 The burial register helps us to identify other stones that are now lost, but which were already in a poor state of repair by the end of the eighteenth century. For example, in 1775 the burial register locates new burials in relation to ledgerstones that could only then be identified by initials carved on them: '13 March The Revd. Dr. Thos. Ashton was Buried in ye Church under ye Stone marked G.G: at ye foot of Mr Hibbert's Stone in ye South Isle'; '23 June Mrs Elizabeth Hawker was Buried in ye Church at ye head of the Stone Mark T:W: by ye Poor Box in ye Middle Isle'. See also '8 December 1785 Mrs Hannah Montgomary was Buried in ye Church by ye Stone mark'd [M] D. by ye Boy's Seats'.

160 Somerset Heritage Centre, D\P\ba.ab/2/1/2, p.242. Penrose noted the location of the font in the South Transept and that the area was not used by the congregation during services, which may have helped preserve the inscriptions on the ledgerstones there: 'The Baptismal Font is [in] a side Isle, quite removed from the Place where Prayers are read; so that the office of Baptism is never read in the Public Congregation' (Penrose, p.111).

161 The following are all used as descriptors of doors to locate burials in 1774–92: the 'Abbey Garden door in ye South Isle', 'ye Abbey House Garden door' in the Middle Aisle, 'ye great [West] Door', 'ye Choir gate', 'ye Closet door in the North Isle', 'ye Library [Vestry] door [in the] S[outh] Isle', 'Mr Taylor's Key-house Door', 'by ye South Tower Door', 'by the Ringers Door', and 'Near Bennett's door'.

162 The following are all used as descriptors of seats to locate burials in 1774–92: 'Charity Girls Seat' (and the 'Charity Boys Seat'), 'the Lady's Seat', 'the Mayor's Seat' in the South Aisle, 'in ye Choir near Mr Bally's Seat', 'in ye Choir close by ye Seat No: 15', 'by ye blue seat', 'in ye Choir under ye s[e]ates. No. 21 ' 25', 'by Mr Trimnel's seat South Isle', 'in ye Choir under ye Clerks Seat', and 'behind ye Closets Seats North Isle'.

163 The following are all used as descriptors of stairs to locate burials in 1774–92: 'Organ loft Stair', 'ye foot of ye Gallery Stairs', and 'South Isle near the Gallery Stairs'.

164 *Bath Chronicle and Weekly Gazette*, 15 January 1795, p.3.

165 *The Poems of John Dryden Volume V 1697–1700*, ed. Paul Hammond and David Hopkins (Harlow: Pearson Education, 2005) p.27.

166 The Ewings' stones in the North Transept are good examples of how stones had

inscriptions added to them and the burials being recorded as under their 'own stone' in the burial register.

167 Somerset Heritage Centre, D/P/ba/ab/9/1/1 Bath Abbey Vestry Minutes 1684–1732, n.p.

168 Ibid. [4 February 1728], n.p.

169 *Bath Chronicle and Weekly Gazette*, 18 June 1761, p.144.

170 See 'Income of the Rectory of Bath 1756–1765', n.p.

171 *Bath Chronicle and Weekly Gazette*, 25 July 1765, p.168.

172 *Bath Chronicle and Weekly Gazette*, 24 October 1765, p.220.

173 *Bath Chronicle and Weekly Gazette*, 13 March 1766, p.44.

174 Penrose, *Letters from Bath 1776–1777*, p.99.

175 Wanda Henry, 'Hester Hammerton and Women Sextons in Eighteenth- and Nineteenth-Century England' in *Gender & History* (Vol. 31, No. 2, July 2019) p.404.

176 H. Gye, *Gye's Bath Directory Corrected to January 1819* (Bath: Gye, 1819) pp.18–21.

177 Penrose, *Letters from Bath 1776–1777*, p.73.

178 Ibid. p.76.

179 *Bath Chronicle and Weekly Gazette*, 4 March 1773, p.1.

180 Penrose, *Letters from Bath 1776–1777*, p.71.

181 *Bath Chronicle and Weekly Gazette*, 31 January 1771, n.p.

182 *Bath Chronicle and Weekly Gazette*, 23 August 1792, p.3. It is unclear whether this William Handcock's wife was allowed to continue in the role of sexton and if so for how long. *The Bath Chronicle and Weekly Gazette* for 1 January 1795 records that an additional guinea (£1 1*s*) from 'A Lady' was added to the collection for the hospital 'by Mrs. Hancock for the Abbey'.

183 *Bath Chronicle and Weekly Gazette*, 15 May 1788, p.2.

184 James Tunstall, M.D., *Rambles About Bath, And its Neighbourhood* (Bath: M. Pocock, 1848, Second Edition, With Map and Illustrations) p.51.

185 *Bath Chronicle and Weekly Gazette*, 22 May 1788, p.1.

186 Thicknesse's views were obviously influenced by those of the character Matthew Bramble in Tobias Smollett's *Humphrey Clinker* (1771), who gives the following opinion of the Abbey to his physician Dr Lewis: 'For my part, I never entered the abbey church at Bath but once, and the moment I stepped over the threshold, I found myself chilled to the very marrow of my bones. When we consider, that, in our churches in general, we breathe a gross stagnated air, surcharged with damps from vaults, tombs and charnel-houses, may we not term them so many magazines of rheums, created for the benefit of the medical faculty, and safely aver that more bodies are lost than souls saved by going to church, in the winter especially, which may be said to engross eight months in the year. I should be glad to know what offence it would give to tender consciences, if the house of God was made more comfortable, or less dangerous to the health of valetudinarians; and whether it would not be an encouragement to piety, as well as the salvation of many lives, if the place of worship was well-floored, wainscoted, warmed, and ventilated, and its area kept sacred from the pollution of the dead. The practice of burying in churches was the effect of ignorant superstition, influenced by knavish priests, who pretended that the devil could have no power over the defunct if he was interred in holy ground; and this indeed is the only reason that can be given for consecrating all cemeteries even at this day.' The state of the floor, wainscoting, warmth and ventilation of the Abbey would continue to be concerns in the nineteenth century.

187 Philip Thicknesse, *The New Prose Bath Guide for the Year 1778* (London: Dodsley, 1778) pp.30–31.

188 *Sepulchral Monuments in Great Britain Applied to Illustrate the History of Families, Manners, Habits and Arts, at the Different Periods from the Norman Conquest to the Seventeenth Century with Introductory Observations*. Part I. (London: J. Nichols, 1786) p.lxx.

189 August 1779 and January 1784 are other examples of this kind of practice when a large number of burials were taking place in the church.

190 *Bath: A Glance at its Public Worship, Style of Dress, Cotillons Masquerades, &c. &c.* (Bath: Meyler, 1814, 2nd edition) p.8.

191 Ibid. p.9.

192 *Bath Chronicle and Weekly Gazette*, 3 June 1802, p.4.

193 *Bath Chronicle and Weekly Gazette*, 2 July 1801, p.2.

194 Penrose, *Letters from Bath 1776–1777*, p.45. See also: 'A handsome fabrick full of monuments of many noble persons' *The Travels through England of Dr. Richard Pococke, Successively Bishop of Meath and of Ossoey During 1750, 1751, and Later Years*, Vol. 1, ed. James Joel Cartwright (London: Camden Society, 1888) p.155. And 'The Abbey-Church is a venerable Pile, and has many Monuments in it' *The Tradesman's and Traveller's Pocket Companion: Or, the Bath and Bristol Guide; Calculated for the Use of Gentlemen and Ladies who visit Bath; The Inhabitants of Bath and Bristol; and All Persons who have Occasion to Travel* (Bath: Boddely, 2nd ed., n.d.) p.2.

195 John Feltham, *A Guide to all the Watering and Sea-Bathing Places* (London: Phillips, 1806) p.45.

196 *Bath: A Glance at its Public Worship*, p.10.

197 Rev. Richard Warner, *The History of Bath* (Bath: Cruttwell, 1801) p.260.

3. Renovation: 'Such undistinguishing accumulations of sepulchral trifling', 1807–1885

1 *Autobiography, Letters, and Literary Remains of Mrs. Piozzi (Thrale)*, Vol. II, ed. and introd. A. Hayward (London: Longman, 1861) p.141.

2 Rev. G.N. Wright, *The Historic Guide to Bath. With a Map and Illustrations* (Bath: Peach, 1864) p.202.

3 Nicholas Penny, *Church Monuments in Romantic England* (Yale: Yale UP, 1977) p.2.

4 *Bath Chronicle and Weekly Gazette*, 8 February 1849, p.2.

5 See: *Historic Floors: Their History and Conservation*, ed. Jane Fawcett (Oxford: Butterworth-Heinemann, 1998) p.26.

6 *Bath Chronicle and Weekly Gazette*, 30 December 1909, p.6.

7 Herbert Russell, 'Bath and its Memories' in *The Quiver* 737.

8 *Pall Mall Gazette*, Thursday, 14 October 1897, p.2.

9 *Bath Chronicle and Weekly Gazette*, 25 January 1816, p.3.

10 *Bath Chronicle and Weekly Gazette*, 22 February 1816, p.3.

11 *Bath Chronicle and Weekly Gazette*, 4 April 1816, p.3. See *Bath Chronicle and Weekly Gazette*, 7 March 1816, p.3, and 21 March 1816, p.3 for complete lists of subscribers. The report on 21 March 1816 incorrectly totalled the previous amount subscribed as £65 19*s* 0*d*, an error of £1 that was carried forward into subsequent totals.

12 *Bath Chronicle and Weekly Gazette*, 6 March 1817, p.3.

13 *Bath Chronicle and Weekly Gazette*, 22 February 1821, p.3.

14 *Bath Chronicle and Weekly Gazette*, 30 January 1823, p.2.

15 As well as those quoted in the main text, see the following reports in *The Bath Chronicle and Weekly Gazette* on monuments created by Thomas King to: Venanzio Rauzzini on 5 November 1812 ('a neat marble drapery Tablet'); Sir Alexander Thomson on

10 December 1818 ('A chaste and elegant monument (designed and executed with his accustomed taste by Mr. T. King, sculptor of this city')); and Caleb Hillier Parry on 3 October 1822 ('A handsome Monument [...] the whole executed in a manner that reflects the highest credit on the taste and talents of Mr. T. King, of Walcot-house'). All reports on these monuments were on p.3 of the newspaper.

16 *Bath Chronicle and Weekly Gazette*, 23 February 1826, p.3 [my emphasis].

17 Richard Warner, *The History of Bath* (Bath: Cruttwell, 1801) p.260.

18 Ibid. p.250.

19 Ibid. p.259.

20 Pierce Egan, *Walks through Bath* (Bath: Meyler, 1819) p.77.

21 Ibid. p. 78.

22 Ibid. p.77.

23 Ibid. p.77.

24 Ibid. p.78.

25 Ibid. pp.79–80.

26 Ibid. p.79.

27 Ibid. p.81.

28 Ibid. p.82.

29 Maria Gertrude Cooper, *Thoughts in Ideal Hours: Poems* (Bath: Peach, 1870) p.56. Cooper's grandmother was Jane Osbaldeston, of Hutton Bushel, Yorkshire, who was buried in the Abbey in 1821. After Scott's works to the floor, Osbaldeston's 'large size' ledgerstone was relocated to the north, between the first two pillars at the west end of the Nave.

30 Pückler-Muskau describes the man simply as the 'clerk'. However, many of the details of his description of him point to the fact that it was William Skrine. The man was present with Pückler-Muskau in the Nave whilst a service took place in the 'sanctuary' and he is mentioned in the context of a sustained description of the church's noteworthy monuments, something Skrine, as sexton, would have been used to pointing out to visitors.

31 There is perhaps a suggestion in his account that the man would have guided Pückler-Muskau around the monuments had he not been 'dismissed'. This was a common task for the sexton. The regard and treatment of the man is similar to that towards other Abbey sextons in the eighteenth and nineteenth centuries. It is hard to imagine Pückler-Muskau treating or being able to dismiss the clerk in the same way. This is further evidence that the identity of the unnamed man in Pückler-Muskau's letters was William Skrine.

32 German Prince [Hermann Ludwig Heinrich von Pückler-Muskau], *Tour in England, Ireland and France in the Years 1828 & 1829*, Vol. II (London: Wilson, 1832) pp.208–13.

33 Rev. G.N. Wright, *The Historic Guide to Bath. With a Map and Illustrations* (Bath: Peach, 1864) p.206.

34 James Storer, *History and Antiquities of the Cathedral Churches of Great Britain. Illustrated with a Series of Highly-Finished Engravings*, Vol. 1 (London: Rivingtons, 1814) n.p.

35 John Britton, *The History and Antiquities of the See and Cathedral Church of Winchester* (London: Longman, 1817) p.79 n.4.

36 John Britton, *The History and Antiquities of Bath Abbey Church: Including Biographical Anecdotes of the Most Distinguished Persons Interred in that Edifice; with an Essay on Epitaphs, in which its Principal Monumental Inscriptions are Recorded. Illustrated in a Series of Engravings* (London: Longman, 1825) pp.95–96.

37 Ibid. p.93.

38 Ibid. pp.95–96.

39 Ibid. pp.96–97.

40 This figure includes the Montagu Tomb.

41 This figure includes the tablet to 'William Gomm' described as 'N.A. Head of the Bishop'.

42 This figure includes the Lichfield Tomb.

43 This figure includes the Waller Tomb.

44 This figure includes descriptions of the location 'Choir, Middle Aisle'.

45 John Britton, The *History and Antiquities* of Bath Abbey Church, p.89.

46 Ibid. p.79.

47 See C. P. Russell's 'Index to the Monuments and Tablets in the Abbey Church Bath' (1876), Bath Abbey Archives, BA/2/BMD/6/1/1.

48 Bath Abbey Archives, MS BA/2/BMD/7/1, p.56.

49 The individuals named are: Venanzio Rauzzini, William Melmoth, Thomas Purnell, Colonel R Walsh, Tobias Venner, Jacob Bosanquet, C.M., Robert Mason, Henrietta Charlotte Byron, Ely Bates, Fletcher Partis, Sarah Currer, James Quin, Sir William Draper, Sarah Fielding, Waller, Richard Nash, Alexander Champion, Caleb Hillier Parry, Baron Thompson, Henry Harington, MD, Lady Miller, Thomas Hawes, John Sibthorpe, Allen, Lord Gardiner, and Josiah Thomas.

50 Bath Abbey Archives, MS BA/2/BMD/7/1, p.61.

51 *The Original Bath Guide, considerably Enlarged and Improved* (Bath: Meyler, 1811) p.38.

52 Bath Abbey Archives, D\P\P\ba.ab/2/9/4 *Sexton's Accounts 1810–36.*

53 Bath Abbey Parish Records, D\P\ba.ab/4/1/1 *Churchwardens' Accounts 1801–1848*, p.134.

54 Bath Abbey Parish Records, D\P\ba.ab/9/1/2 *Vestry Minutes 1819–1884*, 23 September 1824, p.75.

55 Bath Abbey Parish Records, *Bath Abbey Churchwardens' Accounts 1801–1848* D\P\ba.ab/4/1/1, 20 November 1824.

56 The payments for 'overmeasures' for Mr Bingham and Mr Lambert's monuments are entered separately in the accounts in 1808; the main payments for their monuments are made in 1806 and 1807 respectively.

57 In the *Churchwardens' Accounts* the following burial fees were waived 1801–45: 18 December 1814, Dr Thomas Matthew's burial fee waived; 13 February 1817, Wm Lockyer a child burial fee waived 'given up'; 20 May 1817, Geo. Lockyer 'given up'; 1 May 1819, Burial of W W Skrine not charged; 3 June 1820, Burial fee and the fee for permission for a walled grave for the Archdeacon of Bath Josiah Thomas waived (the fee for the overmeasure of his monument is marked 'gratis' in 1823); 1822, Charles Crook makes part payment of the fees for Dr Fordyce's monument himself. The following entries in the *Sexton's Accounts* are recorded: '28 Feby 1833 Do [Permision for a Wall Grave] Elizabeth Skrine –'; '29 May 1833 Rec Monument to Mr Garbitt – '.

58 Bath Abbey Parish Records, D\P\ba.ab/4/1/1 *Churchwardens' Accounts 1801–1848*, n.p. This page of accounts headed 'General Repairs of the Abbey in the Year 1814' precedes the title page of the *Churchwardens' Accounts.*

59 See for example Bath Abbey Parish Records, D\P\ba.ab/4/1/1 *Churchwardens' Accounts 1801–1848* p.245: '12 April 1825 Burial of Martha Cook – allowed being a Poor Parishioner 13s'.

60 *Bath Chronicle and Weekly Gazette*, 12 September 1833, n.p.

61 Bath Abbey Archives, D\P\P\ba.ab/2/9/4 *Sexton's Accounts 1810–36*, '19 September 1833 Burial of Constantia Skrine a par £1 5s 6d'.

62 *Bath Chronicle and Weekly Gazette*, 15 December 1825, p.2.

63 Bath Abbey Parish Records, *Bath Abbey Churchwardens' Accounts 1801–1848* D\P\ba.ab/4/1/1 p. 278. Manners was paid £60 10s for his work at the Abbey in 1825.

64 *Douglas Bernhardt in his study George Phillips Manners: Architect 1789–1866: A Nineteenth Century Bath Practitioner* (Bath: Arbutus Press, 1999) and Ken Hylson-Smith in *Bath Abbey: A History* (Bath: Friends of Bath Abbey, 2003) are both silent on Manners's work to the monuments.

65 All references in this paragraph are to Clark's article in *The Bath Chronicle and Weekly Gazette*, 19 December 1833, p.4.

66 *Eight Letters from Bath*, by The Fidget Family (Bath: Meyler, 1830) p.11.

67 *Bath Chronicle and Weekly Gazette*, 19 December 1833, p.2.

68 Bath Record Office, Philip George, Town Clerk's Papers. Bath Churches 1/8. Bath Abbey. Demolition of houses on the North side of the Abbey. Suggestion for use of void ground as a burial ground. Letter from Earl Manvers proposing clearance of houses on South side of Abbey. 1822–1823.

69 Thomas Haynes Bayley, *Rough Sketches of Bath, Epistles, and Other Poems* (Bath: Meyler, 1819) p.3.

70 See *Bath Chronicle and Weekly Gazette*, 7 August 1834, p.1: 'The houses that were on the south side of the Abbey are completely removed, and the Old Cross Keys Inn, on the other side, is in rapid progress of demolition.'

71 Bath Record Office, Philip George, Town Clerk's Papers. Bath Churches 1/12. Bath Abbey. Minutes of sub-committees of Corporation for Abbey improvements, 1831–40.

72 Bath Record Office, *Council Minute Book No. 15 From the Year 1835 to the Year 1843*, p.11.

73 Ibid. p.12.

74 Bath Abbey Parish Records, *Bath Abbey Churchwardens' Accounts 1801–1848* D\P\ba.ab/4/1/1, 13 April 1837. A Mr Winstone supplied these at a cost of 8s 9d.

75 Bath Record Office, Philip George, Town Clerk's Papers. Bath Churches 1/12. Bath Abbey. Minutes of sub-committees of Corporation for Abbey improvements, 1831–40.

76 Bath Record Office, *Council Minute Book No. 15 From the Year 1835 to the Year 1843*, p.14.

77 Ibid. p.14.

78 Ibid. p.17.

79 Ibid. p.37.

80 Wright, *The Historic Guide to Bath*, pp.212–13.

81 *Bath Chronicle and Weekly Gazette*, 14 August 1834, p.3.

82 Wright, *The Historic Guide to Bath*, p.202.

83 Both letters are found in Bath Record Office, Philip George, Town Clerk's Papers. Bath Churches 1/12. Bath Abbey. Minutes of sub-committees of Corporation for Abbey improvements, 1831–40.

84 See: C. P. Russell's 'Index to the Monuments and Tablets in the Abbey Church Bath' (1876), Bath Abbey Archives, BA/2/BMD/6/1/1. Basey compared Rawlinson's 1719 survey with what he found in the Abbey to compile the list of the following twenty-six monuments: Edward Alchorn, Samuel Bave, John Belingham, Hester Bushell, Susanna Chapman, John Chapman, John Duncombe, Dame Grace Gethin, Elizabeth Grieye, William Heath, Anthony Kingston, Thomas Lychefeild, John Maplet, Dame Damaris Masham, Robert Mason, Jacobo Antonio Miglioruccio, Thomas Morris, George & Elizabeth Norton, John Pearce, Rev. Luke Robinson, Hester Barnes, William Chapman, William Child, Maria Sherwood, Dr Tobias Venner.

85 These are the tablets to Elizabeth Grieye, George & Elizabeth Norton, Hester Barnes, and William Child.

86 John Gough Nichols, *A Bibliographical Review of Works on the Sepulchral Antiquities of England* (Privately Printed: 1867) p.19.

87 Bath Abbey Parish Records, D\P\ba.ab/9/1/2 *Vestry Minutes 1819–1884*, p.267.

88 Bath Abbey Parish Records, *Bath Abbey Churchwardens' Accounts 1801–1848* D\P\ba.ab/4/1/1, p.394.

89 Bath Abbey Archives, BA/3/FIN/4/1/1, *Parochial Fees Book 1816–1837*, 3 May 1836, n.p.
90 Bath Abbey Parish Records, *Bath Abbey Churchwardens' Accounts 1801–1848* D\P\ba.ab/4/1/1, 12 April 1836.
91 *Sir Stephen Glynne's Church Notes for Somerset*, ed. Michael McGarvie. Somerset Record Society Volume 82 (Stroud: Alan Sutton, 1994) p.27.
92 All references in this paragraph to Gibbs's *Bath Visitant; or, New Guide to Bath* (Bath: Gibbs, 1835) pp.41–43.
93 Gibbs's *Bath Visitant*, p.42.
94 John Britton, The *History and Antiquities of Bath Abbey Church*, p.97.
95 See the following payments in *Bath Abbey Churchwardens' Accounts 1801–1848* D\P\ba.ab/4/1/1: 26 June 1836 'Paid Rogers for removing a monument to make room for Dottin Maycocks Monument 9s'; 1 October 1836 'Rogers Bill for raising Pavement of Church &c. £7 14s 1 ½ d'; 13 April 1837 'Rogers for moving Monuments & repairing Pavement £3 18s 6d'; in 1837 'Rogers for Masons Work £1 12s 11d' and '£8 9d 4d'; 'Rogers for Masons Work £6 17s 6d'; 12 February 1839 'Rogers for fixing & Sundries £4'; 'Rogers for Masons Work £10 12s 10d'; 'Rogers for Masons Work to Gass [sic] Work £1 11s 7d'; 'Rogers Bill for repaing [sic] Church paving &c. £3 8s'; 1839 'Rogers for Masons Work £20 15s 5s'; 27 March 1840 'Rogers opening Ground for Gas pipes 12s 6d [when they were repaired]'; June 20 1840 'Rogers for repairing Church Pavement £2 4s 8d' and 'Rogers for Hot Air Stove under Arch £18 17s 4d'; 1840 'Rogers for Masons Work £14 5s 14d'; 10 March 1841 'Rogers for Cleaning the Church £3 10s'; 1841 'Rogers Masons Work £9 6s 2d'; April 1842 'Rogers Bill for Masons Work £4 15s 4d'; 1843 'Rogers for repair of Pavement in the Church £2 17s 4d' and 'Rogers for repair of Pavement & Road £17 9s'; 1842 and 1843 'Bills for Masons Work £18 4s 11d'; March – May 1843 'Rogers for Masons Work to Gas 7 Hot Water pipes £4 13s 2d'; 7 January 1844 'Rogers for Masonry £10 14s 0d' and 'Rogers for Repairing Pavement £2 8s 4 ½ d'; 1843-4 'Rogers £3 6s 11d'; 25 March 1844 'Rogers for repairs of Pavement £23 4s 8d' and 'Rogers for [illegible] & Repy Pavement 14s 11d'; May – November 1844 'Rogers for Cleaning Church & Repairs £12', 'Rogers for Repairs of Pavement £8 0s 2 1/2d', and 'Rogers for Removing Monument 8s 3 ½'; March 25 1845 'Rogers for repy pavement £11 15s 3d'.
96 *Bath Abbey Churchwardens' Accounts 1801–1848* D\P\ba.ab/4/1/1, p.428.
97 See payments in the Churchwardens' Accounts between May and November 1844 to 'Rogers for Cleaning Church & Repairs £12', 'Rogers for Repairs of Pavement £8 0s 2 1/2d' and 'Rogers for Removing Monument 8s 3 ½'.
98 *The Sessional Papers Printed by Order of The House of Lords, or Presented by Royal Command, in the Session 1847*, Vol. XXII, pp.43–46.
99 *Bath Chronicle and Weekly Gazette*, 1 February 1844, p.3.
100 Ken Hylson-Smith, *Bath Abbey: A History* (Bath: Friends of Bath Abbey, 2003) p.174.
101 www.batharchives.co.uk/cemeteries/bath-abbey-cemetery.
102 Ken Hylson-Smith, *Bath Abbey: A History* (Bath: Friends of Bath Abbey, 2003) p.174.
103 James Tunstall, *Rambles About Bath and Its Neighbourhood* (Bath: Peach, 1848) p.115.
104 Ibid.
105 See 'Bath Abbey Cemetery, Lyncombe Vale. Consecrated January 30th, 1844, by the Right Rev. the Lord Bishop of Salisbury. The Right Reverend Bishop Carr, D.D., Rector. Table of Fees and Charges' published on: www.batharchives.co.uk/cemeteries/bath-abbey-cemetery.
106 'On Mural Tablets' in *The Archaeological Magazine of Bristol, Bath, South-Wales, and the South-Western Counties*, No. 1 May 1, 1843, ed. T. H. Sealy (London: Cunningham & Mortimer, 1843) p.8.

107 Rev. John Armstrong, *A Paper on Monuments* (Oxford: Parker, 1844) pp.12, 19.
108 John Britton, *The History and Antiquities* of Bath Abbey Church, p.92.
109 J. H. Markland, *Remarks on English Churches* (Oxford: Parker, 1843, 3rd ed., enlarged) p.xvi.
110 Ibid. pp.82–83.
111 Ibid. p.162.
112 Ibid. p.xvi.
113 *Bath Chronicle and Weekly Gazette*, 14 August 1834, p.3.
114 James Tunstall, *Rambles About Bath and Its Neighbourhood* (Bath: Peach, 1848) p.25.
115 *The Original Bath Guide* (Bath: Meyler, 1841) p.79.
116 Bath Abbey Parish Records, D\P\ba.ab/9/1/2 *Vestry Minutes* 1819–1884, p.285.
117 Buckinghamshire Archives, D-MH/Bishop Carr's diaries. 'Studies in a Devoted Life.' Period 1854. Vol/ XIII/ Thursday 28 December 1854, p.195.
118 Buckinghamshire Archives, D-MH/Bishop Carr's diaries. 'Studies in a Devoted Life.' Period 1854. Vol/ XIV, p.29.
119 *The Bath Chronicle and Weekly Gazette* covered the installation of the following monuments in the late 1850s: 9 December 1858, p.8: A 'simple and unpretending tablet of white marble, decorated with emblems' in the South Transept erected to Lieutenant George Dobson Willoughby, whom the paper called 'The Hero of Delhi'; 19 May 1959, p.8: A 'mural tablet was erected in the north aisle of the Abbey Church, in this city, by the officers of the 85th King's Light Infantry, to the late Colonel [Manley] Power, who died in Bath in 1857'; 7 July 1859, p.3: 'The monument which is about to be erected in the Abbey Church by the Freemasons, to the memory of their departed friend and brother [Mr. Thomas Steele], is completed. The design has been well carried out by the sculptor, Mr. Sheppard, of Dorchester Street. An open Bible surmounts the monument, which is of white marble, and immediately under the inscription are some Masonic emblems.'
120 Carr dined with Markland in October and December 1854. See Buckinghamshire Archives, D-MH/Bishop Carr's diaries. 'Studies in a Devoted Life.' Period 1854. pp.157–58, 184.
121 *Bath Chronicle and Weekly Gazette*, 11 November 1858, p.4.
122 *Bath Chronicle and Weekly Gazette*, 23 October 1856, p.4.
123 *Bath Chronicle and Weekly Gazette*, 16 April 1857, p.5.
124 Carr made the following entries in his diary: 2 May 1858, 'Rogers, the sexton, still very ill, not likely to recover; his brother is to officiate for the present'; 3 May 1858, 'Visited Rogers, who continues in a critical state; - his mind peaceable, resting on the Saviour.'
125 *Bath Chronicle and Weekly Gazette*, 11 November 1858, p.4.
126 *Bath Chronicle and Weekly Gazette*, 4 April 1861, p.6.
127 Bath Abbey Parish Records, D\P\ba.ab/9/1/2 *Vestry Minutes 1819–1884*, p.200.
128 Bath Abbey Parish Records, D\P\ba.ab/9/1/2 *Vestry Minutes 1819–1884*, pp.360–62.
129 Bath Abbey Parish Records, D\P\ba.ab/9/1/2 *Vestry Minutes 1819–1884*, pp.409–10.
130 *Bath Chronicle and Weekly Gazette*, 27 March 1856, p.3.
131 Bath Abbey Parish Records, D\P\ba.ab/9/1/2 *Vestry Minutes 1819–1884*, pp.415–16.
132 *Westminster Abbey: The Monuments, introd. John Physick* (London: Murray, 1989) p.13.
133 It is noteworthy that Thomas Carr's table of fees and charges for the Abbey Cemetery includes higher fees for non-parishioners' burials and monuments laid in open ground over them but one set fee (for both parishioners and non-parishioners erecting tablets in or on the chapel). See: www.batharchives.co.uk/cemeteries/bath-abbey-cemetery.
134 Bath Abbey Parish Records, D\P\ba.ab/4/1/1 *Churchwardens' Accounts 1801–1848*.
135 Bath Abbey Archives, BA/3/FIN/4/1/1.
136 Bath Abbey Parish Records, D\P\ba.ab/4/1/1 *Churchwardens' Accounts 1801–1848*, p.217.

137 Bath Abbey Archives, BA-11-PER/11/1 *Rector's Pocketbook*, n.p.

138 Some overmeasures, like Katencamp's, contain the original dimensions of the monuments. For these monuments, comparison of their current dimensions with those given in the *Churchwardens' Accounts* would allow one to calculate the extent to which they had been reduced in size in the nineteenth century.

139 Bath Abbey Parish Records, D\P\ba.ab/4/1/1 *Churchwardens' Accounts 1801–1848.*

140 This figure includes the two payments for overmeasures for the monuments to Lambert and Bingham that are accounted for separately.

141 This figure includes the 10*s* 6*d* from Mr Moffat, which is a part payment. A note in the account reads: 'part of the fees having been paid before'.

142 This figure includes a payment of 10*s* 6*d* for 'additional fees to Mr Phillips' stone'.

143 John Britton and R.E.M. Peach, T*he History and Antiquities of Bath Abbey Church by John Britton, F.S.A.; Continued to the Present Time, with Additional Notes by R.E.M. Peach* (Bath: Hallett, 1887) p.59.

144 *Bath Chronicle and Weekly Gazette*, 5 April 1860, p.5.

145 *Bath Chronicle and Weekly Gazette*, 12 April 1860, p.8.

146 Somerset Heritage Centre, D/D/cf/1868/4 F*aculty Papers for Bath Abbey*. 1868.

147 Ibid.

148 Edwin Morcombe Hick, *The Cathedral Church of SS. Peter and Paul in the City of Bath commonly called Bath Abbey. An Architectural and Historical Guide*, Homeland Handbooks No. 82 (London: Warne, 1913) p.92.

149 Ibid. p.92.

150 *Bath Chronicle and Weekly Gazette*, 1 April 1869.

151 'Bath Abbey Restoration' reprinted from *The Bath Chronicle and Weekly Gazette*, 7 December 1871.

152 *Bath Chronicle and Weekly Gazette*, 29 January 1903, p.5.

153 Bath Abbey Parish Records, D\P\ba.ab/9/1/2, *Vestry Minutes 1819–1884*, 24 March 1856, p.410.

154 Bath Abbey Parish Records, D\P\ba.ab/9/1/2, *Vestry Minutes 1819–1884*, pp.416 –17.

155 Bath Abbey Parish Records, D\P\ba.ab/9/1/2, *Vestry Minutes 1819–1884*, n.p.

156 *Bath Chronicle and Weekly Gazette*, 29 January 1903, p.5.

157 The article is pasted into the front of C.P. Russell's 'Index to the Monuments and Tablets in the Abbey Church Bath' (1876), Bath Abbey Archives, BA/2/BMD/6/1/1, as an 'Introduction' to the manuscript.

158 See the Monument to Sir Augustine Nicolls (d. 1616) attributed to Nicholas Stone the Elder at the Victoria and Albert Museum, London. collections.vam.ac.uk/item/O77815/monument-to-sir-augustine-nicolls-relief-stone-nicholas-the/.

159 Bath Abbey Archives, 'Bath Abbey Footprint: Post-excavation Assessment and Updated Project Design', Wessex Archaeology (January 2022) p.15

160 Cai Mason and Dr Oliver Taylor, '"A boy sleeping": the discovery of a lost 18th-century sculpture at Bath Abbey' (13 September 2022) www.wessexarch.co.uk/news/boy-sleeping-discovery-lost-18th-century-sculpture-bath-abbey.

161 Bath Abbey Archives, 'Bath Abbey Footprint: Post-excavation Assessment and Updated Project Design', Wessex Archaeology (January 2022) p.21

162 Arthur Jewers (ed.), *The Registers of the Abbey Church SS. Peter and Paul, Bath*, Vol. 2 (London, 1901) p.473.

163 Warner, *History of Bath*, p.261.

164 James Tunstall, *Rambles About Bath and Its Neighbourhood* (Bath: Peach, 1848) p.35.

165 Rev. G.N. Wright, *The Historic Guide to Bath*, p.187.

166 James Tunstall, *Rambles About Bath and Its Neighbourhood* (Bath: Peach, 1848) p.35.

167 Rawlinson, *History and Antiquities*, p.248.
168 *An Historical Description*, p.50.
169 Rawlinson, *History and Antiquities*, pp.257–58.
170 *Bath Chronicle and Weekly Gazette*, 10 November 1881, p.3.
171 *Bath Chronicle and Weekly Gazette*, 5 December 1895, p.8.
172 *Bath Chronicle and Weekly Gazette*, 20 December 1883, p.7.
173 *Bath Chronicle and Weekly Gazette*, 20 December 1883, p.7.
174 *Bath Chronicle and Weekly Gazette*, 3 January 1884, p.8.
175 *Bath Chronicle and Weekly Gazette*, 13 November 1884, p.3.
176 *Bath Chronicle and Weekly Gazette*, 28 May 1885, p.8.
177 *Bath Chronicle and Weekly Gazette*, 20 September 1894, p.8.
178 South West Heritage Trust, Somerset Heritage Centre, D/D/cf/1929/7-8.
179 T*he History and Antiquities of Bath Abbey Church by John Britton, F.S.A.; Continued to the Present Time, with Additional Notes by R.E.M. Peach*, p.59.
180 *Bath Chronicle and Weekly Gazette*, 4 February 1875, p.7.

4. Conservation: 'To restore those which have historic interest or artistic merit', 1895–2021

1 Mary Deane, *Mr. Zinzan of Bath; or, Seen in an Old Mirror. A Novel* (New York: Dutton, 1891) p.2.
2 Ibid. p.36.
3 Ibid. p.37.
4 Ibid. p.146.
5 Ibid. p.148.
6 Ibid. p.148.
7 Ibid. p.188.
8 Ibid. p.188.
9 Ibid. p.189.
10 Ibid. p.190.
11 *Bath Chronicle and Weekly Gazette*, 13 October 1904, p.6.
12 *Bath Chronicle and Weekly Gazette*, 12 April 1877, p.5.
13 See Hick, p.30, Peach p.66, and *Bath Chronicle and Weekly Gazette*, 15 November 1877, p.3.
14 Matthew Holbeche Bloxam, *Companion to the Principles of Gothic Ecclesiastical Architecture* (London: George Bell, 1882) pp.285–86.
15 Odgers Conservation Consultants, 'Bath Abbey: Conservation assessment on the monument to Bishop James Montagu (1618)' (Bath Abbey Archives: Unpub, 2014) p.11.
16 *Bath Chronicle and Weekly Gazette*, 24 February 1881, p.7.
17 *Bath Chronicle and Weekly Gazette*, 5 December 1895, p.8.
18 David Falconer and Peter King, *The Organs and Organists of Bath Abbey* (Bath: Bath Abbey Music Society, 2001) p.19.
19 Ibid. p.20.
20 Ibid. p.21.
21 Ibid. p.21.
22 Ibid. p.21.
23 The 'Tablets removed in 1895 "for New Organ"' listed by Thomas Basey were: Abraham Dixon (1746), William Clement (1790), Hannah Montgomery (1785), Johannis Ellis (1785), Mary Lucy Stoner (1782), John Stoner (1786), William Baker DD (1732), William Trail (1831), Thomas Jones (1793), Jane Holder Alleyne (1842), Thomas Walter Clark Darby (1819), Philp Richards (1798), Thomas Wilkins (1817), Richard Brigden Powell

(1783), Elizabeth Powell (1796), Alicia Henrietta Cotgrave (1829), James Garbett (1832), Elizabeth Jefferies (1792), Richard Peete (1792), Margaretta Georgina Herbert (183?), Henry Cole (1827), Sir John Caldwell (1830), Frances Jolliffe (1802), Lady Elizabeth Cranston (1792), James Kendrick Pyne (1893), Jane Fenwick (1749), Lady Caldwell (1705), Robert Mason (1662), Susanna Jotam (1726), Frances Hare (1806), Thomas Barrow (1807), Anne Barrow (1825), Rebecca Leyborne (1756), Thoebald Bourke (1783), Esther Harington (1829).

24 Falconer and King, p.25.

25 Bath Abbey Archives, Bath Abbey Scrapbook A, Newspaper Cutting 'Bath Abbey Restoration. Public Meeting at Guildhall'. Untitled Newspaper, 29 March 1901.

26 Falconer and King, p.25.

27 Ibid. p.26.

28 South West Heritage Trust, D/D/cf/1913/5. Faculty papers for Bath Abbey, 1913.

29 South West Heritage Trust, D/D/cf/1913/5. Faculty papers for Bath Abbey, 1913.

30 Falconer and King, p.27.

31 *Bath Chronicle and Weekly Gazette*, 15 September 1917, p.6.

32 Jackson's War Memorial Chapel was dedicated by the Bishop of Bath and Wells on Wednesday, 3 October 1923.

33 Jackson's War Memorial Cloister was opened and dedicated by the Bishop of Bath and Wells, who 'unlocked the door of the new cloister and dedicated it' on 11 November 1927.

34 *Bath Chronicle and Weekly Gazette*, 11 August 1923, p.7.

35 *Bath Chronicle and Weekly Gazette*, 13 November 1915, p.7.

36 All references to Dunn's tablet from: *Bath Chronicle and Weekly Gazette*, 22 October 1932, p.12.

37 *Bath Chronicle and Weekly Gazette*, 11 September 1902, p.7.

38 *Bath Chronicle and Weekly Gazette*, 10 July 1943, p.12.

39 *Bath Chronicle and Weekly Gazette*, 24 May 1930, p.14.

40 *Bath Chronicle and Weekly Gazette*, 7 September 1935, p.15.

41 *Bath Chronicle and Weekly Gazette*, 6 January 1912, p.5.

42 *Bath Chronicle and Weekly Gazette*, 7 August 1915, p.5.

43 *Bath Chronicle and Weekly Gazette*, 30 March 1935, p.22.

44 All references to Dunn's tablet from: *Bath Chronicle and Weekly Gazette*, 22 October 1932, p.12.

45 Boyd used the same phrase ('most fitting') to describe the placement of the cenotaph to Sir Arthur Phillip (1738–1814) on the north wall of the Choir in June 1937. It was, he wrote, 'most fitting that his [Phillip's] memory should be honoured in the central church of Bath' (*Bath Chronicle and Weekly Gazette*, 5 June 1937, p.20). Phillip was commemorated elsewhere in the newspaper as 'one of the greatest and most successful of the builders of the Empire'. Phillip was buried at St Nicholas's Church in Bathampton, outside of the city, just as Sir William Baker was buried at St Swithin's Church, Walcot, in 1770. It is possible Boyd knew this. Certainly, the idea of placing a cenotaph in the Abbey was in the same tradition of making monuments to empire builders more visible by placing them in Bath's central church where they would be seen by greater numbers of visitors and worshippers. According to 'Scrapbook A' in Bath Abbey's Archives, Phillip's tablet was 'designed by E. M. Hick' p.73.

46 *Bath Chronicle and Weekly Gazette*, 30 March 1935, p.22.

47 *Bath Chronicle and Weekly Gazette*, 30 March 1935, p.22.

48 *Bath Chronicle and Weekly Gazette*, 29 August 1931, p.18.

49 *Bath Chronicle and Weekly Gazette*, 12 February 1938, p.20. See also p.21 for full-page coverage.
50 *Bath Chronicle and Weekly Gazette*, 1 March 1947, p.9.
51 *Bath Chronicle and Weekly Gazette*, 3 December 1949, p.11.
52 Bath Abbey Archives, 'Bath Abbey Progress of Works Report carried out under the supervision of Messrs. Carpenter and Beresford Smith' (December 1949). 1998/1/27/54. Qtd in Rowena Tulloch, 'Preliminary Report Bath Abbey floor subsidence and interventions 1947–1977' (Bath Abbey Archives, Unpub., July 2014) p.3.
53 Bath Abbey Archives, *Bath Abbey 5th Annual Report (Dec 1952)*. 1998/1/27/54.
54 Bath Abbey Archives, *Bath Abbey 6th Annual Report (Dec 1953)*. 1998/1/27/54.
55 Bath Abbey Archives, *Bath Abbey 7th Annual Report (Oct 1955)*. 1998/1/27/54.
56 Bath Abbey Archives, *Bath Abbey with Saint James PCC Meeting Minutes* (05/10/1959) 2002/45.
57 Bath Abbey Archives, *Bath Abbey Report for 1959* (18.12.1959) 1998/1/27/54.
58 Bath Abbey Archives, *Bath Abbey Report for 1961* (30.07.1962). 1998/1/27/54.
59 Bath Abbey Archives, *Special Meeting, Fabric Committee Minutes* (30 May 1962). 2002/45.
60 See: Bath Abbey Archives 'Special Meeting, Fabric Committee Minutes (30th May 1962). 2002/45 and Meeting held on Monday, 12 November 1962. Fabric Committee Minutes. 2002/45.
61 Bath Abbey Archives, Bath Abbey. *Report on the problem of subsidence of the floor.* (23.01.1963). 1998/1/27/1.
62 Rowena Tulloch, 'Preliminary Report Bath Abbey floor subsidence and interventions 1947–1977' (Bath Abbey Archives, Unpub., July 2014) p.7.
63 Bath Abbey Archives, *Bath Abbey Report for 1962/3* (1962/3). 1998/1/27/54.
64 Bath Abbey Archives, *Bath Abbey with St James PCC Meeting Minutes* (8.04.1963). 2002/45.
65 Bath Abbey Archives, *Bath Abbey Report for 1967* (1967). 2014/1.
66 Bath Abbey Archives, *Bath Abbey 20th Annual Report for the Year 1968* (Dec 1968). 2014/1.
67 *Bath Chronicle and Weekly Gazette*, 8 May 1943, p.9.
68 *Bath Chronicle and Weekly Gazette*, 10 April 1948, p.9.
69 Bath Abbey Archives, Bath Abbey Scrapbook A, p.105. Article from unnamed newspaper, probably *The Bath Chronicle*, dated 28 August 1951, n.p.
70 *Bath Chronicle and Weekly Gazette*, 28 May 1949, p.11.
71 The references in the following three paragraphs follow those given on pp.8 and 9 of the 'Bath Abbey Monument Survey' (Bath Abbey Archives: Unpub., *c.*1997].
72 *Bath Chronicle and Weekly Gazette*, 7 May 1949, p.11.
73 Bath Abbey Archives, *Bath Abbey Scrapbook A*, p.105. Article from unnamed newspaper, probably *The Bath Chronicle*, dated 15 January 1952, n.p.
74 The lettering on George Bolton Eyres's tablet was restored in 2002.
75 *Birmingham Daily Post*, Monday, 25 January 1960, p.5.
76 Alex Morris, 'Bath Abbey Footprint Project: An architect's view of the project objectives and the works' in *Journal of Building Survey, Appraisal & Valuation*, Vol. 10, No. 2 (2021) p.147.
77 Odgers Conservation Consultants, *Bath Abbey Footprint Project: Floor repair trials*, November 2015 (Unpub. Bath Abbey Archives) p.1.
78 Ibid. p.5.
79 Ibid. p.14.

Conclusion

1 *Bath Chronicle and Weekly Gazette*, 4 April 1925, p.19.
2 John Betjeman, *Church Poems*, illustrated by John Piper (London: Pan, 1982) p.61.
3 Two interesting recent studies include: David Littlefield's 'The Living and the dead; an investigation into the status of erasure within the floor of Bath Abbey' in *Interiors: Design, Architecture, Culture*, Vol. 7, Issue 1 (Taylor and Francis, 2016) pp.3–26; and Ian Parkes's 'The Stone Remains: Mapping Place at Bath Abbey' (Unpub. M.A. thesis, University of the West of England, 2014).
4 Betjeman, *Church Poems*, p.63.
5 www.churchofengland.org/news-and-media/news-and-statements/update-church-and-cathedral-monuments.
6 Joan Coutu, *Persuasion and Propaganda: Monuments and the Eighteenth-century British Empire* (Montreal: McGill-Queen's UP, 2006) p.21.
7 Ibid. p.4.
8 *Bath Chronicle and Weekly Gazette*, 4 November 1950, p.13.
9 See: hymnary.org/text/and_must_this_body_die#Author.
10 R. Nicholas Olsberg, 'Ship Registers in the South Carolina Archives 1734–1780', *The South Carolina Historical Magazine*, Vol. 74 (October 1973) p.210.
11 Slavevoyages.org. Voyage ID 100579.
12 Olsberg, 'Ship Registers', p.233.
13 Slavevoyages.org. Voyage ID 100592.
14 Olsberg, 'Ship Registers', p.238.
15 *Sermons Preached in the Abbey Church at Bath, by a Late Dignified Clergyman*. Vol. 1. (Oxford: Jackson, 1790) p.181.
16 *Bath Chronicle and Weekly Gazette*, 21 April 1881, p.5.
17 Jason Edwards, Amy Harris and Greg Sullivan, *Monuments of St Paul's Cathedral 1796–1916* (London: Scala, 2021) p.6.
18 Quoted in *Bath Chronicle and Weekly Gazette*, 29 August 1925, p.20.
19 *Bath Chronicle and Weekly Gazette*, 31 October 1931, p.15.
20 Miranda Carter, 'Dudes in Drapes', *London Review of Books*, Vol. 44, No. 19 (October 2022).

SELECTED BIBLIOGRAPHY

Primary Sources
Bath Abbey Archives:

BA/2/BMD/5/5/1. Notebook listing burial fees, c. 1844.

BA/2/BMD/5/11/9. Designs for memorials to Jesse Mead and Richard England Brooke.

BA/2/BMD/6/1/1. Charles P. Russell, 'Index to the Monuments and Tablets in the Abbey Church Bath' (1876).

BA/2/BMD/6/1/2. 'Inscriptions on the Flat Gravestones in the Bath Abbey Church copied by Charles P Russell (Parish Clerk) at the time of the restoration of the church in 1872'.

BA/2/BMD/6/1/3. Numbered plan of flat gravestones in Bath Abbey.

BA/2/BMD/6/2/1. 'Interments within the Abbey (Mr Basey's book)'

BA/2/BMD/7/1. 'An Abstract Account of the Register Books Belonging to the Rectory of Bath Taken down to 1824'.

BA/3/FIN/4/1/1. Parochial Fees Book, 1816-37.

BA-MS/1. The Benefactors' Book [c.1618-1774].

BA-MS/12/1. Deed of gift of four palls from Benjamin Baber to Bath Abbey, 25 Dec.1705.

BA-PER/8/5. Scrapbooks.

Somerset Heritage Centre, Taunton
Bath Abbey Parish Records:

D/P/ba.ab/2/1/1. Register of Baptisms, Marriages and Burials, 1569-1743.

D/P/ba.ab/2/1/2. Register of Marriages, Baptisms and Burials, 1742-92.

D/P/ba.ab/2/9/3. 'Proffitts arising from the Rectory of Bath', 1768-83.

D/P/ba.ab/2/9/4. Sexton's Accounts, 1810-36.

D/P/ba.ab/4/1/1. Churchwardens' Accounts 1801-48.

D/P/ba.ab/4/1/2. Churchwardens' Accounts 1849-1922.

D/P/ba.ab/9/1/1. Vestry Minutes 1684-1732.

D/P/ba.ab/9/1/2. Vestry Minutes 1819-84.

D/D/cf/1868/4. Faculty Papers for Bath Abbey, 1868.

D/D/cf/1913/5. Faculty papers for Bath Abbey, 1913.

D/D/cf/1929/7-8. Faculty papers for Bath Abbey, 1929.

Bath Record Office:

'[A Cambridge Undergraduate] A Tour from Cambridge to Halifax and Wakefield, returning via Oxford, Bath, and Bristol', 1725. MS in bound vol. Access. No. 38.43, Class: 914.238b.

Council Minute Books, 1684-1843

Philip George, Town Clerk's Papers. Bath Churches 1/5. 'The Income of the Rectory of Bath 1756-1765'

Philip George, Town Clerk's Papers. Bath Churches 1/8. Bath Abbey.

Philip George, Town Clerk's Papers. Bath Churches 1/12. Bath Abbey. Minutes of sub-committees of Corporation for Abbey improvements, 1831-40.

Other archives

Bristol Record Office, 5535/53/d 'Declaration of Joseph William of facts concerning life and death of Thomas Williams, Mary his wife and Thomas Bunter Williams, his son'.

British Library, Add MS 36379 John Buckler Drawings.

British Museum, 1926,1115.25.1-59 An album of original drawings by John Flaxman.

Buckinghamshire Archives, D-MH/Bishop Carr's diaries. 'Studies in a Devoted Life.' Period 1854. Vols. XIII and XIV.

Shakespeare Birthplace Trust, ER 3/2189 'Certificate of Burial of William Ingram in the Abbey Church, Bath; Thomas Coney, rector and James Davis, clerk. 29 April 1737'.

Society of Antiquaries, MS 434 Timothy Baldwin, 'Transcript of several Coates of armes belonging to several Noble Familyes their plaices of Buriall together wth the Epitaphes and Inscriptions upon their several Tablets & Grave Stones.'

The National Archives, HCA 32/55/28, 'Ship: Cornwall Galley (master Bartholomew Stibbs). History: An English vessel with a letter of marque. Ship's papers: letter of marque and undertaking for bail, 1718'.

The National Archives, C 217/123, 'Bill for burial of Bartholomew Stibbs, 1735'.

Wiltshire and Swindon History Centre, 161/125/2 Correspondence between Sir Francis Willes and Thomas King regarding a monument to be erected to Dr. Aubery and wife in Bath Abbey.

Secondary Sources

An Historical Description of the Church Dedicated to St. Peter and St. Paul, in Bath (Commonly called The Abbey) with its Monuments and Curiosities. Designed as a Guide to Strangers, in viewing this Venerable Pile, And, to point out to them the most valuable Remains of Antiquity, contained therein, as well as the Beauties of Modern Statuaries. Bath: Salmon, 1778.

Armstrong, Rev. John. *A Paper on Monuments.* Oxford: Parker, 1844.

Bath: A Glance at its Public Worship, Style of Dress, Cotillons Masquerades, &c. &c. Bath: Meyler, 1814 (2nd edition).

Bayly, Rev. Edward. *A Sermon Preach'd at the Abbey-Church at Bath, on SUNDAY, April 23, 1749, For the SUPPORT of the GOVERNORS of the said HOSPITAL.* Bath: Boddely, 1749.

Bayley, Thomas Haynes. *Rough Sketches of Bath, Epistles, and Other Poems.* Bath: Meyler, 1819.

Bernhardt, Douglas. *George Phillips Manners: Architect 1789-1866: A Nineteenth Century Bath Practitioner.* Bath: Arbutus Press, 1999.

Betjeman, John. *Church Poems,* illustr. John Piper. London: Pan, 1982.

Bloxam, Matthew Holbeche. *Companion to the Principles of Gothic Ecclesiastical Architecture.* London: George Bell, 1882.

Brayley, Edward Wedlake. *The History and Antiquities of the Abbey Church of St. Peter, Westminster.* In Two Volumes. London: Hurst, 1823.

Britton, John. *The History and Antiquities of the See and Cathedral Church of Winchester* London: Longman, 1817.

Britton, John. *The History and Antiquities of Bath Abbey Church: Including Biographical Anecdotes of the Most Distinguished Persons Interred in that Edifice; with an Essay on Epitaphs, in which its Principal Monumental Inscriptions are Recorded. Illustrated in a Series of Engravings.* London: Longman, 1825.

Britton, John. *The History and Antiquities of Bath Abbey Church by John Britton, F.S.A.; Continued to the Present Time, with Additional Notes by R.E.M. Peach.* Bath: Hallett, 1887.

Bush, Amy E and John Hatton. *Thomas Bellott 1534–1611: Steward of the Household of William Cecil, First Lord Burghley, Friend of Bath Abbey, Founder of Bellott's Hospital.* Bath: Friends of Bath Abbey, 1966.

Carter, Miranda. 'Dudes in Drapes' in *London Review of Books*. Vol. 44, No. 19 (6 October 2022).

Carter, Philip. 'Nash, Richard [known as Beau Nash] (1674–1761), master of ceremonies and social celebrity.' *Oxford Dictionary of National Biography*. 24. Oxford University Press. Date of access 22 Feb. 2022, https://www.oxforddnb.com/view/10.1093/ref:odnb/9780198614128.001.0001/odnb-9780198614128-e-19789

Cartwright, James Joel (ed.). *The Travels through England of Dr. Richard Pococke, Successively Bishop of Meath and of Ossoey During 1750, 1751, and Later Years.* Vol. I. London: Camden Society, 1888.

Chandler, Mary. *The Description of Bath. Humbly Inscribed to Her Royal Highness the Princess Amelia.* With several other Poems. London: Leake, 1733 (7th ed. 1755).

Collinson, Rev. John. *The History and Antiquities of the County of Somerset in Three Volumes.* Bath: Cruttwell, 1791.

Chapman, Henry (ed.). Thomas Guidott's *Thermae Redivivae; or, The City of Bath described, &c.* (1673). Bath: Leake, 1725.

[Chapman, John], *Sermons Preached in the Abbey Church at Bath, by a Late Dignified Clergyman.* Two Volumes. Oxford: Jackson 1790.

Cooper, Maria Gertrude. *Thoughts in Ideal Hours: Poems.* Bath: Peach, 1870.

Coutu, Joan. *Persuasion and Propaganda: Monuments and the Eighteenth-Century British Empire.* Montreal: McGill-Queen's UP, 2006.

Croft-Murray, Edward. 'An Account Book of John Flaxman, R.A. (British Museum Add. MSS. 39,784 B.B.)' *The Volume of the Walpole Society*. Vol. 28. The Walpole Society (1939). http://www.jstor.org/stable/41830880

Dalrymple, William. *The Anarchy: The Relentless Rise of the East India Company*. London: Bloomsbury, 2019.

Deane, Mary. *Mr. Zinzan of Bath; or, Seen in an Old Mirror. A Novel.* New York: Dutton, 1891.

Defoe, Daniel. *A Tour Thro' the Whole Island of Great Britain.* Vol. II. London: Birt, 1748.

Davenport, Peter. *Medieval Bath Uncovered.* Stroud: Tempus, 2002.

Davenport, Peter. 'The Church of St. Mary Northgate, Bath' in *Bath History*. Vol. 12. 2011.

Davenport, Peter. 'The Church of St. Mary de Stall, Bath' in *Bath History*. Vol. 15. 2019.

Diary and Letters of Madame D'Arblay, Author of 'Evelina,' 'Cecilia,' &c. Edited by Her Niece. Vol. I. Philadelphia: Carey and Hart, 1842.

Easter, Clive James. 'Church Monuments of Devon and Cornwall c.1660-c.1730'. Ph.D. thesis. U of Plymouth: Unpub., 2006. Vol. 1.

Egan, Pierce. *Walks through Bath.* Bath: Meyler, 1819.

Eight Letters from Bath, by The Fidget Family. Bath: Meyler, 1830.

Edwards, Jason, et. al. *Monuments of St. Paul's Cathedral 1796-1916*. London: Scala, 2021.

'English Cathedrals. Bath' in *All the Year Round. A Weekly Journal.* Saturday June 5 1875. No. 340 (New Series).

Esdaile, Katherine A. *English Church Monuments: 1510-1840.* Introd. Sacherverell Sitwell. London: Batsford, 1946.

Falconer, David Falconer, and Peter King. *The Organs and Organists of Bath Abbey.* Bath: Bath Abbey Music Society, 2001.

Fawcett, Jane (ed.). *Historic Floors: Their History and Conservation*. Oxford: Butterworth-Heinemann, 1998.

Feltham, John. *A Guide to all the Watering and Sea-Bathing Places.* London: Phillips, 1806.

Fuller, Thomas. *The Church History of Britain, from the Birth of Jesus Christ until the Year MDCXLVIII.* Vol. 3. London, 1837.

Gibbs's Bath Visitant; or, New Guide to Bath. Bath: Gibbs, 1835.

Gough, Richard (ed). *Sepulchral Monuments in Great Britain Applied to Illustrate the History of Families, Manners, Habits and Arts, at the Different Periods from the Norman Conquest to the Seventeenth Century with Introductory Observations.* Part I. London: Nichols, 1786.

Gye, H. *Gye's Bath Directory Corrected to January 1819* (Bath: Gye, 1819) 18-21.

Hammond Paul, and David Hopkins (eds.). *The Poems of John Dryden Volume V 1697-1700.* Harlow: Pearson Education, 2005.

Harington, Henry (ed.). *Nugae Antiquae: Being a Miscellaneous Collection of Original Papers, in Prose and Verse; Written During the Reigns of Henry VIII, Edward VI, Queen Mary, Elizabeth, and King James by Sir John Harington, Knt. And by others who lived in those Times.* Vol. 1. London: Vernor and Hood, 1804.

Harington, Henry, and Thomas Park (eds.). *Nugae Antiquae: Being a Miscellaneous Collection of Original Papers, in Prose and Verse; Written During the Reigns of Henry VIII, Edward VI, Queen Mary, Elizabeth, and King James: by Sir John Harington, Knt. And by others who lived in those Times. Selected from Authentic Remains by the Late Henry Harington, M.A. and Newly Arranged, with Illustrative Notes, by Thomas Park, F. S. A.* Vol. II. London: Wright, 1804.

Hayward, A (ed.). *Autobiography, Letters, and Literary Remains of Mrs. Piozzi (Thrale).* Volume II. London: Longman, 1861.

Henry, Wanda. 'Hester Hammerton and Women Sextons in Eighteenth- and Nineteenth-Century England' in *Gender & History*. Vol. 31, No. 2. July 2019.

Hick, Edwin Morcombe. *The Cathedral Church of SS. Peter and Paul in the City of Bath commonly called Bath Abbey. An Architectural and Historical Guide.* Homeland Handbooks No. 82. London: Warne, 1913.

Hickman, David J. *The Religious Allegiance of London's Ruling Elite 1520-1603.* London: University College, Unpub. Ph.D. Thesis: 1995.

Hill, Lockey. *An Appeal to Justice, and the Impartial World. Being a True and faithful Narrative, and just Complaint, of the unparallel'd and unjustifiable Barbarity and hellish Cruelty exercis'd on L. Hill, Esq; a Prisoner in the County Goal* [sic] *of Somerset, at Ilchester, by the Keeper thereof and his Adherents.* Exon: Andre Brice, 1726.

Hobhouse, E (ed.). *The Diary of a West Country Physician [Claver Morris], A.D. 1684-1726.* London: Simpkin Marshall, 1934.

Holland, Elizabeth. 'This Famous City The Story of the Chapmans of Bath 470 Years of History: The Chapmans and Bath Abbey' in *The Survey of Bath and District: The Magazine of the Survey of Old Bath and Its Associates.* No. 7. June 1997.

Hudson, Mark. 'Tablets, Memorials and Flags'. Unpub, Bath Abbey Archives, 2017.

Hylson-Smith, Ken. *Bath Abbey: A History.* Bath: Friends of Bath Abbey, 2002.

Jenkins, Jacqueline. *'Such people As Be Not Letterd In Scripture': Popular Devotion and the Legend of St Katherine of Alexandria in Late Medieval England'.* U of Western Ontario, Ph.D. Thesis, 1996.

Jewers, Arthur J (ed.). *The Registers of the Abbey Church of SS. Peter and Paul, Bath.* 2 Vols. London: Harleian Society, 1901.

Jordan, Kim. 'Monumental Masons in Bath in the 18th and 19th centuries' in *The Proceedings of the History of Bath Research Group.* No. 8. 2019-20. pp. 24-32.

Littlefield, David. 'The Living and the Dead: An Investigation into the Status of Erasure within the Floor of Bath Abbey' in *Interiors: Design, Architecture, Culture.* Volume 7, Issue 1. Taylor and Francis, 2016. pp. 3-26.

Manco, Jean. 'The Buildings of Bath Priory' in *Somerset Archaeology and Natural History* (1993).

Martin, Peter. *Edmond Malone, Shakespearean Scholar.* Cambridge: Cambridge UP, 1995.

Martin, Peter. 'Malone, Edmond (1741–1812), literary scholar and biographer.' *Oxford Dictionary of National Biography.* 25. Oxford University Press. Date of access 28 Feb. 2022, <https://www.oxforddnb.com/view/10.1093/ref:odnb/9780198614128.001.0001/odnb-9780198614128-e-17896>.

Markland, James Hayward. *Remarks on English Churches, and on the Expediency of Rendering Sepulchral Memorials Subserviant to Pious and Christian Uses.* 3rd Edition, Enlarged. Oxford: Parker, 1843.

McGarvie, Michael (ed.). *Sir Stephen Glynne's Church Notes for Somerset.* Somerset Record Society Volume 82. Stroud: Alan Sutton, 1994.

Morris, Alex. 'Bath Abbey Footprint Project: An architect's view of the project objectives and the works' in *Journal of Building Survey, Appraisal & Valuation.* Vol. 10, No. 2. 2021.

Morriss, Roger. *Naval Power and British Culture, 1760-1850: Public Trust and Government Ideology.* London: Routledge, 2004.

Nichols, John. *Illustrations of the Literary History of the Eighteenth Century. Consisting of Authentic Memoirs and Original Letters of Eminent Persons; and Intended as a Sequel to The Literary Anecdotes.* Vol. III. London: Nichols, 1818.

Nichols, John. *A Bibliographical Review of Works on the Sepulchral Antiquities of England.* Privately Printed: 1867.

Norman, Ben. *A History of Death in 17*th *Century England.* Barnsley: Pen & Sword Books, 2021.

Odgers Conservation Consultants. *Bath Abbey: Conservation assessment on the monument to Bishop James Montagu (1618).* Bath Abbey Archives: Unpub., 2014.

Odgers Conservation Consultants, *Bath Abbey Footprint Project: Floor repair trials.* Bath Abbey Archives: Unpub., November 2015.

Olsberg, Nicholas R. 'Ship Registers in the South Carolina Archives 1734-1780' in *The South Carolina Historical Magazine.* Vol. 74. October 1973.

Parker, James Gordon. 'The Directors of the East India Company 1754-1790', Ph.D. thesis. U of Edinburgh, 1977.

Parkes, Ian. 'The Stone Remains: Mapping Place at Bath Abbey'. Unpub. M.A. thesis. U of the West of England, 2014.

Paul, Roland W. *An Account of some of the Incised & Sepulchral Slabs of North-West Somersetshire, with Lithographic Plates.* London: Provost, 1882.

Peirce, Robert. *The History and Memoirs of the Bath.* London: n.p., 1723.

Penny, Nicholas. *Church Monuments in Romantic England.* Paul Mellon Centre for Studies in British Art. New Haven: Yale UP, 1977.

Penny, Nicholas. *The Materials of Sculpture.* New Haven: Yale UP, 1993.

Penrose, Rev. John. *Letters from Bath 1776-1777*, introd. and notes by Brigitte Mitchell and Hubert Penrose. Gloucester: Alan Sutton, 1983.

Perkins, Rev. Thomas. *The Abbey Churches of Bath & Malmesbury and the Church of Saint Laurence, Bradford-on-Avon.* London: Bell & Sons, 1901.

Physick, John (ed. and introd.). *Westminster Abbey: The Monuments.* London: Murray, 1989.

Priest, Gordon. *The Paty Family: Makers of Eighteenth-century Bristol.* Bristol: Redcliffe Press, 2003.

Prior, Sir James. *Life of Edmond Malone, Editor of Shakespeare. With Selections from his Manuscript Anecdotes.* London: Smith, Elder & Co., 1860.

[Pückler-Muskau, Hermann Ludwig Heinrich von], *Tour in England, Ireland and France in the Years 1828 & 1829.* Vol. II. London: Wilson, 1832.

Rawlinson, Rev. Richard. *History and Antiquities of the Cathedral Church of Salisbury, And the Abbey Church of Bath.* London: 1719.

Roberts, Stephen. 'Malone, Edmund (1704–1774), barrister and politician.' Oxford Dictionary of National Biography. 04. Oxford University Press. Date of access 28 Feb. 2022, <https://www.oxforddnb.com/view/10.1093/ref:odnb/9780198614128.001.0001/odnb-9780198614128-e-17895>.

Russell, Herbert, 'Bath and its Memories' in *The Quiver: An Illustrated Magazine for Sunday.* Series 3. Vol. 27. 1892. Pp. 737-42.

Sealy, T. H. 'On Mural Tablets' in *The Archaeological Magazine of Bristol, Bath, South-Wales, and the*

South-Western Counties. No. 1 May 1, 1843. London: Cunningham & Mortimer, 1843.
Shickle, C. W. (ed.). *A Copy of the Chamberlains' Accounts of the City of Bath with a List of Freemen and Other Interesting Matter.* Bath Record Office: Unpub. typescript, 1904.
Shirley, Evelyn Philip. 'The Will, Inventories, and Funeral Expenses of James Montagu, Bishop of Winchester, anno 1618. From the original in the possession of the Baroness North' in *Archaeologia* 44(02): 393-421.
Smith, Edmond. 'The Social Networks of Investment in Early Modern England' in *The Historical Journal, 64(4)*, 912-39.
Smith, Lucy Toulmin (ed.). *The Itinerary of John Leland in or about the Years 1535-1543 Parts I to III.* London: George Bell and Sons, 1907.
Stace, Bernard. *Bath Abbey Monuments.* Millstream Books, 1997.
Stibbs, Bartholomew. 'Journal of a Voyage up the Gambia' (1723/4) in Francis Moore *Travels into the Inland Parts of Africa.* London: Cave, 1738. pp. 235-97.
Storer, James. *The History and Antiquities of the Cathedral Churches of Great Britain*, Vol. 1. London: Rivingtons; Murray; et. al, 1814.
Stow, John, Anthony Munday, Anthony Munday, and Humphrey Dyson. Survey of London (1633): Walbrook Ward. *The Map of Early Modern London, Edition 6.6*, edited by Janelle Jenstad, U of Victoria, 30 Jun. 2021, mapoflondon.uvic.ca/edition/6.6/stow_1633_WALB2.htm. Draft.
Suffling, Ernest R. *English Church Brasses: From the 13*th *to the 17*th *Century: A Manual for Antiquaries, Archaeologists and Collectors.* London: Gill, 1910.
Taylor, Oliver and Cai Mason. 'One of the Most Valuable Women that Ever Lived' in *Current Archaeology* Issue 394 (January 2023) pp. 18-19.
The Gentleman's Magazine for October 1820.
The Original Bath Guide, considerably Enlarged and Improved. Bath: Meyler, 1811.
The Sessional Papers Printed by Order of The House of Lords, or Presented by Royal Command, in the Session 1847. Vol. XXII.
The Tradesman's and Traveller's Pocket Companion: Or, the Bath and Bristol Guide; Calculated for the Use of Gentlemen and Ladies who visit Bath; The Inhabitants of Bath and Bristol; and All Persons who have Occasion to Travel 2nd ed. Bath: Boddely, n.d.
Thicknesse, Philip. *The New Prose Bath Guide for the Year 1778.* London: Dodsley, 1778.
Tunstall, James. *Rambles About Bath, And Its Neighbourhood.* 2nd Edition. With Map and Illustrations. London: Simpkin, Marshall, & Co.; Bath: M. Pocock, 1848.
Ward, Edward. 'A Step to Bath' (1700) reprinted in *The Reformer.* 3rd Edition. London: How, 1708.
Wardle, F. D (ed.). *The Accounts of the Chamberlains of the City of Bath 1568-1602.* Somerset Record Society. Vol. XXXVIII. 1923.
Warner, Rev. Richard. *The History of Bath.* Bath: Cruttwell, 1801.
Warner, Rev. Richard. *A New Guide Through Bath, and its Environs.* Bath: Cruttwell, 1811.
Weaver, F. W. (ed.). *Somerset Medieval Wills (Third Series) 1531-1558.* Somersetshire Archaeological and Natural History Society. 1905.
Wessex Archaeology, *Bath Abbey Footprint: Post-excavation Assessment and Updated Project Design.* Wessex Archaeology, January 2022.
Wood, Anthony. *Monumental Inscriptions in the Churches of Bath, taken in July 1676.* London, 1881.
Wood, John. *A Description of Bath.* Vol. II. 2nd Edition, Corrected and Enlarged. London: Bathoe, 1765.
Wright, Rev. G. N. *The Historic Guide to Bath. With a Map and Illustrations.* Bath: Peach, 1864.
Yarrington, Alison, et al. 'An Edition of the Ledger of Sir Francis Chantrey R.A., at the Royal Academy, 1809-1841.' *The Volume of the Walpole Society.* Vol. 56. The Walpole Society, 1991. http://www.jstor.org/stable/41829570.

INDEX